Joseph Lemuel Chester, Geo J. Armytage

The Parish Registers of St. Antholin, Budge Row, London

Containing the Marriages, Baptisms and Burials from 1538 to 1754...

Joseph Lemuel Chester, Geo J. Armytage

The Parish Registers of St. Antholin, Budge Row, London
Containing the Marriages, Baptisms and Burials from 1538 to 1754...

ISBN/EAN: 9783337047825

Printed in Europe, USA, Canada, Australia, Japan

Cover: Foto ©Andreas Hilbeck / pixelio.de

More available books at **www.hansebooks.com**

THE

Publications

OF

The Harleian Society.

ESTABLISHED A.D. MDCCCLXIX.

Registers.—Volume VIII.

FOR THE YEAR MD.CCC.LXXXIII.

THE

Parish Registers

OF

St. Antholin, Budge Row,

London,

CONTAINING THE

Marriages, Baptisms, and Burials from 1538 to 1754;

AND OF

St. John Baptist on Wallbrook,

London,

CONTAINING THE

Baptisms and Burials from 1682 to 1754.

PARTLY EDITED BY THE LATE

JOSEPH LEMUEL CHESTER, D.C.L., LL.D.,

AND COMPLETED UNDER THE DIRECTION OF

GEO. J. ARMYTAGE, F.S.A.,

HONORARY SECRETARY TO THE SOCIETY.

LONDON:

1883.

Preface.

The following pages contain the registers of the marriages, baptisms, and burials at the Church of St. Antholin, Budge Row, London, from 1538 to 1754, and also the registers of the baptisms and burials at the Church of St. John Baptist on Wallbrook, London, from 1682 to 1754. The transcript of the original MSS. which form this volume was made a few years ago, at the instigation of the late Colonel Chester, and the whole of it was carefully revised by him before his death, and several doubts respecting the earlier entries were cleared up.

The Church of St. Antholin was rebuilt by Sir Thomas Knowles (Lord Mayor of London in 1399 and 1410) and Thomas Knowles his son, who were both buried there; and again rebuilt in 1513 by John Tate, mercer. It was repaired in 1616 at the expense of £1000, raised by seven of the inhabitants. It suffered from the great fire in 1666, but was restored about 1682 by Sir Christopher Wren, and was made the church of the then united parishes of St. Antholin and St. John Baptist, which together were reckoned of the yearly value of £120, in the early part of the eighteenth century, in lieu of tithes to the Incumbent.

Stow says that the Church of St. John Baptist stood upon "the very banks of Walbrook, and from thence it hath been after call'd St. John upon Walbrook." The church was newly built about 1412, and was repaired and adorned in 1621, but was burnt down in the great fire, and being afterwards annexed to that of St. Antholin, the site remained only as a churchyard for the inhabitants of both parishes.

In 1874 the demolition of St. Antholin was determined and carried out, and it was annexed to St. Mary Aldermary, the registers of which church form the fifth volume of this series.

The entries in this volume are full of interest, though there are few to call for special notice. The plague of 1625 seems to have added considerably to the number of deaths, and from August 1666 to the end of 1667 no entries were made, owing, no doubt, to the great fire.

From 1538 to 1724 the registers of births, marriages, and burials have all been entered together, and in a note following an entry of November the 8th, 1724, it is stated "from this time all births and burials belonging to St. John Baptist's parish are registred in ye proper register of that parish." From 1724 to the end of the register of St. Antholin, it will be observed that the marriages are separated from the births and burials; the two latter, however, continue to be entered together. It will be seen, therefore, that previous to 1724 many of the entries of St. John Baptist parish occur in the St. Antholin register, though from the following pages it is clear that the registers of St. John Baptist were in existence from 1682.

The best thanks of the Society are, as before, due to the Rev. Lewis Borrett White, D.D., Rector of St. Mary Aldermary, and to the Churchwardens, for their permission to print these registers and for the facilities they have given for their transcription, which has been carried out with the usual well-known care of the Society's transcriber, Mr. J. Eedes; but more especially are thanks due to Mr. William Hughes, who has corrected the proofs for the press—a labour which Colonel Chester had undertaken, but which unfortunately he was not spared to perform.

GEO. J. ARMYTAGE.

Preface.

The following pages contain the registers of the marriages, baptisms, and burials at the Church of St. Antholin, Budge Row, London, from 1538 to 1754, and also the registers of the baptisms and burials at the Church of St. John Baptist on Wallbrook, London, from 1682 to 1754. The transcript of the original MSS. which form this volume was made a few years ago, at the instigation of the late Colonel Chester, and the whole of it was carefully revised by him before his death, and several doubts respecting the earlier entries were cleared up.

The Church of St. Antholin was rebuilt by Sir Thomas Knowles (Lord Mayor of London in 1399 and 1410) and Thomas Knowles his son, who were both buried there; and again rebuilt in 1513 by John Tate, mercer. It was repaired in 1616 at the expense of £1000, raised by seven of the inhabitants. It suffered from the great fire in 1666, but was restored about 1682 by Sir Christopher Wren, and was made the church of the then united parishes of St. Antholin and St. John Baptist, which together were reckoned of the yearly value of £120, in the early part of the eighteenth century, in lieu of tithes to the Incumbent.

Stow says that the Church of St. John Baptist stood upon "the very banks of Walbrook, and from thence it hath been after call'd St. John upon Walbrook." The church was newly built about 1412, and was repaired and adorned in 1621, but was burnt down in the great fire, and being afterwards annexed to that of St. Antholin, the site remained only as a churchyard for the inhabitants of both parishes.

In 1874 the demolition of St. Antholin was determined and carried out, and it was annexed to St. Mary Aldermary, the registers of which church form the fifth volume of this series.

The entries in this volume are full of interest, though there are few to call for special notice. The plague of 1625 seems to have added considerably to the number of deaths, and from August 1666 to the end of 1667 no entries were made, owing, no doubt, to the great fire.

From 1538 to 1724 the registers of births, marriages, and burials have all been entered together, and in a note following an entry of November the 8th, 1724, it is stated "from this time all births and burials belonging to St. John Baptist's parish are registred in ye proper register of that parish." From 1724 to the end of the register of St. Antholin, it will be observed that the marriages are separated from the births and burials; the two latter, however, continue to be entered together. It will be seen, therefore, that previous to 1724 many of the entries of St. John Baptist parish occur in the St. Antholin register, though from the following pages it is clear that the registers of St. John Baptist were in existence from 1682.

The best thanks of the Society are, as before, due to the Rev. Lewis Borrett White, D.D., Rector of St. Mary Aldermary, and to the Churchwardens, for their permission to print these registers and for the facilities they have given for their transcription, which has been carried out with the usual well-known care of the Society's transcriber, Mr. J. Eedes; but more especially are thanks due to Mr. William Hughes, who has corrected the proofs for the press—a labour which Colonel Chester had undertaken, but which unfortunately he was not spared to perform.

GEO. J. ARMYTAGE.

Inprimis in the yeare of our lord 1538 and in the 30 yeare of the raigne of the most famous prince King Henry the eight, by the grace of God King of England ffrance and Yerland &cet.

This is the booke of the memoriall of the Christnings, Buryings and also weddings newly wrighten for the parrishe Church of Saint Antholins in Budgrow in the Yeare of our Lord 1598 and in the 40th yeare of the Raigne of our soveraine Lady Elisabeth Qveene of England ffraunce & Yreland, Defendor of the fath et cetera.

Master Nicholas ffelton parson in the same yeare.
Alexander Lockwood and Henrye Moodie Churchwardens.
November the twelfthe.

1538.

Jan. 14 Robart Brate & Alis Bugnall, widow, marr.
Jan. 27 M[r] Leonard Hetherington & Francis Wilkinson marr.
Feb. 20 John Woolfe, skinner, bur.
Feb. 27 Christened & bur. the dau. of W[m] Parkins
Mar. 9 Mother Hall bur.

1539.

May 10 William Bower & Johane Dauncy marr.
May 11 William Place & Elisabeth Wild marr.
May 18 The son of Richard Harves chr.
May 29 The son of John Pilchers chr.
June 26 William son of John Hills chr.
June 30 Robart Clovell son of M[r] Clovell chr.
July 25 A child of Thomas Howse's chr. & bur.
Aug. 17 Thomas Smith & Katurne Adcock marr.
Sep. 17 John Coates son of Thomas Cotes chr.
Sep. 19 The dau. of Henry Tomson chr.
Sep. 21 John Smith, skinner, bur.
Oct. 5 Thomas Youly & Elisabeth Hawks marr.
Oct. 9 The son of Bennet Lyghe chr. & bur.
Oct. 15 Joane dau. of M[r] Wilkison chr.
Oct. 19 Richard Parker & Dority Topley marr.
Oct. 25 Richard son of M[r] Banks chr.
Nov. 2 The dau. of William Adams chr.
Jan. 27 William son of John Maxfeild chr.
Feb. 6 Richard James of Beothe & Margarett Hal marr.
Feb. 7 Raphe son of M[rs] Cely, widow, chr.

1540.

[*blank*]20 Elisabeth dau. of William Lansdale bur.
April 25 John Askam & Marie Dickison marr.
May 19 Robart son of John Hill chr.
May 25 William Berry & Christian Cely marr.
May 27 William son of Miles Parkins chr.
June 11 Clement son of Thomas House chr.
July 18 William son of Robart Collins chr.
July 24 Thomas son of Thomas Reede, skinner, bur.
July 29 Hugh Shackerly bur.
Aug. 13 Richard Speite bur.
Aug. 17 Thomas Hills son of John Hills bur.
Aug. 17 Thomas Clifton son of Richard Clifton bur.
Aug. 21 Thomas Hammon, warden of y[e] Skinners, bur.
Sep. 4 William Cooke & Katturne Hamond marr.

Sep. 11 Oswell Faireweather, prentice to Wm Parker, bur.
Sep. 19 Joane wife of Water Boltonne bur.
Sep. 25 Elisabeth Parker bur.
Sep. 27 George Forman & Anne Hammond marr.
Oct. 1 Dorritye Horncliffe, a maiden, bur.
Oct. 4 Lettis dau. of Water Bollton bur.
Oct. 9 John Morton, prentice wth John Toddy, bur.
Oct. 9 Thomas Gibson, prentice wth John Toddy, bur.
Oct. 10 William son of Thomas Cootes bur.
Oct. 11 Sr Clem^{t} Horlistonne & Jane Colson marr.
Oct. 13 Richard Baker, prentice wth John Toddy, bur.
Oct. 15 Margaret wife of John Toddy bur.
Oct. 18 John Arthur, serv^{t} to Water Boulton, bur.
Oct. 19 Marie Allboroughe bur.
Oct. 24 Thomas Morton & Ellen Stowell marr.
Oct. 24 Annis Banks & Henry Davy marr.
Oct. 30 John Parker, a child, bur.
Nov. 1 John Burton, prentice wth Mr Coates, bur.
Nov. 1 John Hill, merch^{t} tailor, bur.
Nov. 1 George Horne, prentice wth Mr How, bur. [see Nov. 19]
Nov. 8 Elisabeth dau. of John Cootes chr.
Nov. 19 George Horne, prentice wth Mr How, bur. [*sic*]
Nov. 23 Raphe Umphery, prentice wth Collins, bur.
Nov. 24 John Varrow, prentice wth Toson, bur.
Nov. 26 Thomas Uprobarte, prentice wth Toson, bur.
Nov. 26 John Clark, prentice wth How, bur.
Nov. 27 Elisabeth How, a child, bur.
Dec. 11 Barnard son of John Cootes bur.
Dec. 19 Margaret dau. of Collins bur.
Dec. 19 Thomas son of Wm Adams chr.
Dec. 24 Christopher Goodman, prentice, bur.
Dec. 24 Alice Borrow, Collins' maid, bur.
Dec. 26 Rose Hetherington chr. & bur.
Dec. 30 Elisabeth West, Collins' maid, bur.
Jan. 7 Ameis Austin, Mr Smith's maid, bur.
Jan. 9 Bennet Leigh, skinner, bur.
Jan. 28 Christian dau. of Richard Harves chr.
Jan. 28 Larrance Hodson & An Blacksly marr.
Jan. 29 Annis dau. of Wm Parker chr.
Feb. 23 The dau. of Jane Richardson bur.
Feb. 27 Anne dau. of Mr Reede bur.
Mar. 2 William Richardson, brewer, bur.
Mar. 2 William Johnsonne, skinner, bur.
Mar. 17 Anthonie Mertam, serv^{t} to Mr Weldan, bur.

1541.

April 1 Annis dau. of Nicholas Tailor chr.
April 5 Martha Banks' child chr. & bur.
May 13 John Sperin & Katurne Shushe marr.
May 17 William Lansdale & Joane Lyghe marr.
May 19 Nicholas Aldie & Spicely [*sic*] Hill marr.
May 19 Roger Gammadge & Elisabeth Fisher marr.
Aug. 6 Raphe son of Mr Averson [?]
Aug. 7 William Flemming & Ellen Richardson marr.
Aug. 8 John Cannon, skinner, bur.
Aug. 8 Robart Hill son of John Hill bur.

Aug. 12 John Bro'les,* ^{ist} warden of the Skinners, bur.
Aug. 16 Bernard son of Thomas Blunt chr.
Sep. 20 John Myn, serv^{t} to Mr Gammadge, bur.
Sep. 29 Dennis son of Miles Parkins chr.
Oct. 9 William Smith & Elisabeth Okely marr.
Oct. 10 John Ady & Margaret Johnson marr.
Oct. 17 Timothie Clifton chr. & bur.
Nov. 24 Jane dau. of William Toades chr.
Nov. 25 John Haward bur.
Dec. 31 Anne dau. of Wm Adams chr.
Jan. 14 William Beston & Elisabeth Milborn marr.
Jan. 22 Mr Thomas Darell & Mrs Mary Roydon marr.
Jan. 28 Thomas Rider & Anne Pamberton marr.
Jan. 28 Robart Wodyfe & Magery [*sic*] Treton marr.
Mar. 3 Anne dau. of Nicholas Aldy chr.

1542.

Mar. 27 The child of Thomas Cootes named Timothi chr. & bur.
Mar. 31 Thomas son of Mr Weldon chr.
April 1 Raphe son of William Adams bur.
April 5 John son of Henry Daveys chr.
April 26 John son of Mr Sperin chr.
April 27 Anne dau. of John Bells chr.
April 30 John Bolster, goldsmith, & Cristones Wolfe marr.
May 1 Johane dau. of Mr Maxwell chr.
June 16 Mistris Dancy wife of Alderman Dancy bur.
June 25 Adam Grevis & Johane Luas marr.
July 7 Dority Trassey bur.
July 27 William son of Mr Curchman chr. & bur.
Aug. 1 John Skinnings, serv^{t} to John Cootes, bur.
Aug. 26 Thomas son of Richd Mays chr.
Sep. 8 Umphery son of Mr Edward Bowland chr.
Sep. 8 Johan Russell, serv^{t} to Mrs Boulton, bur.
Sep. 20 Elisabeth Bonner, serv^{t} to Mrs Bolton, bur.
Sep. 20 Ede Bush, serv^{t} to Mrs Boulton, bur.
Oct. 2 Thomas Brigitt, a scholar, bur.
Oct. 9 Richard Wilkinson & An Sinnis marr.
Oct. 10 John son of John Bankes ye younger chr.
Oct. 25 Richard Wilkinson, mercer, bur.
Nov. 3 William son of Roger Gammadge chr.
Nov. 7 Richard Adlin, servant, bur.
Nov. 11 Raphe son of Mr Hetherington chr.
Nov. 29 Anne dau. of Thomas Roodes chr.
Sep.† 6 John son of Thomas Blunt chr.
Jan. 20 George Heath & Alice Evans marr.
Jan. 30 John Bank ye elder, merch^{t} tailor, bur.
Feb. 1 Thomas son of Mr Weldon chr.
Feb. 2 Thomas son of Mr Weldon bur.

1543.

Mar. 26 George Welpleis his wife bur.
April 12 John Jackson, a poor blind man, bur.
April 24 Thomas son of Robart Collins chr.

* On enquiry at the Skinners' Hall, the Clerk kindly informed the Editor that the name no doubt was Bromley. † *Sic.* ‡ December.

April 26 William Hough, skinner, bur.
April 27 Mr William Dauncy, alderman, bur.
May 12 William Adams his wife was delivered of ij children, ye one buried, ye other christned & named Margaret ye 12 May
May 19 Cisley dau. of Mr Aldy chr.
May 20 Elisabeth dau. of John Maxfeild chr.
May 29 Richard Chapman, servt to Mr Maxfeild, bur.
July 20 Frederick dau. of William Adams bur.
July 31 Jane dau. of Miles Parkins chr.
Aug. 5 Henry Warnar, prentice wth Wm Parker, bur.
Aug. 7 Elisabeth Atkinson, servt wth Thomas Tailor, bur.
Aug. 20 John Weathered, Thomas Tailor's servt, bur.
Sep. 6 Mr William Wilkinson, mercer, bur.
Sep. 6 Thomas son of Richard Churchman chr.
Sep. 7 Alce dau. of William Lansadale bur.
Sep. 9 John Brabin, prentice wth Thomas Tailor, bur.
Sep. 13 John Corbit, servt of Thomas Blunt, bur.
Sep. 23 William son of Richard May chr.
Sep. 27 John Tauntlin, a child, bur.
Sep. 28 Nicholas Errable, Mr May's servt, bur.
Oct. 6 Sibble dau. of John Bels chr.
Oct. 28 John Mace, servt to Wm Parker, bur.
Oct. 30 William son of John Clollins bur.
Nov. 6 Margerie Johnson wife of Mr John [*sic*] bur.
Nov. 12 Edward son of Mr Bowland chr.
Nov. 17 Grace dau. of Ritchard Churchman bur.
Dec. 14 Nicholas son of Roger Gamadge chr.
Dec. 15 Thomas Addington, ye King's skinner, bur.
Dec. 18 Nicholas son of Roger Gammadg bur.
Dec. 25 Awdrian wife of Ritchard [*sic*] bur.
Jan. 4 Thomas Tailor's child chr. & bur.
Jan. 20 Andrew Banberry & Annis Cumbery marr.
Jan. 21 Cutbert Worpcop & Anne Wilkinson marr.
Feb. 24 William son of Thomas Cootes chr.
Mar. 5 Katerine dau. of John Perrin chr.

1544.

April 2 Richard son of Wm Tod chr.
May 15 Marthat dau. of Mr Lambard bur.
May 19 Katturne dau. of Mr Blunt chr.
May 21 George Welply bur.
May 24 Joane wife of Robart Collins bur.
May 27 Nicholas Tailor, sexton, bur.
July 7 William Dowell & Margaret Body marr.
July 12 Alse Gibbs bur.
July 15 Thomas Halslopp & Joane Bolter marr.
Aug. 12 Joane dau. of Mr Atherington chr.
Aug. 30 Mistris Allen bur.
Sep. 9 Dorety dau. of Mr Lambard chr.
Sep. 12 Annis Tailor, a child, bur.
Sep. 30 William son of Nicholas Aldaies chr.
Oct. 16 Rainebrowne son of John Banks chr.
Oct. 29 The wife of Thomas Lane bur.
Nov. 16 William Benning & Margaret Sebrock marr.
Nov. 16 Jone dau. of Cutbert Warcop chr.
Dec. 22 Thomas son of Wm Adams bur.

Dec. 25 Rowland son of W[m] Adams chr.
Jan. 8 Doritye Lake, widow, bur.
Jan. 13 John Cusworth & Dority Hill marr.
Jan. 13 Thomas son of M[r] Tailor chr.
Jan. 25 William Hide & Alse Tailor marr.
Jan. 27 William Porrege & Ames Copwell marr.
Feb. 18 A poore man y[t] died in the street was buried
Feb. 28 John Parke bur.
Mar. 10 Katturn dau. of Thomas Perrius chr.
Mar. 11 William son of Nicholas Alday bur.
Mar. 14 Katturne dau. of Edward Bowlaud chr.

1545.

Mar. 27 John son of [*blank*] Luggs chr. & bur.
May 17 Water Marlar & Mary Dale marr.
June 4 Daniell son of Thomas Cootes chr.
June 27 Marye dau. of Rich[d] Clifton chr.
July 4 Rainebrowne son of M[r] Curchman chr.
July 11 Katturne dau. of Edward Blunt bur.
July 16 William son of Thomas Cootes bur.
July 18 Richard son of W[m] Tood bur.
Aug. 15 Joane dau. of Roger Gamadge bur.
Sep. 17 M[r] William Weldon bur.
Sep. 22 William son of Thomas Blunt chr.
Oct. 10 Thomas Tailor bur.
Oct. 31 Raphe son of Cutbert Warcup chr.
Nov. 4 Thomas Perrin's child bur.
Nov. 28 William Meldnall & Elisabeth Tailor marr.
Dec. 3 Steven Raynam bur.
Dec. 9 Annis Giffersonne bur.
Dec. 13 Katurne dau. of Leonard Etherington chr.
Dec. 20 Thomas son of M[r] Toods chr.
Jan. 14 Christian dau. of Thomas Reed chr.
Feb. 14 Thomas Whipp & Katturn Ampleford marr.
Feb. 25 Thomas son of John Maxfeild chr.
Feb.* 12 John Smith bur.

1546.

April 3 Evan Ellis bur.
May 1 Ritchard May, merch[t] tailor, bur.
May 30 Ambros son of M[r] Lambard chr.
June 21 Alse dau. of John Banks chr.
Sep. 9 Cutburt son of John Lugs chr.
Sep. 16 Margery wife of John Singlehurst bur.
Oct. 16 William son of [*blank*] Mednot chr.
Nov. 17 M[r] Underhill & Joane Downes marr.
Nov. 17 Leonard son of Cutbert Worcup chr.
Dec. 7 Ester dau. of Thomas Blunt chr.
Dec. 24 John, Doctor Krome's serv[t], bur.
Jan. 16 John Best & Joane Hopkin marr.
Jan. 16 Christian, M[r] Etherington's child, chr.
Jan. 30 James Sillafer & Alce Mercer marr.
Feb. 3 John Singlehurst & Sibble [*blank*] marr.
Feb. 4 John son of John Sperin bur.
Feb. 22 Ames Bell dau. of John Bell bur.

* *Sic.* ? March.

1547.

April 30 Phillip son of Robart Collins bur.
May 8 Christopher Ward & Nem [*sic*] Nelson marr.
May 20 Edward son of Mr Bowland bur.
May 26 Ambros son of Wm Lambart bur.
June 16 William Whetely & Clement Norton marr.
July 14 Edward Saxby, gentleman, and [*blank*] Bowland, wedow, marr.
July 15 Thomas son of Richard Churchman bur.
July 23 Richard Rise & Phillipp Mercy marr.
July 30 Thomas Lane, wax-chandler, bur.
Aug. 4 Margery dau. of Thomas Wippe chr.
Aug. 8 John Purvay & An Wedliffe marr.
Aug. 16 Edmond Stringer's child chr.
Aug. 18 Phillipp son of John Churchman chr.
Sep. 6 Fulke son of Richard Richardson bur.
Sep. 13 John son of Roger Gammade [*sic*] chr.
Sep. 16 John son of Mr Dickison chr.
Sep. 24 John son of Mr Richardson chr.
Sep. 27 Raiburne son of Mr Bank bur.
Oct. 1 Thomas son of John Sperin bur.
Oct. 21 Katturne dau. of John Singlehurst chr.
Nov. 11 Edward son of Thomas Tollwin bur.
Dec. 13 William son of Mr Midnall chr.
Jan. 7 Jesper son of William Lambert chr.
Jan. 22 Leonard Roberdine & Margaret Archer marr.
Jan. 28 Elsabeth dau. of John Bancks chr.
Feb. 9 Austin Hanson & Jane Rawlins marr.
Feb. 23 Margaret dau. of Robart Benfeild [?]
Feb. 26 Nicholas son of Cut. Warcuppe chr.
Feb. 28 Jone dau. of Mr Hetherington chr.
Mar. 19 Richard son of Thomas Blunt chr.

1548.

April 17 Als dau. of John Sperin chr.
April 23 Custones Hough, widow, bur.
April 27 Mr Stile, physician, bur.
May 1 John Ruese & Maudlin Smith marr.
June 4 Elisabeth dau. of Edward Saxbey chr.
July 8 Joane dau. of Richard Clifton bur.
July 9 Katerine dau. of Thomas Cootes chr.
July 15 Margery dau. of Mr Lugs chr.
July 16 Jane dau. of Wm Tod bur.
July 23 Sisly Tod, and Soky her serv. wth her, bur.
July 25 John Edmond, hoshier, bur.
Aug. 2 Thomas son of Wm Tod bur.
Aug. 4 Thomas Gest, prentice, bur.
Aug. 5 Joane of godsending was buried [*sic*]
Aug. 13 Thomas Ballander, tailor, bur.
Aug. 15 Thomas the Flemming's boy bur.
Aug. 17 Frauncis Walker bur.
Aug. 24 Anne Stavely bur.
Sep. 1 Richard Hall bur.
Sep. 12 Nicholas Finch bur.
Sep. 18 Alexander Charnock bur.

Sep. 22 Joane dau. of Robart Collins chr.
Sep. 25 Thomas Brigell bur.
Sep. 27 Jane, serv[t] wth M[r] Shushe, bur.
Sep. 30 Thomas Hevy bur.
Sep. 30 John son of Thomas Whip chr.
Oct. 9 Anne Chiverall bur.
Oct. 10 Roger Gammadge, merch[t] tailor, bur.
Oct. 13 Richard son of John Bancks bur.
Oct. 17 Jone Chadwell bur.
Oct. 18 Thomas Bocks, prentice, bur.
Oct. 20 Annis Bancks bur.
Nov. 4 John, serv[t] of John Bancks, bur.
Nov. 5 Jeames Grenade bur.
Nov. 9 John Warren bur.
Nov. 12 James son of Robart Dickison chr.
Nov. 15 Elisabeth dau. of M[r] Richarson chr.
Nov. 17 Katerin dau. of M[r] Coper chr.
Nov. 18 Thomas Scott, a child, bur.
Nov. 20 John Simson & Joane Hornecliffe marr.
Dec. 5 Mary Churchman, a child, bur.
Dec. 7 Richard Churchman's child chr.
Dec. 17 Thomas son of M[r] Miduall chr.
Dec. 19 Roger son of Roger Gammadge chr.
Dec. 21 Annis dau. of Thomas Ludway chr.
Dec. 22 William son of John Singlehurst chr.
Dec. 27 Maudlyn Richardson bur
Jan. 6 Edward Blend bur.
Jan. 27 Susan dau. of Thomas Ballander chr.
Jan. 29 William Tod & Johan Ridly marr.
Jan. 30 Steven son of Edmond Stringer chr.
Mar. 3 Thomas Bannister & Elisabeth Gamadge marr.
Mar. 7 John son of M[r] Hanson chr.
Mar. 18 Raphe Sprate's child chr.
Mar. 19 Als Sperin, an old woman, bur.

1549.

Mar. 25 Thomas son of M[r] Hetherington chr
April 28 Taylboys son of Thomas Blunt chr.
April 29 Margarett Cannon, widow, bur.
May 5 Christian dau. of Cutbert Warcup chr.
May 14 Maudlin Darsy bur.
May 24 Elisabeth Huis bur.
May 26 John son of M[r] Maxfeild chr.
June 25 Baltasar son of M[r] Lambard chr.
June 28 Richard Blunt, servant, bur.
July 9 Thomas Tate & Elisabeth [*blank*] marr.
July 13 Miles Raven & Anne Ballander marr.
July 17 James Heath & Elisabeth Brafeild marr.
July 23 Mihill Assherst & Christian Bowin marr.
Sep. 10 Millisant Monocks & Thomas Agriffeth marr.
Oct. 15 Alee dau. of Robert Collins chr.
Oct. 28 Issable dau. of Thomas Ludway chr.
Nov. 24 Robart son of M[r] Dickison chr.
Dec. 8 Emma dau. of W[m] Cooper chr.
Dec. 18 M[r] Middleton's wife bur.
Dec. 19 Richard son of Mihill Christen chr.

Jan. 1 Richard Churchman's child chr.
Jan. 5 Dannell son of Edmund Stringer chr.
Jan. 7 William Pott bur.
Jan. 11 Edward son of Thomas Bet chr.
Feb. 16 Joane Jacksonne bur.
Feb. 23 Marie dau. of John Singglehurst chr.
Mar. 2 William son of Austin Hausons chr.
Mar. 2 Timothy son of Mr Raven chr.
Mar. 2 Sarah dau. of Wm Bancks chr.
Mar. 8 Sisly Dorner bur.
Mar. 9 Anne dau. of Mr Mernat chr.
Mar. 9 Annes dau. of Thomas Whip chr.
Mar. 17 Ravey's child bur.

1550.

April 11 Eme Nixsanne bur.
April 20 Jeames Meriall & Margeret Shingleton marr.
May 18 Sibble Shingleton bur.
June 14 William son of John Cootes chr.
Aug. 2 John Rawlins & Joane Ellis marr.
Sep. 8 Thomas Sperin's child chr. John
Sep. 16 Anne dau. of Cutber Warcup chr.
Oct. 20 William Howis & Joan Beabson marr.
Nov. 2 Mary dau. of Ro. Colins chr.
Nov. 9 Samuell son of Mr Ludway chr.
Nov. 12 A child was chr. & named Thomas
Nov. 19 Cristones wife of John Bolter* bur.
Jan. 11 Edward son of Mr Saxby chr.
Jan. 11 Richard Richardson's child chr.
Jan. 24 Hew Parker & Katerin Sims marr.
Jan. 25 George Nuson & An Martiall marr.
Jan. 27 Allen Writhby & Alis Gould marr.
Feb. 8 Elsabeth dau. of Thom. Pullison chr.
Feb. 24 William son of Mr Coper chr.
Mar. 18 Aplin the child of Robert Dickison chr.
Mar. 22 Anne dau. of Edmund Stringer chr.

1551.

April 12 Judeth dau. of Mr Twiford chr.
May 1 Simond son of Mr Bancks chr.
May 24 Frauncis son of Wm Hawes chr.
June 9 Thomas Watton & Mary Jarrall marr.
June 14 Christofer Fath & Joane [*blank*] marr.

In the time of ye sweating July.

July 10 Thomas Hot, skinner, bur.
July 10 Thomas Pile, prentice, bur.
July 10 Richard Churchman, skinner, bur.
July 11 Anne Tolwinne bur.
July 11 Martin Foxley, prentice, bur.
July 12 Lewis Foxley bur.
July 13 Ellis Wimarke bur.
July 13 William Lawton, tailor, bur.
July 13 John Bancks, merch^t tailor, bur.

* Bolster; see April 30, 1542.

July 15 John son of Mr Bancks bur.
July 18 Sarah dau. of Wm Bancks bur.
Aug. 12 Katerin dau. of Mr Brigot chr.
Sep. 14 Raphe son of Mr Spratt chr.
Oct. 16 John son of Mr Maxfeild bur.
Nov. 15 William Pitcher & Elisabeth Collins marr.
Nov. 17 John son of Alen Srathbys [*sic*] chr.
Nov. 22 John Brigdale & Joane Rokennan marr.
Nov. 23 William Holl & Elisabeth Warren marr.
Dec. 12 Margaret Ady, wch destroyed herself, bur.
Dec. 13 William son of Thomas Hodwell chr.
Dec. 25 Margeret dau. of John Maxfeild chr.
Feb. 2 John Ampleforth's child chr.
Feb. 3 William Alard & Margaret Churchman marr.
Feb. 3 Joane Marsam bur.
Feb. 7 Joane Wale bur.
Feb. 11 Timothy son of Wm Mednall chr.
Mar. 18 Jane dau. of Mr Richardson chr.

1552.

Mar. 30 Mother Ellen bur.
April 3 Henry Shush, skinner, bur.
April 21 Raphe Baxton bur.
May 4 Mistris Addington, the King's skinner [?]
May 4 Samuell son of Thomas Ludwell bur.
May 5 Jane dau. of Robert Collins chr.
May 28 Mr Bernard Gennings, skinner, bur.
June 3 Grace, Cutberd Wareup's maid, bur.
June 5 Richard son of Wm Howes chr.
June 18 Anne dau. of Mr Dickison chr.
July 3 Richard Westray & Joane Fullon marr.
Aug. 21 Unica dau. of Cutbert Wareup chr.
Sep. 12 Anne dau. of Raphe Spratt chr.
Sep. 24 Richard son of Thomas Sanders chr.
Sep. 25 William son of Edmund Stringer chr.
Oct. 16 Mary dau. of Richard Brigot chr.
Oct. 17 Thomas son of Mr Whip chr.
Nov. 18 Francis son of Wm Hawes bur.
Nov. 23 Mr George Rowles bur.
Dec. 11 Sarah dau. of Mr Clement chr.
Dec. 11 John son of Thomas Lodway chr.
Dec. 18 Samuell son of Robart Twiford chr.
Jan. 14 Susanna dau. of Wm Dowfeild chr.
Feb. 11 Sarah dau. of Wm Bancks chr.
Feb. 12 Robert son of Thomas Pullison chr.
Feb. 17 Robart son of Thomas Pullison chr. [? bur.]
Mar. 2 Henry Booth, servt, bur.
Mar. 5 William son of Mr Singglehurst chr.
Mar. 14 Thomas Whip's wife bur.
Mar. 19 Ane bur. [*sic*]
Mar. 19 Susan dau. of Mr Westray chr.

1553.

Mar. 25 Nicholas son of Richard Rand chr.
April 8 A woman named Elsabeth bur.
April 17 Margaret wife of Mr Ady bur.

April 22 Joane dau. of Mr Rasby chr.
April 23 William son of Mihill Christian chr.
May 7 Richard Greene & Jone Clark marr.
June 18 William son of Thomas Stone chr.
June 24 William son of John Ampleforth chr.
July 11 Thomas Rumnie bur.
July 13 Anes dau. of William Througod chr.
July 22 Mary dau. of Robert Diconson chr.
Aug. 6 Richard son of Raphe Sprat chr.
Sep. 9 Timothy son of John Collins bur.
Sep. 16 Elisabeth dau. of Mr Stone bur.
Oct. 5 Jone dau. of Wm Holland chr.
Oct. 10 Briget dau. of Mr Richardson chr.
Oct. 27 Peter Johnson & Elisabeth Tottle marr.
Nov. 5 William Dountton & Julias Gold marr.
Nov. 11 Fridaysweede dau. of Mr Southworth chr.
Dec. 9 Harry son of Richard Brigot chr.
Dec. 13 Alse dau. of Henry Glover chr.
Dec. 31 Anne dau. of Thomas Ludwell chr.
Jan. 14 Daniell son of Mr Milnill chr.
Feb. 13 Susan Maxfeild chr.
Feb. 17 Richard Brickit bur.
Feb. 26 John son of Mr Bancks chr.
Mar. 16 Anne dau. of Wm Bancks chr.

1554.

April 11 Sarah dau. of Robert Thiford chr.
May 8 Elisabeth dau. of Thomas Stone chr.
July 26 John son of Mr Maxfeild bur.
July 26 William son of Richard Rave chr.
Aug. 15 Thomas Parker & Ames Clarke marr.
Aug. 15 Margaret dau. of Mr Alessander chr.
Aug. 30 Thomas son of Richard Vestray chr.
Sep. 6 Susanna dau. of Allen Rattoslyes chr.
Oct. 3 John son of Mr Ampelford born [*sic*]
Nov. 3 Annis dau. of Richard Richardson born [*sic*]
Nov. 4 Margery Dickison's maid bur.
Nov. 10 Mr Sudworth's child named Elizabeth chr.
Nov. 12 Sibble Nodegate, gentlewoman, bur.
Dec. 11 Alse dau. of Thomas Pullison chr.
Jan. 10 John son of Robert Collins chr.
Jan. 25 Susanna dau. of Thomas Ludwell chr.
Feb. 6 Jone dau. of John Singlehurst chr.
Feb. 8 William son of Robert Dickison chr.
Feb. 18 Sarrah dau. of Wm Througod chr.
Feb. 24 Rooffe Bowell's child chr.

1555.

Mar. 28 Jone dau. of Mr Singlehurst bur.
Mar. 29 Millisant dau. of Georg Nosset [*sic*] chr.
May 6 Millisent dau. of Georg Mosset [*sic*] bur.
May 18 Thomas Trighton & Joane Mossell marr.
July 14 Thomas Morton, gentleman, bur.
July 21 Mr Weston & Mistris Addington marr.
Aug. 17 Elisabeth dau. of Robart Twiford chr.

Sep. 16 One Fishe's dau. of Water Fish bur.
Sep. 26 Richard son of Water Fish bur.
Sep. 30 Wm Bancks' child chr. & bur.
Nov. 17 John Mansfeild & Katerin Clere marr.
Nov. 20 John Ampleford's child chr.
Nov. 22 Joane dau. of Allen Rathby chr.
Nov. 24 Anne dau. of Thomas Whipp chr.
Nov. 30 Thomas Seer & An Locknell marr.
Dec. 4 William son of Raphe Sprat chr.
Dec. 6 John son of Richard Richardson chr.
Dec. 18 Raphe wife [*sic*] of Thomas Rede bur.
Dec. 20 Marie dau. of Wm Holland chr.
Jan. 10 Robert Vickers & Elisabeth Bancks marr.
Jan. 12 Thomas son of Rafe Sprat bur.
Feb. 6 Elisabeth & John [*sic*] the children of Bell were born both at a birth, & Jone [*sic*] was bur.
Feb. 14 Thomas son of Richard Sudworth chr.

1556.

April 6 Thomas son of Davy Evans chr.
April 7 Winefrid dau. of John Hous chr.
April 8 John son of Thomas Sander chr.
April 14 Winifrid dau. of Mr Howes bur.
April 16 John Singlehurst bur.
April 23 William Bancks bur.
April 24 John Roduld bur.
April 26 Grace Spratt bur.
July 3 John son of Robart Collins chr.
July 26 Bessell Johnson & Elisabeth Whitchurch marr.
Aug. 1 Jone dau. of Thomas Ludwell chr.
Aug. 11 Annes dau. of Willm Hates chr.
Aug. 19 John son of John Singlehurst chr.
Sep. 12 Barbary Jackson bur.
Sep. 21 Margaret Cottes [?]
Oct. 3 Water Fishe's child bur.
Nov. 28 Jone Saunders, widow, bur.
Dec. 1 Jacobin Smith, widow, bur.
Dec. 19 William Tod, tailor, bur.
Jan. 15 Anne dau. of Robart Tailor chr.; her name was Elisabeth, for so she is cald, and therfore this semeth to be an error
Jan. 17 Robert Pennerton & Mary Slipperton marr.
Jan. 17 Daniell son of Robart Diconson chr.
Jan. 20 Henry son of Edward Warner chr.

1557.

May 17 John Brand bur.
May 18 John Wilford bur.
May 25 George son of Richard Southwell chr.
June 18 Richard Davy bur.
June 20 Christofer Bellingham & Elisabeth Scott marr.
July 1 John Humble & An Bricket marr.
July 3 Jone King, widow, bur.
July 20 Arthur Bing bur.
Aug. 23 Margery dau. of Water Handleys chr.
Aug. 30 Francis son of Mr Bassill chr.

Sep. 8 Kinborough son of Raphe Spratt chr.
Dec.*10 William Batcheler bur.
Oct. 19 Dority Througood chr.
Oct. 21 Elisabeth, Johnson's wife, bur.
Oct. 23 Frauncis Stone chr.
Oct. 23 Thomas Fish chr.
Nov. 5 John Dixson & Dority Doson marr.
Nov. 6 George Ausley bur.
Nov. 6 Hugh Alessander bur.
Nov. 20 Mary Martin dau. to Mr Alderman Martin chr.
Dec. 2 Robart Twiford chr.
Dec. 28 Steven Howish chr.
Jan. 29 Annis Howish bur.
Feb. 13 Anthony Silver chr.

1558.

Mar. 27 Jone Draper chr.
April 18 Elisabeth Hind chr.
April 25 Thomas Bull chr.
May 1 William Stockes & Margaret Deane marr.
May 12 Ellen Baldwin chr.
May 16 Winefrid Pullison chr.
May 27 John Mate chr.
June 2 Alse Dickison chr.
June 22 Thomas Robison chr.
June 28 Robart Tailor bur.
July 5 Susanna Tailor chr.
July 11 Roger Woodom & Margery Yong marr.
July 13 Thomas Banckes bapt.
Aug. 10 Robert son of Robart Dickison bur.
Aug. 11 Katerin Stringer bur.
Aug. 14 Andrew Stevenson & Mary Reede marr.
Aug. 28 Marye White bapt.
Sep. 7 Jane Rathesoby bapt.
Sep. 9 Water Handberry bapt.
Sep. 29 Nicholas Dounton bapt.
Oct. 18 Frauncis Spratt & his brother Edward bapt.
Nov. 13 Georg Eliot & Jane Underwood marr.
Nov. 19 Katerin More bur.
Nov. 19 Elisabeth Fish bapt.
Dec. 17 William Whipp bapt.
Jan. 15 George Smith & Isbell Fox marr.
Jan. 16 George Carr & Margaret Farrer marr.
Jan. 17 John Didlesoul & Als Rigal marr.
Jan. 19 Mother South bur.
Jan. 20 Mother Elsabeth, widow, bur.
Jan. 21 Isbell Whipp bur.
Jan. 23 Thomas Rede & Elsabeth Rigdall marr.
Feb. 11 Margaret Simple bur.
Mar. 19 Elsabeth Throwgod chr.
Mar. 24 Thomas Smith bur.

1559.

April 7 Katerin Cox bur.
April 13 William Dowfeild chr.
April 17 Sigisimus Broke & An Gerningham marr.

* *Sic.*

May 4 Thomas Kinsman bur.
May 15 Katerin Draper chr.
June 14 Elsabeth dau. of John Bull chr.

Queene Elizabeth.

The first yeare of the raine of our Soveraine Queene.

July 6 Richard Baker of Shrewsbery bur.
July 13 Samuell son of Mr Robinson chr.
Aug. 10 Elisabeth Mayats chr.
Sep. 18 The child of Wm How chr. in the house & bur.
Sep. 23 Anthony Browne bur.
Sep. 23 Augustine son of John Baudwin chr.
Sep. 24 Susan dau. of Robert Dickson chr.
Sep. 30 Thomas Mayots burd 20 Oct. but decd 30 Sep.
Oct. 18 Sr Roger Martin Alderman his child was buried and his wiffe brought a bedde ye same daye
Nov. 1 Katerin dau. of Water Handbery bapt.
Nov. 5 An dau. of Thomas Pullison chr.
Nov. 26 Thomas son of Mr Stone chr.
Nov. 26 Thomas son of Alen Rasby chr.
Jan. 19 Robart son of Edmund Stringer chr.
Jan. 29 Thomas son of Mr Dunkin chr.
Feb. 1 Thomas Stringer bur.
Feb. 12 Elisabeth dau. of John Whit chr.
Feb. 18 Elisabeth dau. of Wm Banckes chr.
Mar. 6 Katerin dau. of Mr Johnson bapt.
Mar. 12 John Hill bur.

1560.

April 8 Richard Shawell, prentice wth Mr Parker [?]
April 8 Elsabeth dau. of Newton, a clothworker, dwelling in St Mary Buthol's parish, chr.
April 8 A child wch found at Ludgate at five of the clocke in ye morning was bapt.
April 10 Margery Shaw bur.
April 12 Ames Hudson bur.
April 16 Hester dau. of Thomas Whip chr.
May 1 Nicholas Purser, servt to Crosse, bur.
May 4 Elisabeth dau. of George Fisher chr.
May 5 Griffin Evans bur.
May 15 Roger son of Raphe Sprat [?]
May 19 Roger Martin's child chr. in ye house & bur.
Aug. 26 John son of Water Lancaster chr.
Aug. 29 Susanna dau. of Wm Wanton chr.
Aug. 30 Dority dau. of Ambros Smith chr.
Sep. 1 John son of Mr Draper chr.
Sep. 21 Barnick Dericke, servt wth John Draper, bur.
Oct. 7 Jone dau. of Francis Robinson chr.
Oct. 13 Richard Dod & Elisabeth Oliar marr.
Oct. 21 Als dau. of John Baudlin chr.
Oct. 28 William son of Robart Dickison bapt.
Nov. 9 Thomas Pullison's child bur.
Nov. 10 John son of Thomas Stone bapt.
Nov. 10 Susan dau. of Wm Piburnes chr.
Dec. 16 John Notshaw & Ellen Patgit marr.
Dec. 18 Mary dau. of Wm Dickison chr.

Oct.* 14 Augustine son of John Hindes chr.
Jan. 4 Susan dau. of Thomas Dickison chr.
Mar. 1 Thomas son of John White chr.
Mar. 1 Margery dau. of Roger Atkins chr.
Mar. 14 Edward son of Mr Harlow chr.
Feb.* 24 Mary Robinson bur.
[*blank*]3 Richard Clarck & John [*sic*] Parker marr.

1561.

April 5 Jane dau. of Allen Rasby bur.
May 4 William Howe's child born & bur.
May 4 Edward Roche & Dority Dortun [*sic*] marr.
May 18 Thomas Torner & Alis Constable marr.
May 28 George Mutton son of Nicholas Mutton of Haddam, Herts, husbandman, serv^t to Allen Rathby, bur.
June 8 John son of Edmund Stringer chr.
June 24 Johane ye daughter of Sr Roger Martin chr.
July 5 Catterin Tailor *alias* Caterin Cardmake bur.
July 17 John Foxall & Sibble Whipp marr.
July 24 Water son of Thomas Pullison chr.
July 30 Thomas son of John Marshall chr.
Aug. 2 Harry son of John Isam chr.
Sep. 4 Edward son of Richard Sudworth chr.
Oct. 9 Elisabeth dau. of Wm Worship chr.
Oct. 10 Bartholmew Gorbit bur.
Oct. 14 Francis son of John Baldin chr. & bur.
Oct. 24 William Care & Als Draper marr.
Oct. 31 Margaret dau. of Raphe Sprat chr.
Nov. 8 Annes dau. of Allen Rathby chr.
Nov. 9 Water son of Wm Fish chr.
Nov. 9 Ambros son of Thomas Stone chr.
Nov. 9 Thomas son of Robt Dickison bur.
Dec. 3 William Sherrington & Elisabeth Mayot marr.
Dec. 6 John son of Wm Througood chr.
Dec. 21 Elisabeth dau. of Mr Robinson chr.
Jan. 4 Anne Poole, gentlewoman, bur.
Jan. 11 Margaret dau. of Mr Smith chr.
Jan. 17 Richard son of Thomas Dounton chr.
Mar. 16 William Worship bur.

1562.

Mar. 27 Goodman Bell's child was bur., named Jone Vedaull
Mar. 30 Mary dau. of Mr Ludway bur.
April 4 William Gibs, servant, bur.
April 10 Allen Rathby bur.
May 17 Joane dau. of Water Lancaster chr.
May 18 Umphery Ramsden & Als Pickins marr.
May 28 Elisabeth Througood bur.
June 6 Elisabeth dau. of Water Lancaster bur.
June 14 John Nale & Sisley Barlow marr.
June 21 Thomas Robinson & Jane Morlish marr.
June 21 Katerin dau. of John Silver chr.
June 30 Roger Mountague & Alse Smith marr.
July 25 Margaret dau. of Georg Fisher chr.
Aug. 16 William son of John Marshall chr.

* *Sic.*

Aug. 27 Susan dau. of Umphery Ramsden bur.
Sep. 1 William Tollwin, parson of ye parish, bur.
Sep. 2 Harry Cheyney bur.
Sep. 6 William Beckwith & Margaret Day marr.
Oct. 11 Francis son of Thomas Stone chr.
Nov. 4 Harry Maxfeild bur.
Nov. 8 Mihill son of Thomas Pullison chr.
Nov. 20 John son of Raphe Sprat chr.
Nov. 27 Margaret Cheyney bur.
Nov. 27 Francis Hiham & Jane Perkins marr.
Nov. 29 Euseby child of John Isam chr.
Nov. 30 Robert Collins bur.
Dec. 1 Harry Greene, serv^t to Mr Isam, bur.
Dec. 2 Eusebe child of John Isam bur.
Dec. 20 Maud Widdrick's child bapt., serv^t to Mr Brigs
Jan. 17 John son of John Whit bapt.
Feb. 2 Francis son of Christofer Bevell bapt.
Feb. 7 William Godding, servant, bur.
Feb. 7 Elsabeth dau. of John Pales chr.
Feb. 21 Elsabeth dau. of Edmund Stringer [?]
Mar. 18 Jone dau. of Richard Sudworth chr.
Mar. 18 Henry son of Wm Perris chr.

1563.

Mar. 30 Sarah Baldwin's child bapt. & named Sarah
April 4 Anne dau. of Mr Roger Martin bapt.
April 18 Richard son of Wm Pibrune chr.
April 23 William son of Francis Robinson chr.
April 26 Richard son of Wm Pilburne bur.
May 30 Nathaniell son of Richard Est chr.
June 27 Harry Willman & Als Worship marr.
July 4 Thomas son of Ambros Smith chr.
July 4 William son of Water Lancaster chr.
July 30 Valentine Worst, servant, bur.
Aug. 1 Mary Whithed, serv^t of John Morgain, bur.
Aug. 7 Francis son of John Draper bapt.
Aug. 13 Water Right, serv^t to Ri. Clarke [?]
Aug. 17 Joane Roberts bur.; of the plague
Aug. 18 Robart Diconson's child bur., not chr.
Aug. 19 John How, serv^t to Wm Hodson, bur.
Aug. 26 Als Burden, serv^t to Richard Clark, bur.
Aug. 26 Thomas son of Thomas Dounton bur.
Aug. 27 Edward, serv^t to Alderman Martin, bur.
Aug. 28 Abraham son of Robart Dickison chr.
Aug. 28 Caterin Morris, serv^t to John Morris, bur.
Aug. 30 Elisabeth Worship bur.
Sep. 1 James Hale, serv^t to Raffe Sprat, bur.
Sep. 2 Richard Nudigate, serv^t to Rich. Clarck, bur.
Sep. 3 Barbery Dalia, serv^t to Wm Througood, bur.
Sep. 3 Harry Milman bur.
Sep. 4 Thomas Kickmer, serv^t to Raphe Sprat, bur.
Sep. 5 Thomas Fuston, sexton, bur.
Sep. 8 William Rascock's boy bur.
Sep. 9 Rose Dauson, serv^t to Wm Througood, bur.
Sep. 11 William Atkinsonne, parson of this parish, bur.
Sep. 12 Edward Barber, brother-in-law to Mr Stringer, bur.

Sep. 14 Robart Eltonhed, serv[t] to Rob[t] Collins, bur.
Sep. 14 Maudlin Gemo, serv[t] to the parson of the parish, bur.
Sep. 17 Nathaniell Atkinson bur., parson's son
Sep. 17 George son of Thomas Dounton bur.
Sep. 17 Allen Rathby's child chr.
Sep. 18 Nathaniell son of Richard Est bur.
Sep. 19 Jane Atkinson dau. of y[e] parson of the parish bur.
Sep. 21 Edmund Pedly, serv[t] to W[m] Parker, draper, bur.
Sep. 22 William Newton bur.
Sep. 23 Richard Est, householder, tailor, bur.
Sep. 23 John Morris, clothworker, bur.
Sep. 25 John How, son-in-law to Thomas Donton, bur.
Sep. 26 Giles Batson, serv[t] to George Fisher, bur.
Sep. 27 Joane Barber, dau.-in-law to Ed. Stringer, bur.
Sep. 27 Jane dau. of Robart Diconson bur.
Sep. 28 Raphe Anslowe's wife bur.
Sep. 28 William Piborne, tailor, bur.
Sep. 28 Susanna dau. of Tho. Donton bur.
Sep. 28 Mary dau. of Water Lancaster bur.
Sep. 29 Michaell son of Thomas Donton bur.
Sep. 29 Betteris Popplewell, serv[t] to Rob. Diconson, bur.
Sep. 29 Sarah dau. of M[r] Lancaster bur.
Sep. 30 Maudlin Grigs, serv[t] to W[m] [*blank*], bur.
Sep. 30 Susan dau. of Rob[t] Dickison, draper, bur.
Oct. 1 Margery Whip bur.
Oct. 2 Elisabeth Hammon bur.
Oct. 2 Jane Brickle, dwelling wth M[r] Hooke, bur.
Oct. 2 Jane Hooke, dwelling wth W[m] Hooke, bur.
Oct. 3 Als, serv[t] to Richard Sudworth, bur.
Oct. 4 Annis Hillton bur.
Oct. 5 Maudlin Grigs bur. [see Sep. 30]
Oct. 6 George Browin bur.
Oct. 7 Richard Fisher, serv[t] to W[m] Stevens, clothworker, bur.
Oct. 9 Thomas son of Edmund Stringer bur.
Oct. 13 Elisabeth Sanders bur.
Oct. 13 Elisabeth Fisher bur.
Oct. 16 John Hudson, serv[t] to Water Lancaster, bur.
Oct. 16 John Bradford, serv[t] to John Foxall, bur.
Oct. 18 James Finall, serv[t] to Rob[t] Dickison, bur.
Oct. 22 W[m] Yong, serv[t] to John Kemp, bur.
Oct. 22 Annes, John Draper's wife, bur.
Oct. 23 John Carlel, serv[t] to John Pell, bur.
Oct. 27 Elisabeth Pullison bur.
Oct. 27 Elisabeth Austin bur.
Oct. 28 George Cooper, serv[t] to W[m] Stevens, clothworker, bur.
Oct. 31 Elisabeth dau. of Richard Sudworth bur.
Nov. 9 Winifrid wife of John Ampilford bur.
Nov. 11 Edward Manering, serv[t] to W[m] Hudson, draper, bur.
Nov. 12 Water Lancaster's child Jone bur.
Nov. 13 John Talor, serv[t] to John Draper, bur.
Nov. 14 John Draper's child Katerin bur.
Nov. 16 John Draper bur.
Nov. 22 Rise Pulton, serv[t] to John Isam, bur.
Nov. 28 Richard Fox, serv[t] to Richard Southworth, bur.
Dec. 5 Winifrid Sudworth bur.
Dec. 6 Katerin Woodward bur.
Dec. 24 Water Downe, serv[t] to Thomas Spirim, bur.

Jan. 22 Bartholmew son of John Whit chr.
Feb. 7 Robart White & Alse Morris marr.
Mar. 2 Wm Cock *alias* Cox, of St Pancridg parish, & Alls Leake, of St Olive's, Southwark, marr.
Mar. 8 William Howis' child born & bur.
Mar. 19 Katerin dau. of George Eliot chr.

1564.

June 18 Edward Gergis & Jone Brid marr.
June 25 William Chapman & Als Eton marr.
June 26 Elisabeth Pouling, serv^t^ to Wm Dues, bur.
July 16 Nicholas Brigman & Als Milmon marr.
July 19 Samuell son of Thomas Stone chr.
July 24 Jane dau. of Francis Robinson chr.
July 24 Allen child of John Baudwin chr.
Sep. 3 Thomas son of Thomas Douton chr.
Oct. 4 Francis son of Mr Beverly chr.
Oct. 14 Mother Julian bur.
Oct. 28 Joyce dau. of Mr Maxfeild chr.
Oct. 29 The same child bur.
Nov. 4 Harry son of Thomas Wright bur. [see Nov. 19]
Nov. 5 William Atkinson ye clothworker's child born & bur.
Nov. 12 Allein child of Allen Rathby chr.
Nov. 19 Harry son of Thomas Wright chr. [*sic*]
Dec. 6 Prudence dau. of Thomas Pullison chr.
Jan. 12 Richard son of John Isam chr.
Jan. 12 John son of Anthony Robinson chr.
Jan. 28 Margaret dau. of Robart Dickinson chr.
Jan. 28 George son of Wm Dewis chr.
Feb. 24 Wm Flemming & Als Atkinson marr.

1565.

Mar. 25 Winefrid dau. of Thomas Davys chr.
April 8 Joane son [*sic*] of Raffe Spratt chr.
April 15 Elisabeth dau. of Thomas Smith chr.
May 10 Richard Wells & Elisabeth Holland, both of Feversam, Kent, marr.
May 14 Thomas Bird & Annis Wrake marr.
May 14 Mathew son of Richard Clark chr.
May 17 Elisabeth dau. of Thomas Sanders chr.
May 27 Raphe Daniell & Jone Chapman marr.
June 10 Elisabeth dau. of Wm Througood chr.
June 15 John Bungey, preacher, & Margaret Parkes marr.
June 17 John son of John Marshall chr.
July 1 Robart Longly & Ellen Watkinson marr.
July 5 Gudwife Robarts, nurse, bur.
July 18 Joane Cliffe bur.
Aug. 6 John Slorres & Rosse Martin marr.
Aug. 18 Frances dau. of John Harrison chr.
Aug. 22 Joane dau. of Wm Horns chr.
Sep. 3 Frances dau. of Francis Robinson chr.
Sep. 18 Margaret Pratt bur.
Nov. 4 Jone dau. of Edward Stringer chr.
Nov. 12 Alderman Martin's child was christned w^th^in the house, and died ye same ower & bur. ye sam day
Dec. 9 W^m^ son of Francis Kemp chr.

Dec. 9 Winifrid dau. of Thomas Stone chr.
Dec. 15 Tovall Iver's child, an Irishman, named Roger, chr.
Jan. 7 Als dau. of Thomas Right chr.
Jan. 12 Christofer Stanton & Elisabeth Piborn marr.
Jan. 20 Frances dau. of Wm Harriot chr.
Jan. 22 John Barker & Margaret Charles marr.
Feb. 2 Edward son of George Eliot chr.
Feb. 20 Larrance son of Wm Davis chr.
Feb. 22 W^m^ son of Christofer Beverly chr.
Feb. 30* Richard Hammon, serv^t^ to Mr Harrison, bur.
Mar. 5 Dority dau. of John Bauldwin chr.
Mar. 6 Wm Atkinson's child born & bur.
Mar. 17 Sible dau. of Richard Suthwell chr.

1566.

April 25 John son of John Penson chr.
May 9 John Tailor bur.
May 21 Nicholas Wicks bur.
Aug. 3 Edward son of Allen Rathby chr.
Aug. 21 John Phillips had two maiden children bapt., one named Elisabeth, and the other Joane
Aug. 24 Frances dau. of Wm Horne chr.
Aug. 28 Joane dau. of Thomas Bird bur.
Sep. 1 Thomas son of Anthony Robinson chr.
Sep. 1 Annis dau. of Thomas Davis chr.
Sep. 5 Mr Thomas [*sic*] & Elisabeth Cox marr.
Sep. 17 Thomas Madder & Margery Gould marr.
Sep. 29 Robart Clifton & Als Perin marr.
Sep. 29 Mary dau. of Mr Wm Througood chr.
Oct. 6 Thomas son of Thomas Sanders chr.
Oct. 6 Thomas son of the s^d^ Thomas Sanders bur.
Oct. 23 Thomas son of Robart Wright chr.
Oct. 25 Robart son of Mr John Isam chr.
Nov. 1 Judeth dau. of Christopher Stanton chr.
Nov. 10 Nicholas son of Mr Thomas Pullison chr.
Nov. 10 John son of Robart Dickison chr.
Nov. 22 William Norman, serv^t^ of Thomas Ludwell, bur.
Dec. 16 Francis son of Francis Kemp chr.
Dec. 22 Elisabeth dau. of John Marshall chr.
Dec. 23 Richard Fowlsam & Elisabeth Swanne marr.
Jan. 23 Jordan son of Francis Robinson chr.
Feb. 2 Roger son of Wm Harriot chr.
Feb. 3 Francis Cockwell & An Ludwell marr.
Feb. 9 Nicholas Roodes & Elisabeth Story marr.
Feb. 10 Thomas son of Thomas Wright bur.
Feb. 11 John Hutton & An Castlen marr.
Feb. 24 W^m^ son of Thomas Stone chr.
Mar. 6 Elisabeth dau. of John Harrison chr.

1567.

April 18 Master John Bull bur.
May 4 Valentine son of John Penson chr.
May 5 Margaret dau. of Wm Dewis chr.
May 8 Elsobeth dau. of Roger Austin chr.
May 28 Dority dau. of Francis Hihan [*sic*] chr.

* *Sic.*

June 8 Johannar dau. of Tho. Rawlins chr.
June 14 Richard Clifton bur.
July 17 Elias son of M[r] Starkowe chr.
July 30 Winefrid dau. of Robart Clifton chr.
Aug. 17 Elisabeth dau. of Robart Maxfeild chr.
Aug. 22 Winifrid dau. of Tho. Stone bur.
Aug. 29 Edward son of Anthony Robison chr.
Sep. 7 Abraham son of Reynold Woster, stranger, chr.
Sep. 16 Abigall dau. of Tho. Robison bur.
Oct. 11 W[m] Segar & Kathering Hetherington marr.
Nov. 26 Elisabeth dau. of Thomas Bird chr.
Dec. 22 Geffry son of George Vaine chr.
Jan. 4 Als dau. of M[r] Davis chr.
Jan. 17 M[rs] Hudson wife of W[m] Hudson bur.
Feb. 17 Thomas son of M[r] Sprat bur.
Feb. 9 Robart Warcup & Annis Beram marr.
Mar. 3 Thomas son of Thomas Sander chr.
Mar. 4 Als dau. of Robart Right chr.

1568.

Mar. 27 Susan dau. of John Penson chr.
April 18 William son of W[m] Hariot chr.
May 23 W[m] Grenam, serv[t] to Mathew Cros, bur.
May 27 Thomas son of Rob[t] Diconson chr.
May 30 S[r] Roger Martin, alderman, in the yeare of his maralty had maried out of his house his made named Anne Whaplet unto Richard Feirsey
May 30 The same day was maried Richard Pitts unto another of his maids named Jone Rooke
May 30 Water son of Francis Robinson chr.
July 15 John Gilbert, serv[t] to M[r] Througood, bur.
July 19 Richard Pert and Jone Knowles were maried out of S[r] Roger Martin's house in his maralty
Aug. 14 Roger son of John Marshall chr.
Aug. 2... Elsabeth dau. of Thomas Bird bur.
Sep. 20 Thomas son of Allen Rathby bur.
Sep. 25 Sible dau. of Thomas Hornes chr.
Oct. 3 Susan dau. of Allen Rathby bur.
Oct. 3 Water son of John Phillips chr.
Oct. 4 Joane dau. of Allen Rathby bur.
Oct. 17 W[m] son of Thomas Pullison chr.
Oct. 17 Dowsebell dau. of W[m] Dickison chr.
Oct. 21 John son of Robart Clifton chr.
Oct. 29 Annes Afford y[e] child of John Marshall bur.
Oct. 31 Thomas Archdale & Mary Clifton marr.
Nov. 1 Nathaniell son of Thomas Rawlins chr.
Nov. 1 Anthony son of Rob[t] Warcup chr.
Nov. 10 Rody dau. of Allen Rathby chr.
Nov. 22 John Castlin, marchant, maried to Martha the daughter of S[r] Roger Martin, Knight
Nov. 22 Robert Bye, marchant, maried Susan the daughter of Roger Martin
Nov. 22 Elisabeth wife of John Harrison bur.
Jan. 6 Elisabeth dau. of Thomas Wright chr.
Jan. 15 Elisabeth dau. of W[m] Care chr.
Jan. 16 Martha dau. of Robart Maxfeild chr.
Jan. 23 Margaret dau. of Anthony Robison chr.
Jan. 27 Grace dau. of Raphe Sprat chr.

Feb. 20 Thomas son of Francis Hiham chr.
Mar. 6 Jone dau. of Mr Davis chr.
Mar. 15 George Rathby bur.

1569.

April 9 Goodman Beverly bur.
April 17 Marye dau. of Tho. Wright bur.
April 18 Benson [*sic*] son of John Benson chr.
April 22 Jane dau. of Thomas Davis bur.
April 23 Tonkinson [*sic*] dau. of James Tonkinson chr.
April 24 John Token & Dority Kemp marr.
May 4 Annis Gotsley, serv^t to Mr Ludwell, bur.
May 9 Wm Stone, serv^t to Thomas Stone, bur.
May 15 Robart Aplegath & An Buckle marr.
May 21 Francis Beverly bur.
May 24 Margaret dau. of Ro. Wright chr.
June 5 Water son of John Phillips bur.
June 5 Annis dau. of Wm Hariot chr.
June 12 Joane dau. of Robt Hetherington chr.
June 26 Elsabeth dau. of Mother Lowton bur.
Aug. 10 John Sperin, skinner, bur.
Aug. 10 Thomas son of Thomas Bird chr.
Aug. 31 George son of Wm Anslow chr.
Sep. 14 Paull Burgis, serv^t to Mr Hudson [?]
Oct. 1 Mr John Kemp bur. in the chancell at his pew door
Oct. 5 Richard Greene, serv^t to Mr Kemp, bur.
Oct. 9 Francis son of Francis Robinson chr.
Oct. 16 Christofer Glasse & Jane Beverly, widow, marr.
Oct. 20 Thomas Edmundes, minister, & Als Perin marr.
Nov. 6 Thomas son of Thomas Rawlins, skinner, chr.
Nov. 6 Margaret dau. of Thomas Archdale chr.
Nov. 6 W^m son of Mr Cox, of St Pancridg parish, chr.
Nov. 28 Christian dau. of Wm Horne chr.
Nov. 30 Amos son of Robart Warcup chr.
Dec. 11 Wm Hudson & Joane Bull, both of this parish, marr.
Jan. 11 Water son of Robart Dickison chr.
Jan. 22 William Turner & Annis Robartes marr.
Jan. 29 John Gilborne & Anne Coker marr.
Feb. 5 Edward son of Mr Pullison chr.
Feb. 15 Michaell son of Anthony Robison chr.
Feb. 21 Als dau. of Robart Dickison bur.
Feb. 24 Anthony son of George Thean chr.
Mar. 10 James son of Robart Dickison bur.
Mar. 14 Peter Foster, sexton of this parish, bur.

1570.

Mar. 25 Thomas son of Thomas Wright chr.
April 15 Davy Jones & Margaret England marr.
April 18 George Thean bur. in ye little chapel
May 4 W^m son of John Benson chr.
June 1 Margaret dau. of Harry Jay chr.
July 1 Susan dau. of Thomas Hornes chr.
July 17 Thomas son of Thomas Sanders [?]
July 22 George, serv^t of Roger Austin, bur.
Aug. 6 Joane dau. of Thomas Bird chr.
Aug. 13 Katerin dau. of Wm Harriot chr.

Aug. 16 Robart son of Robart Martiall chr.
Aug. 23 Wm Shaw, serv^t^ with Wm Dickson, bur.
Sep. 16 Wm Foote & Jane Jack marr.
Sep. 19 Elsabeth dau. of Robart Hetherington chr.
Sep. 21 Ellen Sodon, serv^t^ of John Bell, clothworker, bur.
Sep. 23 Susan dau. of Allen Rathby chr.
Oct. 22 John Appit & Joane Hipkins marr.
Nov. 5 Harry son of Robart Right chr.
Nov. 10 Annis dau. of Wm Harriot bur.
Nov. 23 Margery, serv^t^ of John Bell, bur.
Dec. 8 Abigall dau. of Thomas Rawlins chr.
Dec. 8 Elsabeth dau. of Wm Care bur.
Dec. 11 John Petly, serv^t^ to Wm Hudson, bur.
Dec. 17 Margaret dau. of John Harrison, laborer, chr.
Dec. 26 Margery wife of Mr Wm Parker bur.
Dec. 29 W^m^ son of Wm Hariot bur.
Jan. 22 Thomas Wright, clothworker, bur.
Jan. 30 A child, found in the parish, bur.
Feb. 11 Elsabeth dau. of Mr Hiham chr.
Feb. 15 Mr Eles bur. out of this parish, new churchyard
Feb. 19 John Goose & Annis Farmar marr.
Feb. 22 Edward son of Alen Rathby bur.
Feb. 25 John Bowland & Elsabeth Theyney marr.
Feb. 26 Raphe [? Everit] & An Maxfeild marr.

1571.

April 2 Joane wife of Thomas Davis bur.
April 22 Thomas son of Thomas Howton chr.
June 24 Thomas Davis & Annis Savey marr.
July 19 Water son of Robt Clifton chr.
Aug. 6 Mary dau. of James Harman chr.
Sep. 4 Mathew Crosse, one of ye churchwardens, bur.
Sep. 22 John Sanders & An Wright marr.
Sep. 23 George Transum & Jane Carow marr.
Sep. 29 Annis dau. of Robt Warcup chr.
Oct. 10 William son of Thomas Bird chr.
Oct. 14 Jane dau. of Robert Dickison chr.
Nov. 14 Water son of Robart Dickison bur.
Nov. 15 W^m^ son of Hugh Parsons chr.
Nov. 25 Annis dau. of Wm Harriot chr.
Dec. 2 John son of Thomas Archdale chr.
Dec. 16 A poore woman y^t^ dwelt in the contrye was brought a bed in this parish whose name was Browne, her child was baptized and named Anthony
Jan. 6 Thomas son of Robert Maxfeild chr.
Jan. 6 John Jonson & Elisabeth Rawlins marr.
Jan. 15 Steven Scarborough & Elizabeth Eaton marr.
Jan. 20 Nodia son of Thomas Raulins chr.
Feb. 10 Thomas Swift & Tabitha Harriot marr.
Mar. 8 Joane dau. of Mr Marshall, cousin to Mr Marshall, chr.

1572.

Mar. 25 Alse Basset, a poor woman, bur.
April 2 John Sutton & An Palmer marr.
April 19 Jeffry son of Allen Rathby bur.

April 20 Francis son of M[r] Sanders chr.
May 1 Thomas Rich & Jane Clarck marr.
May 11 Edmund Granger & Dority Holder marr.
May 17 An dau. of M[r] Cuts, gent., chr., w[ch] child after dec. in Kent
May 24 Ellen Ford, serv[t] to M[r] Skarborough, bur. in the new churchy[d]
June 2 Jone Wilson, serv[t] to Allen Rathby, bur.
June 29 W[m] son of Henry Jay chr.
July 5 W[m] son of Thomas Davy chr.
July 6 W[m] Jay son of Henry Jay, draper, bur.
July 12 Joane dau. of Richard Sudworth bur.
Sep. 9 Nicholas Smith & Margaret Wenden marr.
Sep. 17 Allen son of Rob[t] Wright chr.
Sep. 26 Alexander Mason & Rose Lancaster marr.
Oct. 2 John son of Rob[t] Maxfeild, draper, bur.
Oct. 6 W[m] Crouch & Alce Wright marr.
Oct. 12 Edward Edwardson & Margery Thorp marr.
Oct. 14 W[m] Osborne & Katerin Hamore marr.
Oct. 15 John Crowly & Olive Hind marr.
Oct. 18 Francis son of Georg Hiham chr.
Oct. 20 W[m] Tolinson & Mary Shingle marr.
Oct. 23 W[m] son of John Sanders, drawer, chr.
Oct. 24 Edmund Lodge & Sence Cox marr.
Oct. 26 Robart Maxfeild bur.
Oct. 28 Elisabeth dau. of Thomas Hawton chr.
Nov. 1 A child of M[r] Parson, drawer, w[ch] was born dead, bur.
Nov. 6 Peter son of Steven Scharborough chr.
Nov. 11 Umphery Martin & Alce Pullison marr.
Nov. 17 Thomas Paget & Barbery Bradbery marr.
Nov. 17 John Walker, tailor, & Mary Robart marr.
Nov. 30 The dau. of W[m] Dickison chr.
Dec. 10 Alce Boulton bur.
Dec. 14 Daniell son of Francis Robinson chr.
Dec. 16 Margaret dau. of W[m] Griffin chr.
Dec. 16 Amos son of Rob[t] Warcup chr.
Dec. 23 Thomas Stone, warden of the Skinners, bur.
Jan. 1 Robert Streton & Joyce Gostelo marr.
Jan. 0* The son of John Palmer chr.
Jan. 26 Edwin Babington & Sarah Throughgood marr.
Jan. 29 M[r] Samuell Knowles & Elisabeth Hind marr.
Feb. 22 Susan dau. of Anthony Robison chr.
Mar. 19 Francis Yeomans, merch[t] tailor, & Ursula Sondon marr.
Mar. 19 Joane dau. of Raphe Spratt bur.
Mar. 22 Thomas son of Robart Hetherington chr.

1573.

Mar. 25 Calib son of Thomas Rawlins chr.
April 10 Elisabeth dau. of Thomas Haughton bur.
April 12 John son of Thomas Bird chr.
April 12 Jane dau. of John King chr.
April 19 Dorcas dau. of James Harmon chr.
May 6 M[r] Water Penistone bur.
May 7 Edward son of Rowland Cole chr.
May 8 Elisabeth dau. of John Penson chr.
May 14 Thomas Howton, merch[t] of this parish, bur.
May 31 John Parker & Ellen Crosse marr.

* *Sic.*

June 8 Alessander Denton & Mary Martin marr.
June 14 Elisabeth dau. of Thomas Davis chr.
June 19 The child of Henry Lee bur.
July 5 Agnes dau. of Robt Wareup bur.
July 6 George Ive, serv^t^ to Raphe Glasse, bur.
July 7 Geane Heath, serv^t^ to Wm Onshew, bur.
July 9 Elisabeth dau. of Thomas Davis bur.
July 12 Robart son of Robt Maxfeild chr.
Aug. 7 Thomas up Thomas, serv^t^ wth Thomas Davis, bur.
Aug. 11 Phillip Tailor bur.
Aug. 14 Thomas Penson, serv^t^ to Thomas Davis, bur.
Aug. 14 Margaret Guet bur.
Aug. 14 Anne dau. to Thomas Davis bur.
Aug. 15 Winifrid Davis bur.
Aug. 16 W^m^ son of John Walker chr.
Aug. 18 Jaine Adlington, serv^t^ wth John Parker, bur.
Sep. 4 Abraham Glossup bur.
Sep. 12 Samuell & Michaell Houghton chr., born both at a birth
Sep. 14 Thomas Gould, serv^t^ wth Thomas Davys, bur.
Sep. 19 Michaell Houghton bur.
Sep. 21 Robt Scarborough & Barbery [? Sing] marr.
Sep. 29 Samuell Houghton bur.
Sep. 30 Robart Maxfeld bur.
Oct. 25 W^m^ son of Thomas Scarborow bapt.
Nov. 10 Steven Daniell & Elisabeth Holt marr.
Nov. 23 John Life & Elisabeth Cole marr.
Nov. 28 Sarah dau. of John Marshall chr.
Dec. 17 Thomas son of Mr Griffin chr.
Dec. 24 Edward Bromley, serv^t^ wth Mr Ludwel, bur.
Jan. 9 W^m^ son of Mr Scarborough bur.
Jan. 12 Sr Roger Martin, alderman, bur.
Jan. 18 John Wheler & Agnes Haughton marr.
Feb. 2 Robart Lion & Margaret Wilcox marr.
Feb. 7 John Newsam & Susan Ludwel marr.
Feb. 8 Harry son of Hugh Parson chr.
Feb. 8 Raphe Glashop bur.
Feb. 11 Edward Glashop bur.
Feb. 22 Nicholas Hill & Rose Biell marr.
Mar. 7 Persevall son of Wm Harriot chr.

1574.

April 15 John Milborn & Allis Jones marr.
April 22 Edward Applefast & Luce Bodworth marr.
April 29 Peter Delabolia, serv^t^ to Mr Robinson, bur.
May 30 Robart son of Thomas Bird chr.
June 20 John son of Robt Wareup chr.
June 21 John Lucas & Elisabeth Stone marr.
July 8 John son of John King chr.
July 12 Thomas Lowin & An Throwgood marr.
Aug. 3 Sarah dau. of Thomas Archdale chr.
Aug. 22 Henry son of Henry Lee chr.
Sep. 5 Francis son of Francis Hiham chr.
Sep. 11 Mabell Boull, serv^t^ to Mr Througood, bur.
Sep. 19 Brigit Wallis, serv^t^ to Widow Cheeke, bur.
Sep. 24 Joane Cope bur.
Sep. 26 Tabitha Rawlins dau. of Thomas chr.

Oct. 10 Frauncis Eston & Mary Dickison marr.
Oct. 24 Henry Bennetland & Winefrid Poynes marr.
Nov. 20 Michaell son of Anthony Robinson bur.
Dec. 18 The wife of Hugh Parson, drawer, bur.
Dec. 20 Doryty Sivedale, serv[t] to M[r] Robison, bur.
Dec. 25 Thomas son of W[m] Dyose chr.
Dec. 25 W[m] son of W[m] Griffen chr.
Jan. 2 Jacob son of Steven Scarboroh chr.
Jan. 6 Thomas son of Thomas Davis chr.
Jan. 16 Anthony Robison bur.
Jan. 17 Thomas son of John Penson chr.
Jan. 30 Thomas son of John Waker chr.
Jan. 30 John son of Rob[t] Right chr.
Feb. 2 John Kicksham, serv[t] to Alexander Lockwood, bur.
Feb. 6 Thomas son of Anthony Robison bur.
Feb. 6 Margaret Penne, servant, bur.
Feb. 11 Edward son of Tho. Power chr.
Feb. 11 Margaret Robison bur.

1575.

[*blank*] 24 Sarah dau. of W[m] Austin chr.
May 25 Roger Austin & Joane Marshall marr.
May 25 Rebecka dau. of John Spence bur.
June 5 Samuell son of Harry Siles chr.
June 18 Thomas Bradbrooke & An Wright marr.
July 3 Elisabeth dau. of Robart Clifton chr.
July 10 Mary dau. of W[m] Harriot chr.
July 24 Anne dau. of John King chr.
Aug. 29 Charles Hales & Elisabeth Fish marr.
Sep. 8 W[m] son of Edward Lodge chr.
Sep. 14 Thomas Tindell, serv[t] to Richard Nicholas, bur.
Sep. 25 Simon son of W[m] Dickison chr.
Oct. 9 W[m] son of Nicholas [*sic*] bur.
Oct. 9 W[m] son of Edward Lodge bur.
Oct. 23 W[m] Shore & Margaret Harrison marr.
Oct. 30 Richard son of John Marshall chr.
Oct. 30 John Slatur & Elisabeth Maxse marr.
Nov. 4 Grace dau. of John Martin bur.
Nov. 7 Edmund Thomas & Au Sprat marr.
Nov. 19 W[m] Martin bur.
Nov. 20 Thomas son of Rob[t] Warcop chr.
Jan. 3 Roger son of W[m] Harriot bur.
Jan. 5 Richard son of Thomas Bird chr.
Jan. 29 W[m] son of Thomas Knowles chr.
Jan. 29 Frauncis son of W[m] Griffen chr.
Jan. 29 Ursula Pore dau. of Tho. Poore chr.
Feb. 4 Margaret wife of Tho. Scot bur.
Feb. 5 Steven son of Steven Scarborough chr.
Feb. 13 John son of Francis Hiham chr.
Mar. 3 Harry Hiham & Jane Jastlin marr.
Mar. 4 Roger Jonson & Katerin Gub marr.
Mar. 6 Katerin dau. of W[m] Hariot bur.
Mar. 10 Margaret dau. of W[m] Kins chr.
Mar. 11 Elisabeth dau. of Richard Nicholas chr.
Mar. 12 Martin Smith & An Bothby marr.
Mar. 14 Jane Robison, serv[t] of Tho. Barton, bur.

1576.

April 1 Richard son of Tho. Daves chr.
May 7 Daniell Chamberlaine, William Parker, & Jone Robinson bur.
June 3 Rebecka dau. of Henry Felie chr.
June 17 Agnes dau. of Allen Rathby bur.
July 1 Susan dau. of Nicholas Whelar chr.
July 3 William Walker & Elisabeth Almon marr.
July 13 Grissell dau. of M[r] Cobhed, minister, chr.
July 13 Dority Finch bur.
July 15 Robart son of Robert Everington chr.
July 19 Thomas, a foundling, chr.
Aug. 30 Thomas Whelar bur. in new chy[d]
Sep. 16 Steven son of Charles Hales chr.
Sep. 20 Elisabeth Throwgood bur.
Sep. 29 Raphe Spratt bur.
Sep. 30 Mary Harriot chr.
Oct. 20 Annis Warcup bur.
Oct. 21 Sabatian King chr.
Oct. 28 Joane Hill chr.
Oct. 28 Elisabeth Slatur chr.
Nov. 17 Hester Whip dau. to M[r] Foxall, marr. to one M[r] W[m] Francklin, gentleman
Dec. 9 Thomas Tailor & Jellian Tagus marr.
Dec. 20 Peter son of John Penson chr.
Dec. 22 Edward son of Francis Griffen chr.
Jan. 28 Richard Tailor & Elisabeth Stone marr.
Jan. 29 Umphery Corbit & Agnes Parcar marr.
Feb. 18 Robart Baines & Elisabeth Sprat marr.
Mar. 9 Amos Warcup bur.
Mar. 10 George Paiton bur.
Mar. 17 Richard son of John Walker chr.

1577.

April 4 John Griffin son of W[m] Griffin chr.
April 6 Marye Paiton dau. of George Paiton chr.
April 25 Robart son of W[m] Turner chr.
May 5 Richard Tod & Mary Baker marr.
May 21 Rafe Sprat & Robart Turner bur.
June 2 Samuell son of Steven Scarboroh chr.
June 13 Allen Rathby bur.
June 14 Sarah Turner bur.
June 14 John Wilson bur.
July 18 William son of Edwin Babington chr.
Aug. 4 Roger son of W[m] Jennings chr.
Aug. 4 Steven Davis son of Thom. Davis chr.
Aug. 5 Raph Seely & Margaret Bedle marr.
Aug. 8 Margaret wife of Henry Right bur.
Aug. 20 [*blank*] son of Water Fish bur.
Aug. 22 Hellen dau. of W[m] Atkison bur.
Aug. 25 Henry son of Henry Siles chr.
Aug. 27 Margaret dau. of Robart Wright bur.
Aug. 29 Alicua Wright dau. of Rob[t] Right bur.
Sep. 3 Thomas son of Rob[t] Wright bur.
Sep. 7 Thomas Davis son of Gregorie Massy bur.
Sep. 8 William Massey bur.
Sep. 21 Thurstan Hill son of Robart Wright bur.

Sep. 28 Francis son of Gregory Massy bur.
Sep. 29 Jaine Check dau. of Mr Cheeck bur.
Oct. 2 An Willaby dau. of Wm Glos bur.
Oct. 6 Francis Grimston bur.
Oct. 16 Jacob son of Nicholas Hill chr.
Oct. 20 John son of Nicholas Hill chr.
Oct. 20 Jacob Hill son of Nicholas Hill bur.
Oct. 24 John son of Nicholas Hill bur.
Oct. 26 An dau. of John King bur.
Nov. 1 An dau. of John Bird chr.
Nov. 14 John son of Wm Francklin chr.
Nov. 15 John son of Wm Francklin bur.
Jan. 5 Elisabeth dau. of John King chr.
Jan. 9 Tabitha Harrison chr.
Jan. 19 Juda dau. of Robt Warcup chr.
Jan. 20 Margaret wife of Mr Penson bur.
Jan. 26 Robt Pogge & Agnes Camden marr.
Feb. 9 Sarah dau. of Wm Dickison chr.

1578.

April 1 Sarah dau. of Thomas Archdal chr.
April 2 Edward son of Gregory Massy chr.
April 13 Calid [*sic*] son of Thomas Rawlins chr.
May 4 John Hatterly & Joane Crosse marr.
May 16 Thomas son of Edward Lodg chr.
May 18 Samuell son of Steven Scarborough chr.
May 18 Robart son of Wm Harriot chr.
May 25 John son of Wm Griffin chr.
May 25 Thomas son of Edward Lodge bur.
June 1 Robert Davilin & Merin Maxfeld marr.
June 1 Robt Hall & Mildred Clarck marr.
June 21 Ann wife of Tho. Davis bur.
June 22 Roger Cumber & Joyce Ardin marr.
June 29 Wm son of Wm Turner chr.
Aug. 7 An dau. of Thomas Bird bur.
Aug. 16 Wm Simons, servt to Mr Hiham, bur.
Aug. 17 George Millitton bur.
Aug. 21 Steven son of Mr Scarborough bur.
Aug. 24 Henry Tailor, stranger, bur.
Aug. 24 George son of Francis Hiham bur.
Aug. 30 Elisabeth wife of George Millington bur.
Aug. 31 Robt Breichley, servt to Mr Hensbew, bur.
Aug. 31 John son of Nicholas Hill chr.
Sep. 2 John Hiham bur.
Sep. 7 Nicholas son of Henry Siles chr.
Sep. 12 John son of Tho. Bird bur.
Sep. 18 Nicholas Walsh, servt to Mr Scarboroug, bur.
Sep. 27 An wife of Thomas Bird bur.
Sep. 27 Edward Roodes & Jane Francis marr.
Oct. 3 Bennet dau. of Wm Fancey chr.
Oct. 3 Robt son of Thomas Bird bur.
Oct. 17 Cristofer son of John Tore bur.
Oct. 19 Luis Jenkinson & Katerin Wilkinson marr.
Oct. 28 Charles son of Charles Hales chr.
Oct. 30 John son of Thom. Archdale bur.
Nov. 4 John son of Robt Clifton bur.

Nov. 26 Mary wife of Thomas Archdale bur.
Nov. 28 Jone wife of Water Duar bur.
Nov. 30 Joane dau. of Thomas Mason chr.
Dec. 2 John Lucas bur.
Dec. 14 Thomas Conway & Elisabeth Gray marr.
Jan. 1 Alee Rathby bur.
Jan. 11 Elisabeth dau. of Ri. Rosdale chr.
Jan. 22 Randoll Foster & Martha Bishop marr.
Jan. 25 Winithrid dau. of Edwin Babington chr.
Jan. 25 Rebecka dau. of Henry Syles chr.
Feb. 19 Christofer Rosdale, minister of the church, & An Felie [?] marr.
Mar. 1 W[m] son of Rob[t] Warcup chr.
Mar. 8 Rob[t] Warcup bur.

1579.

Mar. 31 Elisabeth Hudson, serv[t] to M[r] Wright, bur.
April 1 W[m] Osland, serv[t] to M[r] Right, bur.
April 4 W[m] Robison, serv[t] to the same M[r] Right, bur.
April 10 Sence wife of Edward Lodge bur.
April 26 W[m] son of Thomas Lodwin chr.
May 4 Susan dau. of Steven Scarboroug bur.
June 8 Anthony Culpeper & An Martin marr.
June 11 Elisabeth Anderson bur.
June 19 Samuell Scarboroh bur.
June 28 George Burton & Joane Audry marr.
June 28 An dau. of W[m] Griffin chr.
July 6 Thomas Davis & An Taboll marr.
July 18 An dau. of George Stansmore chr.
Aug. 2 Elisabeth dau. of Jone Walker chr.
Aug. 30 Bartholmew son of Steven Scarboroh chr.
Sep. 6 Tomisin dau. of Henry Siles chr.
Sep. 15 W[m] Arvy & An Southwark marr.
Sep. 18 Henry son of Rob't Henshew chr.
Sep. 27 Richard Sanders & Margery Petyfir [?] marr.
Oct. 12 Nicholas son of Nicholas Hill chr.
Nov. 29 John son of W[m] Hariot chr.
Dec. 6 Jane dau. of Francis Hiham chr.
Feb. 1 Joane [*sic*] Baker & Elisabeth Maxfeld marr.
Feb. 7 Margaret wife of Rob't Wright bur.
Feb. 16 Ould M[rs] Fish, called An, bur.
Feb. 24 Richard Hoskin & Margaret Maxfeld marr.

1580.

Mar. 27 Edward son of John Peck chr.
April 13 Thomas son of Rob[t] Clifton chr.
April 14 Joane Lucas bur.
April 24 W[m] Cawly & Joane Tore marr.
May 4 Rob't son of Rob't Netmaker chr. & bur.
June 12 Alce dau. of Richard Sanders chr.
June 19 Alce dau. of Thomas Davis chr.
June 20 Abigall dau. of Thomas Rawlins bur.
July 3 John son of W[m] Griffin chr.
July 6 Beamond Marlar bur.
July 16 Cristofer son of Christofer Rosdale, parson of this church, chr.
July 17 Christofer son of M[r] Rosdale bur.
Sep. 4 Joane [*sic*] Rot & Martha Wise marr.

Sep. 18 Thomas son of Wm Turner chr.
Sep. 28 The said Tho. Turner bur.
Oct. 6 An dau. of Giles Ruance, a stranger, bur.
Oct. 8 Thomas son of Wm Dickison chr.
Nov. 2 Mary Larance & Henry Sanderson marr.
Nov. 6 Jane dau. of Henry Siles bapt.
Nov. 13 Edwin son of Rob't Warcup chr.
Nov. 14 Richard Mahan & Jane Dickison marr.
Jan. 20 Henry Otwell & Joane Smith marr.
Jan. 25 Edward Tomson & Mary Haward marr.
Jan. 29 Elisabeth dau. of Wm Harriot chr.
Feb. 1 Joane dau. of Wm Cawley chr.
Feb. 12 John son of Steven Searborowh chr.
Feb. 16 Grace dau. of George Stainsmore chr.
Mar. 14 Elisabeth dau. of Nicholas Hill chr.

1581.

April 10 John Allen & Joane Raime marr.
April 14 Winifred dau. of Rob't Clifton bur.
April 16 Wm Smith & Alce Akerland, servt to Mr Jay, marr.
April 16 Wm son of Wm Gold chr.
May 2 Peter son of Giles Evans chr.
May 19 Jane dau. of Joane Bussell bur.
May 21 Thomas Godfrey & Ellen Brasly marr.
June 14 Jane wife of Francis Hiham bur.
July 4 Thomasin dau. of Robt Netmaker chr.
July 25 Androw Huntington & Marget Bruer marr.
July 25 Henry Thorlon bur.
Aug. 4 Christofer son of Thomas Bird chr.
Aug. 6 John son of John Peck chr.
Aug. 9 Rob't son of Thomas Davys chr.
Aug. 12 Christofer son of Tho. Bird bur.
Aug. 20 Jane dau. of Rob't Page chr.
Aug. 23 Margaret Plumer, Mr Atkinson's servt, bur.
Aug. 30 Richard Latley, servant to Mr Banister, bur.
Sep. 6 Elisabeth dau. of John Walker bur.
Sep. 10 Jane dau. of John Walker chr.
Sep. 17 Penellopen Leycrof dau. of Mrs Leycrof bur.
Sep. 18 Winifrid dau. of Edwin Babington bur.
Sep. 27 John dau. [*sic*] of Joane Walker bur.
Oct. 3 Alce dau. of Margaret Leycrof bur.
Oct. 3 Mary dau. of Rich. Sanders chr.
Nov. 4 John Halfton, the clark of this parish, bur.
Nov. 5 Francis son of Francis Bower chr.
Nov. 19 John Francklin son of Wm Francklin chr.
Nov. 26 Thomasin Robartes son [*sic*] of Tho. Robartes chr.
Jan. 11 J[illegible], a foundling [?]
Jan. 22 Jo[illegible] Riddle & Mary Cherry marr.
Feb. 7 Wm Grosse & Barbery Marbeck marr.
Feb. 11 Blanch dau. of Richard Robison chr.
Feb. 18 Michaell Scruggam & Issable Nortines marr.

1582.

Mar. 25 Margaret Cornhill bur.
Mar. 26 Margaret dau. of Rob't Warcup chr.
April 15 Cristofer Hudson & Elisabeth Bustard marr.

April 22 Richard son of Wm Griffen chr.
April 30 Joane dau. of Tho. Ludwell bur.
May 3 An dau. of Giles Luis chr.
May 6 John son of Henry Siles chr.
May 13 Edward Richardson & Ellen Burrows marr.
May 30 W^m^ son of Thomas Browne chr.
June 14 Jane wife of Rob't Dickson bur.
June 27 Thomas son of Cristo^r^ Rosdale chr.
July 4 Wm Blaball, serv^t^ of Mr Honsell, bur.
July 22 Steven son of Mr Scarboroh chr.
July 22 Ame dau. of Rob't Right bapt.
Aug. 3 Brian son of Wm Clarcke chr.
Aug. 12 John son of Thomas Bird bapt.
Aug. 18 John Hounsell & Alce Reed marr.
Aug. 26 John son of Umphery Camden bapt.
Aug. 27 Bartholm. son of Mr Stansmor chr.
Aug. 29 John, a foundling, chr.
Aug. 29 Margaret dau. of John Peck chr.
Sep. 2 W^m^ son of Rob't Clifton chr.
Sep. 2 An dau. of John Walker chr.
Sep. 13 Wolston son of Cornellis Fish chr.
Sep. 14 The said Wolston Fish bur.
Sep. 16 Roger son of Wm Harriot chr.
Sep. 18 Brian son of Wm Clarke bur.
Sep. 23 John Annis & Margaret Bromley marr.
Sep. 29 Margaret dau. of Roger Page bapt.
Oct. 30 Margaret Cheeck bur.
Nov. 28 Michaell, serv^t^ of Tho. Collins, bur.
Dec. 1 Thomas son of Richard Sanders chr.
Dec. 2 An dau. of John Allington bapt.
Dec. 10 Rob't Crosley & Elisabeth Eaton marr.
Dec. 22 Mary dau. of John Honsell chr.
Dec. 29 Tho. Renoldes, serv^t^ to Mr Jew [?], bur.
Jan. 14 Wm Luis bur.
Jan. 23 Henry Stevens & Ellenor Cholmley marr.
Jan. 26 Mary Cakebread bur.
Jan. 28 The dau. of Thomas Roberts bur.
Jan. 29 Thomas son of Francis Hiham bur.
Feb. 3 Thomas Holding & Elisabeth Tirar marr.
Feb. 3 Jeffry Hall & Jane Rider marr.
Mar. 8 My Lady Martin bur.
Mar. 15 Raphe Griffen, serv^t^ wth Tho. Davis, clothwo., bur.
Mar. 23 Robert son of Wm Harriot bur.

1583.

April 3 John Jackson, servant, bur.
April 13 Alce dau. of Thomas Davis bur.
April 25 Edward son of Peter Jenkins bur.
April 26 Annis Taler, serv^t^ to Tho. Davys, bur.
May 1 W^m^ son of Tho. Davis bur.
May 6 Robart Joyner, serv^t^ to Thomas Davis, bur.
May 12 Thomas son of Thomas Davis bur.
May 12 Joseph son of Wm Bowin chr.
May 13 Nicholas Clackson, serv^t^ to Mr Craven, bur.
May 21 Wm Cawly, sexton of St Antholin's, bur.
May 28 An wife of Raphe Everat bur.
June 9 Edwin son of Wm Griffin chr.

June 23 Morgaine Hubble & Tomison Halestone marr.
June 24 Owin Banister bur.
July 8 Edward son of Rob[t] Netmaker chr.
July 9 Annis, serv[t] to Thomas Robart, bur.
Aug. 2 Ester Francklin, widow, bur.
Aug. 12 Elisabeth Gelaster, serv[t] to M[r] Dobson, bur.
Aug. 28 An dau. of Umphery Tandin bapt.
Sep. 16 W[m] Loye & Mary Jay marr.
Sep. 22 An dau. of W[m] Clarke chr.
Sep. 29 W[m] Bower son of Francis Bowyer chr.
Sep. 29 Thomas son of John Pinnin [?]
Oct. 6 W[m] son of Rob't Warcup chr.
Oct. 7 Thomas Richardson & Francis Harriot marr.
Oct. 8 Joane dau. of Nicholas Hill chr.
Nov. 11 Francis son of Thomas Davis chr.
Nov. 11 A child of Thomas Davys bur.
Nov. 13 Elisabeth Curteis, serv[t] to Umphery Camden, bur.
Nov. 16 The son of Anthony Marlar bur.
Nov. 19 Jane Evan dau. to Giles Evan, a stranger, bapt. at the French Church
Dec. 4 An dau. of Rob't Page chr.
Dec. 29 Thomas Archdale & Blith Wilfred marr.
Dec. 29 An wife of Henry Convers bur.
Jan. 7 Henry Knevit & Frances Elsin marr.
Jan. 19 Richard son of Reynold Gye chr.
Jan. 25 John Wharton & Margery Hunt marr.
Feb. 3 Gregory Griffin & Elisabeth Sanders marr.
Feb. 23 John son of Thomas Knowles chr.
Feb. 23 Margaret dau. of W[m] Dickison chr.
Feb. 23 Elisabeth dau. of Ric. Sanders chr.
Feb. 23 Elisabeth dau. of Thomas Bird chr.
Mar. 8 Luceslat dau. of W[m] Francke bur.

1584.

April 19 William son of Thomas Richardson chr.
April 19 Thomas son of W[m] Harriot chr.
April 20 Steven Cardinall, serv[t] to M[r] Griffin, bur.
April 23 George Dorell & Joane Pimme marr.
May 10 Henry son of John Allington chr.
May 10 Francis son of Thomas Richardson bur.
May 11 Dority dau. of Thomas Wicks chr.
June 11 Richard Harebut, serv[t] to M[r] Babington, bur.
June 17 Robart son of W[m] Spratt chr.
June 18 Rob't son of W[m] Spratt bur.
July 12 Richard Cencis & An Dalis marr.
Aug. 2 Thomas son of Rob[t] Wright chr.
Aug. 4 W[m] son of W[m] Bowin bur.
Aug. 9 Susan dau. of Daniell Simson chr.
Sep. 2 Elisabeth dau. of Jeffry Powell chr.
Sep. 6 Samuell son of Ste. Scarboroh chr.
Sep. 10 George son of Georg Stansmor chr.
Sep. 10 John Escock bur.
Oct. 29 John Davis & Joane Blighton marr.
Nov. 8 Susan dau. of Umphery Camden chr.
Dec. 6 Martha dau. of John Peck chr.
Dec. 22 William Loye bur.
Jan. 26 Mary dau. of Rob[t] Warcup chr.

Jan. 28 Howill Jones & Avis Floye marr.
Jan. 31 Anthony Smith & Joane Cally marr.
Feb. 2 Elisabeth dau. of Roger Page chr.
Feb. 14 Elisabeth wife of John Lucas bur.
Feb. 17 Rob[t] son of Tho. Knowles chr.
Feb. 24 Mary dau. of Gregory Griffin chr.
Mar. 3 Henry son of John Allington bur.
Mar. 7 W[m] son of Henry Convers chr.
Mar. 19 Anthony son of Rob't Netmaker chr.
Mar. 21 John son of Reynold Gye chr.
Mar. 24 Francis son of W[m] Griffin bur.

1585.

April 15 Urye Babington & Annis Heath marr.
April 18 Ester dau. of John Walker chr.
April 26 Mary dau. of John Hounsell bur.
May 2 Larance son of Larance Camp chr.
May 17 Joane Friar, serv[t] to M[r] Hariot, bur.
May 24 Thomas Row & Mary Loye marr.
May 24 Georg son of W[m] Hariot chr.
June 29 W[m] son of W[m] Bowin chr.
July 21 Richard son of Nicholas Hill chr.
July 26 M[r] Water Fish bur.
July 29 Richard Sanders bur.
July 31 Roger son of W[m] Hariot bur.
Aug. 4 Elisabeth dau. of Tho. Bird bur.
Aug. 7 Mary dau. of John Housel chr.
Aug. 11 An dau. of W[m] Sprat chr.
Aug. 15 Elisabeth dau. of M[r] Scarborough chr.
Aug. 29 Martha dau. of Rob't Wright chr.
Sep. 6 Thomas Watson & An Swift marr.
Sep. 25 John Parnall & Margaret Leycrof marr.
Oct. 4 W[m] son of W[m] Jones chr.
Dec. 14 Jane wife of M[r] Simpson bur.
Dec. 16 Richard Hopp & Mary Carpentur marr.
Jan. 16 Richard Jaylor & Margaret Brickwood marr.
Jan. 24 Owen Semps & Margery Sane marr.
Jan. 30 William Hewis & Als Owin marr.
Feb. 13 Rob't Wilson & Elisabeth Kitson marr.
Feb. 13 Susan dau. of W[m] Grifin chr.
Feb. 19 Jane dau. of W[m] Clark bur.
Mar. 20 An dau. of Ury Babington chr.

1586.

Mar. 25 John Buckland & Elisabeth Ware marr.
April 10 Rowland son of Harry Convers chr.
April 14 M[r] W[m] Harding & M[rs] Katerin White marr.
April 20 John Hounsell sister [*sic*] to John Housel bur.
May 6 An dau. of Tho. Boothby chr.
May 8 Paull son of Rob't Warcup chr.
May 8 Alce dau. of Jeffry Powell chr.
May 30 Richard son of Rob't Walker chr.
June 1 Burton, serv[t] to W[m] Tood, bur.
June 8 Harry Shepard & An More marr.
June 12 Thomas son of Reynold Gye chr.
June 29 Magdelin dau. of John Allinton chr.

July 2 John Hanson bur.
Sep. 13 Ambros Comes & Annis Clark marr.
Sep. 15 Joseph son of Wm Bowin bur.
Sep. 18 An dau. of Nicholas Hill chr.
Sep. 29 Wm son of Wm Hariot chr.
Oct. 9 John son of John How chr.
Oct. 16 John son of Wm Dickson chr.
Nov. 5 Mary dau. of John Housell bur.
Dec. 9 Susan dau. of Thomas Davys chr.
Dec. 13 Samuell Wellar & Susan Stedman marr.
Dec. 18 Anthony son of Rob't Right chr.
Dec. 25 Jane dau. of Wm Clarke chr.
Dec. 26 Janne dau. of Wm Bowin chr.
Jan. 26 Jaine dau. of Wm Clere bur.
Feb. 5 Rowland son of Edwin Semp chr.
Feb. 19 Water Saltar & Dority Roffe marr.
Feb. 27 Henry Sukar & Sarah Dutfild marr
Mar. 6 Elsabeth Patson bur.
Mar. 12 Henry son of Henry Convers chr.

1587.

April 23 Benjamin son of Wm Griffin chr.
April 23 Elsabeth dau. of Tho. Boothby chr.
June 13 Steven son of Mr Searboroh bur.
June 22 Richard son of Wm Jones bur.
Aug. 3 Wm son of Reynold Gye chr.
Aug. 23 Katerin dau. of Thomas Richardson chr.
Aug. 31 Lois Vahon, servt to Richard Ivy, bur.
Sep. 9 Allis Jay wife of Henry Jay bur.
Sep. 18 Jentile son of Wm Larance chr.
Oct. 31 Margaret Clifton bur.
Oct. 18 Elisabeth Babington dau. of Urias chr.
Nov. 6 John Danson & Joane Horne marr.
Nov. 8 Sarah dau. of Rob't Washborne chr.
Nov. 13 Richard Burrel & Jane Jay marr.
Nov. 26 Bridget dau. of Roger Gamadg chr.
Dec. 11 John Comb & Margaret Archdale marr.
Dec. 31 Wm son of Wm Clarke chr.
Jan. 1 James Smith & Mary Jiles marr.
Jan. 9 Winifred dau. of Nicho. Hill chr.
Jan. 13 Henry son of Thomas Davyes chr.
Mar. 4 John Bell bur.
Mar. 17 Marian Morla. dau. of Ri. Morla. chr.

1588.

April 14 Elisabeth dau. of Henry Covers chr.
May 12 Elisabeth dau. of John Vovert chr.
May 19 Katerin dau. of Daniel Elsmore chr.
June 9 Dority dau. of Wm Jones chr.
June 15 Margery Lancton bur.
June 24 John son of Thomas Richardson chr.
June 24 Thomas Glasse & Margaret Dickison marr.
June 27 Joane Ludwell wife of Mr Ludwell bur.
June 28 A child of Jeffry Powell born and bur.
June 30 Peter son of Robt Barnes chr.
July 5 John son of Tho. Richardson bur.

July 29 John Miles & Brigit Tomson marr.

Aug. 5 Wm Lestar & Frances Lithdale marr.

Aug. 20 Alce dau. of John Walker chr.

Sep. 25 Elizabeth dau. of Thomas Boothby chr.

Oct. 29 Margaret Austin, widow, bur.

Nov. 3 Morris Tidder & Alce Davis marr.

Nov. 5 An infant of Rob. Washborne's bur., not chr.

Nov. 13 Wm Spratt & Rose Turner marr.

Nov. 22 An infant of Wm Franclin's bur., not chr.

Dec. 15 Wm son of John Danson chr.

Dec. 26 John son of Wm Francklin bur.

Jan. 12 Wm Himman & Agnes Bright marr.

Jan. 26 Alce dau. of John Honsell chr.

Jan. 28 Thomas son of John Allington chr.

Jan. 31 The same Thomas bur.

Feb. 2 Vincent Antholins, so named because he was fond in the church porch upon St. Vincent's Day, chr.

Feb. 3 Anthony Marlar & Mary Wolworth marr.

Feb. 5 John Tinkerson & Sibell Le marr.

Feb. 9 Francis dau. of John Jay chr.

Feb. 10 Richard Pit & Mary Bates marr.

Feb. 23 Robt son of John Morle chr.

Feb. 23 Mary dau. of Wm Dickison chr.

Feb. 25 Sarah dau. of Nicholas Hill chr.

Feb. 28 Bridgit dau. of Roger Gammadg bur.

Mar. 16 Johne Pavy dau. of Mr Pavy bapt.

1589.

Mar. 30 Francis dau. of Wm Clarck chr.

April 2 Raphe Everit & An Bird marr.

April 12 Alce Walker, an infant, bur.

April 20 An dau. of Thomas Richardson chr.

April 21 Miles Leonard & Joyce Basley marr.

April 23 Rob't Clifton bur.

May 25 Harry son of Richard Levit chr.

June 2 John son of Henry Couvers chr. the 1st day & bur. 2d

June 8 Margaret dau. of Daniel Elsmore chr.

June 26 John Walker bur.

June 29 Mr Henry Jay, widr, & Mrs Elsabeth Fish marr.

July 13 Thomas Davys, clothworker, bur.

July 31 Edward son of Tho. Cox chr. 25 day & bur. 31

Sep. 2 A man-child of Thomas Tailor's, unchr., bur.

Oct. 5 Edwin son of Reynold Gye chr.

Oct. 24 Thomas Figge & Dority Burden marr.

Oct. 25 Anchoret dau. of John Cundell chr.

Oct. 2.. Mr Cundale's dau. bur.

Oct. 31 Jane dau. of Wm Bowin bur.

Nov. 6 Elisabeth dau. of John Vavert chr.

Nov. 9 Wm Sanders & Agnes Hunt marr.

Nov. 9 Thomas son of Tho. Boothby chr.

Nov. 9 Dority dau. of Roger Jones chr.

Nov. 29 John Adams & Elisabeth Maxfeild marr.

Nov. 29 Wm Benberry & An Marsh marr.

Jan. 13 Mary dau. of John Danson chr.

Jan. 18 Henry Hartshed & Susan Hickman marr.

Jan. 18 Thomas Stirrop & Katturne Getting marr.

Jan. 30 Elisabeth dau. of John Jay chr.

Feb. 7 Richard Nicholas & An Davys marr.
Feb. 16 John Horsenden & Margaret Ansteide marr.
Mar. 8 Ellen dau. of Richard Lee chr.
Mar. 14 A child of John Homsel's, unchr., bur.
Mar. 21 Rose wife of W[m] Spratt bur.
Mar. 22 Roger son of Roger Gammadge chr.
Mar. 22 John son of Andrew Skell chr.

1590.

April 5 Dorcas dau. of Tho. Treate chr.
April 10 Radax Rathby bur.
April 13 Thomas West & Elisabeth Drayot marr.
April 19 Alce dau. of Phillip Browne chr.
May 10 An dau. of Rob[t] Washborne chr.
May 10 John Keene & Jane Denton marr.
May 19 Henry Mason & Joyce Hunt marr.
May 24 W[m] son of Richard Levit chr.
June 8 Rob't Burdet & Mary Homsell marr.
June 8 Randvill Palmer bur.
June 28 Francis dau. of John Peck chr.
July 5 Rob[t] Moule bur.
July 8 Richard Quereк & Jane Palnes marr.
July 15 Sisly dau. of Umphery Camdin bur.
July 21 Bye Hill dau. of Nich. Hill bapt.
July 28 Sarah dau. of Nicholas Hill bur.
Aug. 9 Mary dau. of John Honsell chr.
Aug. 24 Richard son of W[m] Sanders chr.
Aug. 30 Richard son of W[m] Jones chr.
Aug. 30 Dorques dau. of W[m] Bowin chr.
Sep. 26 Mary dau. of W[m] Dickison bur.
Sep. 30 Willyam son of Danyell Dyconson bapt.
Oct. 9 Gaberell Ducket & Rose Isop marr.
Nov. 2 An wife of John Peck bur.
Nov. 8 Hugh son of John Allington chr.
Nov. 27 Elisabeth dau. of M[r] Windover chr.
Dec. 6 Richard son of Phill. Pick chr.
Dec. 11 Hugh son of M[r] Allington bur.
Dec. 12 Nicholas Williams, M[r] Jones's man, bur.
Dec. 13 An dau. of Henry Convers chr.
Dec. 13 Martha dau. of Rob[t] Barnes chr.
Dec. 28 Jane wife of W[m] Horne bur.
Jan. 3 Dence dau. of Reynold Gye chr.
Jan. 4 Rowland Haward & An Offild marr.
Jan. 31 Henry Fanthurpe & Joane Boys marr.
Feb. 2 Christofer Jackson & Elisabeth Tillar marr.
Feb. 3 James Milles & Margaret Crill marr.
Feb. 16 John, a foundling, bur.

1591.

Mar. 25 Thomas son of John Danson chr.
April 25 Edmund Penicoke & Als Hopkins marr.
April 26 Elisabeth wife of John Slatur bur.
April 30 John Fathers, serv[t] to M[r] Rawlins, bur.
May 23 Rob't Moule chr.
June 8 Daniell son of Daniell Elsmor chr. & bur.
June 13 Raphe son of Andrew Skeele chr.

June 27 Elisabeth dau. of Mr Richardson chr.
July 1 Blasse Bate son of Thomas bur.
July 18 Martin son of Martin Billingly chr.
July 18 Mary dau. of Daniell Dikison chr.
July 31 George Fisher bur.
Aug. 8 Alce dau. of Henry Moody chr.
Aug. 10 Thomas Ransmont & Mary Convers marr.
Aug. 22 Edward Dickison & Cysly Ceycome marr.
Aug. 23 Rowland Crouder, servt to Mr Morely, bur.
Aug. 26 Annis Robarts, widow, bur.
Oct. 13 Wm son of Henry Moody bur.
Oct. 13 Katerin Rideard chr.
Oct. 18 Thomas son of Wm Sander chr.
Dec. 10 John Foxall bur.
Dec. 12 Rob't son of Thomas Boothby chr.
Jan. 23 Thomas Ludwell, mercht tailor, bur.
Jan. 30 James Kill & George [*sic*] Warton marr.
Feb. 9 Thomas Sperin bur.
Feb. 17 Mr Dickison, skinner, bur.
Mar. 1 John son of Nicholas Felton chr.
Mar. 5 Elisabeth dau. of Jeffry Powell chr.
Mar. 11 John Felton son of Mr Felton, parson, bur.

1592.

Mar. 26 Elemar dau. of Henry Convers chr.
April 7 Reynold Gye, grocer, bur.
May 14 Susanna dau. of Hugh Morris chr.
May 21 Anthony Robison & Isbell Hall marr.
May 22 Joane wife of Henry Camdin bur.
June 4 James son of Tho. Richardson chr.
June 4 Dorcas dau. of Robt Washborne chr.
June 18 An dau. of Roger Spratt chr.
July 2 Elisabeth dau. of Richard Lee chr.
July 9 Robt Vause & Amy Hobby marr.
Aug. 5 Morganne Hubble bur.
Aug. 20 Thomas Lander, servt to Mr Slatur, bur.
Aug. 25 John Fels, servt to Mr Nicholas, bur.
Sep. 9 Richard brother to John Slatur bur.
Sep. 10 John Slatur, mercht tailor, bur.
Sep. 17 Mary dau. of Reynold Gye chr.
Sep. 20 Elisabeth wife of Tho. Boothby bur.
Sep. 20 Elisabeth dau. of Tho. Througood bur.
Oct. 15 Elisabeth dau. of Henry Convers bur.
Oct. 19 Mary dau. of Edmund Langnell chr.
Nov. 5 Sibill dau. of Henry Moodey chr.
Nov. 26 Elisabeth wife of Thomas Sanders bur.
Nov. 26 Wm son of Martin Billingsly chr.
Dec. 1 John Wood, servt to John Hounsell, bur.
Jan. 9 Robart Dickison, draper, bur.
Jan. 14 Thomas son of Robt Barnes chr.
Feb. 19 Mary wife of Daniell Dickison, draper, bur.
Feb. 19 Dorcas dau. of Wm Bowin bur.
Feb. 25 Ellen dau. of John Danson bapt.
Feb. 26 Robt Gifford & Lettis Atturbury marr.
Mar. 3 Dority wife of Robt Washborn bur.
Mar. 4 James son of Tho. Richardson bur.
Mar. 11 Daniell son of Daniell Elsmore bapt.

1593.

April 1 Arthur son of Arthur Jackson chr.
April 1 An dau. of Wm Sherly chr.
April 25 Thomas Rawlins & Joane Reade marr.
May 11 Thomas Marlot bur.
May 13 Wm Greene & Mary Husbands marr.
July 22 Alce dau. of Richard Levit chr.
July 29 Ralph son of Andrew Skeele bur.
July 29 Isbell Dorlaton, serv^{t} to Widow Walker, bur.
Aug. 5 Dority wife of Mr Powell bur.
Aug. 12 An & Ester daus. of Mary Walkere bur.
Aug. 12 Jane dau. of John Moule chr.
Aug. 15 Jane dau. of John Moule bur.
Aug. 16 Elisabeth Babham, dau.-in-law to Umphery Camdin, bur.
Aug. 16 Simon son of Mr Dickison bur.
Aug. 18 Richard Cradock, merch^{t}, out of Mr Jackson's house, bur.
Aug. 20 Rob't son of John Moule bur.
Aug. 22 Elisabeth dau. of Jeffry Powell bur.
Aug. 26 W^{m} son of Henry Convers bur.
Aug. 29 Umphery Camdin, merch^{t} tailor, bur.
Aug. 29 Thomas Constantine, serv^{t} to Henry Convers, bur.
Sep. 1 Benjamin son of Henry Convers chr.
Sep. 6 Constant Morton, serv^{t} to Mrs Foxall, bur.
Sep. 7 Thomas son of Phillip Dickison bur.
Sep. 7 An Gardner, widow, bur.
Sep. 8 Wm Babham, son-in-law to Umphery Camdin, bur.
Sep. 8 Ellen wife of Henry Converse bur.
Sep. 14 John son of Phillip Dickison bur.
Sep. 21 John Hamon, serv^{t} to Umphery Camdin, bur.
Sep. 22 Mary Sanders, dau.-in-law to Mr Semp, cook, bur.
Sep. 30 Hugh son of Hugh Lee chr.
Sep. 30 Robt son of Phillip Browne chr.
Sep. 30 Rich. Kerming, serv^{t} to Daniel Elismor, bur.
Oct. 2 James Athborne, serv^{t} to Daniell Elsmor, bur.
Oct. 4 Phillip Dickison, widow, bur.
Oct. 7 Rowland son of Henry Convers bur.
Oct. 13 Richard Robartes bur.
Oct. 13 Edmund Railton bur.
Oct. 14 Christian dau. of Tho. Richardson chr.
Oct. 21 George Melton & An Cannings marr.
Oct. 22 Robt Washborn & Mary Harriot marr.
Nov. 15 Avis dau. of Owin Semp bur.
Nov. 17 Adiel Rawlins bur.
Nov. 19 Martin Clarck & Jane Dickison marr.
Jan. 12 The son of Mr Richard Burrell bur.
Jan. 15 The son of Wm Jones bur.
Feb. 2 Wm Joanes & Dority Hamlock marr.
Feb. 3 John son of Anthony Hodson chr.
Feb. 8 Margaret dau. of Rich. Lee chr.
Feb. 9 The same child bur.
Feb. 11 Thomas Sanders, beadle of the ward, bur.
Feb. 21 W^{m} son of Roger Sprat chr.

1594.

April 1 Robart son of Sachery Dove chr.
April 2 Thomas Boothby & An Grafton marr.
April 21 Daniell Alkinton & Margery Weare marr.

June 15 Elisabeth dau. of Rich. Lee bur.
July 28 Dority dau. of Henry Jay ye younger chr.
Sep. 12 Edward Person & Alce Clifton marr.
Sep. 15 John son of Tho. Richardson chr.
Sep. 17 Christian wife of Thomas Richardson bur.
Sep. 18 Robart son of Daniell Dickison chr.
Sep. 20 Henry Convers & Blanch Turnbull marr.
Sep. 29 John Mussenden & Katterin Cooly marr.
Oct. 1 Ralfe Rowse & Mary Dent marr.
Oct. 3 Wm Hariot, draper, bur.
Oct. 20 Robart son of John Moule chr
Oct. 27 Dority dau. of Robt Judson chr.
Nov. 7 Elisabeth dau. of Mar. Billingsly bapt.
Nov. 10 Wm Spencer & Margaret Griffin marr.
Nov. 28 Rob't son of Daniell Dickison bur.
Dec. 3 Wm Bennet & Johannar Rawlins marr.
Dec. 26 Wm Kirrin & Alce Harriot marr.
Jan. 19 William son of Anthony Nicholas chr.
Jan. 19 Sible dau. of Simon Porridge chr.
Feb. 19 An dau. of Wm Sherly bur.

1595.

Mar. 25 John son of Arthur Jackson chr.
Mar. 30 Robt son of Rich. Lee chr.
April 30 William son of William White chr.
April 21 Joane wife of Wm Atkison bur.
May 4 Edward son of John Danson chr.
May 18 Mary dau. of Tho. Boothby chr.
June 29 William Hodgkinson & Doryty Cakebread marr.
June 29 Margaret dau. of Roger Sprat chr.
July 13 William son of Wm Tailor chr.
July 15 James son of Rich. Ven chr.
Sep. 14 A child of Mr Henry Jay the younger bur.
Sep. 20 Elisabeth wife of Thomas Rawlins, skinner, bur.
Oct. 1 Christofer son of Sachery Dove chr.
Oct. 5 Raphe son of Wm Sprat chr.
Oct. 19 Anna dau. of Robt Judson chr.
Nov. 9 Katerin dau. of Martin Billinsly chr.
Nov. 19 Wm Peares, a stranger, bur.
Nov. 27 John Conyers, a gentleman stranger, bur.
Jan. 1 Als dau. of Robart Worshborne chr.
Jan. 6 Wm son of Wm Sherly bapt.
Jan. 11 Gregory son of Thomas Ballard chr.
Jan. 12 The dau. of Henry Convers (not bapt.) bur.
Feb. 9 Wm son of Roger Sprat bur.
Mar. 7 Mary dau. of Daniell Dickison bapt.

1596.

Mar. 29 William Stone, doctor, bur.
April 2 John Ampleforth bur.
May 18 A child of Henry Jay ye younger (unchr.) bur.
May 30 Henry son of Hugh Lea chr.
June 9 Agnes dau. of Umphery Slinn chr.
June 18 Henry son of Daniell Elsmor bur.
June 22 Dority wife of Wm Jones bur.
June 29 Richard Bunbery & Elisabeth Sanders marr.
July 6 William Warren & Elisabeth Jaque marr.

Aug. 27 Martha dau. of Thomas Boothby chr.
Sep. 7 Elisabeth dau. of Wm Tailor bapt.
Sep. 12 Richard son of John Danson chr.
Sep. 14 Robart Gibson, minister, bur.
Sep. 17 Robart son of Richard Lee bur.
Sep. 27 Wm Ferendow & An Fish marr.
Sep. 30 Robert son of Richard Ven chr.
Oct. 24 Guilbart Wilkison & Geritrude Augustin marr.
Oct. 24 Mary Nimes, cousin to Mr Hounsell, bur.
Nov. 7 Sarah dau. of Cleofus Smith chr.
Nov. 14 William Bowin, joyner, bur.
Nov. 28 Elisabeth dau. of Richard Lee bapt.
Dec. 4 Allice Sprat, widow, bur. from Mr Elsmor's house
Dec. 12 Wm, a child that died in the church door, bur.
Dec. 19 Susan dau. of Rob't Washborn chr.
Jan. 16 Nathaniell son of Richard Hall chr.
Jan. 16 Elisabeth dau. of Henry Convers bapt.
Jan. 30 Richard son of Wm Sherly bapt.
Jan. 31 William Allen & An Babington marr.
Feb. 5 Nicholas Borradle, servt to Mr Homsell, bur.
Feb. 9 A girl, left in Mr Joanes's gate, bur.
Feb. 10 John Reede & Margery Gye marr.

1597.

Mar. 28 Raphe son of Ismell Collingwood chr.
Mar. 30 Ruth dau. of Georg Johnson chr.
April 9 Mr Joseph Lambard, dying in Aldermary, bur.
April 10 Elisabeth dau. of Wm Sprat bapt.
May 1 Dority dau. of Arthur Jackson chr.
May 1 Geames Wine & Elisabeth Barbar marr.
May 8 Mariell dau. of Israell Collingwood bur.
May 16 Edward son of John Peck bur.
June 5 Mary dau. of Simon Porridg bapt.
June 18 Henry Convers, mercht tailor, bur.
June 18 An dau. of Robt Judson bur.
July 2 Robart Judson, clothworker, bur.
July 8 Elisabeth Rooke, out of Mr Sprat's house, bur.
July 9 Magdeulin Goffe bur. out of his [*sic*] son's house
July 24 John Torill, servt to Mr Sprat, bur.
July 24 An dau. of John Palmer bapt.
July 27 Rob't son of Rob't Chanflowre chr.
July 27 Hestar wife of Rob't Chanflowre bur.
July 28 An dau. of Martin Billingsly chr.
Aug. 27 Leonard Dolton, servt to Mr Sherly, bur.
Sep. 3 George Cretoffe, servant to Thomas Ballard, bur.
Sep. 7 John Talor & An Austin marr.
Oct. 9 An dau. of Wm Whit chr.
Nov. 2 William Sherly bur.
Nov. 8 Judith wife of John Pecke bur.
Dec. 11 William son of Thomas Boothby bapt.
Dec. 18 An dau. of William Craven bapt.
Dec. 18 Jane dau. of Richard Lee chr.
Dec. 25 Harriot dau. of Robt Washborn bapt.
Jan. 12 Eleasor son of John Palmer chr.
Jan. 15 John son of Roger Baker chr.
Jan. 22 John Quarre, servt to Widow Sherly, bur.
Feb. 5 Thomas Tomson & Judith Wilkison marr.

Feb. 24 John son of Wm Sherly chr.
Mar. 6 Clemmant Forman, bellman, bur.
Mar. 9 Edward Jones, bachr of divy & parson of Streetum, co. Cambr., bur.
Mar. 18 Elsabeth dau. of Richd Lee bur.

1598.

Mar. 29 Elsabeth dau. of Augustin Garland chr.
April 8 The son of Mr Dickison (unbapt.) bur.
May 8 Richard Nicholas, clothworker, bur.
May 25 Annes Roocke bur.
June 5 Katturne dau. of Rich. Ven bapt.
July 23 Sarah dau. of Cleophas Smith bapt.
July 29 Richard son of Phillip Browne bapt.
Aug. 12 Richard son of Israell [? Collingwood]* bapt.
Sep. 17 Elenar dau. of Alexander Pistor bapt.
Sep. 18 Estar dau. of Christofer Lancaster bapt.
Sep. 25 Katturn wife of Phillip Patson bur.
Sep. 27 Christofer Lancaster & Mary Crips marr.
Oct. 23 Ester dau. of Christofer Lancaster bur.
Oct. 29 Precilla wife of Rob. Chanflowre bur.
Nov. 1 Thomas Huckly & Mary Austin marr.
Nov. 7 Mary dau. of Israel Collingwood bur.
Dec. 5 Elenar dau. of Alexander Pistor bur.
Dec. 10 Elisabeth dau. of Mr Jay ye younger bapt.
Jan. 8 Annis dau. of William White bur.
Jan. 14 Thomas Shepard & Jone Parker marr.
Feb. 8 Elizabeth dau. of Philip Fysher bur.
Feb. 11 Philip Patson & Madelyn Cox marr.
Mar. 4 Mychaell son of Robert Yaateman bapt.
Mar. 4 Catheryne dau. of Symon Porridge bapt.

1599.

April 10 Richard son of Thomas Boothbye bapt.
April 13 Arthur son of Arthur Jackson bur.
April 15 Elizabeth dau. of Frances Dorington bapt.
April 15 George Walmsley & Margerett Kynge marr.
April 18 John Stephens & Margerett Barker marr.
April 21 Will'm son of Will'm Whitte bur.
April 22 George son of Roger Baker bapt.
April 27 Richard son of Phillipe Browne bur.
April 30 Thomas son of Daniell Dickenson bapt.
May 1 Henrie son of Martin Billingsley chr.
May 2 Thomas son of Daniell Dickenson bur.
May 18 John son of Barnard Saunders bapt.
May 19 Jno son of Barnard Saunders bur.
May 20 Jno son of Robertt Washbourne chr.
May 30 Phillipe Wallys & Margerett Clarke marr. by lic.
June 5 Annes Foremane, widow, bur.
June 10 Samuell son of Richard Hollewase chr.
June 10 Anne dau. of Augustine Garland chr.
June 10 Elizabeth dau. of Jno Palner bapt.
July 27 A child born 26 & bur. the next day
Aug. 2 Margett, mother of the sd child & servt to Richard Venn, bur.
Aug. 26 Robarte son of William Kempton bapt.
Sep. 21 Edward son of Iseralle Collynwoode bapt.

* The surname omitted in the original, but see previous year, and also other entries.

Sep. 30 Marye dau. of Arthuer Jackson bapt.
Oct. 21 John Troowbridge, serv[t] to M[r] Yaye [? Jay] the elder, bur.
Oct. 21 Frainces Smyth & Marie Judson marr.
Nov. 4 Thomas Burves & Joue Knight marr.
Nov. 4 Sarae dau. of John Ryla bapt.
Nov. 26 Richard son (as we are informed) of Richard Clarke bapt.
Dec. 2 Thomas Sharpe, serv[t] to John Danson, bur.
Dec. 26 Thomas son of Thomas Spencer bapt.
Jan. 7 Elizabeth dau. of William Craven bapt.
Jan. 22 Merine dau. of Simonde Poorige bur.
Jan. 27 Marie dau. of Alexsander Pistore bapt.
Feb. 29 An Turnbull dau. of Widow Converes bur.
Mar. 2 Anna dau. of Clefas Smythe bapt.

1600.

April 3 An infant son to Daniell Diconsonne bur.
April 5 Dorite dau. of Symond Pooridge bur.
April 13 Robart son of Christifer Lanckister bapt.
April 15 Joan wife of Thomas Burows bur.
May 2 John Hownsell bur.
May 5 Mathyas Westmerland & Elyzabethe Pecke marr.
May 9 Elizabethe dau. of Lodwicke Briskett bapt.
May 25 Elizabethe dau. of George Walmslaye bapt.
June 25 Thomas Raulines, skinner, bur.
June 29 Ane dau. of Marten Billingslaye bapt.
Aug. 10 Henrye Jacksonne bur. out of M[r] Aarter Jacksonne's house
Sep. 2 George Sampton & Marye Drie marr.
Sep. 3 The son of Margerite Hitin (not bapt.) bur.
Sep. 14 Sara dau. of Awstin Garland bapt.
Sep. 24 Margerit Hogsone, widow, mother to Allexsander Lockwood, bur.
Sep. 29 Noadiah Rawlin & Joan Danson marr.
Nov. 1 Joan dau. of Frances Dorington bapt.
Nov. 7 Richard Emsone bur. out of M[r] Dickinson's house
Nov. 9 Robart son of Robarte Yatman bapt.
Nov. 12 Helthy Croocke & Sara Welsh marr.
Dec. 21 Thomas son of Iserall Colinwood bapt.
Mar. 11 Mary dau. of Jane Cretofe bur.
Mar. 19 Thomas Jenett bur.
Mar. 22 William son of W[m] Kempton bapt.

1601.

April 26 Elizabeth dau. of W[m] Hawes bapt.
May 10 Adrian dau. of Thomas Ballord bapt.
June 1 John Dade & Joyes Bothbr marr.
June 1 Sara dau. of Phill. Patson bur.
June 14 William son of George Walmsley bapt.
June 17 Anne dau. of Simon Porridge bapt.
June 28 Thomas Baskervile & Anne Bullma' marr.
July 5 Nathaniell & Lyddia son & dau. of W[m] White bapt.
July 26 Jeane dau. of Danyell Dickinson bapt.
Aug. 2 Mary dau. of William Sprott bapt.
Aug. 9 Tzeby [*sic*] dau. of Noadia Rawlin bapt.
Aug. 16 Richard Bennett bur.
Aug. 26 George Jarvis, gent[n], of Woodchurch, Kent, & Dennis Frebodie marr.
Aug. 28 Sara wife of Thomas Wates bur.
Sep. 1 Thomas Breell & Elyzabeth Modye marr.

Sep. 9 An infant of M^r^tine Billingsly bur.
Sep. 11 Edward Babington bur.
Sep. 20 Jeane dau. of Henry Jay bapt.
Sep. 27 Mary dau. of Francis Wickes bapt.
Oct. 18 William son of Arther Jackeson bapt.
Oct. 28 Wm Harte & An Hunte marr.
Nov. 19 John Cutt & Margaret Elston marr. by lic.
Nov. 24 Robert Hawes, parish^r^, died w^th^in o^r^ parish, bur. at Ald^r^mary par. by . . . ves his wife was bur. there
Jan. 2 Richerd Richerson bur. out of Mr Bates's house
Jan. 6 Mary dau. of Cleophas Smyth bapt.
Jan. 7 Elyzabeth dau. of George Dorrington bapt.
Jan. 19 Nathaniell son of William White bur.
Feb. 7 Alics dau. of Tomas Borrowes chr.
Feb. 14 John son of John Ryley chr.
Feb. 18 Rachele dau. of Thomas Griffen chr.
Feb. 18 Richard son of John Parkinson chr.
Feb. 21 Susan dau. of Rease Bellfeld
Mar. 2 Mr Hendereye Jaye bur.
Mar. 9 Jesebell Foxcall bur.

1602.

April 18 Samewell son of Robbart Washborne chr.
April 22 John Mounford, serv^t^ to Ser Richard Bartlete, bur.
April 22 Samewell son of Robbart Washborne bur.
April 25 Tomas son of Robbart Goodall chr.
July 5 Alise Lewes wife of Willyam Lewes bur.
July 11 Willyam son of Willyam Hayes chr.
July 11 Anne dau. of John Dayde chr.
July 12 Tomas Bolde, clark of this parish, bur.
Aug. 1 Richard son of Richard Harvye chr.
Aug. 1 Sussanaye dau. of Zacarye Dowe chr.
Aug. 5 Allexsander Dolenton son of Francis Dolenton chr.
Aug. 20 Frances Daves bur.
Sep. 26 Soussene Bellenesly dau. of Marten Bellenesly chr.
Sep. 26 Allen Morles & [*blank*] Rosse, serv^t^ with Bates, marr.
Oct. 13 Ane Lankkester dau. of Crestofer Lankester chr. 13 Oct. & bur. 17 Oct. after
Oct. 17 Marye Craven the dater of Mr Will'm Craven, Alderman, chr.
Nov. 11 Richard Vene son of Richard Vene chr.
Jan. 2 Ales Dorington dau. to Mr Gorge Dorington chr.
Jan. 13 Augustin son to Mr Augustin Garland chr.
Jan. 23 A child of Mr Henry Jaye's bur. before it was chr.
Jan. 23 On Mary, a stray, christined ye 23 Jan. 1602
Feb. 11 Margret dau. of Robert Yateman chr.
Feb. 13 James Gob^r^oine & Margeritt Huet, serv^t^ to Mr Raullins, marr.
Feb. 13 Eevan Jones & Alis Falver marr.
Feb. 13 Richard Levitt son to Richard Levitt chr.
Feb. 14 Thomas Fulwode & Ales Munckus, serv^t^ to Mr Moodye, marr.
Feb. 15 Mr John Harvye bur.
Mar. 20 Francis son of Francis Smith chr.

1603.

April 3 John of St Antholin's, laid in the parish, chr.
April 24 Benjamin son of Richar Goodalle chr. Easterday
April 25 Mary Parke bur.

May 15 Ferdonando son to John Gooef chr. 15 & bur. 22 May
May 17 One Mary, a stray, bur.
June 1 Katherine dau. to John Parkinsone chr.
June 13 Thomas Hayward & Aenn Buttler, serv[t] to M[r] Venn, marr.
June 28 Elizabeth dau. to M[r] William Joons bur.
July 3 Margrett dau. to William Staniuale chr.
July 15 William Craven, kinsman to M[r] All. Craven, bur.
July 22 Jane Sanders, serv[t] to Alderman Craven, bur.
July 25 James son to Francis Weeks chr.
July 30 Mary Neale & Mother Houbble bur.
Aug. 1 Grace Saitas, serv[t] to Francis Smith, bur.
Aug. 4 Elsabeth Crabe, a child, bur.
Aug. 5 A young man, a glazier, newly come to the parish, bur.
Aug. 7 Dorithy Judsonne bur.
Aug. 9 Sible Poridge dau. to Simon Poridge bur.
Aug. 12 Christopher son to William Lewes bur.
Aug. 16 John Davisone, prentice to Daniel Elsmore, bur.
Aug. 17 Roger Steevinson, prentice to French y[e] turner, bur.
Aug. 17 Elsabeth dau. to Richard Jagger bur.
Aug. 22 Elline Griffine sister to M[r] Willi. Jones bur.
Aug. 22 Margeritt wife to Micaell French, turner, bur.
Aug. 23 Suzan dau. to Zacary Dove bur.
Aug. 26 William Quinten, serv[t] to Danyell Elsmore, bur.
Sep. 1 Jane dau. of Simon Pottage [*sic*] bur. [see Aug. 9]
Sep. 4 Toby Laen, serv[t] to John Daed, bur.
Sep. 13 Hary son to Martin Billinsly bur. [see Oct. 5]
Sep. 18 Mary dau. to Christopher Lauckester bur.
Oct. 2 Israyell Collingewod bur.
Oct. 3 Margerit Spencer & Hew Griffine bur.
Oct. 5 Hary son to Martine Billinsly chr. [*sic*]
Oct. 6 Annis Jones, serv[t] to M[r] Dickiousou, bur.
Oct. 11 Robert son to Zacrey Dove bur.
Oct. 11 Arthur Maberly, serv[t] to Danyell Dickinson, bur.
Oct. 20 Robert Davis son to M[rs] Nickolas bur.
Oct. 28 Ayme dau. to Nicolas Hayden chr. & bur. y[e] 30th
Nov. 11 Mary dau. to Daniell Dickinesonn bur.
Nov. 13 M[r] Daniell Dickinesonn bur.
Nov. 14 John Hayfield & Mary Smith, strangers, marr.
Dec. 9 Thomas Corsby bur.
Jan. 1 Mary dau. to Richard Haell chr.
Jan. 8 One Sara, a bast., bur.
Jan. 20 James Higgly, turner, bur.
Jan. 30 William Cunnet and Elner Darby marr.
Feb. 12 Thomas Yeomans & Eliza. Wiecn marr.
Feb. 16 Jone Chambers bur., out of Holborne
Feb. 19 Anna dau. to William Ufflitt chr.
Feb. 20 William Flecher & Grace Muffut marr.
Mar. 11 Margeritt dau. to Robert Yeatman chr.
Mar. 12 Rebecka dau. to Will. Staninall bur.
Mar. 13 Annis Attkinson, serv[t] to Will. Staninall, bur.

1604.

April 1 George Heb, serv[t] to Will. Stanynall, bur.
April 5 John Yonge, serv[t] to Will. Stanynall, bur.
April 19 Thomas Craven, serv[t] to S[r] Will. Craven, bur.
April 26 Thomas Morley & Rebeckae Bridges marr.
May 6 Mary dau. to John Pecke chr.

May 9 Androw son to William Muffett bur.
June 17 Cleophas son to Cleophas Smith chr.
Aug. 19 James son to Richard Jagger chr.
Sep. 13 Thomas Dey bur.
Sep. 13 Hawis dau. to Francis Doringtonn chr.
Sep. 23 Nathaniell son to John Haell chr.
Oct. 3 Gressam son to Nicolas Hayden bur.
Oct. 7 Aen dau. to Thomas Simsonne chr.
Oct. 18 Elizabeth Antholins chr., 2 years old, a foundling
Nov. 4 Simon Stocke & Elline Prate marr.
Nov. 6 Richard Cooke & Aeun Wonly marr.
Nov. 20 Arther Yeomansonn & Jone Dowell marr.
Dec. 3 Richard Gille & Margrett Simes marr.
Dec. 9 Sara dau. to Robbertt Goodale chr.
Dec. 25 Anne dau. to Richard Harvy chr.
Dec. 26 William Starky & Anne Blackborn marr.
Dec. 30 Margeritt dau. to Richard Attwell chr.
Jan. 1 William son to William Benitt chr.
Jan. 6 Ithamar dau. to Noadiah Rullins chr.
Jan. 6 Mary dau. to Hen. Hamersly chr.
Jan. 20 Henry son to Martine Billinsly chr.
Jan. 21 Rebecka dau. to Agustine Garland chr.
Jan. 27 Henry son to Henry Jaye chr.
Feb. 8 Ithamar dau. to Noadiah Rallins bur.
Feb. 10 John Griffin & Jane Williames marr.
Feb. 14 Henry son to M[r] John Jaye bur.
Feb. 17 Francis dau. to Nicolas Hayden chr.
Feb. 21 Old John Davis, serv[t] to M[rs] Jaye, bur.
Feb. 24 Isacke son to Thomas Ballard chr.
Feb. 24 Joyce dau. to Francis Wickes chr.
Feb. 28 Sara dau. to Augustin Garland bur.
Mar. 24 Katherin Sperrine, from Pancras, bur.

1605.

April 2 Humphery Haukins & Bathsua Wilcokes marr.
April 5 A child of M[r] Moor's, stillborn, bur.
April 14 Mathew Thornhull & Margery Newton marr.
April 18 Margrett wife to M[r] Andryan Moore bur.; of childbed
April 21 Elizabeth dau. of William Connitt chr.
May 5 Thomas son to Robert Worsoncrafte chr.
May 25 Aeun dau. to M[r] Augustin Garland bur.
June 1 John son to Henry Skeritte bur.
June 2 Arthur son to Arthur Jacksonn chr.
June 19 John Wade & Avis Parkers marr.
June 23 John son to Christopher Lancaster chr.
Aug. 4 Peeter Willsonn & Margrett Mathew marr.
Aug. 11 Humphry son to Thomas Humble chr.
Sep. 1 Thomas Attwater & Jane Page marr.
Sep. 10 Elizabeth Robinsonn bur.; of the plague
Sep. 11 Jane Hews, bur.; plague
Sep. 15 Mary dau. to John Bourmann chr.
Sep. 22 A child, stillborn, of Richard Levet's bur.
Sep. 27 John son to Christopher Lanckester bur.
Sep. 29 Thomas Whitly & Margrett Barksdall marr.
Oct. 1 John Ford & An Dansonn marr.
Oct. 1 Mathew Blith bur.; plague
Oct. 11 John Greathed bur.; plague

Oct. 19 John Farthinge & Elizabeth Olaude marr.
Oct. 28 Robert Yeattman bur.; plague
Oct. 29 Miridith Mady & Jone Peeters marr.
Nov. 24 John son to Robert Goodaell chr.
Nov. 25 Willi. son to Sr Willia. Craven chr.
Nov. 26 Nicolas Hayden & his dau. Jane bur.
Nov. 26 Alls dau. to Henry Mondy bur.
Dec. 3 George Wats & Susan Davis marr.
Dec. 19 Steeven Fuller & Isabell Sanders marr.
Dec. 21 Abigall dau. to Noadiah Rallins chr.
Dec. 22 Abigall dau. to Noadiah Rallins bur.
Dec. 23 A bastard child of Nicola. Hayden bur.
Dec. 24 William Keellinge bur.
Jan. 4 Elizabeth wife to Martin Billinsly bur.
Jan. 4 Mary dau. to Martin Billinsly chr.
Jan. 5 Mary dau. to John Daed chr.
Jan. 9 Elizabeth wife to Mr Doctor Felton bur.
Jan. 12 Anne dau. to Henry Skerritt chr.
Jan. 26 Timothy Cannon & Maudlin Shepherd marr.
Jan. 26 Walter son to Mathew Thornhull [?]
Feb. 4 Thomas Perry & Als Hall marr.
Feb. 16 Ursala, a base child, the mother in the porch, chr.
Feb. 17 John Pary, serv^t^ to Nicolas Hayden, bur.
Feb. 18 Anna dau. to Hew Hamersly chr.
Feb. 19 Elizabeth dau. to John Lewes, clark, bur.
Feb. 25 William Ayre & Jone Jacsonn marr.
Mar. 4 An dau. to Sr William Craven bur.
Mar. 5 Margrett dau. to Richard Attwell bur.
Mar. 9 Sara dau. to Roger Oulton chr.
Mar. 23 Maudlin Inggram, the mother in ye church porch, chr.

1606.

Mar. 25 An dau. to William Hausse chr.
April 3 William son to Sr Willi. Craven bur.
April 4 Winyfrid lady to Sr Thomas Pullison bur.
April 8 Arter son to Arter Jacson bur.
April 20 Thomas Simpson son to Thomas Simpson chr.
April 22 Mrs Jone Hudsonn, from the Strand, bur.
April 27 An dau. to Edward Raply chr.
April 27 Androges son to Valliutyn Griffin chr.
May 1 Androges son to Vallintyn Gryffin bur.
May 7 Abraham Savage, serv^t^ to Mrs Yeattman, bur.
May 23 Thom. son to Thom. Bayly chr. 23 & bur. 26th
June 24 John Rudducke & Katharin Elsmore marr.
June 27 Margrett Coulloom, from Old Change, St Mary Maudlin's, bur.
July 26 John Jackson bur.
July 27 Thomas Sargent & Penelopy Startine marr.
Aug. 14 Bento Asswerowe, a Spaniard, bur.
Aug. 24 Ann dau. to Richard Jagger chr.
Aug. 26 Ann dau. to John Peeke chr. 26 & bur. the 30th
Sep. 7 Thomas son to Augustine Garland chr.
Sep. 21 Robert son to Robert Washborne chr.
Sep. 21 John son to George Watts chr.
Sep. 22 John Piggott, serv^t^ to Willi. Connet, bur.
Sep. 24 John son to George Watts chr.
Sep. 29 Georg Dixe bur.
Oct. 4 Mr William Younge, silkman, bur.

Oct. 5 Walter son to Mathew Thournhull bur.
Oct. 5 Charls son to Robert Worsoncrafte chr.
Oct. 5 Robert son to Richard Munsey chr.
Oct. 14 A stillborn of Robert Crettof's bur.
Oct. 17 Margrett Yearly, serv[t] to M[r] Goughs, bur.
Oct. 18 Ann Barlow bur.
Oct. 20 Ann dau. to Richard Jagger bur.
Oct. 21 Isack son to Thomas Ballard bur.
Oct. 22 John Spirine bur.
Nov. 2 Edward Hochkins & Margery Webb marr.
Nov. 2 Henry son to Willi. Benitt chr.
Nov. 15 John son to Richard Linnis chr.
Nov. 23 John son to M[r] Henry Jaye chr.
Jan. 2 Benjamin son to Robert Goodall bur.
Jan. 6 John son to John Boorman chr.
Jan. 29 Robert son to George Quiny bur.
Feb. 3 David, a bastard, son to David Leake chr.
Feb. 5 John Wise & Maudline Merston marr.
Feb. 8 Henry Atkins & Mary Harper marr.
Mar. 22 Mary dau. to Richard Attwels chr.
Mar. 23 George Quiny bur.

1607.

Mar. 29 Joseph son to Arthur Jacksonn chr.
April 6 Anna dau. to Noadiah Raulins chr.
April 12 Thomas son to John Daed chr.
April 12 Anna dau. to M[r] Rich. Ven chr.
April 12 Ellizab. dau. to John Rudduck chr.
May 10 S[r] Peeter Saltalstall & Christian Pettus marr.
May 14 Richard Field & Christian Newton marr.
May 25 Samuell Tucker & Eliza. Jaye marr.
May 25 Eliza. dau. to M[r] Hen. Hamersly chr.
June 1 Mary dau. to Richa. Atwels bur.
June 21 Elizabeth dau. to Mathew Thornhull chr.
Aug. 2 Thomas Locker & Jane Nelson marr.
Aug. 9 Nicolas son to Thomas Ballard chr.
Sep. 6 [*blank*] dau. to John Lewes, clerk, chr.
Sep. 22 Jone wife to Richard Levett bur.
Sep. 29 Richard Bright & Winifrid Vickers marr.
Nov. 9 Robert son to Robert Cretoff chr.
Nov. 22 Lewes Morgaun & Luce Jones marr.
Dec. 11 Elitzur son to George Barnard bur.
Dec. 13 Margery dau. to Edward Sherington chr.
Dec. 20 William son to Robert Washborne chr.
Dec. 27 Thomas son to Robert Vace, from M[r] Washborne's, chr.
Jan. 1 Thomas son to Robert Goodale chr.
Jan. 3 George son to Richard Jagger [?]
Jan. 12 John Kintonn & Margret Dutton marr.
Feb. 29 Elizabeth dau. to William Rankin chr.
Mar. 9 John son to M[r] Henry Jay bur.

1608.

April 7 Elizabeth Wright, a maid-serv[t], bur.
May 5 Jane dau. to John Linnis chr.
May 16 William Stacey & Margrett Yeatman marr.
June 1 John son to John Daed chr.

June 23 George son to Richard Jagger bur.
June 28 Mary dau. to Augustine Garland chr.
July 19 Humphery Saulsbury & Joyce Poole marr.
July 23 Mary dau. to George Woodward chr.
July 26 Mary dau. to George Woodward bur.
Aug. 23 Henry son to Martine Billinsley bur.
Sep. 1 Ann dau. to Robert Netmaker chr.
Sep. 4 Elizabeth dau. to Mr Cleophas Smith chr.
Sep. 8 Ann dau. to Mr Martin Billinsley bur.
Sep. 19 Margery Perrine, servt to Mr Billinsley, bur.
Sep. 26 John son to John Linnis bur.
Oct. 2 John son to Hew Parnell chr.
Oct. 6 Charles Cossinne & Ann Paine marr.
Oct. 31 Francis son to Mr Francis Dorringtonn chr.
Nov. 7 Lewes son to Henry Scerrett chr.
Nov. 7 A stillborn of Mr Richard Hobbie's bur.
Nov. 7 Margrett Woollet, servt to Mr Garland, bur.
Nov. 15 William Gilly and Saray Parris marr.
Nov. 19 Ann wife to Mr John Gough bur.
Nov. 23 Ellin Puller, servt to Mr Gough, bur.
Nov. 27 Roger Weston, a minister, a stranger, bur.
Dec. 27 Thomas Rock & Mary Clark marr.
Jan. 6 George son to Thomas Humble chr.
Jan. 13 Susanna dau. to Henry Carcleell chr.
Jan. 19 Nicolas Chuna & Catherinn Hac marr.
Jan. 27 Mary dau. to Martine Billinsly bur.
Feb. 9 William Sharpe & Elizabeth Sandford marr.
Feb. 12 William son to William Tolly chr.
Feb. 14 Thomas son to Thomas Humble bur.
Mar. 3 A stillborn child of Robert Goodall's bur.
Mar. 7 Hauwas dau. to Francis Dorrington bur.
Mar. 15 Elizabeth dau. to Francis Weekes chr.

1609.

Mar. 30 David son to Mathias Foule, at Mr Henry Jaye's, chr.
May 1 Mary dau. to John Daed bur.
May 10 Francis Prior, prentice to Roger Oultonn, bur.
June 1 Dorcas dau. to Hew Hamersly chr.
June 13 Henry son to Henry Sherrington chr.
June 18 Joseph son to Joseph Cock chr.
June 24 A child, unbapt., of John Pecke's bur.
Aug. 18 Bazzill son to William Bennitt chr. 18 & bur. 20 Aug.
Aug. 23 Ann wife to Mr Richard Venn bur.
Sep. 21 Leonard son to Richard Jagger chr.
Sep. 24 Sara dau. to Robert Cretoff chr.
Sep. 26 Ephraim son to Edmund Willis chr.
Oct. 15 Ann dau. to Thomas Wetherall chr.
Oct. 17 Richard Ratheram his child (unbaptd) bur.
Oct. 28 John son to Randall Greaton chr.
Nov. 1 Nicolas son to Nicolas Chuna chr.
Nov. 5 Thomas son to Noadiah Raullins chr.
Nov. 19 William son to Matthew Thornhull chr.
Nov. 30 Thomas Cranfield, taylor, in St Thomas the Apostle, & Margret Griffin, of this parish, marr. by lic.
Dec. 4 John Applebee, from Mr Baker's, bur.
Dec. 16 Ephraime son to Edmund Willis bur.
Dec. 21 Mr Humphery Corbet, from Nuwington, bur.

Jan. 1 Mary dau. of Richard Levit chr.
Jan. 14 Thomas son to Richard Hoby chr.
Jan. 20 Martha Lukin, serv[t] to the Lady Denny, bur.
Jan. 29 John son to Randall Greaton bur.
Feb. 3 Judith Snooke, at M[r] Hobbi's, bur.
Feb. 12 William Deane, of S[t] Andrew's, Holborne, taylor, & Margret Clarke, of this parish, marr.
Feb. 28 Elizabeth wife to M[r] Henry Jaye bur.
Mar. 10 Thomas Rivet, of Rattlesden, Suffolk, & Jone Savill, of Nethertonn in Yorkshire, marr. by lic.
Mar. 11 Mary dau. to John Dade chr.
Mar. 12 Elizabeth dau. of Martine Billinsly bur.

1610.

Mar. 29 Robert son to Robert Creatoff bur.
April 10 Thomas Claye, S[t] Clem., Temple bar, & Elizabeth Gander, of Rigate in Surrey, marr. by lic.
April 29 Martha dau. to Isack Griffinn chr.
May 12 Robert son to Thomas Humble chr.
June 17 Richard son to Robert Goodalle chr.
June 20 A stillborn of M[r] Arthur Jackson's bur.
June 21 M[rs] Elizabeth Joye the elder, widow, bur.
June 22 Alis Goodalle, sister to Robert Goodalle, bur.
June 25 Robert Parkes bur.
July 15 Richard Wood & Mary Beverly marr. by lic.
July 18 David Powell, serv[t] to M[r] William White, bur.
July 30 A child found dead at the church door bur.
Aug. 2 M[r] William White bur.
Aug. 2 William Pitts, prentice to M[r] Hale, bur.
Aug. 12 Thomas son to Robert Washborne chr.
Aug. 15 Edward Banburye & Mary Goodale, both of this par., marr. by lic.
Aug. 19 Bartholomew Guilliams & Ann Walle marr. by banns.
Aug. 20 Richard son to Robert Goodalle bur.
Aug. 21 Phillip Johnsonn, prentice to William Spencer, bur.
Aug. 26 John son to William Bennitt chr.
Aug. 28 Andrew Draughton, of S[t] Steeven's in Walbrooke, & Anne Tennant, of S[t] Grigorye's by Paule's, marr. by lic.
Sep. 2 John son to John Lewes, the clark, chr.
Sep. 24 John Hagly, a sojourner, bur.
Oct. 7 Ann dau. to Anthony Woode chr.
Oct. 26 William Tolly, upholster, bur.
Oct. 28 William Howell, of Westminster, tailor, & Mary Saule, of this par., marr. by banns
Nov. 14 Jane dau. to John Linnis bur.
Dec. 4 Elizabeth dau. to William Woodrofe chr.
Jan. 13 John son to William Tolly chr.
Jan. 16 Humphery son to John Norgrave chr.
Feb. 4 Richard Dike & Dority Jaye, of this par., marr. by lic.
Mar. 17 Robert son to Richar Hobby chr.

1611.

April 7 Umphery Write, taylor, & Lettis Grigg marr. by banns
April 8 William Robinsonn, gent., of the Temple, & Elizabeth Burrell, of Benit Gracechurch, marr. by lic.
April 18 John Dewman, taylor, of St. Thomas Apostle, & Alice Webster, of Aldermary, marr. by lic.

May 5 Margrett dau. to Izacke Griffine chr.
May 5 Hester dau. to Edward Banbury chr.
May 19 John son to Mr Cleophas Smith chr.
May 21 John son to Mr Cleophas Smith bur.
May 23 Richard Keeling, gent., a lawyer's clerk, in Dunston's West, & Elizabeth Penn, of this par., marr. by lic.
June 3 Margrett dau. to Henry Skerrow chr.
July 7 Joyce dau. to John Dade chr.
July 9 Anthony Young, servt to Sr William Craven, bur.
July 25 Thomas son to Thomas Wetherall chr.
Sep. 15 James son to Thomas Grove chr.
Sep. 22 Gabriell Pennington, glazier, of St John Baptist, & Anne Redman, of this par., marr.
Oct. 6 James son to Robert Washborn chr.
Oct. 6 John son to Thomas Browne chr.
Nov. 11 Sara dau. to Robert Cretoft bur.
Nov. 17 Robert son to Robert Goodall chr.
Nov. 18 Margret dau. to Henry Skerrow bur.
Nov. 19 Robert son to Robert Goodall bur.
Nov. 19 Edward Moody bur.
Nov. 20 Magdalin dau. to Henry Fisher, gent., of the Midd. Temple, lodger in this parish, chr.
Nov. 23 Amy Ellis bur.
Nov. 27 Mr Thomas Archdale, from Aldermanbury, bur.
Dec. 8 Hannah dau. to Joseph Cock chr.
Dec. 15 Edward son to Mathue Thornhull chr.
Dec. 22 Sara dau. to Noadiah Raulins chr.
Dec. 24 Mary Walker, an old widow, bur.
Jan. 5 Thomas son to Thomas Waren chr.
Jan. 9 Sara dau. to Noadiah Raulins bur.
Jan. 27 William Leygh, gent., & Margery Michelborne, both of S 'Steen's [*sic*], Walbrooke, marr. by lic.
Jan. 28 Henry son to Richard Dicke chr.
Feb. 14 Bartholomew son to Thomas Griffeth chr.
Feb. 16 The same Bartholomew bur.
Feb. 18 Richar Organ, gent., of Lincoln's Inn, and Lucy Dove, of Badsly, co. Southampton, marr. by lic.
Mar. 8 Thomas son to Thomas Humble chr.
Mar. 9 Mr Edward Hinnidge, our minister, bur.
Mar. 18 John son to Mr William Butler, gent., bur.
Mar. 24 John son to Richard Hobby chr.

1612.

May 10 Ann dau. to Robert Lucey, from Mr Bothbi's, chr.
May 17 Elizabeth dau. to John Peck chr.
May 18 Edward son to Mathew Thornhull bur.
June 2 Thomas son to Robert Goodalle bur.
June 4 John son to Anthony Wood chr.
June 7 Anna dau. to William Benuitt chr.
June 14 Richard son to Richard Jaggard chr.
June 27 Roger Oultonn bur.
July 1 Magdalin Strange, a foundling in this parish, chr.
July 5 Thomas son to Mr Hugh Hamersly chr.
Aug. 7 Mr Hugh Broughtonn, from Tatnam high Cross, bur.
Aug. 7 Hester dau. to Edward Banbury bur.
Aug. 10 Micaias Wellum, of Benit's, Poule's Wharf, & Susanna Smith, of this parish, marr. by banns

Aug. 19 A foundling, unbapt., bur.
Aug. 24 Michell son to Thomas Dunn chr.
Aug. 27 M[r] Edward Sprot, from Aldermary, bur.
Sep. 2 Mary dau. to Richard Levit bur.
Sep. 3 Anne dau. to Isaac Griffin chr. 3[d] & bur. 7th
Oct. 4 Rebecca dau. to Henry Skerrow chr.
Oct. 20 Elizabeth dau. to Sampsonn Cotton chr.
Oct. 23 Thomas son to M[r] John Dade bur.
Oct. 28 Jeremy Warner & Jone Whitmoor marr. by banns
Oct. 28 Jhon son to John Lewes, the clark, bur.
Oct. 30 Rachell wife to Ralph Huffe bur.
Nov. 14 A child (unbapt.) of Noadiah Raulins bur.
Nov. 22 Ann Compton, servant, bur.
Nov. 29 Martha dau. to John Dade chr.
Dec. 6 William Dickinsonn & Mary Faulkner marr. by banns
Dec. 13 George Stockall & Sarah Hunnicote marr. by banns
Dec. 19 Jerimy son to M[r] Hopkinsonn, sometime our minister, bur.
Dec. 29 Susanna dau. to Nicolas Beales chr.
Jan. 5 Randulfe Austonn bur.
Jan. 10 Elizabeth dau. to Edmond Willis chr.
Jan. 17 Alice wife to Simon Pordage bur.
Jan. 26 Mary dau. to John Dade bur.
Jan. 30 Mary dau. to Thomas Grove bur.
Jan. 31 Nicolas Bonner & Alice Levit marr. by banns
Jan. 31 Susanna dau. to Robert Goodalle chr.
Feb. 2 John Wilde, father to M[rs] Willis, bur.
Feb. 5 Susanna dau. to Robert Goodall bur.
Feb. 8 Phillip Pattson, our old sexton, bur.
Feb. 11 Thomas Coe, grocer, at S[t] Mary Hill, & Dorath Cardwell, of this parish, marr. by lic.
Mar. 14 Mary dau. to Edward Banbury chr.

1613.

Mar. 29 Rebecca dau. to Henry Skerrow bur.
April 12 Robert Kindersly, of Margret Moyses, & Mary Auston, of this parish, marr. by lic.
April 18 Robert Smith, merch[t], of S[t] Thomas Apostle, & Elizabeth Sharpulls, of Gabraell Fanchurch, London, marr. by lic.
April 25 William Lamb, of Magdalins Barmsey, & Sara Judson, of this parish, marr. by banns
April 28 M[r] Thom. Raulins, D[r] of Physic, from Sepulcher's, bur.
May 18 Dorathy wife to Richard Jagger bur.
June 7 Thomas Streame, of S[t] Martin's le graunde, & Fraunces Savidge, marr. by lic.
July 1 M[r] William Jones bur.
July 5 Richard Levit bur.
July 7 Jerimy Butler bur.
July 11 Thomas son to William Dicke chr.
July 13 Richard son to Richard Hobbey chr.
July 19 Danniell son to Robert Washborne bur.
July 23 Anna dau. to Thomas Aunderson, a lodger at M[rs] Saul's, chr.
July 25 Peninnah dau. to Joseph Cocke chr.
Aug. 17 William Downes & Elizabeth Morris, both of Westminster, marr.
Aug. 30 Richard Knowles bur.
Sep. 10 Alce dau. to Sammuell Plaifoote bur.
Sep. 13 John Barnard & Ann Pennington marr. by banns
Sep. 16 A child, unbapt., of M[r] Ralins, bur.

Sep. 19 William son to Christopher Rily chr.
Oct. 7 Owen Sempeer, from Alphage parish, bur.
Oct. 10 Mary dau. to Matthew Thornhull chr.
Oct. 14 James Browne & Bridget Terrey marr.
Oct. 24 Frauncis son to Hugh Hamersly chr.
Nov. 4 William Barron & Judith Piggott marr.
Nov. 5 Margret wife to Thomas Craufilde bur.
Nov. 21 Elizabeth dau. to Nicolas Cleggett chr.
Nov. 26 Mary Browne, found in the parish, chr.
Dec. 10 A stillborn child of Thomas Aldersey's bur.
Dec. 17 Judith Eaton died here, & at S[t] Swithin's bur.
Dec. 25 Ann dau. of Thomas Ives chr.
Jan. 28 Margret dau. to Izaac Griffin bur.
Jan. 30 John son to Edward Chelsam chr.
Feb. 2 Thomas son to Thomas Browne chr.
Feb. 4 Mary dau. to Thomas Grove chr.
Feb. 11 M[rs] Burton, from S[t] Dunston's East, bur.
Feb. 23 William son to Henry Skerrow chr.
Mar. 5 John Lewes, a foundling, chr.
Mar. 9 John son to Thomas Wetherall chr.
Mar. 9 Thomas Collingwood bur.

1614.

Mar. 27 John son to Thomas Wetherall bur.
April 7 Ann dau. to Robert Goodall chr.
April 7 Mary dau. to Anthony Wood chr.
April 19 A child, found dead, bur.
April 25 Margret Bradford bur.
June 14 Thomas son to Thomas Dunn chr.
June 16 Steeven Foster & Alice Houncell marr.
June 21 Thomas son to Thomas Dunn bur.
June 26 Edward Burgis & Maude Goorde marr.
July 24 A stillborn of M[r] Hugh Hamersly bur.
July 27 Hannah dau. to Joseph Cock bur.
July 31 Ezechiell son to Robert Washborn chr.
Aug. 5 James son to Robert Washborn bur.
Aug. 12 Elizabeth dau. to Edward Atkinsonn bur.
Sep. 4 Thomas son to Joseph Cock chr.
Sep. 14 A stillborn of Albion Jugsonn bur.
Sep. 25 Robert son to Anthony Burton chr.
Sep. 29 John Dent & Ann Carver marr.
Oct. 3 John Michell & Catherin Fouler marr.
Oct. 5 Robert son to Anthony Burton bur.
Oct. 15 Eedy Varnam, from S[t] Andrew Wardrobe, bur.
Oct. 16 Hannah dau. to Peeter Hazard chr.
Nov. 1 Elizabeth dau. to Noadiah Raulins chr.
Nov. 13 Sammuell son to Richard Crooke, our minister, chr.
Nov. 13 Mary dau. to John Ragg chr.
Nov. 20 Aaron son to Aaron Linnacar chr.
Dec. 14 M[r] Thomas Smith, of Lincoln's Inn, bur.
Dec. 18 Thomas son to Thomas Edmons chr.
Jan. 1 John Jonsonn & Alice Haine marr.
Jan. 2 Mary dau. to Nicolas Clegat chr.
Jan. 18 Vahhan Floyd, born in the church porch, chr.
Jan. 25 George Brooksby, serv[t] to M[r] Moore, bur.
Feb. 10 Susanna dau. to Nicolas Beales bur.
Feb. 21 Robert Dighton & Elizabeth Washborne marr.

Mar. 7 Margery dau. to Mathew Thornhull bur.
Mar. 14 A stillborn of Nicolas Beales bur.
Mar. 18 Mary dau. to Richard Ginnings bur.
Mar. 22 M[rs] Alce Vace, widow, bur.

1615.

Mar. 28 Anna dau. to Richard Hobby chr.
April 10 Thomas Bettersby & Sara Pitcher marr.
April 30 Bridget & Elizabeth daus. to Raphaell Gooddin chr.
May 15 Elizabeth dau. of Raphaell Gooddin bur.
May 21 Edward son to Edward Banbury chr.
May 30 Thomas Pardnall & Margret Crampton marr.
May 31 Anna dau. to Richard Hill chr.
June 4 Liddia dau. to William Bennit chr.
June 10 James son to Thomas Grove bur.
June 15 Thomas son to Richard Gennings chr.
June 18 Margret dau. to Edward Chelsam chr.
June 29 Richard Lilly & Joane Smith marr.
Aug. 27 John Cullamoore & Alice Wilde marr.
Sep. 30 Rebecca dau. of William Best chr.
Oct. 15 Humphery son to Thomas Wetherall chr.
Nov. 13 Mary dau. to John Wragg bur.
Nov. 15 Nathaneell son to Noadiah Raulins chr.
Nov. 17 Henry son to Cleophas Smith bur.
Dec. 4 Thomas Grove bur.
Dec. 6 Thomas Allin, serv[t] to M[r] Sherrington, bur.
Dec. 7 Hanna dau. to Joseph Cock chr.
Dec. 12 A child, unbapt., of Mathew Thornhull bur.
Dec. 24 Leonard Hale bur.
Jan. 7 Richard son to Anthony Burton chr.
Jan. 17 Sara dau. to Thomas Browne chr.
Jan. 28 Thomas son to Thomas Ives chr.
Jan. 30 Richard son to Richard Dike chr.
Feb. 26 Zachary son to Micaell Bryann chr.
Mar. 1 Margret dau. to Anthony Woode chr.
Mar. 4 M[r] Mathew Salloway bur.
Mar. 11 Edwarde Sherringtonn bur.
Mar. 11 Joyce dau. to John Dade bur.
Mar. 13 Francis Walker, a foundling, chr.

1616.

Mar. 30 Elizabeth dau. to Noadiah Raulins bur.
Mar. 30 James Pindle bur. at Pancrose, Soper Lane
April 2 William Dunn & Ann Grove marr.
April 5 Rachell dau. to Richard Hobby chr.
April 8 John Osborne & Mary Sprot marr.
April 10 Thomas Hobson & Fraunois Ferne marr.
May 9 Sammuell son to Robert Washborne chr.
May 21 Timothy Elwicke & Sara Smith marr.
May 24 Sara dau. to Steeven Foster chr.
May 25 Fraunois Yeomans bur.
May 27 Doraty dau. to Aaronn Linicar chr.
May 30 Sara dau. to Steeven Foster bur.
June 17 Maudeline Pattson & Edward Osborne marr.
July 3 Sara dau. to Edward Banbury chr.
July 5 Ann Howell bur.

Aug. 6 John son to Martin Billinsley chr.
Aug. 20 Margery Semper, from Alphage by the Wall, bur.
Aug. 27 Isaac son to Peeter Hasser chr.
Oct. 18 Anna dau. to John Sharrow chr. 18 & bur. 21
Oct. 28 William Lusher & Ellinn Merrideth marr.
Nov. 3 William son to Edward Moss chr.
Nov. 5 Mr Cleophas Smith bur.
Nov. 10 Edward son to Edward Chelsam chr.
Nov. 27 Mary Slaughter, a prentice, bur.
Nov. 28 Christian dau. to John Haukins chr.
Dec. 5 Alice Hounsell, widow, bur.
Jan. 9 Margret wife of Thomas Bradford bur.
Jan. 16 William Collingwood & Bridget Collingwood marr.
Jan. 17 Tomazin Patsonn, a foundling, chr.
Jan. 22 Ann dau. to Robert Slaughter chr.
Jan. 26 Thomas son to Robert Walker chr.
Jan. 26 Susanna dau. to Nicolas Beales chr.
Feb. 9 Richard Jaggard & Eedy Arnall marr.
Feb. 9 Elizabeth dau. to William Kilborne chr.
Feb. 11 Henry Cartwrit & Ann Ailmer marr.
Feb. 13 Sara dau. to Robert Walker bur.
Feb. 20 Ann dau. to William Allinn chr.
Mar. 2 William son to William Dunn chr.
Mar. 10 Richard son to Richard Hill chr. 10 & bur. 11
Mar. 20 Andrew Bance, a mercer of Oxford, bur.
Mar. 24 William son to Raphaell Gooddin chr.
Mar. 24 Bridget dau. to Raphaell Gooddin bur.

1617.

Mar. 31 Elizabeth dau. to Thomas Davice bur.
April 1 Ann dau. to Vaspasian Bradford bur.
April 16 Thomas son to Hugh Perry bur.
April 25 Margret Gibsonn bur.
May 18 John Crosse & Elizabeth Bartleme marr. by banns
May 18 Jane dau. to John Atkins chr.
May 21 Elnor wife to William Cunnett bur.
June 11 John Parris bur.
June 26 Steeven son to Steeven Foster chr.
June 27 Alice wife to Steeven Foster bur.
Aug. 3 Ann dau. to Fraunci Bickley chr.
Aug. 12 Elizabeth dau. to Henry Browne chr.
Aug. 23 Thomas son to Thomas Ive bur.
Sep. 16 Old Mrs [*blank*] Parris bur.
Sep. 16 Mr Fraunci Dorrington bur.
Oct. 1 John Sertaine & Mary Deane marr.
Oct. 4 Sara dau. to Thomas Browne bur.
Oct. 5 Richard son to Thomas Wetherall chr.
Oct. 12 John son to Edward Moss chr. 12 & bur. 18
Oct. 12 Ann dau. to John Goddard chr.
Oct. 17 John son to John Sharrow chr. 17 & bur. 20
Oct. 21 Joseph Negus & Dorkas Washborne marr.
Oct. 31 John Cooke, a foundling, chr.
Nov. 2 Jone dau. to William Collingwood chr.
Nov. 16 Thomas Brickell & Ann Isbell marr.
Nov. 30 John son to Aaron Linicar chr.
Jan. 1 Thomas Crouch & Hanna Smith marr.
Jan. 11 Richard Simcott & Mercey Reisonn marr.

Jan. 13 Elizabeth dau. to John Haukins chr.
Jan. 23 Susann dau. to Anthony Woode chr.
Feb. 11 Mr John Peck bur.
Feb. 15 Susan dau. to Matthew Thornehull chr.
Feb. 16 John Itchener, a prentice, bur.
Feb. 22 Robert son to John Bland chr.
Feb. 27 Mary Staudish, a maid-servt, bur.
Feb. 27 Issabell Bankes, a foundling, chr.
Mar. 8 Sibbell dau. to Thomas Ive chr.
Mar. 13 John son to Anthony Burtonn chr.
Mar. 13 Aaron son to Aaron Linicar bur.
Mar. 15 Larance son to Thomas Browne chr.
Mar. 17 Ann dau. to Edmund Willis bur.

1618.

April 2 Susan Brian, a servant, bur.
April 11 Vaspatian Bradford, from Ratlife, bur.
April 12 William Jereme & Mary Ayre marr.
April 12 William son to Thomas Davice chr.
April 21 James Grove, a child, bur.
May 13 William son to William Slaughter chr.
May 16 Richard son to Anthony Burton bur.
May 31 Richard son to Richard Wikes chr.
June 3 Ralfe Litler & Sara Reade marr. by lic.
June 3 Martha dau. to Nicolas Clegat chr.
June 8 Sara dau. to Edward Baubury bur.
June 24 Sammuell son to Cristopher Roily chr.
July 1 Dority dau. to Aaron Linnicar bur.
July 2 Ann dau. to Roger Hatton chr. 2 & bur. 3
July 19 Richard Jennings bur.
July 25 Thomas Michelboorne & Barbara James marr.
Aug. 11 Jane dau. to Mr William Hunton, son-in-law to Alderman Jay, bur.
Aug. 30 Edward Agborrow & Catherin Davice marr.
Sep. 17 Anne dau. to Thomas Ives bur.
Sep. 24 Peeter son to Peeter Hasser chr.
Sep. 25 Mary Grange, a servt, bur.
Sep. 28 A child, new born, of William Allin's bur.
Oct. 7 Issabell Baukes, a foundling, bur.
Oct. 15 Peninna dau. of Joseph Cock bur.
Oct. 15 Ann dau. to Mr Zachary Evans, a preacher at Alhollowes Stainings, bur.
Oct. 20 A stillborn of William Cranfild's bur.
Oct. 22 William Heuman, a lodger, bur.
Oct. 30 Richard Walker, prentice to Mrs Smith, bur.
Nov. 1 William Trulock & Elizabeth Ursala marr.
Nov. 1 Thomas son to Thomas Chrouch chr.
Nov. 1 William son to William Sorricole chr. 1 & bur. 3
Nov. 1 Thomas son to Henry Browne chr.
Nov. 1 Margret dau. to William Dunn chr.
Nov. 5 Jane dau. to Hugh Perry chr.
Nov. 9 Henry Parkehurst & Gartwrite Wetherall marr.
Nov. 13 Frauncis son to Edward Mosse chr.
Nov. 20 Mrs Mary Parker, dau. to Sr Nicolas Parker, bur.
Nov. 27 Alice Roules, prentice to Mr Browne [?]
Nov. 27 Hanna dau. to William Allin [?]
Dec. 6 Steeven son to Steeven Foster chr. 6 & bur. 9
Dec. 15 James son to John Sharrow chr.
Dec. 16 Jhon Chalcraft, the father, bur.

Dec. 16 Jhon son to John Chalcrafte chr.
Dec. 23 Tzeby dau. to Noadiah Raulins bur.
Dec. 25 John son to John Chalcraft bur.
Jan. 8 Margery dau. to William Semer, his wife or quene a vagrant came out from turnebull street, & thether went againe, till hir belly bee full, shee was delivered at Mrs Smith's doore one Christmas day, hir child was chr. 8
Jan. 27 Izaack son to Peeter Hasser bur.
Feb. 4 Joseph Belgrave & Alice Smith marr.
Feb. 7 Israell son to William Collingwood chr.
Feb. 9 Elizabeth dau. to Thomas Martin chr.
Feb. 14 Aymee dau. to Frauncis Bickley chr.
Feb. 25 Israell son to Thomas Browne chr.
Mar. 7 William son to Edward Banbury chr.

1619.

Mar. 31 Sara dau. to Henry Whaly chr.
April 12 Mary dau. to William Slaughter bur.
April 15 Mary dau. to Noadiah Raulins chr.
April 29 Thomas Tedder & Rose Challiner marr.
May 6 Elizabeth dau. of William Slaughter chr.
May 13 Robert Abram, a prentice, bur.
May 26 Ann dau. to John Blande chr.
May 30 John son to John Atkins chr.
June 10 Ann wife to Frauncis Hill bur.
June 15 William Bennit bur.
June 17 Thomas Artice, died in Civill in Spain, & was here bur.
June 19 Abigaile Seger, a servt, bur.
June 23 Benedict Viner & Marian Adice marr. by banns
June 24 Andrew Knapp & Ann Sparkes, both of Sunbury, marr. by lic.
July 4 Thomas son to Joseph Cock chr.
July 24 John son to John Hawkins chr.
July 25 Elizabeth dau. of Thomas Wetherall chr.
July 29 Mr John Frewen, a minister, & Mrs Susan Burdon marr.
Aug. 2 John son to John Haukins bur.
Aug. 7 John Vickers & Bridget Garrey marr. by lic.
Sep. 2 James Raulinson & Elizabeth Walsingham marr.
Sep. 4 Frauncis Jaggard, a foundling in the parish, chr.
Sep. 14 Robert son to Robert Walker chr.
Sep. 19 Josias Urlin & Ellinor Thorpe marr.
Sep. 23 Ann dau. to William & Jone Passand chr.
Sep. 28 Margrett wife to Henry Carelile bur.
Sep. 28 Mary Jones, a child from Mr Washborn's, bur.
Sep. 30 John Cother & Martha Warren marr.
Oct. 24 William son to William & Ann Sorricoll chr.
Oct. 28 Elizabeth dau. to Timothy & Sarra Elwick chr.
Nov. 4 William son to William & Ann Sorricole bur.
Nov. 4 William son to William & Anna Allin chr.
Nov. 7 John son to William & Elizabeth Hale chr. 7 & bur. 17
Nov. 7 Richard son to Raphaell & Rebecca Gooddin chr.
Nov. 14 Sisley dau. to Edward & Jane Mosse chr.
Nov. 19 Revet Ragg son to Dorathy Goddard bur.
Nov. 28 Jone dau. to John & Ann Bradford chr.
Dec. 9 William Boules & Blanch Abell marr.
Dec. 12 Elizabeth dau. to William & Rebecca Cranfilde chr.
Dec. 21 Samuell son to Robert & Mary Washborne bur.
Dec. 26 Thomas son to Roger & Ann Hatton chr.

Dec. 28 Barnaby Smith & Ann White marr.
Jan. 9 Elizabeth dau. to Steeven & Eedy Foster chr.
Jan. 19 Two new-born child[n] of William & Anne Middleton's bur.
Jan. 27 Cleophas son to Thomas & Hanna Crouch chr.
Feb. 13 Ann dau. to Thomas & Ellin Ives chr.
Feb. 22 Ruth dau. to Richard & Duance Perry chr.
Mar. 5 Fraunces dau. to Joseph & Doreity George chr.
Mar. 9 Samuell son to Hugh & Catherin Perry [?]

1620.

April 2 Henry son to Thomas & Easter Browne chr.
April 17 Frauncis Flier & Martha Boothby marr. by lic.
April 17 Robert son to Anthony & Alice Burtonn chr.
April 30 Humphery son to Thomas & Ann Hortonn chr.
May 1 Elizabeth wife to John Haukins bur.
May 30 Robert son to Robert & Catherin Walker bur.
June 29 James Darbishire & Mary Mosse marr.
July 22 William son to Edward & Mary Banbery bur.
Aug. 20 Elizabeth dau. to John & Susanna Blande chr.
Aug. 27 Ellin dau. to Anthony & Ann Wood chr.
Oct. 9 Robert Hulson & Ann Dade marr.
Oct. 26 Edward Holmwood & Elizabeth Blaude marr.
Nov. 5 Elizabeth dau. to John & Dority Goddard chr.
Nov. 5 Sara dau. to Thomas & Jane Davice chr.
Nov. 26 Sammuell son to William & Ann Sorricoaie chr.
Nov. 29 M[r] Henry Jaye, Alderman, by night bur.
Dec. 17 Mary dau. to Frauncis & Mary Bickley chr.
Dec. 23 Eedy wife to Richard Jaggar bur.
Dec. 31 Thomas son to William & Ellin Westrow chr.
Jan. 7 Elizabeth dau. to Cristopher & Elizabeth Reily chr.
Jan. 14 Robert Greene & Priscilla Thornehull marr.
Jan. 14 Thomas son to William & Jone Passand chr.
Jan. 24 John son to John & Mary Sharrow chr.
Feb. 4 George Lumbly & Jone Tatuam marr.
Feb. 16 Robert son to Anthony & Alice Burtonn bur.
Mar. 2 Elizabeth dau. of Richard & Elizabeth Boothby chr.
Mar. 13 Sara dau. to Nicolas & Mary Clegatt chr.

1621.

April 17 M[rs] Alice Whitehorne *alias* Jones bur.
April 30 Elizabeth Standley, a maid-serv[t], bur.
May 6 Peeter son to Richard & Duance Perry chr.
May 6 William son to William & Elizabeth Halle chr.
May 9 Mary dau. to Frauncis & Dority Hill chr. 9 & bur. 11
May 27 Mary dau. to Robert & Catherin Walker chr.
June 10 Giles son to John & Ann Bradford chr.
June 21 M[rs] Jone Smith, widow, from S[t] Giles, Cripplegate, bur.
July 3 Ann wife to John Bradford, at Alphage by the Wall, bur.
July 8 Judith dau. to Ralfe & Susan Fenton, a lodger, chr.
July 16 M[r] John Oakes, gen., a lodger, bur. by night
July 18 William Edwards & Jaue Dickinsonn marr.
July 28 Thomas Hudson & Ann Salvin marr.
Aug. 4 Nathan Tailor, a prentice, bur.
Aug. 8 Richard Glascock & Catherin Banbury marr.
Aug. 14 M[r] William Carpenter, a merch[t], by night bur.
Aug. 17 Edward son to Thomas & Ann Hortonn bur.

Aug. 20 A stillborn child of John & Susan Bland's bur.
Aug. 24 John Evereden, gen., & Mary White marr.
Aug. 30 Elizabeth dau. of Henry & Margret Whaly chr.
Sep. 9 Mary dau. to John & Thomazin Cooke chr.
Sep. 26 Martha dau. to Noadiah & Jone Rawlins chr.
Oct. 13 Robert Netmaker, an old man, bur.
Oct. 14 John son to Edward & Mary Banbury chr.
Oct. 14 Ralfe son to Miles & Mary Newton chr.
Oct. 20 William son to deceased William & Martha Carpenter chr.
Oct. 21 John son to Thomas & Ann Hortonn chr.
Oct. 22 A son, unbapt., of John & Dorathy Goddard's bur.
Nov. 4 Anna dau. to William & Hanna Allin chr.
Nov. 8 Mr John Burgis & Sara Smith marr.
Nov. 17 Elizabeth dau. to Edward & Jane Mosse chr.
Nov. 18 Mary dau. to William & Rebecca Cranfilde chr.
Nov. 23 Nicolas son to Bartholomew & Patience Waight chr. 23 & bur. 26
Dec. 6 Peeter Blackhurst & Catherin Ryding marr.
Dec. 8 Mary dau. to John & Thomazin Cooke bur.
Dec. 19 Daniell Elsmor the elder bur.
Jan. 21 John son to Thomas & Ann Horton bur.
Feb. 3 Sara dau. to Raphaell & Rebecca Gooddin chr.
Feb. 14 John son to Thomas & Hannah Crouch chr.
Feb. 17 Sr Edward Duke & Mrs Jane Jay, widdow to Alderman Jay, marr.
Feb. 24 Elizabeth dau. to Cristopher & Ann Mancer chr. 24 & bur. 27
Feb. 26 Samuell Harsnet & Martha Washborne marr.
Mar. 1 William son to Mathew & Margery Thornehull bur.
Mar. 5 Thomas Edwards & Jone Cage marr.
Mar. 16 Emm Gay, a maid-servt, bur.
Mar. 20 Catherin dau. to Hugh & Catherin Perry chr.

1622.

Mar. 28 Thomas Plarer & Rebecca Cutburne marr.
Mar. 28 Sara dau. to Thomas & Jane Davice bur.
Mar. 31 Frauncis son to Edward & Jane Mosse bur.
April 10 Alice, a bastard born in the porch, dau. to John & Jone Walker, chr.
April 11 Robert Reeve & Elizabeth Warren marr.
April 14 Ann dau. to Mr Robert & Ann Hulsonn chr.
May 12 Elizabeth dau. to Arthur & Audry Guie chr. 12 & bur. 14
May 17 Henry son to Steeven & Eedy Foster chr. 17 & bur. 29
June 7 William Darby, a lodger, bur.
July 7 Henry son to Thomas & Elizabeth Wetherall chr.
Aug. 3 William Soane, a prentice, bur.
Aug. 22 David Polhill & Mary Campe marr. by lic.
Aug. 25 Elizabeth dau. to Richard & Duance Perry chr.
Sep. 7 Ralfe son to Miles & Mary Newtonn chr.
Sep. 15 Roger son to Roger & Ann Hattonn chr.
Sep. 27 John Jagger, a foundling in the parish, chr.
Oct. 8 John Curle & Margret Annley marr.
Oct. 15 Margret dau. to William & Ann Dunn bur.
Oct. 17 William son to William & Jone Passand chr.
Oct. 20 James Burningsould & Debora Clarke marr.
Oct. 26 Fraunicis son to Fraunicis & Mary Bickley chr.
Oct. 30 William Dunn bur.
Nov. 4 Mr William Sprott bur.
Nov. 7 Robert son to Richard & Elizabeth Greenowes chr.
Nov. 30 Thomas son to Thomas & Ann Hortonn chr.
Dec. 3 John son to William & Ellin Westrow chr. 3 & bur. 13

Dec. 5 George son to George & Elizabeth Griffith chr.
Dec. 8 Mary dau. to Joseph & Hanna Cock chr.
Dec. 17 Elizabeth dau. to Richard & Alice Burtonn chr.
Dec. 26 William son to Thomas & Susan Bland chr.
Dec. 29 Samuell son to Joseph & Dorathy Ewer chr.
Jan. 1 Henry Hore & Jone Barber marr.
Jan. 3 Mr John Rowles, a minister, bur.
Jan. 4 Thomas son to Robert & Catherin Walker bur.
Jan. 9 Edward Thorntonn & Mary Tovy marr.
Jan. 9 John son to William & Dorathy Jefford, gent., of Twiford in Midd'x, chr.
Jan. 14 Richard Hale the elder bur.
Jan. 15 Thomazin wife to Martin Billinsly bur.
Jan. 16 Ann wife to Mr Thomas Boothby bur.
Jan. 22 Robert son to Anthony & Alice Burtonn chr.
Jan. 22 Mrs Elizabeth Sprott, widow, bur.
Jan. 31 Richarde Gooddin, a stranger, bur.
Feb. 7 Elizabeth dau. to Thomas & Elizabeth Brangum chr.
Feb. 14 Thomas son to John & Doraty Goddard chr.
Feb. 23 Fruuncis son to Thomas & Jane Davice chr.
Feb. 26 Bridget Reynales, a serv^t^, bur.
Mar. 5 Elizabeth dau. of Cristopher & Elizabeth Ryley bur.
Mar. 20 Mrs Judith Granger, a stranger, bur.

1623.

Mar. 30 Thomas son to John & Mary Sharrow chr.
April 3 Edward son to Edward & Ann Collingwood bur.
April 8 Thomas Ives bur.
May 1 Thomas Franklin & Barbara Mullins marr.
May 9 Richard Strange, a foundling in the parish, chr.
May 18 Steeven son to George & Alice Davice chr.
May 29 Peeter son to Peeter & Ann Girling, a stranger, bur
May 30 Richard Smith, from Fullum, bur.
June 8 Jonathan son to Steeven & Eedy Foster chr.
June 15 John son to Robert & Catherin Walker chr.
July 22 Zachery son to Zachery & Sara Sims chr.
July 23 Elizabeth wife to Richard Greenowes bur.
July 24 John Bransonn, a prentice, bur.
Aug. 9 John son to Edward & Sibbell Oliver bur.
Aug. 10 John son to John & Tomazin Cooke chr.
Aug. 18 Zachary son to Zachary & Sara Sims bur.
Aug. 24 Jane dau. to Henery & Margret Whaly chr.
Aug. 25 John Petter, of Breade, & Elizabeth Hay, of Rie, both in Sussex, marr.
Sep. 9 Susanna dau. to Richard & Duance Perry chr.
Sep. 14 Mary dau. to Edward & Mary Haukins chr.
Sep. 21 Hennery son to Edward & Jane Mosse chr.
Sep. 24 Sammuell son to Thomas & Hanna Crouch chr.
Sep. 25 Mrs Jane Burrell, from Lamber Street, & Richard Greenowes bur.
Sep. 28 John son to Thomas & Ann Scalesbrooke chr.
Oct. 7 Elizabeth dau. to Humphery & Mary Oneby chr.
Oct. 19 Ann dau. to Thomas & Ann Brickhill chr.
Oct. 23 John son to James & Ann Parkes chr. 23 & bur. 29
Oct. 26 John son to Edward & Ann Collingwood chr.
Nov. 9 Rebecca dau. to Hugh & Catherin Perry chr.
Nov. 17 William Arkinstall & Bridget Greenegrasse marr.
Dec. 7 John son to William & Ellin Westroe chr.
Dec. 25 George son to Thomas & Martha Reeve chr.

Jan. 6 Arthur Mayo, a silkman & a bachelor, bur.
Jan. 17 John son to Edward & Mary Banbury bur.
Jan. 18 Hester dau. to John & Susann Bland chr.
Jan. 24 A fondlyng founde dead in the parrish bur.
Jan. 29 Mr Robert Halloway, from Benit Sheerhogg, bur.
Jan. 31 Ann Hayward, a maid-servt, bur.
Feb. 9 John Norton & Susan Langhorne marr.
Feb. 22 John son to Raphaell & Rebecca Gooddin chr.
Feb. 22 Hester dau. to William & Rebecca Cranfilde chr.
Feb. 28 Thomas Brickhill, clothworker, bur.
Mar. 6 Elizabeth dau. to Danniell & Phillip Elsmoor bur.
Mar. 13 Robert son to Anthony & Alice Burton bur.

1624.

April 5 Hugh Tracy & Tomazin Ellistone, from Erith, marr.
April 11 Thomas Slade & Elizabeth Hone marr. by banns
April 11 Frauncis son to William & Elizabeth Hall chr.
April 19 Henry Pitter son to Jone Maudie bur.
May 8 Thomas Joyner, a stranger coming to see his brother, bur.
May 23 John son to Henry & Ann Shawe chr.
May 30 Hanna dau. to Edward & Sibble Olliver chr.
June 6 George Mayo & Margret Hassall marr.
June 9 Ann dau. to the Widow Brickhill bur.
June 30 Thomas Loe, a prentice, bur.
July 8 Richard Ouldum & Mary Cliftonn marr.
July 25 Thomas son to Thomas & Ann Scalesbrooke chr.
Aug. 1 Ann dau. to John & Alice Leesonn chr.
Aug. 10 Elizabeth dau. to Francis & Mary Bicklie chr. 10 & bur. 21
Aug. 14 Mr Nathniell Halle, a minister, bur.
Sep. 18 Elizabeth dau. of John & Doraty Goddard bur.
Sep. 27 Mary dau. to William & Rebecca Cranfilde bur.
Sep. 28 Elizabeth dau. to Humphery & Mary Oneby bur.
Oct. 28 Elizabeth dau. to George & Elizabeth Griffeth chr.
Nov. 10 Frauncis son to John Farrer & Abigaile Lambert, a common woman, born in the street, chr.
Nov. 11 Jone wife of Richard Swindall bur.
Nov. 15 John son to Edward & Ann Collingwood bur.
Nov. 21 Margerye, maid-servt to Mr Cock, bur.
Nov. 30 Walter White & Mary Dannsonn marr.
Nov. 30 Margret dau. to Anthony & Alice Burton chr.
Nov. 30 Mary dau. to Thomas & Jane Harloe chr.
Dec. 3 John Cooke, a lodger in the parish, bur.
Dec. 14 Danniell Pennington & Elizabeth Risby marr.
Dec. 21 Richard Warner & Rebecca Masonn marr.
Dec. 25 Timothy son to Thomas & Hanna Crouch chr.
Dec. 25 Jone Cole, servt to Anthony Burton, bur.
Dec. 26 Annis dau. to James & Annis Parkes chr.
Jan. 19 Elizabeth dau. to Richard & Duance Perry bur.
Jan. 24 Sara dau. to Zachary & Sara Sims chr.
Jan. 28 Mary dau. to Simon & Mary Edmons chr.
Jan. 30 John son to Roger & Ann Hattonn chr.
Feb. 8 Luce dau. to Richard & Elizabeth Joyner chr.
Feb. 11 Richard son to John & Susan Bland chr.
Feb. 17 Roger Eburne & Ellin Chivers marr.
Feb. 22 Frauncis Burton, a son laid in the parish, chr.
Feb. 24 Aun dau. to William & Jane Lodge chr.
Feb. 27 Thomas son to John & Thomazin Cooke chr

Feb. 27 William son to William & Sara Newet chr.
Feb. 28 Sara dau. to Joseph & Hanna Cock chr.
Mar. 2 Sara dau. to Joseph & Hauna Cock bur.
Mar. 4 Jethro Scott bur.
Mar. 4 Frauncis Hill, a prentice, bur.
Mar. 7 John son to John & Thomazin Cooke bur.
Mar. 13 Nathaniell son to Richard & Duance Perry chr.
Mar. 13 William son to Richard & Debora Houland chr.
Mar. 20 Elizabeth dau. to Cristopher & Elizabeth Riely chr.
Mar. 22 Cristopher Riely aforesaid bur.

1625.

Mar. 28 John son to Raphaell & Rebecca Gooddin bur.
Mar. 29 John son to Henry & Ann Shaw bur.
April 8 Mr George Close, one of our lecturers, bur.
April 11 Thomas son to John & Dorraty Goddard bur.
April 11 A stillborn child of Steven & Eedie Foster's bur.
April 14 Ann dau. to William & Jane Lodge bur.
April 20 Charles son to John & Mary Sharrow chr. 20 & bur. 28
May 3 John son to William & Alis Woodcock bur.
May 5 Rose dau. to Thomas & Martha Reeve chr.
May 11 John son to Noadiah & Jone Raulins chr.
May 13 Sara dau. to Thomas & Hester Browne chr.
May 14 Thomas Evans, an ould lame souldier, bur.
May 15 Ruith dau. to William & Mary Smith chr.
May 18 Edward Foxley & Judith Doubleday marr.
May 26 Thomas Johncock & Dority Peckham marr.
May 26 Henry Lacie & Mary Steele marr.
May 26 Edward son to Edward & Mary Haukins chr.
May 30 Mrs Elizabeth Close, from Great Alhollowes, bur.
June 7 Edward Haukins son to Edward & Mary Haukins bur.
July 12 Robert Parker bur.; plague
July 14 James Brooksbanke bur.; plague
July 26 Richard Parker, prentice, bur.; plague
July 29 Alice Tither, a maid-servt, bur.; plague
July 30 William Onion, prentice to Mr Raulins, bur.
July 30 Edward Oulton bur.; plague
Aug. 7 Alice wife to Peregrin Moore bur.; plague
Aug. 8 Oliver Cherton, housekeeper, bur.; plague
Aug. 9 George son to Edward & Jane Mosse chr.
Aug. 14 Sammuell son to Audrian & Elizabeth Merry chr.
Aug. 16 William French & Elizabeth Cannon marr. by lic.
Aug. 18 Susan dau. to Mathew & Margery Thornehull, bur.; plague
Aug. 20 Elizabeth dau. to Mathew & Margery Thornhull bur.; plague
Aug. 20 Joseph Yorke, Mr Peerris' man, bur.; plague
Aug. 21 Silbell dau. to Widow Ires bur.; plague
Aug. 23 Ann Netmaker bur.
Aug. 25 Eedy wife to Steeven Foster bur.; plague
Aug. 27 Harim dau. to John & Ursala Lewes, the clark, bur.
Aug. 28 Thomas Harlow bur.; plague
Aug. 28 Henry Rands bur.; plague
Aug. 29 Alice dau. to Widow Brickhill bur.; plague
Aug. 30 William Crooker bur.; plague
Aug. 30 Thomas Draper bur.; plague
Sep. 1 John King, prentice, bur.; plague
Sep. 7 Prissilla wife to Richard Eires bur.; plague
Sep. 7 Prissilla dau. to Richard & Prissilla Eires chr. 7 & bur. 17; plague

Sep. 9 George Tireman, prentice, bur.; plague
Sep. 12 John Trent, prentice, bur.; plague
Sep. 14 Martin Billinslie bur.; plague
Sep. 14 Steeven Foster bur.; plague
Sep. 15 Ann Griffin dau. to the aforesaid Prissilla Eire bur.; plague
Sep. 17 Richard Wood, prentice, bur.; plague
Sep. 19 Frauncis son to Thomas & Jane Davice bur.; plague
Sep. 19 Sara Platt bur.; plague
Sep. 21 John Earle bur.; plague
Sep. 26 William son to Marmaduke and Martha Keddall bur.
Oct. 1 Martha dau. to Mr Charles & Martha Ofspring, parson, chr.; and a son of theirs, unbaptized, the same day bur.
Oct. 1 Liddia Mullinex, a maid-serv^t, bur.
Oct. 11 Eve dau. to Thomas Hust, a Frenchman, bur.
Oct. 18 Mr Thomas Boothby bur.
Oct. 29 Edward Fisher, a prentice, & Issabell Haines, a child, bur.
Nov. 5 William son to William & Ellin Westrow chr. 5, & his son Thomas bur. (plague) 6
Nov. 5 A stillborn of Widow Harlowe's bur.
Nov. 7 William Jerman & Alice Mounture marr.
Nov. 17 John Hanson & Elizabeth Aires marr.
Nov. 17 Sara wife to Isaac Griffin bur.
Nov. 19 Francis Smith, the sexton, bur.
Nov. 19 Martha dau. to Nicolas & Mary Clegat bur.
Nov. 29 William Pemberton & Catherin Guye marr.
Nov. 30 Ralfe Browne & Alice Sharrowe marr.
Dec. 8 Mary dau. to Harriot & Ann Washburne chr.
Dec. 18 Rebecca dau. to William & Rebecca Cranfilde chr.
Jan. 5 Heaster dau. to John & Susanna Bland bur.
Jan. 26 John Hedges & Emme Robinsonn marr.
Feb. 9 William Covet & Ann Rennals marr.
Feb. 13 Martha dau. to Marmaduke & Martha Keddar bur. [see "Keddall," 26 Sep.]
Feb. 16 William Smith & Ann Wright marr.
Feb. 16 Richard Aires & Ellin Ives marr.
Feb. 16 Thomas Russell, a stranger, bur.
Feb. 20 Thomas Peett, from Mr Boothby, a stranger, bur.
Feb. 24 Jane dau. to Thomas & Jane Davis chr.
Feb. 27 Elizabeth Wilson, a foundling in the parish, chr.
Mar. 8 Sr Arthur Smithes & Jane Rowland marr.
Mar. 9 John son to Simon & Mary Edmouns chr.
Mar. 14 Robert Walker bur.
Mar. 19 William son to Anthony & Alis Burton chr.

1626.

April 4 Jone dau. to Thomas & Martha Reeve chr. 4 & bur. 5
April 11 Richard Baker & Elizabeth Pendry marr.
April 11 Robert son to William & Jone Passand chr.
April 22 Thomas son to Raphaell & Rebecca Gooddin chr.
April 23 Constance dau. to James & Ann Parkes chr.
May 9 Nicolas Darling & Mary Skidmore marr.
May 16 William Hutchins & Martha Growt marr.
June 5 Margret dau. to Antony & Alis Burton bur.
June 8 Emmanuell Proby & Mary Bland marr.
June 13 Richard Chandler & Emm Marshall marr.
June 16 William son to John & Mary Sharrow chr.

June 19 Daniell Ellitt & Margret Kedders marr.
June 30 John son to John & Mary Sharrow bur.
July 2 Joseph son to Thomas & Hanna Crouch chr.
July 9 Thomas son to Henry & Ann Shaw chr. 9 & bur. 17
July 25 Mary dau. to Thomas & Susan Kenniston chr.
July 27 Richard Davice & Martha Glascock marr.
July 29 Ruith Elsmore, widow, bur.
Aug. 2 Mary dau. to Thomas & Susan Kennistone bur.
Aug. 27 Mary dau. to Miles & Mary Newtonn chr.
Aug. 27 Bennit Hattonn, a country gent., bur.
Sep. 2 Richard son to Fraunçis & Mary Bickly bur.
Sep. 3 Mary dau. to Miles & Mary Newtonn bur.
Sep. 15 Elizabeth wife to Raffe Nutting bur.
Oct. 1 Thomas Tounzin & Ann Brickhill marr.
Oct. 5 Nicolas Smith & Elizabeth Scott marr.
Oct. 6 Mr Nicolas Felton, D^r^ & Bishop of Ecly, bur.
Oct. 17 Anthony Griffin & Elizabeth Stallonn marr.
Nov. 3 Mr John Smith, a lodger, bur.
Nov. 14 Rachell dau. to John & Susanna Bland chr.
Nov. 19 Ann dau. to John & Thomazin Cooke chr.
Nov. 30 William Hix & Elizabeth Sharrow marr.
Dec. 13 Elihue Estonn & Ellin Boise marr.
Dec. 14 Richard Turner & Fraunces Bradford marr.
Dec. 15 William son to Anthony & Alice Burton bur.
Dec. 21 Jane Flaxue, a child, bur.
Dec. 21 A stillborn child of Thomas & Margret Hales bur.
Dec. 29 Mr Robert Leasly, gent., & the Lady Fraunces Packington marr.
Jan. 7 Debora dau. to Richard & Debora Houland chr.
Jan. 10 Walter Woodward & Mary Foster marr.
Jan. 14 Mary dau. to Roger & Ann Hatton chr.
Jan. 17 Abigaile Porter, a maid-serv^t^, bur.
Jan. 28 Thomas Masonn & Issabell Anslow marr.
Jan. 30 John son to John & Jone Glover chr.
Feb. 2 Thomas son to Fraunçis & Mary Bickley chr.
Feb. 11 Thomas son to Thomas & Elizabeth Salmon chr. 11 & bur. 19
Feb. 11 Mary dau. to Thomas & Jone Broomfild chr. 11 & bur. 16
Mar. 4 Joseph son to Richard & Duance Perry chr.
Mar. 4 John son to Richard & Margret Hopwood chr.
Mar. 6 James son to George & Elizabeth Griffeth chr.
Mar. 9 John Sheton & Ann Cumbers marr. by Mr Peeters
Mar. 10 Richard Williams, a foundling in the parish, chr.
Mar. 11 Eliza. dau. to Audrian & Elizabeth Merry chr.
Mar. 14 Eliza. dau. to Richard & Jone Weekes chr.
Mar. 22 Mary Grove dau. to Widow Dunn bur.

1627.

Mar. 25 Elizabeth dau. to Nicolas & Margret Beales chr., and the mother Margret Beales bur. at night
Mar. 28 Robert Smith, a prentice, bur.
April 1 Margret dau. to Henry & Jone Hore chr,
April 4 Debora dau. to Richard & Debora Houland bur.
April 4 William Kedgwin, a stranger, bur.
April 24 Phillip son to Fraunçis & Eedith Taylor chr.
May 1 Fraunçis Gardner & Rebecca Rott marr.
May 1 Thomas Carver, a prentice, bur.
May 6 Jann dau. to Richard & Ellin Aires chr.

May 17 William Bissh & Jone Sharrow marr.
May 18 Mr John Dade bur.
May 26 George son to Edward & Jane Moss bur.
June 26 Elizabeth dau. to James & Ann Parkes chr.
July 1 John son to William & Sara Nuett chr.
July 1 Thomas & William sons to Thomas & Ann Tounzin chr.
July 17 Thomas son to Thomas & Susanna Kennistone chr.
July 20 John son to William & Alis Woodcock chr.
Aug. 12 William son to James & Jane Reade chr.
Aug. 28 William Bankes & Mary Brookes marr.
Sep. 8 Elizabeth Nicoles, widow, bur.
Sep. 15 Nicolas Ballard bur.
Sep. 17 Ellin Aires bur.
Sep. 18 Edward Bond & Margret Padnall marr.
Sep. 23 Ann dau. to Ralfe & Alis Browne chr.
Sep. 25 John Browne & Mary Sallis marr.
Oct. 18 John Birde & Alis Halle marr.
Nov. 3 Thomas son to Thomas & Ann Tounsin bur.
Nov. 8 Joanna dau. to Thomas & Ann Rastall chr.
Nov. 11 Thomas Jones & Ellin Gibbs marr.
Nov. 20 Elizabeth dau. to Mr Charles & Doraty Boorne, minister, chr.
Nov. 29 Elizabeth dau. to Thomas & Margret Halle bur.
Nov. 30 Sara dau. to Henry & Ann Shawe chr.
Dec. 3 Mary dau. to Tho. & Martha Reeve chr. 3 & bur 5
Dec. 4 Edward Bishop & Bridget Catchpoole marr.
Dec. 14 Sara dau. to Edward & Mary Haukins chr.
Dec. 14 John son to John & Mary Sharrow chr.
Dec. 31 Mary Melborne, from Mr Newton's, bur.
Jan. 20 Judith dau. to Richard & Catherin Laitonn chr.
Jan. 26 Jone dau. to Thomas & Jone Broomfield chr. 26 & bur. 29
Feb. 10 John son to William & Elizabeth Hix chr.
Feb. 14 Mary dau. to Robert & Aymy Osburne chr.
Feb. 24 Steeven Winnibote & Alis Eshbeach marr.
Feb. 24 Arnall son to John & Susan Bland chr.
Feb. 24 Hugh son to Richard & Debora Houland chr.
Mar. 2 John son to Thomas & Elizabeth Salmon chr.
Mar. 2 Tomazin dau. to John & Tomazin Cooke chr.
Mar. 18 Charles son to Mr Charles & Martha Ofspring chr.

1628.

April 6 Richard son to Thomas & Ann Yates chr.
April 17 Sibble wife to Thomas Taverner bur.
April 27 Christopher Hulme & Catherin Howard marr.
April 29 William Remnant & Ann Wilkinsonn marr.
May 11 Rebecca dau. to Nicolas & Susanna Beales chr.
May 18 Jane dau. to Henry & Sara Daunson chr.
May 19 Charles son to Mr Charles & Martha Ofspring bur.
June 29 Ann Anslow, a maid-servt bur.
July 10 A stillborn of Sara Uproberts, a quean by cha'ce, bur.
July 12 Robert son to William & Jone Passand bur.
July 30 John Winterboorne & Jane Hill marr.
July 31 Mary dau. to Roger & Ann Hatton bur.
Aug. 7 Mary wife to Nicolas Clegat bur.
Aug. 13 Mary dau. to Thomas & Margrett Halle chr. 13 & bur. 25
Aug. 27 John Hinckessell & Elizabeth Franklin marr.
Aug. 27 John son to William & Elizabeth Hix bur.
Aug. 30 Ann dau. to Will'm & Ann Davenport chr.

Aug. 31 Henry son to Richard & Margret Hopwood chr.
Sep. 21 Jone dau. to Thomas & Ann Tounzin chr.
Sep. 24 Richard Leake, a foundling in the parish, chr.
Oct. 3 M[rs] Joice Dade, widow, bur.
Oct. 10 John son to Fraunecis & Mary Bickly chr.
Oct. 13 A stillborn dau. of Thomas & Martha Reeves bur.
Oct. 28 Edmond son to Thomas & Jane Davice chr.
Nov. 10 Daniell Rogers & Alice Thorpe marr.
Dec. 4 Simonn King & Grace Cunny marr.
Dec. 11 Mary dau. to George & Elizabeth Griffeth chr.
Dec. 20 Sara dau. to William & Ann Remnant chr.
Jan. 7 William Streete, a prentice, bur.
Jan. 9 Benjamin son to Thomas & Hanna Crouch chr.
Jan. 22 Ann dau. to Thomas & Ann Rastall chr.
Jan. 27 William Shore & Margret Buckley marr.
Jan. 27 Elizabeth dau. to John & Jone Glover chr.
Feb. 15 Samuell King & Sara Washborne marr.
Mar. 4 Sara dau. to William & Sara Newet chr.
Mar. 6 Mary dau. to John & Mary Sharrow chr.
Mar. 14 Hanna wife to Will. Smith, of Issleworth, bur.
Mar. 18 Thomas son to Thomas & Jone Broomfield chr.
Mar. 23 Jone wife to John Armin bur.

1629.

Mar. 27 Charles son to M[r] Charles & Martha Ofspring chr.
April 2 John Derewall & Prissilla Reynals marr.
April 10 M[r] Sammuell King, minister, bur.
April 23 James Sneller & Audry Beeston marr.
April 23 Sara dau. to John & Margret Mayo bur.
April 25 Ann wife to Richard Jagger bur.
May 3 Mary dau. to Will. & Elizabeth Hix chr.
May 6 Mary wife to Edward Banbury bur.
May 7 Timothy son to Roger & Ann Hattonn chr.
May 31 Rebecca dau. to John & Elizabeth Smith chr.
June 14 John Watmore & Jane Oliver marr.
June 24 John Watkins & Margery Corker marr.
June 24 George son to Walter & Catherin Boothby chr. 24 & bur. 26
July 1 Martha Fletcher, a maid-serv[t], bur.
July 2 Hanna dau. to Henry & Ann Shawe chr.
July 12 Edmond son to Richard & Catherin Laytonn chr.
July 28 Martha Tomlins, from M[r] Willis, a stranger, bur.
Aug. 2 Mary dau. to Audrian & Elizabeth Merry chr.
Aug. 10 A stillborn male of Thomas & Ann Tounezane bur.
Aug. 23 Edward son to Fraunecis & Edith Taylor chr. 23 & bur. 26
Aug. 26 A stillborn male of Steeven & Mercy Simpson bur.
Aug. 27 Susann wife to James Venn bur.
Aug. 29 Thomas Hugbone, a stranger, bur.
Sep. 13 Edward son to Thomas & Susanna Kennistone chr.
Sep. 16 Mary dau. to James & Ann Parks chr.
Sep. 17 Jonathan Buck & Catherin Berry marr.
Sep. 25 Perregrin son to Kellum & Elizabeth Willoby chr.
Oct. 23 A stillborn son of Timothy & Sarah Elwick's bur.
Oct. 30 Anthony Burtonn bur.
Nov. 1 John son to Thomas & Ann Yates chr.
Nov. 8 Thomas Ballard, beadle of the ward, bur.
Nov. 8 Mary dau. to Nicolas & Susanna Beales chr.
Nov. 16 M[rs] Mareeah Doubler, M[rs] Bland's mother, bur.

Dec. 1 Edward son to Thomas & Martha Reeves chr. 1 & bur. 2
Dec. 1 Mr Thomas Bradford bur.
Dec. 11 Samuell son to Will. & Ann Remnant chr.
Dec. 21 Sara dau. to Will. & Alice Woodcock chr.
Dec. 29 Edward Browne & Faith Peacock marr.
Jan. 2 Richard son to Thomas & Ann Yates bur.
Jan. 6 Richard Glover & Alice Faulkner marr.
Jan. 6 Jone wife to Will. Passand bur.
Jan. 6 Theoderet son to John & Susan Bland chr.
Jan. 8 Ann dau. to Frauncis & Rebecca Gardner chr.
Jan. 9 Joseph son to Richard & Duance Perry bur.
Jan. 11 Jonathan son to Steeven & Mercy Simpson bur.
Jan. 29 Nathaniell son to Jeffery Callis bur.
Feb. 1 Thomas son to Thomas & Ann Rastall chr.
Feb. 7 Isaac son to John & Margret Mayo chr. 7 & bur. 15
Feb. 21 Sara dau. to Thomas & Margrt [*sic*] Halle chr.
Feb. 26 Edward son to Thomas & Ann Yates bur.
Feb. 26 Doraty wife to Aroun Linicar bur.

1630.

April 1 Barnaby Wetherall & Elizabeth Greene marr.
April 22 Danniell Callis & Hellin Kettleboorrow marr.
April 28 William son to William & Elizabeth Hix chr.
May 4 Jeffery Howland & Grizegonn Langly marr.
May 18 William Bartlemew & Ann Laycock marr.
May 20 John Laffell & Hester Maior marr.
May 27 Mary dau. to Steeven & Mercy Simpsonn bur.
May 28 Margret dau. to Henry & Jone Hoare bur.
May 29 Richard Bathurst, prentice to Henry Shawe [?]
June 1 Ann Hix, a maid, bur.
June 4 Will. son to William & Elizabeth Hix bur.
July 15 Susan dau. to Anthony & Ann Wood bur.
Aug. 3 John Lole & Ann Stone marr.
Aug. 6 Henry son to Thomas & Hester Browne chr.
Aug. 7 Mary dau. to Thomas & Ann Townzin chr.
Aug. 23 Jane wife to Thomas Davice bur.
Aug. 25 Alice dau. to John & Elizabeth Smith chr.
Aug. 29 William son to Roger & Ann Hattonn chr.
Sep. 20 Martha dau. to Thomas & Martha Reeve chr. 20 & bur. 24
Oct. 10 Elizabeth dau. to Edward & Mary Haukins chr.
Oct. 22 Sammuell son to Willi. & Sara Newit chr. 22 & bur. 27
Oct. 27 William Jones & Elizabeth Walker marr.
Oct. 31 Sammuell son to Fraundis & Eedith Taylor chr.
Nov. 14 John Risley & Mary Chasie marr.
Dec. 1 A stillborn of John & Catherin Hiyate's bur.
Dec. 5 Sara dau. to Thomas & Ann Yates chr.
Dec. 11 Mr Edward Spendlove, a lecturer in this place 45 years, bur.
Dec. 25 Elizabeth dau. to Fraundis & Mary Bickley chr.
Dec. 26 Steeren son to Steeven & Mercy Simpsonn chr.
Dec. 27 James Denewe bur.
Jan. 12 Abigaile dau. to George & Abigaill Jones chr. 12 & bur. 17
Jan. 28 Ursala Maynard, a foundling, chr.
Feb. 6 John son to William & Sara Newett bur.
Feb. 7 Tobit Wildebore & Prissilla Jonsonn marr.
Feb. 13 Walter son to Walter & Catherin Oake chr.
Feb. 13 Matthew son to Thomas & Jone Broomfield chr.
Feb. 14 Hanna dau. to Henry & Ann Shawe bur.

Feb. 21 William Ritch & Luce Jaquis marr.
Feb. 25 Rebecca dau. to George & Elizabeth Griffith chr.
Feb. 28 Edward Egerle & Elizabeth Langdenn marr.
Mar. 20 Hester dau. to Andrew & Hester Coleman chr.
Mar. 22 Robert Eire & Ann Aldersey marr.

1631.

April 6 Fraunces dau. to Frauncis & Rebecca Gardner chr.
April 14 Mr Ezekiell Culverwell, minister, bur.
April 24 Richard Coish & Mary Luptonn marr.
May 8 John Anderton & Eedith Pedder marr.
May 11 Elizabeth dau. to Edward & Mary Haukins bur.
May 15 Frauncis son to Richard & Catherin Laitonn chr.
May 18 George May, a prentice, bur.
May 25 John son to Willi. & Elizabeth Hix chr.
May 29 Cornelius son to Micaell & Constance Castell chr.
May 30 Thomas Daviee & Elizabeth Clarke marr.
June 11 Martha dau. to Roger & Ellin Bridgis bur.
June 16 Cornelius son to Micaell & Constance Castell bur.
June 24 Robert Kennistone, a factor, bur.
June 30 Ralfe Eve & Ellin Eborne marr.
July 2 John son to Andrian & Elizabeth Merry chr.
July 7 John son to William & Elizabeth Hix bur.
July 16 Jone Gibbins, widow, a stranger, bur.
July 26 John Goodall & Theodosia Fowler marr.
July 31 A stillborn of Thomas & Ann Tounzine bur.
Aug. 18 Andrew Broughtonn & Mary Barran marr.
Sep. 1 Nathaniell Hanfoorth & Elizabeth Bradbant marr.
Sep. 5 Edward Hopkins & Ann Yearle marr.
Sep. 19 Elizabeth Walker, a poor old maid, bur.
Sep. 23 Anthony Sounde, laid in the parish, chr.
Sep. 25 George Ongley & Alice Benboe marr.
Oct. 9 Jane dau. to Nicolas & Susan Beales chr.
Oct. 10 Mary Smith, the old sexton's widow, bur.
Oct. 12 Abraham son to Henry & Jone Hore chr.
Oct. 13 Sammuell Tomlin & Sara King marr.
Oct. 13 Samuell Hale, from Aldermanbury, bur.
Nov. 4 Thomas Waire, a stranger, bur.
Nov. 9 William Clarke & Elizabeth Oflie marr.
Nov. 10 A stillborn dau. of Frauncis & Eedith Tailor bur.
Nov. 17 John Bickley & Julian Mountford marr.
Nov. 20 Ann wife of Anthony Woode bur.
Nov. 22 Benjamine Halle, from Boe in Chepe, bur.
Nov. 24 John Arnold & Bridget Bosserd marr.
Nov. 29 Nicolas Heath & Grace Holcombe marr.
Dec. 7 John Wood & Margret Fitzrichards marr.
Dec. 17 Hanna Chester, a foundling, chr.
Dec. 18 Israell son to John & Margret Mayo chr.
Dec. 22 Martine Cobbs, a lodger in the parish, bur.
Dec. 29 John son to Andrian & Elizabeth Merry bur.
Jan. 4 Robert Goodall, our sexton, bur.
Jan. 6 Frauncis son to George & Grace Hill chr.
Jan. 10 Joneane [*sic*] dau. to John & Susanna Bland chr.
Jan. 15 John son to William & Sara Newet chr. 15 & bur. 19
Jan. 16 John Morris, a stranger, bur.
Jan. 18 Cleophas Smith, from Putney, bur.
Feb. 12 Elizabeth dau. to Thomas & Margret Halle chr.

Feb. 14 Henry Barton & Elizabeth Clegat marr.
Feb. 23 Margret dau. to Thomas & Martha Reeve chr. 13 & bur. 26
Feb. 25 Alice Turpin, a child from Mrs Linnis, bur.
Mar. 6 John Morris & Ann Bell marr.
Mar. 20 A stillborn female of William & Ann Remnant's bur.
Mar. 21 Benjamine son to John & Mary Sharrow chr. 21 & bur. 25
Mar. 23 Sammuell son to Mr Charles & Martha Ofspring chr.
Mar. 23 Judith dau. to Steven & Mercy Simpson chr.

1632.

Mar. 25 John son to William & Lucie Passand chr.
Mar. 28 Ralfe son to Thomas & Ann Yates chr.
April 8 Edward son to Edward & Jane Sumner chr. 8 & bur. 14
April 25 John son to Thomas & Elizabeth Davice chr.
April 26 Matthew son to Thomas & Jone Broomfield bur.
April 27 Ann dau. to James & Ann Rennald, dwelling at the Bridge house, fell in labor at William Nuet's house coming for silk, chr.
April 29 Edward son to Edward & Mary Haukins chr.
April 29 Daniell son to Roger & Elline Bridgis chr.
May 3 Debora dau. to Walter & Judith Dekins chr.
May 5 Mr John Bland & his youngest dau. Joneane, both together bur.
May 15 Ann sister to John Bickley bur.
May 17 Sammuell son to William & Alice Woodcock chr.
May 18 Catherin dau. to John & Theodosia Goodall chr. 18 & bur. 23
May 29 Mary dau. to Thomas & Ann Tounzin bur.
May 30 Lucy wife to William Passand bur.
June 2 John Andrewes & Mary Lane marr.
June 7 Ursala wife of John Lewes, our clark, bur.
June 22 Daniell Purchas, a prentice, bur.
June 22 Richard son to James & Ann Fenn chr.
June 24 Thomas son to Frauncis & Rebecca Gardner chr.
June 25 William Cradler & Ann Broomann marr.
June 26 Sara dau. to Thomas & Margret Halle bur.
July 7 Sara Tounsend bur.
July 22 Abigaile dau. to George & Abigaile Jones chr. 22 & bur. 23
July 25 Henry son to Thomas & Hester Browne bur.
Aug. 8 Thomas Halsey, a bastard, chr.
Aug. 17 Ann Dunn, widow, bur.
Aug. 26 John Lewes, our clark, & Mary Pepper marr.
Sep. 5 Elizabeth dau. to William & Elizabeth Hixe chr.
Sep. 18 William son to Thomas & Hanna Walker chr.
Sep. 29 Elizabeth dau. to George & Elizabeth Griffeth chr.
Oct. 1 Job Boorman, a prentice, bur.
Oct. 10 Bridgitt Collingwood, widow, bur.
Oct. 26 William son to Walter & Catherine Oake chr.
Oct. 26 John Okely, prentice to Walter Oake, bur.
Oct. 28 Mary dau. to John & Julian Bickeley chr.
Nov. 4 John son to Audrian & Elizabeth Merry chr.
Nov. 9 John son to Richard & Duance Perry bur.
Nov. 15 Walter son to Walter & Catherin Oake bur.
Nov. 29 Benjamine Berry & Sisly Sorrell marr.
Dec. 4 Mr John Leigh & Margret Harris marr.
Dec. 13 Edward Somes & Mary Tiffin marr.
Dec. 13 Ann Goddard, a young maid, dau. to John Goddard, from Boe, bur.
Dec. 26 Gilbert Cleter & Margret Bickley marr.
Dec. 27 John Clewloe & Jane Bartonn marr.
Dec. 29 Benjamine son to Richard & Jone Lazonby chr. 29 & bur. 31

Dec. 31 Elizabeth dau. to Umphery Oneby, from Aldermanbury, bur.
Jan. 1 Elizabeth dau. to Roger & Ann Hattonn chr.
Jan. 8 John son to John & Ann Smith chr.
Jan. 20 Walter son to Walter & Catherin Dannum chr.
Jan. 24 Thomas Swallow & Jone Bond marr.
Jan. 29 William Collinsonn & Elizabeth Beadle marr.
Feb. 11 A stillborn of Thomas & Ann Tounsend bur.
Feb. 17 Rachell dau. to Steven & Mercy Simpsonn chr.
Mar. 1 Ann Collingwood, a young maid, bur.
Mar. 3 John son to Nicolas & Susanna Beales chr.
Mar. 19 Jane dau. to Henry & Frannces Browne chr.

1633.

Mar. 29 Thomas son to Thomas & Ann Yates chr.
April 5 William Whotes, a bastard for ought we know, chr.
April 16 William son to Thomas & Jone Broomfield chr. 16 & bur. 18
May 1 Mary & Martha daus. to Will. & Ann Remnant chr. 1 & both bur. 4
May 8 Thomazin wife to Willi. Ince & her stillborn dau. both bur.
May 11 Ann wife to Willi. Remnant bur.
May 23 Jane dau. to Edward & Jane Sumner chr.
May 27 Christopher son to Thomas Taverner bur.
May 30 James son to James & Ann Fenn chr.
June 2 John son to Nicolas & Mary Higginbottom chr.
June 7 William son to William & Sara Newett chr.
June 7 Margret Willis, widow, bur.
June 24 Benedict Scott & Ann Crue marr.
June 26 Roger son to George & Abigaile Jones chr.
July 19 Judith dau. to Walter & Judith Dekins chr.
Aug. 4 Joseph son to John & Mary Sharrow chr.
Aug. 5 John son to Humphery & Mary Oneby bur.
Aug. 15 Bridget Masonn, a young maiden, bur.
Aug. 23 Rachell dau. to Susanna Bland, widow, bur.
Aug. 27 Thomas son to William & Elizabeth Hixx chr.
Aug. 28 Josuan wife to John Strange bur.
Sep. 11 Julian wife to John Bickley bur.
Sep. 13 Judith wife to William Houlte bur.
Oct. 4 Elizabeth Fielde, a maid-serv[t], bur.
Oct. 22 Sammuell Eve & Ann Bulby marr.
Oct. 23 Elizabeth dau. of Thomas & Elizabeth Cage chr.
Nov. 8 William son to Thomas & Hanna Walker bur.
Nov. 14 Editha dau. to Frauncis & Editha Tailor chr.
Nov. 17 John Strange & Catherin Farman marr., & he bur. 25
Nov. 19 Edward son to Frauncis & Ann Dorringtonn chr.
Nov. 21 Elizabeth Mascall, from M[r] Washburn's, bur.
Nov. 28 Thomas Walker & Elizabeth Colemann marr.
Dec. 6 John son to Nicolas & Mary Higginbottom bur.
Dec. 15 Grace dau. to Edward & Mary Haukins chr.
Dec. 24 Alexander Bishop & Margret Ambrose marr.
Dec. 26 Joseph son to Richard & Prudence Dimond chr.
Jan. 1 Joseph son to Richard & Prudence Dimond bur.
Jan. 13 Liddiah dau. to Catherin Farman, widow, bur.
Jan. 20 Thomas son to Nicolas & Jone Clegat chr. 20 & bur. 22
Jan. 23 Nathanaell Carter & Ann Leather marr.
Jan. 26 John son to Richard & Alice Heath chr.
Jan. 26 Mary dau. to John & Margret Mayo chr.
Jan. 27 Elizabeth wife to Jarvice Smithsonn bur.
Jan. 28 George Nelsonn & Ann Nettlefold marr.

Jan. 30 Thomas son to Thomas & Margret Halle chr.
Jan. 30 Joice Robinsoun, a foundling, chr.
Feb. 2 Thomas Bucket & Susanna Booth marr.
Feb. 23 Richard son to Thomas & Ann Yates chr.
Feb. 27 Sara dau. to Sammuell & Sara Tomlins chr.
Mar. 6 Thomas son to Frauncis & Rebecca Gardner bur.
Mar. 12 Martha Williams, a foundling, chr.

1634.

April 13 Joseph son to Audrian & Elizabeth Merry chr.
April 20 William son to William & Mary Smith chr.
April 28 Erasmus Laude & Mary Griffith marr.
May 1 Danniell son to William & Alice Woodcock chr.
May 4 John Canncer & Ann Ambler marr.
May 21 John Aggard & Mary Adderly marr.
May 25 Constance dau. to Thomas & Jone Broomfielde chr.
June 12 Richard Saunibery & Rebecca Peck marr.
June 14 Richard Bauldwine, from Mr Shaw's, bur.
June 21 Sara dau. to Richard & Jone Lazonby chr. 21 & bur. 23
June 25 Old Mr Robert Washborn bur.
June 27 James son to James & Ann Fenn chr.
July 1 Elizabeth Collingwood, a young maid, bur.
July 3 John Cornelius & Jane Davice marr.
July 18 Sara Goodall, a young maid, bur.
July 28 Doraty dau. to Henery & Jone Higginbottom chr. 28, & the mother Jone bur. 31
Aug. 5 Anna dau. to Thomas & Anna Owin chr.
Aug. 16 Hanna wife to Thomas Crouch bur.
Aug. 17 Martha dau. to Roger & Ellin Bridges chr.
Sep. 3 Jerimy son to John & Mary Sharrow chr.
Sep. 16 Grace dau. to George & Grace Hill chr.
Sep. 30 John son to Thomas & Elizabeth Davice bur.
Oct. 9 Edmond Whitefoot & Martha Walker marr.
Oct. 16 Elizabeth dau. to Thomas & Elizabeth Davice chr.
Oct. 18 Arnall son to Susanna Bland, widow, bur.
Oct. 23 Mary dau. to Mr Charles & Martha Ofspring chr.
Oct. 24 Nicolas son to Nicolas & Mary Higginbottom chr.
Oct. 24 Elizabeth dau. to Thomas & Elizabeth Cage bur.
Nov. 9 Elizabeth dau. to Thomas & Elizabeth Davis bur.
Nov. 14 George Hyat & Jone Hedden, both prentices, bur.
Nov. 15 Elizabeth Williams, a servant, bur.
Nov. 30 . . . Baily & Ann Procter marr.
Dec. 2 Edward Wallis & Sara Seele marr.
Jan. 2 Ann wife to Henry Shawe bur.
Jan. 12 Elizabeth dau. to George & Elizabeth Griffeth bur.
Jan. 19 Joseph son to Audrian & Elizbeth Merry bur.
Jan. 20 Jeremy son to John & Mary Sharrow bur.
Jan. 24 Margaret dau. to Frauncis & Mary Bickly chr. 24 & bur. 27
Feb. 1 Ann dau. to Nicolas & Susanna Beales chr.
Feb. 10 Roger Oake & Margret Tresswell marr.
Feb. 11 Robert son to Richard & Elizabeth Hunt, was taken as she was passing through the parish, chr.
Feb. 19 Ann dau. to Edward & Ann Nevit chr.
Feb. 27 Thomas son to Thomas & Ann Yates bur.
Mar. 13 John Sharrow bur.
Mar. 22 Walter son to Walter & Katherin Oake chr.

1635.

Mar. 29 William son to William & Sara Newit chr.
Mar. 30 John Voie & Rohda Bull marr.
April 2 Bartholomew Nicolsonn & Kather. Savern marr.
April 3 Doraty wife to Richard Dike bur. in ye church
April 8 William Passand bur.; church
April 8 John Collins, a young man, bur. in churchyard
April 9 George Elsmore & Ann Gossage marr.
April 12 John son to William & Elizabeth Hix chr.
April 13 Judith dau. to Steeven & Mercie Simpsonn bur. in ye yard
April 18 Walter son to Walter & Katarin Oake bur. in ye church
May 5 Hanna dau. to Thomas & Hanna Walker chr.
May 10 William son to John & Ann Smith chr.
May 11 Richard Jaggar, a pensioner, bur.; churchyard
May 17 Fraunncis son to Thomas & Ann Yates chr.
May 23 William son to William & Sara Newet bur.; church
June 24 John son to William & Fraunces Ince chr.
July 16 John son to William & Elizabeth Hix bur.; church
July 19 Phillip dau. to Richard & Mary Moorcraft chr.
July 21 Sammuell son to James & Ann Venn chr.
July 31 Kendrick son to Richard & Ann Edesbury chr.
Aug. 1 Ann dau. to Thomas & Ann Owin bur.; church
Aug. 2 Hanna dau. to Edward & Mary Haukins chr. & bur.; church
Aug. 4 John son to William & Fraunces Ince bur.; church
Aug. 6 Humphery Windsor & Martha Atkins marr.
Aug. 9 John son to John & Faith Tent chr.
Aug. 21 Robert Kerby, from Mr Smithsonn's, bur.; churchyard
Sep. 5 William Burdett, a foundling, chr.
Sep. 17 Alexander Ladd & Elizabeth Applebee marr.
Sep. 25 Thomas son to Thomas & Ann Owin chr.
Oct. 9 Edward son to Edward & Jane Sumner chr.
Oct. 20 William Hoult & Jone Smith marr.
Oct. 26 John son to Launslat & Sara Granger bur.; church
Oct. 27 Humphery son to John and Anne Bickley chr.
Oct. 31 Thomas son to Thomas & Jone Lazonby chr. 31 Oct., bur. 2 Nov church
Nov. 3 Robert Sharpe & Jane Nevisonn marr.
Nov. 19 Sampsonn Morris & Elizabeth Gouldsmith marr.
Nov. 19 Anthony Drew & Elizabeth Ash marr.
Nov. 28 Faith wife to John Teint bur.
Nov. 30 Mary [*blank*], born in the limehouse, chr.
Dec. 1 Roger Price & Elizabeth Busby marr.
Dec. 7 Mary wife to Fraunncis Bickley bur.
Dec. 9 Thomas son to Nicolas & Jone Clegat chr.
Dec. 9 Fraunces dau. to Henery & Jone Higginbottom chr.
Dec. 11 Mr Jhon Smithsonn, D^r of the Civil Law, bur.
Dec. 17 Harman Terrill & Jane Laifever marr.
Dec. 20 Ann dau. to Adrian & Elizabeth Merry chr.
Dec. 30 Hanna dau. to Roger & Ann Hattonn chr.
Jan. 2 Fraunncis Hill bur.
Jan. 8 A stillborn of Thomas & Mary Chrouche's bur.; yard
Jan. 26 Thomas Hunt & Ann Jonsonn marr.
Feb. 2 Mr Robert Wicks, minister, & Fraunces Thurloe marr.
Feb. 3 John Quince, a child from Mr Wood's, bur.; churchyard
Feb. 16 Hanna dau. to Thomas & Margret Halle chr.
Mar. 5 Elizabeth dau. to Hugh & Jone Haines, a straggler in the outhouse, chr.

Mar. 10 William Wheately bur.; church
Mar. 11 Mary dau. to George & Elizabeth Griffith bur.; church
Mar. 11 Henry son to Henery & Margret Speed chr.
Mar. 17 Mary dau. to Edward & Ann Nevet chr.

1636.

Mar. 31 Ann & Mary daus. to Edward & Ann Nevet both bur.; church
May 5 Damaris dau. to Walter & Katherin Oake chr.
May 11 John son to Richard & Alis Heath bur.; yard
May 23 Richard son to Paule & Mary Browne, from Mr Mosse's, bur.; yard
May 26 Charles Houlte, a prentice, from Mrs Washborne's, bur.; yard
May 29 Elizabeth dau. to Steeven & Mercy Simpsonn chr.
June 30 Mathew Thornehull bur.; church
July 9 John Heron & Margret Chambers marr.
July 13 Alice wife to Richard Heath bur.; yard
July 14 Mercy wife to Steeven Simpsonn bur.; yard
Aug. 14 Edward son to a vagrant delivered in the street chr.
Sep. 7 Ann dau. to Nicolas & Susann Beales bur.; yard
Sep. 24 Elizabeth dau. to Nicolas & Margret Beales bur.; yard
Oct. 12 Isaac son to Lewis & Ann Price chr.
Oct. 12 Rebecca dau. to Nicolas & Susan Beales chr.
Oct. 18 Alice Farman, a young maid, bur.; yard
Oct. 19 John son to Andryan & Elizabeth Merry, bur. 19 (plague); & the said Audrian Merry himself bur. 22 (plague); yard
Nov. 2 Sammuell & Mary & Ann son & daus. to the Widow Merry bur. (plague) 2, 7, & 9 Nov.; yard
Nov. 10 Daniell son to Roger & Ellin Bridgis bur.; church; plague
Nov. 10 Mrs Ann Barnes, from Mr Owin's, bur.; church
Dec. 15 George son to Edward & Mary Haukins chr. 15 & bur. 19; church
Dec. 21 John son to Henry & Jonne Higgenbottom chr.
Jan. 12 William son to Richard Tomsonn, of Ditton, bur.; churchyard
Jan. 17 Elias Fairefield & Elizabeth Catherin [*sic*] marr.
Feb. 11 Marmaduke Tennant & Eunis Bennitt, widow, marr.
Feb. 23 Henery Moore & Elizabeth Gouldgay marr.
Feb. 28 Will. son to Frauncis & Editha Tailor chr.
Mar. 5 Thomas Scottle & Susanna Ashtonn marr.
Mar. 19 John son to John & Mary Bute chr. 19 & bur. 24; church

1637.

April 20 Sr John Meltonn & Mrs Margaret Aldersey marr. Mar. 20
May 3 Solomon Peeke, a bastard child, chr.
May 3 Rachell dau. of Stephen & Mary Simpson bur.
May 4 John Lewes, the parish clerk, bur.
May 15 Mr Thomas Hoe & Mrs Mary Bickly marr.
June 2 Barnet Charnico, a stranger from Goodage's, bur.
June 9 Isaack son to William & Judith Gibson chr.
July 4 Annis dau. of John & Ann Bickly chr.
Aug. 13 John son of Henry & Elizabeth Shaw chr.
Aug. 15 Katherine Billinsley bur.
Sep. 17 Hannah dau. of Stephen & Mary Simpson chr.
Sep. 26 Mr John Kedgwin, from Mr Ofspring's, bur.
Oct. 1 Thomas son of Thomas & Jane Joyte chr.
Oct. 5 A strange woman & her child, from Jagger's, bur.
Oct. 21 Henry Costell & Mary Dew marr.
Oct. 22 Robert Sharpe & Jone Nevinson marr.
Oct. 28 Philip son of John & Elizabeth Adams chr.

Nov. 12 George son of Edward & Mary Hawkins chr.
Nov. 14 Urian Oakes & Joan Collingwood marr.
Nov. 21 Sarah dau. of William & Elizabeth Hix chr.
Nov. 28 Sarah dau. of William & Sarah Newitt chr.
Nov. 30 William Bridges & Joan Merick marr.
Dec. 4 Ralph son of Ralfe & Margret Hinchin chr.
Dec. 7 John Dorman & Elizabeth Hatton marr.
Dec. 11 Sarah dau. of William & Sarah Newitt bur.
Dec. 12 A bastard child, born in ye street, chr.
Dec. 17 John Crewkerne & Elizabeth Watts marr.
Jan. 2 Marke Stanton & Elizabeth Pepper marr.
Jan. 6 Jane dau. of Nicolas & Susan Beales bur.
Jan. 8 Ann dau. of Noadiah & Jone Rawlins bur.
Jan. 12 Thomas son of Thomas & Ann Yates bur.
Jan. 16 Jane dau. of Edward & Jane Sumner bur.
Jan. 18 Barnard Connier & Katherine Goowin marr.
Jan. 28 Edward son of Edward & Jane Sumner bur.
Feb. 4 Thomas Palmer & Margery Thornhill marr.
Feb. 4 Judith dau. of Nicolas & Susan Beales chr.
Feb. 12 Jeremy Dike & Joyce Fenner marr.
Feb. 18 Ann dau. to Edward & Ann Nevett chr.
Mar. 1 Ann dau. of Edward & Ann Nevett bur.
Mar. 4 Mary dau. of Thomas & Margrett Hall chr.
Mar. 13 Mr Roger Hatton, one of our parishioners, bur.
Mar. 15 Barnard son of Barnard & Katherine Coniers chr.
Mar. 21 Jane dau. of Abraham & Mary Ottgar chr.

1638.

April 12 Mary dau. of Charles & Martha Ofspring bur.
April 20 Mary dau. of Thomas & Ann Yeats chr.
April 24 Edward son of Nicolas & Joan Clegat chr.
April 29 Dorothy dau. to David & Susan Godfrey chr.
May 2 Mary dau. to Thomas & Hannah Walker chr.
May 5 Elizabeth dau. to Elizab. & George Griffin bur.
May 8 Francis Leake, a stranger from Mr Speed's, bur.
May 14 Samuel Enderby & Elizabeth Newberry marr.
May 17 Samuel Gillibrand & Obedience Cruttenden marr.
May 26 Thomas son of Thom. & Margrett Hall bur.
June 4 Elizabeth dau. of Thomas & Margrett Hall bur.
June 4 Mary dau. of Thomas & Joan Brumfield bur.
June 7 Jone wife of Mr Thomas Brumfield bur.
June 23 A stranger from Mrs Washborne's bur.
June 29 Katherine dau. to Walter & Katherine Oake chr.
July 8 John son to Henry & Elizabeth Shaw chr.
July 14 Alice Burras *alias* Mrs Lightfoot, out of ye alley, bur.
July 19 Anthony Langley, serv^t to William Remnant, bur.
July 25 Tobie Band & Elizabeth Abram marr.
Aug. 12 Mary dau. of George & Alice Tayler, ye seedman, chr.
Aug. 28 Hugh Hollingsworth, serv^t to John Adams, bur.
Aug. 29 George Warner, serv^t to John Adams, bur.
Sep. 1 Martha dau. to Roger & Ellin Bridges bur.
Sep. 6 Adam son to Adam & [*blank*] Head chr.
[*blank*] Anthony Wood, out of ye alley, bur.
Sep. 18 James son to Edward & Jane Sumner chr.
Sep. 21 Y^e said James Sumner bur.
Sep. 24 James son to Nicolas & Mary Clegatt bur.
Sep. 29 Jane Cooper, serv^t-maid to Mr William Gibson, bur.

Oct. 10 Ann dau. to William & Ann Butterworth chr.
Oct. 12 Mr William Woodcock bur.
Oct. 18 Jane dau. to Urian & Jone Oakes chr.
Oct. 20 Peter son to John & Mary Butts chr.
Oct. 29 Mary wife of John Butts bur.
Nov. 12 Richard Burrus & Grace Greene marr.
Nov. 18 Elizabeth Tuff & William Ridgway marr.
Nov. 22 Mr Jarvis Smithsonn bur.
Nov. 29 Mrs Mary Taverner bur.
Dec. 16 Elizabeth dau. to Launcelett & Sara Granger
Dec. 18 Jane dau. to Urian & Jone Oakes bur.
Dec. 23 Ralfe Bold & Mary Fairy marr.
Jan. 3 William Dangerfield & Ann New marr.
Jan. 8 A child bur.
Jan. 15 Mr Thomas Newton & Mrs Amie Bickly marr.
Jan. 22 Thom. & Hannat Hawkins twins to Edward & Mary Hawkins chr.
Feb. 20 Amie dau. to Richard & Mary Moorcraft chr.
Mar. 10 Elizabeth dau. to [*blank*] Fox [?]
Mar. 11 Hannah dau. to Edward & Mary Hawkins bur.
Mar. 20 Hannah dau. to George & Grace Hill chr.
Mar. 21 Martha dau. to George & Elizab. Griffeth [?]

1639.

Mar. 25 Thomas son to Edward & Mary Hawkins bur.
April 1 Mary dau. to Thomas & Hannah Walker bur.
April 2 Hannah dau. to Ann Hatton bur.
April 5 A stranger from Mr Goodage's bur.
April 16 Margret dau. to Anthony & Susan Luling chr.
April 25 John Glover & Jone Thomson marr.
May 5 William Turner & Ann Sparkes marr.
May 21 Old Mrs Sumner, Mr Edward Sumner's mother, bur.
June 18 Frances dau. to William & Frances Ince chr.
June 24 Sarah dau. to Richard & Jane Heath chr.
June 24 Roger, a brother of Mr John Adams, bur.
July 2 Joseph son to Francis & Editha Tayler chr.
July 6 A female bastard child bur.
July 12 William son of Lewes & Ann Price chr.
July 18 John son to Thomas & Margrett Hall chr.
July 25 Ellen dau. to Roger & Ellen Bridges chr.
July 26 Thomas West, a wine-cooper, bur.
July 30 Alice dau. to William & Ann Nevett chr.
Aug. 12 Richard Melton & Judith Wood marr.
Aug. 12 Elizabeth dau. to Henry & Elizabeth Shaw [?]
Sep. 6 Robert Childe & Ann Leyton marr.
Sep. 13 Elizabeth dau. to Edward & Jane Sumner chr.
Sep. 14 Mr Fox his wife, in the alley, bur.
Sep. 23 Edward son to William & Sarah Newitt chr.
Sep. 30 William son to Robert & Elizabeth Sheeld bur.
Oct. 1 Sarah dau. to Nicolas & Susan Beales chr.
Oct. 1 William son of Will. & Elizab. Sheeld bur.
Oct. 14 Sarah dau. to Nicolas & Susan Beales bur.
Oct. 25 Grace Antholins, a foundling child, chr.
Oct. 31 Ezechiell Calsby & Ellen Beeke marr.
Nov. 7 Obadiah Allen & Bridgett Pickford marr.
Nov. 24 John son of John & Elizab. Adams chr.
Dec. 1 Samuel son to Francis & Bridget Genvy [?] bur.
Dec. 13 Dorothy dau. to Elizabeth & William Jones chr.

Dec. 16 Mr William Newitt bur.
Dec. 19 Richard Ridgar & Em Padnall marr.
Dec. 22 Thomas son to Thomas & Mary Roe chr.
Jan. 5 Henry son to Lancelett & Sarah Granger chr.
Jan. 12 Ann dau. to Francis & Elizab. Row chr.
Jan. 15 Mary wife to Mr Miles Newton bur.
Jan. 30 John son to Thom. & Margrett Hall bur.
Jan. 31 Judith dau. to Nicolas & Susan Beales bur.
Feb. 6 Edward son to William & Sarah Newitt bur.
Feb. 16 John son of Henry & Margrett Speed chr.
Feb. 29 Martha dau. to John & Elizab. Scott chr.
Mar. 7 Margery Hoare, a stranger, out of ye alley, bur.
Mar. 14 John son to Henry & Margret Speed bur.
Mar. 22 Cleophas son to Edward & Mary Hawkins chr.

1640.

Mar. 27 Christian Freeman, widow, sister to Mrs Pitts, bur.
Mar. 28 Mrs Susan Shackbolt bur.
April 7 Thomas son to Henry & Elizabeth Shaw bur.
April 9 John son to Henry & Elizabeth Shaw bur.
April 16 John Hodson & Wilsford Hoskins marr.
April 17 Sarah dau. to William & Joane Smith chr.
April 19 Susan dau. to Anthony & Susan Luling chr.
April 30 Elizabeth dau. to Susan Sympson bur.
May 7 Francis son to Richard & Ann Edgberry chr.
May 14 William Nevill & Ann Wilkinson marr.
May 16 Robert Davis, a stranger, from Mr Banburye's, bur.
May 26 John Stokes & Joyce Wheeler marr.
May 28 John son to Henry & Elizabeth Barten bur.
June 11 Thomas Edgly & Elizabeth Gale marr.
June 13 Ann dau. to Thomas & Jone Brumfield bur.
June 30 Mary Edwards, from Gardiner's in ye alley, bur.
July 14 A stillborn dau. of Thom. & Amie Newton bur.
Aug. 5 Ann dau. to Richard & Elizabeth Thorne bur.
Aug. 16 Bartholomew son to David & Susan Godfrey chr.
Aug. 18 Bartholomew the same child bur.
Aug. 23 Urian son to Urian & Jone Oakes chr.
Sep. 6 Elizabeth dau. to Edward & Ann Nevett chr.
Sep. 14 Ralfe son to Edward & Jane Sumner chr.
Sep. 15 Elizabeth Antholins, a foundling, chr.
Sep. 25 Joan dau. to Thomas & Ann Townsend bur.
Oct. 4 Sarah dau. to Thomas & Hannah Walker chr.
Oct. 11 Edward son to John & Mildred Tint chr.
Oct. 19 Hannah dau. to George & Grace Hill bur.
Oct. 19 Katherine dau. to Gwalter & Katherine Oake bur.
Nov. 6 Mary dau. to Richard & Margery Moorcraft bur.
Nov. 14 Ralfe son to Edward & Jane Sumner bur.
Nov. 15 John Allen & Dorothy Whitmore marr.
Nov. 28 Mr Lyonell Wake, from Mr Butterworth's, bur.
Dec. 11 Mary dau. to Katherine & Walter Oake chr.
Dec. 13 Ann dau. to Urian & Ann Cryer, an inmate, chr.
Dec. 15 Mrs Margaret Stacy, widow, out of ye alley, bur.
Dec. 16 William son to Lewes & Ann Price bur.
Dec. 18 Mary dau. to Fran. & Elizab. How chr.
Dec. 22 Em wife to Mr Rich. Ridgar bur.
Dec. 23 Henry son to Henry & Elizab. Barten bur.
Dec. 31 Mr Timothy Elwick, from Putney, bur.

Jan. 6 Thomas son to Rich. & Elizab. Thorn chr.
Jan. 20 Thomas son to Henry & Elizab. Barten bur.
Jan. 26 John Howdisly & Luce Langworth marr.
Jan. 30 Grace dau. to George & Grace Hill bur.
Feb. 2 Augustine Symmes & Elizab. Bembrick marr.
Feb. 3 Mary Halfehide, from Mr Eden's, bur.
Feb. 9 Thomas son to Richard & Margery Moorcraft chr.
Mar. 3 William, father to Mr Ince of this parish, bur.
Mar. 24 Thomas Warren & Hester Newton marr.

1641.

Mar. 28 Francis son to Nicolas & Susan Beales chr.
Mar. 31 Edward son to Edw. & Ann Shield chr.
April 3 Cisley dau. to Edw. & Jane Mosse bur.
April 14 Vincent son to Anthony & Susan Luling chr.
April 16 Nicolas son to George & Cisly Brookes, at Mr Beale's, chr.
April 17 Mr Henry Shaw bur.
April 21 John Arnold & Elizabeth Robinson marr.
May 9 William Newberry & Elizab. Treimer marr.
May 15 A son to Fran. & Editha Tayler, stillborn, bur.
May 17 Francis Newton & Jane Philips marr.
June 6 Elizabeth dau. to Edw. & Elizab. Hodierne chr.
June 10 Thomas Burges & Mary Newman marr.
June 29 Nicolas Skillin & Ann Amis marr.
July 4 Henry son to Henry & Margery Speed chr.
July 22 William Dashwood & Susan Hanviues [*sic*] marr.
Aug. 3 John son to William & Francis Ince chr.
Aug. 5 Susan dau. to Rich. & Jane Heath chr.
Aug. 5 Frances dau. to Francis & Rebecca Gardener bur.
Aug. 5 A son to David & Susan Godfrey, stillborn, bur.
Aug. 11 Ezra son to Thom. & Hester Browne bur.
Aug. 14 Margaret Gasty, from Mr Case, in Mr Welding's house, bur.
Aug. 31 Edward son to Edward & Mary Hawkins bur.
Sep. 6* Elizabeth dau. to Edward & Ann Nevet chr.
Sep. 14 Ralfe son to Edward & Jane Sumner chr.
Sep. 15 Elizabeth Antholins, a foundling, chr.
Sep. 26 Jone dau. of Mrs Townsend bur.
Oct. 4 Sarah dau. to Thomas & Hannah Walker chr.
Oct. 11 Edward son to John & Mildred Tint chr.
Oct. 19 Hannah dau. to George & Grace Hill bur.
Oct. 19 Katherine dau. to Katherine & Walter Oake bur.
Nov. 6 Mary dau. of Richard & Margery Moorcraft bur.
Nov. 14 Ralfe son to Edward & Jane Sumner bur.
Nov. 15 John Allen & Dorothy Whitmore marr.
Nov. 28 Lionell Wake, from Mr. Butterworth's, bur.
Dec. 11 Mary dau. to Walter & Katherine Oake chr.
Dec. 13 Ann dau. to Urian & Ann Cryer chr.
Dec. 15 Mrs Stacy, out of ye alley against the pump, bur.
Dec. 16 A child of [*blank*] Price bur.
Dec. 18 A child of Fran. How & Elizab. bur.
Dec. 22 A kinswoman of Mrs Wilkinson's bur.
Dec. 23 A child of Mr Barten's bur.

* From Sept. 6 to Dec. 23 of this year the entries in the Registers are nearly the same as from Sept. 6 to Dec. 23 of 1640. They are retained only to shew the few variations, and to account for the absence of fresh entries in the same period of 1641.

Jan. 1 Joan dau. to Nathaniel & Jane Rawlins bur.
Jan. 3 Mary dau. to Katherine & Walter Oake bur.
Jan. 5 A child from ye houses besides Mr Newman's chr.
Jan. 10 James son to Jeremiah & Elizab. Deane, barber, chr.
Jan. 15 A child stillborn from an inmate at Mr Goodage's bur.
Jan. 22 Sarah dau. to Ephraim & Sarah Thorne chr.
Jan. 25 Sarah dau. to Ephr. & Sarah Thorne bur.
Feb. 20 John son to John & Elizab. Butts chr.
Feb. 22 A child of Mr Luling's bur.
Feb. 24 A child of the bodymaker's, Mr Greene's prentice, chr.
Mar. 16 Mary dau. to William & Margery Ormaudy chr.

1642.

Mar. 29 A child of Mr Moorcraft's bur.
April 5 James son to Henry & Ann Colbran chr.
April 12 John son to John & Sense Duncon chr.
April 19 Henry Hatton & Elizab. Pitts marr.
April 22 Hannah dau. to Stephen & [*blank*] Sympson chr.
April 25 William son to Francis & Elizab. How chr.
May 1 Roger son to John & Cisly Spilman chr.
May 11 James Heames & Mary Hale marr.
May 12 Francis Gardener, out of ye alley, bur.
May 16 William son to Francis & Editha Tayler bur.
June 3 Editha dau. to Francis & Editha Tayler bur.
June 5 Frances dau. to Francis & Editha Tayler bur.
June 9 Mr Danson, of St Thom. Apostle's, bur.
June 11 John son to Edward & John [*sic*] Sheild, at Mr Mosse's, bur.
June 28 Mr Richard Moorecraft bur.
July 2 A stillborn child of Mr Hill's bur.
July 17 William Lane & Mary Drue marr.
July 21 Thomas Roberts & Mary Witherden marr.
July 23 Katherine wife of Walter Oake bur.
Aug. 11 Mary dau. to Noadiah & Joan Rawlins bur.
Aug. 23 John Stapelerd & Mary Crampe marr.
Aug. 28 Samuel son to Thom. & Margret Hall chr.
Sep. 1 Sarah dau. to Urian & Jone Oakes chr.
Oct. 9 Thomas son to Nicolas & Susan Beales chr.
Oct. 9 William son to John & Mildred Tint chr.
Oct. 26 Henry son to Lancelett & Sarah Granger bur.
Oct. 29 A stillborn child of Mr Mormye's bur.
Oct. 30 Abram & Jacob twin sons to Lewis & Ann Price chr.
Nov. 3 A stranger, out of ye alley, from Widow Chester's, bur.
Nov. 20 A child of Mr Abram & Mary Otgar bur.
Nov. 24 William Hatly & Elizabeth Harrison marr.
Dec. 15 Mrs Goodage bur.
Dec. 20 John son to John & Margery Mayo bur.
Jan. 5 Syr Francis Swift & Mary Johuson, Mr Waterhouse's dau., marr.
Jan. 9 A child of Richard Heath, ye carpenter, bur.
Jan. 11 Thomas son to John & Elizabeth Butts chr.
Jan. 19 A child bur.
Jan. 21 John son to John & Mary Shipley chr.
Jan. 29 Hannah dau. to Roger & Ellen Bridges chr.
Feb. 1 Hannah ye same child of Roger & Ellen Bridges bur.
[*blank*] A child of one out of ye alley bur.
Mar. 4 [*blank*] to Edward & Jane Sumner chr.
Mar. 8 Noadiah Rawlins bur.
Mar. 12 John son to John & Dorothy Mason chr.

1643.

April 12 Ann dau. to Edward & Ann Nevet chr.

April 13 Benjamin son to Nathaniel & Jane Rawlins chr.

April 13 Sarah Clegat marr. by a Captain of New Engl. at home

April 13 Judith Pitts marr. also in the like maner

April 14 Ann dau. to William Passand bur.

April 26 John Robinson & Samuel Robinson sons of John Robinson, but one about 6 weeks before the other, bur.

April 28 Susan wife of David Godfrey bur.

May 2 Old Goodman Holt bur.

May 5 Dorothy Weekes, from Mrs Wood's, bur.

May 14 Sara dau. to John & [*blank*] Smith chr.

May 16 Gabriell Carpenter & Ann Harris marr.

May 22 William Herne, Mr Butterworth's man, bur.

May 22 Sara dau. of Eliz. & George Tie chr.

May 23 Hamnet Hide, from Mr Hollinsworth's, bur.

May 23 [*blank*] of Thom. & Margret Hall bur.

June 1 Thom. son to Nicolas & Susan Beales bur.

June 2 Tabitha Baynard, Mr Baynard's wife, bur.

June 13 John Yates bur.

June 16 Mr Godard bur.

June 27 Thom. Rix, from Mr Bridges', bur.

July 15 Francis dau. to Hen. Browne bur.

July 27 William Turner, out of the alley, bur.

Aug. 8 Sara dau. of John & Mary Robinson bur.

Sep. 9 Mrs Wilkinson bur.

Sep. 24 Henry Morgan & Jone Holt marr.

Oct. 16 Elizabeth a child of Mr How's chr.

Oct. 16 Elizabeth a child of Mr Christopher Leader's chr.

Oct. 22 Thomas son to Thomas Woodard chr.

Oct. 26 James son to Thom. & Sence Duncon chr.

Nov. 2 Robert Jole & Elizabeth Dennis marr.

Nov. 12 One Ann, from Mr Butterworth's, chr.

Nov. 30 Sylvester Deane & Mary Blower marr.

Dec. 9 Mary Lewes, Mr Beale's maid, bur.

Dec. 19 John son to George & [*blank*] Mayo chr.

Dec. 20 Benjamin son to Lewis & Ann Price chr.

Dec. 24 Jane dau. to Fran. & [*blank*] Mormay chr.

Jan. 1 Abraham Bestwick & Dorothy Vitty (by Mr Death) marr.

Jan. 19 Jane dau. to Francis Mormay bur.

Jan. 20 George son to Margret Prideox, from Mr Bridges', bur.

Mar. 8 William son to Fran. How, ye glazier, bur.

Mar. 14 Richard son to Rich. & Jane Heath chr.

Mar. 15 Mr John Tinte bur.

1644.

Mar. 26 Thomas son of John & Mary Shipsey chr. [see Jan. 21, 1642-3]

April 9 Daniell son of John & Eliz. Butts chr.

April 13 Elizabeth dau. to John & Katherine Greene chr.

April 15 A child of Mr. Woodard's bur.

May 4 Mr Sympson bur.

May 6 A child of Mr Greene's, ye bodymaker, bur.

May 9 A child of Mr Oak's bur.

May 10 A child of Mr Potter's chr.

June 4 Mary dau. to Urian & Jone Oakes chr.

June 10 David, Mr Godfrye's child, chr.

June 10 A child of Mr Potter's bur.

June 14 Dorcas dau. to Rich. & Dorothy Inman chr.
June 19 Martha dau. to George & Mary Web bur.
June 20 Thomas son to Henry & Eliz. Fowler chr.
July 15 John son to John Mason, from Goodage's, bur.
July 28 Samuel son to George Martir chr.
July 30 John son to Mr Griffith chr.
Aug. 19 Samuell Willy, from Gardener's out of the alley, bur.
Sep. 1 William son to William & Eliz. Rutt chr.
Sep. 3 Margret, ye foundling that went to Compton's, chr.
Sep. 7 William son of William & Eliz. Rutt bur.
Sep. 8 Sara dau. to William & Margery Ormandy chr.
Sep. 9 Dorothy dau. to David & [*blank*] Godfrey bur.
Oct. 26 William son to Francis How chr.
Nov. 13 M^rs^ [*blank*] Styles bur.
Nov. 21 Thomas Witherall bur.
Dec. 19 Mrs Godard bur.
Dec. 24 Mr Griffith's son bur.
Jan. 1 Sara dau. of Urian Oaks [?]

1645.

Mar. 25 Edward Goodage bur.
April 1 A child of Abraham Otgar's (not bapt.) bur.
April 7 Ann dau. to Lewes & An Price chr.
April 11 A child of [*blank*] bur.
April 26 Mr Rawson bur.
May 11 John son to Will. & Alice Burt chr.
June 16 John son to William & Alice Burt chr. [*sic* ? bur.]
June 24 John son to Thomas & Barbara Woodard chr.
July 6 Elizabeth dau. to Jeremy & Eliz. Deane chr.
July 12 Caleb Rawlins bur.
July 15 Mr Leech, a courtier, bur.
July 17 Margret Worthington, Mr Beal's maid, bur.
July 22 Robert Bold & Bennet Bishop marr.
July 28 Sara dau. of Henry & Eliz. Barten bur.
Aug. 21 John Dawny & Elizab. Melton marr.
Aug. 24 Mary dau. of Edward & Ann Hains, at Mr Bridges', chr.
Aug. 31 Rebecca dau. of James & Ann Rigg chr.
Aug. 31 Mary dau. of Tobias & Mary Allin [?]
Aug. 31 William son to Dorothy & Rich. Inman chr.
Sep. 1 Henry Cleiton & Elizab. Reeve marr.
Sep. 6 William son to Rich. & Dorothy Inman bur.
Sep. 7 Mary dau. to Edmund & Elizab. Webberly bur.
Sep. 11 Margret dau. to Thomas & Mary Potter chr.
Sep. 21 John son to William & Eliz. Rutt chr.
Sep. 21 Edward Coe & Mary Lacy marr.
Sep. 25 Margret dau. to Christopher & Eliz. Leader chr.
Oct. 10 John son to Francis & Eliz. How chr.
Oct. 20 A child out of the alley bur.
Nov. 22 Francis ye child of Francis & An Mormy chr.
Dec. 9 Margret wife to Mr Thom. Potter bur.
Dec. 19 Nicolas son to Lancelot & Sara Granger chr.
Dec. 23 Stephen Pig & Elizab. Horne marr.

1646.

May 17 Joseph son to John & Mary Shipsey chr.
May 18 Symon Edmunds, Alderman, & Susan Nudigate marr.
May 21 Thom. Greene & Jane Grove marr.

May 24 Robert son to Robert Hudson, in yᵉ alley, chr.
June, July, August, September, 1646, sick at Hackny.
Oct. 10 Abell Kelly & Mary Ellis marr.
Dec. 6 A son of Thom. Cooper's, yᵉ carpenter, chr.
[*blank*] A child of John & Mary Butts chr.
[*blank*] A son of Colonel Mancring's bur.
[*blank*] A stranger, from Beal's house, bur.
Feb. 4 Thom. Cartar & Ann Vanley marr.
Feb. 7 Philip Upton & An Rawbone marr.
Feb. 23 Edward Win & Mary Smith marr.
Mar. 6 Thomas Cooper's son bur.
Mar. 8 Mʳˢ Eliz. Grimes bur.
Mar. 10 Mʳˢ Thornton bur.

1647.

Mar. 28 Robert son to George & Mary Web chr.
April 16 Mary dau. to Nicolas & Susan Beals bur.
April 18 William Mason & Ann Machernes marr.
April 19 Elenor Nightingale, my own maid, bur.
April 26 Mʳ Bridges, yᵉ salesman, bur.
April 29 John son to Francis & Eliz. How bur.
April 29 Sara dau. to George & Lucy Mayo chr.
May 6 Ralfe Gun & Ann Palmer, by Mʳ Haviland, marr.
May 7 A servant-man of Mʳˢ Bridges bur.
May 11 Mary dau. to Urian & Jone Okes chr.
June 28 Nicolas Brasmore & Jone Morgan marr.
June 28 Frances dau. to Edmund & Eliz. Webberly chr.
July 11 John son to John & Ann Palmer chr.
July 13 Ann dau. to William & Jone Smith chr.
Aug. 15 Benedict son to John & Mary Shipsey chr.
Aug. 18 Mʳ Abraham Mayo, yᵉ old man, bur.
Aug. 23 Martha dau. to Fran. & Eliz. How chr.
Sep. } Oct. } Mʳ Ince had a child bapt. while I was at Bristol
Nov. 12 Thomas Passand bur.
Dec. 10 Elizabeth Hatton bur.
Dec. 18 About this time Mʳ Thom. Browne bur.
Jan. 1 Mary dau. to John & Mary White chr.
Jan. 6 Melon Stacy & Elizab. Bickly marr.
Jan. 6 A child of Mʳ Jeremy Dean's chr.
Jan. 6 A child of Mʳ Christopher Leader's chr.
Jan. 10 Mʳ Rawson's wife bur.
Jan. 16 Ann dau. to Roger & Ann Hunt chr.
Jan. 27 Abigall dau. to Nick. & Abigall Jackson chr.
Feb. 11 Triphena dau. to Rich. & Triphena Hill chr.
Feb. 29 Elizabeth Leech, from Aldermary parish, bur.
Mar. 2 A child of Mʳ Rutt's bur.
Mar. 6 A child of Francis How's bur.
Mar. 6 William Harris & Sara Browne marr.
Mar. 12 Thomas Jordan & Ann Paris marr.
Mar. 16 Joseph son of John & [*blank*] Butts chr.

1648.

Mar. 26 William son of Edward & Anne Sheild chr.
April 3 John Williams & Margret Lovell marr.
April 11 Richard Hole & Ann Hobby marr.

April 30 Mary dau. to Thom. & Rebecca Cooper chr.
May 5 A child of Mr Rogers, ye plumber, bur.
May 8 Mrs Rogers, his wife, bur.
May 28 Elizabeth dau. to John & Eliz. Bennet chr.
June 8 Judith dau. to Lancelott & Sara Granger chr.
June 10 Mr George Blande bur.
June 23 A child from Mr Shawe's bur.
July 19 Mrs Deliller bur.
July 22 A child from Mr Mormy's bur.
Aug. 9 Mrs Pavier, from Mr Edishbury's, bur.
Aug. 29 Joseph Norris & Ann Woodall marr.
Sep. 6 Martha Ofspring & Thom. Blackall marr.
Nov. 26 Joseph Royce & Abigaile Chappell marr.
Dec. 10 Mr Chelsey the vintner's mother bur.
Dec. 14 Elizabeth dau. to Mr Thom. Potter chr.
Dec. 29 A maid from Mr Russell's bur.
Dec. 30 A child from Mr Darbie's bur.
Jan. 2 George son of John & Mary Shipsey chr.
Jan. 3 Widow Jaggar bur.
Jan. 4 William Graves & Jone Smith marr.
Jan. 25 Thom. Hall son of Thom. Hall bur.
Jan. 29 Mary dau. to J. Hudson chr.
Feb. 25 Hester dau. to Thom. & Eliz. Heath chr.
Feb. 26 Barbary dau. to Thom. & Barbary Woodard chr.
Mar. 19 Mary Sheepey & John Nelham marr.
Mar. 20 Mr Thomas Hall ye elder bur.

1649.

April 2 Thom. son to Urian & Jone Okes chr.
April 3 A child of Lancelot & Sara Granger's bur.
April 13 Joseph Potter, from Mr Jackson's, bur.
May 1 Robert Rash & Mary Lee marr.
May 6 Benjamin son to Isack & Mary Legue chr.
May 12 Samuel Jackson & Christian Lane marr.
May 14 Francis son to John & Susan Harper chr.
May 17 Valentine son of Valentine & Jane Crome chr.
June 3 John Brocket & Elinor Wolfe marr.
July 11 William son to Edward Mosse, ye clark, bur.
Aug. 14 Nathaniel son to John & Ann Palmer chr.
Aug. 14 Thomas son to Robert & Mary Web chr.
Aug. 22 Martha wife of Charles Ofspring, parson, bur.
Oct. 3 A dau. of Mr Henry Eden's chr.
Oct. 9 Sr Peter le royre Mortimer & Sara Artson marr.
Oct. 19 Edward Guin & Mary Colloum, of Bride's, marr.
Oct. 20 A dau. of Mr Denewe's bur.
Oct. 28 Sara dau. to James & Sara Russell chr.
Jan. 12 Mr Richard Perry bur.
Feb. 10 A child of one Redman's bur.
Feb. 12 Mr George Mayo & Julian Cruse marr. at Hackny by me

1650.

Mar. 31 James son to Thom. & Margery Potter chr.
April 19 Mr John Browne, from Mrs Harris', bur.
April 30 Eliz. Ginder, Mrs Eden's sister, bur.
April 30 Will. James & Mary Wattell, Mr Cooper's friends, marr.
May 6 Sara dau. of Mr Abraham Otgar bur.

June 12 Sara dau. of Roger & Jane Oake chr.
June 17 Walter Miles & Margret Johnson marr.
June 20 William son to William & Francis Ince chr.
June 22 William the same son of Will. & Fran. Ince bur.
June 24 Daniel Forth & Ann Edwards marr.
Aug. 2 James Sampson & Ann Wells, of Chapham, marr.
Aug. 11 A child of Mr Williamson's, stillborn, bur.
Aug. 12 William Townsende bur.
Sep. 17 Mr Richard Hill, mercht, bur.
Oct. 16 Mary dau. to William & Eliz. Cox chr.
Oct. 21 Ann dau. to John & Mary White chr.
Oct. 21 Samuel Sillesby, vice-president of Queen's Coll., Cambr., bur.
Oct. 25 Samuel son to John & Mary Shipsey chr.
Oct. 27 John Thomas, servt to Mr Chambers, bur.
Oct. 31 Charles son to Thom. & Martha Blackall, of Gregorie's, chr.
Nov. 3 Margret dau. to Rich. & Ann Fleetwood, Mr Mayo's son-in-law, chr.
Nov. 4 A child of Mr Eburne's bur.
Nov. 13 Rebecca dau. to Mr Barten bur.
Nov. 14 Thomas son to Mr Francis Bickly bur.
Nov. 28 Ellen dau. to Nicolas & Abigaile Jackson chr.
Dec. 6 Robert son to Robert & Eliz. Hulbert chr.
Dec. 17 Hannah dau. to Urian & Jone Oke chr.
Dec. 22 Isack son to George & Julian Mayo chr.
Jan. 5 Ann dau. to Lancelot & Sara Granger chr.
Jan. 6 William son to William & Eliz. Rutt chr.
Jan. 8 Sara dau. to George & Mary Webb chr.
Jan. 11 Henry Mosse son of Edward Mosse, ye clerk, bur.
Jan. 30 Thom. son to George & Mary Web bur.
Mar. 8 A child of Mr Pamplin's, stillborn, bur.
Mar. 18 Edward son to John & Abigaile Randoll chr.

1651.

Mar. 25 Christopher son to Christopher & Eliz. Leader chr.
April 11 A child of Mr Pamplin's bur.
May 5 The child of a stranger lodging at Mr Mosse's bur.
May 15 Thom. Pritchard & Jone Luke marr.
May 22 John son to John & Eliz. Key chr.
May 27 Mary dau. to John & Ann Palmer chr.
June 13 Rebecca dau. to Thom. & Rebecca Cooper bur.
July 6 Roger son to Roger & Ann Hunt chr.
July 13 Thomas Maynard & Margret Alford marr.
Aug. 6 Francis Parsons & Mary Perwitch marr.
Aug. 13 Mrs Mary Otgar wife of Abraham Otgar bur.
Something about a child of Mr Okes, I being then at Bristoll
Sep. 12 A dau. of Mr Henry Eden's bur.
Oct. 8 Samuel son to Thomas & Barbary Woodard chr.
Oct. 10 Mr Paul Russell, minister at Hackney, bur.
Oct. 13 Mr Lewes Price, of Thom. Ap'l's side, bur.
Nov. 20 Sara Somister, from Mr Hen. Crispe's, bur.
Dec. 2 Mr Thom. Brumfield, junr, bur.
Dec. 10 Mary dau. to James Denew bur.
Dec. 17 William James & Jane Brigs marr.
Dec. 24 Mary dau. to Will. & Eliz. Cox bur.
Jan. 1 Elizabeth dau. to John & Mary White chr.
Jan. 1 Gualter son to Francis & Eliz. How chr.
Jan. 20 Samuel Warner & Mary Davenport marr.
Jan. 22 Jane May, an infant, from Nicolas Beal's, bur.

Feb. 8 Ann dau. to John & Sara Rogers chr.
Feb. 10 Peter son to Henry & Eliz. Crisps chr.
Feb. 12 Jane dau. to Samuel & An Holled bur.
Feb. 13 Joseph son of Joseph More chr.
Feb. 24 Susan dau. to Nicolas & Abigaile Jackson chr.
Mar. 2 Mr Thomas Middleton & Mrs Constance Bru'field marr.

1652.

Mar. 25 Stephen Read & Eliz. [*blank*], Beal's friends, marr.
April 6 Elizabeth dau. to James & Sara Russell bur.
April 13 Elizabeth dau. to Philip & Mary Perkins, in ye alley, chr.
April 15 Elizabeth dau. to Henry & Eliz. Crips bur.
April 19 Edward Searle & Hannah Harvie marr.
April 20 Martha dau. to Will. & Eliz. Rutt chr.
April 27 John son to Rich. & Ann Fleetwood chr.
May 3 Christopher son to Christopher & Eliz. Leader bur.
May 7 Mr Thomas Kinastane bur.
May 27 John Skrachar & Sara Hinde marr.
June 6 John son to Richard & Ann Fleetwood bur.
June 8 Henry son to Jeremy & Elizab. Deane bur.
June 10 James son to Urian & Jone Okes chr.
June 21 A child of Mr Dickeson's bur.
June 26 Judith dau. to Cutberd James bur.
July 31 Mr Manering, from Foxhall, bur.
July 31 Rebecca James, from Mr Cooper's, bur.
Aug. 11 A man of Mr Miles Newton's bur.

I myself was this month at Bristoll

Sep. 11 Editha wife of Mr Francis Tayler bur.
Sep. 15 A child of Eburne's bur.
Sep. 25 A stillborn child of Sam. & Hanah Pole's bur.
Sep. 30 Turlo Bride & Ann Harding marr.
Oct. 13 Mr Edward Brumfield, out of Cheapside, bur.
Oct. 15 Elizabeth dau. to Edward & Eliz. Austine bapt.
Nov. 2 John son to John & Eliz. Bradney bapt.
Nov. 4 Colonell Randoll Manering bur.
Nov. 4 Frances dau. to John & Frances Butts bapt.
Nov. 5 Frances dau. to John & Frances Buts bur.
Dec. 1 George Kettleby & Elizabeth Kinaston marr.
Dec. 7 John son of James & Mary Denew bur.
Dec. 30 Jonathan son of John & Mary Shipside bapt.
Dec. 30 Samuel son to Roger & Ann Hunt bapt.
Jan. 9 Edward Watson & Elizabeth Paul marr.
Jan. 9 Thom. Harding & Sara Goodman marr.
Jan. 16 Thom. son to Thomas & Rebecca Cooper bapt.
Jan. 20 Mr Purland, Mr Edgberrye's partner, bur.
Jan. 25 Rebecca dau. to Nicolas & Susan Beales bur.
Jan. 27 Erasmus Greenoway & Eliz. Cruse marr.
Jan. 30 Sara dau. to Thom. & Joan Clarke bapt.
Feb. 23 Robert Sellers & Sarah Peacock marr.
Feb. 24 Elizabeth dau. to John & Eliz. White bur.
Mar. 21 Elizabeth Royly, from Mr Banburye's, bur.

1653.

Mar. 28 John son to John & Abigaile Randoll bapt.
April 5 Thomas Cramphorne & Mary Crosse marr.
April 26 A stranger from Mr Deliller's bur.

May 4 Isack son to Isack & Elizabeth Collier bapt.
May 6 Constance dau. to Thom. & Constance Middleton bapt.
May 8 William Purse & Mary Wakam marr.
May 11 Jane dau. to George & Mary Web bapt.
May 14 Mr William Painter, from Mr Colbran's, bur.
May 19 Charles Ofspring son to Char. Ofspring, our minister, bur.
May 16 Martha dau. to Thom. & Martha Blackall bapt.
May 28 Ann dau. to Lancelot & Sara Granger bur.
June 11 Mr Thomas Taverner, out of Southwark, bur.
June 13 Susanna dau. to Christopher & Elizab. Leader bapt.
July 18 Heath, in Sight's Lane, himself, & his wife ye 25, bur.
July 24 Hester dau. to John & Eliz. White bapt.
Aug. 9 John Edwards & Margery Swift marr.
Aug. 11 John Atars & Mary Harris marr.
Aug. 23 Henry Mayday son to Rich. & Frances Mayday bur.
Aug. 26 Hannah dau. to Urian & Joan Okes bapt.
Sep. 18 Thomas son of Henry & Christian Meele bapt.
Sep. 27 Mrs Remnant wife of William Remnant bur.

Memorandum. The Christnings, Burialls, and also Weddings from October 1653 to May 1663 are entered in a Booke by Mr Mosse, then Parrish Clerke of St Antholyn, and were in the yeare 1666 written in this booke by John Clutterbuck, Churchwarden, by the order and at the request of Thomas Sheerman, Rector, and the Parishioners of St. Antholyn.

ANTHONY DAFFYIE, } Churchwardens in
JOHN CLUTTERBUCK, } the same yeare.

Oct. 4 William son to Henry & Elizabeth Cripps bapt.
Oct. 7 William son to William & Frances Iuce, born 27 Sep., bapt. 7 Oct.
Oct. 13 Sarah dau. to John & Mary Dent born
Oct. 20 Elizabeth dau. to Thom. & Eliz. Malin bapt.
Oct. 23 Hannah dau. to John & Elizabeth Bradney bapt.
Nov. 8 Richard son to Jeremy & Elizabeth Deane bapt.
Nov. 13 George Hill bur.
Nov. 16 Two abortives sons to George & Julian Mayo bur.
Nov. 17 James son to Abraham & Mary Otgar bapt.
Nov. 20 Joseph son to Robert & Mary Hudson bapt.
Nov. 29 Alice wife of Alexander Sharpe bur.
Nov. 30 Elizabeth dau. to Edward & Elizabeth Austin bapt.
Jan. 9 Jane wife to Peter Lyle bur.
Jan. 10 Thomas Hart & Mary Bowyer marr.
Jan. 19 Duence Perry bur.
Jan. 20 George Daby bur.
Jan. 22 Edward Banbury bur.
Jan. 23 Robert Holden bur.
Jan. 30 Philip Perkins bur.
Feb. 10 Nolivia Masday bur.
Mar. 1 George Fowler & Mary Robuck marr.
Mar. 2 Elizabeth dau. to Richard & Frances Masday bur.
Mar. 2 Elizabeth Cooke, servt to Richard Masday, bur.
Mar. 17 Barbary wife to Richard Broome bur.

1654.

Mar. 29 Charles Crowch & Frances Langhorne marr.
Mar. 29 James son to Abraham & Mary Otgar bur.
April 12 Sarah dau. to Francis & Elizabeth How bapt.
April 19 Peter White, chymist, bur.

April 20 Anthony son to Thomas & Jane Hall bapt.
April 21 Thomas son to Thomas & Constance Middleton bapt.
April 23 Samuell son to Samuell & Hannah Poole bapt.
April 25 John Mustars & Sarah Biddolph marr.
April 28 Elizabeth dau. to William & Elizabeth Rutt bur.
May 9 John son to Thomas & Barborah Woodward bapt.
May 9 Nathaniell Hart & Elizabeth Holled marr.
May 16 Gideon de Spaine & Mary Leleu marr.
May 22 William Carbonnell & Elizabeth Delillors marr.
May 25 Henry Crispe bur.
July 8 Richard son to Richard & Frances Maysday bapt.
July 14 Elizabeth dau. to Richard & Barborah Smyth born
July 14 Thomas Harding & Elizabeth Layston marr.
July 15 Sarah dau. to William & Ann Pilkington bapt.
July 16 Marcellis son to John & Mary Dent bapt.
July 20 Jane dau. to George Webb bur.
Aug. 7 Peter son to Henry & Elizabeth Crispe bur.
Aug. 20 Ann dau. to Peter & Ann Lylly bapt.
Aug. 24 John Clutterbuck & Allice Fox marr.
Sep. 5 Ann Taylor, from Mr Webb's, bur.
Sep. 10 Elizabeth dau. to Thomas & Rebecca Cooper bapt.
Sep. 14 Thomas Davis bur.
Sep. 17 James son of Edward & Frances Edmonds bapt.
Sep. 28 George son to George & Ann Davis bapt.
Oct. 2 Yeoman Camp, from Mr Sands', bur.
Oct. 3 Nicholas Granger, from St Saviour's, bur.
Oct. 19 Martha dau. to William & Julian Taylor bapt.
Oct. 28 Hosea Dorrington, widow, bur.
Nov. 21 Thomas son to John & Sarah Bland bur.
Nov. 25 James son to Thomas & Joane Clerke bapt.
Nov. 26 Elizabeth dau. to Henry & Elizabeth Crispe bapt.
Nov. 29 Edmond Rowley & Sarah Spencer marr.
Dec. 4 Elizabeth dau. to John & Elizabeth Bradney bur.
Dec. 4 Anthony Wood, apprentice to Mr Dent, bur.
Dec. 8 Richard Edisbury bur.
Dec. 18 Peter Perrey bur.
Dec. 18 Edward White & Mary White marr.
Dec. 25 Hester dau. to John & Allice Layston bapt.
Jan. 9 Judith Bennett, from Hackney, bur.
Jan. 17 George Bassill, from Mr Edmonds', bur.
Jan. 20 Martha dau. to William & Julian Taylor bur.
Jan. 20 [*blank*] son to Henry & Isabell Jackson bapt.
Feb. 19 Thomas Evans & Mary Rand marr.
Feb. 26 Sarah dau. to Abraham & Mary Otger bapt.
Feb. 26 Francis Taylor, from St Michael Royall, bur.
Mar. 1 James Russell bur.
Mar. 6 Mr Edward Peachy & Allice Hester marr.
Mar. 6 Thomas son to Urian & Joane Oakes bur.
Mar. 14 John son to Edward & Elizabeth Austin bapt.

1655.

Mar. 25 Rebecca Gardiner bur.
Mar. 27 William Ryley bur.
Mar. 29 Rachell dau. to Henry & Elizabeth Barton bur.
Mar. 29 Mathew son to John & Abigaile Randall bapt.
April 5 Thomas son to John & Alice Layston bur.
May 5 Thomas son to Urian & Joane Oakes bur.

May 6 Sarah dau. to William & Ann Pilkington bapt.
May 29 Mr John Butts his son bur.
June 15 Marcellis dau. [*sic*] to John & Mary Dent bapt.
June 18 Alice dau. to John & Allice Clutterbuck bapt.
July 26 Mary wife to Francis Isackson bur.
July 29 An abortive son to Thomas & Elizabeth Malyn bur.
Aug. 7 Ann wife to William Pilkington bur.
Aug. 18 Alice dau. to John & Alice Clutterbuck bur.
Aug. 22 Ann dau. to Peter Camphare bapt.
Sep. 9 Edmund son to Edmond & Sarah Rowley bapt.
Sep. 22 Elizabeth Mayes bur.
Oct. 1 William son to William & Frances Ince bur.
Oct. 16 Thomas son to Daniell & Mary Edwards bapt.
Oct. 19 William son to Richard & Mary Chiverton bapt.
Oct. 20 Ann dau. to Samuell & Joane Ledginham bapt.
Oct. 23 Walter son to Francis & Elizabeth How bur.
Nov. 18 Elizabeth dau. to Richard & Rebecca Smith bur.
Nov. 27 Richard son to Roger & Ann Hunt bapt.
Dec. 24 Edward son to Edward & Alice Peachy bapt.
Dec. 25 Mary dau. to Richard & Rebecca Smith bapt.
Dec. 27 [*blank*] wife to Nicholas Jackson bur.
Dec. 30 Richard Broome bur.
Jan. 13 Francis son to George & Elizabeth Palmer bur.
Jan. 13 Hannah dau. to Samuell & Hannah Pole bapt.
Feb. 6 Michael Clerke bur.
Feb. 13 Mrs Salter bur.
Feb. 15 Judith dau. to John & Alice Layston bapt.
Mar. 4 Richard son to Thomas & Joane Clerke bapt.
Mar. 15 Rebecca Gardiner bur.
Mar. 17 William Ryley bur.
Mar. 18 Rachell dau. to Henry & Elizabeth Barton bur.

1656.

Mar. 28 John son to Richard & Ann Wilford bapt.
April 5 Thomas son to John & Alice Layston bur.
April 21 William Remnant bur.
April 29 Marcellis son to John & Mary Dent bur.
May 26 Frances wife to William Ince bur.
June 2 Deborah dau. to John & Alice Clutterbuck bapt.
June 12 Susanna Leader bur.
June 13 Elizabeth dau. to John & Mary White bapt.
June 21 John son to Abraham & Mary Otger born & bapt.
June 22 Elizabeth dau. to Thomas & Susanna Whittaker bapt.
June 28 Charles son to Robert & Mary Whitechurch bapt.
July 2 Elizabeth Banbury bur.
July 18 Elizabeth dau. to Edward & Frances Edmonds bapt.
July 23 Mary dau. to Francis & Mary Bickley bur.
Sep. 11 Margarett dau. to John & Mary Shipside bapt.
Sep. 22 John Bryan bur., from Mr Hall's
Sep. 25 Mathew son to John & Abigaile Randall bur.
Oct. 1 Margarett dau. to John & Mary Shipside bur.
Oct. 8 Mary dau. to Thomas & Elizabeth Boothby bur.
Oct. 11 Mary dau. to John & Mary Dent bapt.
Oct. 16 Easter dau. to William & Susanna Whittaker bapt.
Oct. 24 Thomas son to Edmond & Sarah Rowley bapt.
Oct. 30 An infant son to John & Sarah Rogers bur.
Nov. 25 Isaack son to John Butts bapt.

Nov. 27 Susanna wife to William Whittle bur.
Dec. 1 Isaack son to John Butts bur.
Dec. 12 [*blank*] son to Samuell & Katharin Remnaut bur.
Dec. 30 An infant found dead in the church bur.
Jan. 13 Peter son to Peter & Ann Lilly bapt.
Jan. 25 Ralph son to Samuell & Joane Ledginham bur.
Mar. 14 Sarah dau. to Thomas & Elizabeth Malyn bapt.
Mar. 17 Susanna wife to George Vaughan bur.
Mar. 21 Mary dau. to Alexander & Mary Sharpe bapt.

1657.

May 10 John son to W^m^ & Jane Raven bur.
May 13 Thomas Lygon bur.
May 26 Daro Katherina dau. to John Dury bapt.
June 6 Margarett Harrison bur.
June 18 Easter dau. to Wm Whittle bur.
June 22 Elizabeth dau. to Thomas & Susanna Whittaker bapt.
July 7 Rebecca wife to Richard Smyth bur.
July 15 Samuell son to John & Alice Clutterbuck bapt.
July 28 Amy dau. to Francis & Mary Bickley bur.
Aug. 5 Jane dau. to George & Mary Webb bur.
Sep. 4 Robert Martin bur.
Sep. 25 Ann dau. to Robert & Margarett Sanderson bapt.
Sep. 31 Sarah dau. to William & Martha Turner bapt.
Oct. 1 Robert Whitechurch bur.
Oct. 3 Nicholas son to Mr Morse bapt.
Oct. 6 Jane dau. to Samuell & Joane Ledgingham bapt.
Nov. 8 Christian dau. to William & Jane Raven bapt.
Nov. 8 Henry son to Henry & Judith Eden bapt.
Nov. 19 Samuell Offspringe bur.
Dec. 4 Ann Stonn bur.
Dec. 9 Francis son to George & Elizabeth Palmer bapt.
Jan. 4 William Roberts & Elizabeth Denner marr.
Jan. 5 Francis Decker & Sarah Crickett marr.
Jan. 5 Martha Rogers bur.
Jan. 7 Francis son to George & Elizabeth Palmer bur.
Jan. 9 William Taylor bur.
Jan. 22 An infant dau. to Charles & Mary Herbert bur.
Jan. 29 Jeremiah Deane bur.
Jan. 30 Thomas Addams, gentleman, bur.
Jan. 31 Isaac son to Abraham & Mary Otger, born 31 Jan. & bapt. 16 Feb.
Feb. 18 Margarett Leigh bur.
Feb. 21 Sarah dau. to Alexander Sharp bapt.

1658.

April 22 John son to Benjamin & Elizabeth Albin bapt.
April 24 Katharin Walker bur.
April 29 Mary wife to Alexander Sharpe bur.
May 4 Thomas son to Thomas & Susanna Whittaker bapt.
May 4 William Chambers bur.
May 6 Nathaniell Box & Mary Mayo marr.
May 21 John son to John & Mary Parrey, born 21 May, bapt. 3 June
May 22 William Foster & Lettice Beadle marr.
June 8 Elizabeth dau. to Francis & Mary Bickley bur.
June 10 . . . . dau. to Thomas & Susanna Whittaker bur.
June 11 An abortive son to Mathew & Martha Mereton bur.

June 16 John Linn bur.
June 20 Humphry Felstia & Ann Welsh marr.
June 27 Abell son to Abell & Mary Ould bapt.
July 2 Thomas Crouch bur.
July 6 Henry son to Henry & Judith Eden bur.
July 9 Alice Antilbey bur.
July 12 Jane dau. to Samuell & Joane Ledginham bur.
July 16 Susanna Sands bur.
July 21 John son to William & Rebecca Antilby born
Aug. 14 Sarah dau. to Edward & Frances Edmonds bapt.
Aug. 25 Isaac son to Abraham & Mary Otger bur.
Sep. 8 Sarah dau. to John & Sarah Rogers bapt.
Sep. 10 Daniell son to M[r] Morse bapt.
Sep. 23 Margarett Sanderson bur.
Sep. 27 A chrisom dau. to Edward & Alice Peachy bur.
Sep. 28 Josuah son to John & Mary White bapt.
Sep. 30 Edward Antholyn, a foundling, bapt.
Oct. 5 Thomas son to John & Mary Dent bur.
Oct. 10 Joseph son to Thomas & Joane Clerke bapt.
Oct. 23 Richard Hall bur.
Oct. 26 Mary wife to John Dent bur.
Nov. 3 Elias son to John & Mary Thompson bapt.
Nov. 22 An infant son to George Webb bur.
Dec. 15 John son to John & Mary Parrey bur.
Feb. 9 Daniell Reeve bur.
Mar. 5 Thomas Cooper bur.
Mar. 6 Richard son to Edmond & Sarah Rowley bapt.
Mar. 8 Susanna wife to Nicholas Beale bur.

1659.

Mar. 30 Francis Lyon bur.
April 30 John son to William & Rebecca Antilby bur.
May 4 Joseph son to Richard & Ann Wilford bapt.
May 7 Elizabeth dau. to John & Elizabeth Alexander bapt.
May 28 A chrisome son to Mathew & Martha Mereton bur.
June 2 Mathew Palmer bur.
June 3 John Lylley bur.
June 9 Sarah Antholyn, a foundling, bapt.
June 9 William Whittle bur.
July 2 Sarah Turner bur.
July 13 Alice Healy bur.
July 28 Robert Boothby bur.
Aug. 2 Isaac son to George Mayo bur.
Aug. 16 Mary Parrey bur.
Aug. 16 A foundling female bur.
Aug. 27 Mathew Geerey, serv[t] to M[r] Benjamin Davis, bur.
Aug. 27 Benjamin son to Benjamin & Lucretia Davis bapt.
Sep. 3 Thomas son to Thomas & Elizabeth Rawlinson bapt.
Sep. 16 Samuell son to Samuell & Katharin Remnant bapt.
Sep. 17 William Thatcher bur.
Sep. 23 Robert Jones bur.
Oct. 6 Richard Deane & Mary Franklin marr.
Oct. 14 Peter Wainwright bur.
Oct. 16 John son to John & Sarah Rogers bapt.
Oct. 30 Elizabeth dau. to Thomas & Joane Clerke bapt.
Nov. 2 Edward son to Doctor John Betts bapt.
Nov. 6 Elizabeth Clerke bur.
Nov. 11 George son to Samuell & Joane Ledgingham bapt.

Nov. 15 M[r] Beale's child buried, from Hackney
Nov. 15 Rachell Davis bur.
Nov. 17 Ann dau. to Lancelott & Mary Granger bapt.
Nov. 30 John son to Thomas & Susanna Whittaker bapt.
Dec. 22 Joseph Surbutt & Mary Craston marr.
Dec. 27 Thomas Higgs & Judith Smyth marr.
Dec. 27 John Dixson & Katharin Guppy marr.
Jan. 4 Hans Jacob Verpoorven bur.
Jan. 12 Martha Rawlins bur.
Jan. 13 Isaac Legay bur.
Feb. 22 John son to Stephen & Elizabeth Cosford bapt.
Feb. 27 John Mathewes & Mary Walker marr.
Feb. 28 An abortive son to Mathew Mereton bur.
Mar. 9 M[r] [*blank*] Rawlins bur.
Mar. 10 Elizabeth Legay bur.
Mar. 13 Charles Offspringe, Rector of S[t] Antholyn's, bur.
Mar. 22 James Antholyn, a foundling, bapt.

1660.

April 3 Elizabeth dau. to Abraham Otger bapt.
April 3 Mary dau. to Richard & Ann Smyth bapt.
April 9 William Hall & Phœbe Allcock marr.
April 9 Francis Mills & Elizabeth Pledger marr.
April 25 Thomas son to John & Elizabeth Dent bapt.
April 25 Elias son to Elias Pledger bur.
April 25 Susanna Burrage bur.
June 4 Joane Healy bur.
June 10 James son to James & Mary Thompson bapt.
June 15 Elizabeth Griffith bur.
July 24 A chrisom dau. to George & Elizabeth Webb bur.
Aug. 3 Sarah dau. to John Butts bapt.
Aug. 7 Sarah Butts bur.
Aug. 12 Thomas Dent bur.
Aug. 15 Susan dau. to Peter & Isabella Soone bapt.
Aug. 16 Andrew Marlo & Martha Gullom marr.
Sep. 4 Henry Browne bur.
Sep. 4 Nicholas Beale bur.
Sep. 14 John Forman bur.
Sep. 17 Philip son to John & Mary Parrey bapt.
Sep. 27 Leonard son to Leonard & Elizabeth Bower bapt.
Sep. 28 Samuell son to Samuell & Ruth Salter bapt.
Oct. 9 William son to Edward & Alice Peachy bapt.
Oct. 28 Jane dau. to Alexander & Jane Sharp bapt.
Oct. 28 Rebecca dau. to Edward Edmonds bapt.
Oct. 28 Sarah dau. to John & Alice Clutterbuck bapt.
Nov. 12 Mary Antholyn, a foundling, bapt.
Dec. 4 Amy Eford bur.
Dec. 22 Rachell Antholyn, a foundling, bapt.
Dec. 23 Daniell son to Thomas & Joane Clerke bapt.
Jan. 1 Richard Cale & Mary Hawkins marr.
Jan. 24 William Cooper & Elizabeth Stratfeild marr.
Feb. 8 Jane wife to Edward Mosse bur.
Feb. 24 Hannah dau. to Samuell & Hannah Pole bapt.
Feb. 26 William Styles & Hannah Pensonn marr.
Mar. 5 Sarah dau. to Edmond & Sarah Rowley bapt.
Mar. 10 Elizabeth dau. to Peter & Ann Lilly bapt.
Mar. 23 Elizabeth dau. to Benjamin & Lucretia Davis bapt.

1661.

April 1 James son to James & Mary Town bapt.
April 4 Samuell son to William & Rebecca Antilby bapt.
April 16 Anthony Winter & Elizabeth Jollett marr.
April 18 John Feilder & Jane Mynsterne marr.
April 24 Samuell son to Richard & Ann Wilford bapt.
April 24 Jethro Chelsham bur.
April 30 Ann dau. to Nicholas & Ann Jackson bapt.
April 30 John son to Mr John Betts bapt.
May 8 Thomas Woodward bur.
May 9 Robert son to John & Alice Green bapt.
June 3 Thomas Whittaker bur.
June 15 A crisome son to Capt. Beale bur.
June 16 Sarah Dent bur.
June 19 John Betts bur.
July 7 James Thompson bur.
July 12 Nathaniell Knipe bur.
July 12 A maid from Mrs Woodward's bur.
July 14 [*blank*] wife to Herbert bur.
July 26 John Whittaker bur.
July 30 Thomas Osborne & Julian Taylor marr.
Aug. 1 A stillborn son to Mr Pratt bur.
Aug. 11 Thomas Sherloe & Elizabeth Smyth marr.
Aug. 15 Rachell Pott bur.
Aug. 20 Sr Thomas Boothby bur.
Aug. 24 Francis Mormay bur.
Aug. 29 Edward Damaske & Dorothy Dent marr.
Aug. 30 Elizabeth wife to Anthony Daffie bur.
Sep. 3 Ann dau. to John & Elizabeth Alexander bapt.
Oct. 3 Thomas son to John Dent bapt.
Oct. 11 Siceley dau. to Edward & Elizabeth Cox bapt.
Oct. 25 Henry Eden bur.
Nov. 6 Urian Oake bur.
Nov. 13 Jane Sharpe bur.
Nov. 14 Thomas son to John & Alice Clutterbuck bapt.
Nov. 25 Alice dau. to Edward & Alice Peachy bapt.
Dec. 4 Thomas Clutterbuck bur.
Dec. 10 William Peachy bur.
Dec. 12 Thomas Hall bur.
Dec. 15 Mary dau. to Lancelott Granger bapt.
Dec. 22 Elias Thompson bur.
Dec. 26 A stillborn son of John Rogers bur.
Jan. 1 Anthonie Daffie & Ellin Harwood marr.
Jan. 15 Richard Gore & Jane Broome marr.
Jan. 15 Sarah wife to John Rogers bur.
Jan. 17 [*blank*] son to Richard Wilford bur.
Jan. 20 Mary dau. to John & Jane Gowner bapt.
Feb. 6 Edward Parrey & Ann Phitts marr.
Feb. 17 Mary dau. to Samuell Salter bapt.
Mar. 1 Ann Ling bur.
Mar. 9 Joanna dau. to Thomas & Joanna Clerke bapt.
Mar. 10 Elizabeth dau. to Francis & Elizabeth Thursfield bapt.

1662.

Mar. 30 Richard Richstonn & Mary Locker marr.
April 15 Henry Knight & Mary Bishop marr.

April 16 Richard Swanston & Katherin Raven marr.
April 16 John Johnson bur.
April 18 George Stubbs bur.
April 18 James Deane bur.
April 28 John Kent bur.
May 6 Nicholas son to Nicholas & Ann Jackson bapt.
May 8 Thomas Shettereon & Elizabeth Plummer marr.
May 22 Thomas son to Leonard & Elizabeth Bower bapt.
May 30 Frances dau. to John & Frances Butts bapt.
June 8 Mary dau. to Francis & Mary Coppinger bapt.
June 15 Mary dau. to James & Mary Thompson bapt.
June 19 Susanna wife to Richard Anderson bur.
July 14 Leonard Shittleworth & Frances Houlton marr.
July 15 Rachell dau. to Thomas Whittaker bapt.
July 17 Elizabeth dau. to John & Dorothy Betts bapt.
July 19 Ann Levesley bur.
July 22 Peter Whaley & Elizabeth Fitzwilliams marr.
July 30 Caleb Graver & Mary Linder marr.
Aug. 6 John Meakins & Ann Hilliard marr.
Aug. 19 Thomas Malyn & Elizabeth Merywether marr.
Aug. 21 Richard son to Arthur & Ann Bettsworth bapt.
Aug. 24 Robert son to Alexander & Jane Sharpe bapt.
Aug. 26 Robert son to Alexander Sharpe bur.
Sep. 9 [*blank*] wife to Abraham Otger bur.
Sep. 23 John Read & Mary Collins marr.
Sep. 26 Thomas Shipton bur.
Sep. 28 Joane, servt to Mr Inch, bur.
Oct. 7 Rebecca dau. to George & Rebecca Mander bapt.
Oct. 8 Charles Herbert bur.
Oct. 16 Lawrence Powell bur.
Oct. 24 John Cross & Abigaile Benge marr.
Oct. 27 Joseph Chamberlin & Sarah Clerke marr.
Nov. 4 Thomas Throughton bur.
Nov. 5 Robert Coulsom & Mary Perrey marr.
Nov. 6 Jane Townesend bur.
Nov. 7 Joseph son to Anthony & Hellen Daffie bapt.
Nov. 23 Jeremiah son to Richard & Ann Willford bapt.
Nov. 23 Lucretia dau. to Benjamin & Lucretia Davis bapt.
Nov. 25 A stillborn dau. to Mr Pratt bur.
Nov. 26 Richard Neave & Avery Mason marr.
Dec. 4 John Kellick & Isabell Couell marr.
Dec. 9 Mary Hawkins bur.
Dec. 12 John son to John & Alice Clutterbuck bapt.
Dec. 15 Richard Buckley bur.
Dec. 15 Mary Hart bur.
Dec. 19 Mary dau. to Edmond & Sarah Rowley bapt.
Dec. 19 Frances dau. to Francis Win bapt.
Jan. 13 Thomas Ward & Sarah Surrey marr.
Jan. 22 William Pusey & Mary Goode marr.
Jan. 28 Elizabeth Wetherall bur.
Feb. 1 Joseph son of Anthony & Helin Daffie bur.
Feb. 10 Mathew [*blank*] & Joane [*blank*] marr.
Feb. 14 A stillborn son to Edward Peachy bur.
Mar. 1 William son to Joseph & Elizabeth Cleeve bapt.
Mar. 18 Rebecca wife to George Mander bur.
Mar. 20 Elizabeth dau. to John & Elizabeth Wright bapt.

1663.

April 19 Thomas Lawrence & Elinor Spycer marr.
May 6 Robert son to Roger & Katharine Arkingstal bur.
May 6 Elias son of George & Mary Webb bapt.
May 6 Hannah dau. to Leonard & Elizabeth Bowers bapt.
June .. Frances & Priscilla daus. to Anthony & Priscilla Sadler bapt.
June .. Frances & Priscilla daus. to Anthony & Priscilla Sadler bur.
July 1 Thomas Houghton & Hannah Walford marr.
Aug. 2 John son of Mathias & Margaret Child bapt.
Aug. 16 Mary dau. of Stephen & Elizabeth Cosford bapt.
Aug. 20 William son of John & Abigall Randoll bapt.
Aug. 22 Dorothie dau. of D[r] John & Dorothie Betts bapt.
Sep. 13 Abraham son of Abraham & Mary Williams bapt.
Sep. 14 Mary dau. of Lancelot & Mary Granger bur.
Sep. 18 John son of John & Elizabeth Alexander bapt.
Sep. .. Abraham son of Abraham & Mary Williams bur.
Oct. 8 Mary dau. of John & Anne [*blank*]
Oct. 9 Edward Mosse, parish clerk, bur.
Oct. 15 Susanna dau. of George & Sarah Brian bapt.
Nov. 6 Doct[r] Willis bur.
Nov. .. Nicholas son of Nicholas & Ann Jackson bur.
Nov. 9 John Gold, an Irishman, bur.
Nov. 10 Mathew son of Mathew & Mary Merriton bapt.
Nov. 13 Rachell dau. of Thomas & Susanna Whitikar bur.
Nov. 28 John son of John & Mary Parrie bapt.
Nov. 30 John son of John & Margaret Barton bapt.
Dec. 4 Elizabeth dau. of John & Jane Waters bapt.
Dec. 18 Mathew son of Mathew & Mary Merriton bur.
Dec. 21 Mary dau. of Thomas & Susanna Whitikar bapt.
Dec. 28 William son of Edward & Alice Peachie bapt.
Dec. .. William son of John & Abigall Randoll bur.
Jan. 3 Joan wife of Samuell Legingam bur.
Jan. 7 Mary dau. of Thomas & Susanna Whitikar bur.
Jan. 19 Henry son of Charles & Martha Richards bapt.
Jan. 31 Sarah dau. of Lancelot & Mary Granger bapt.
Feb. 4 Elizabeth wife of Henry Barton bur.
Feb. 14 Sarah dau. of Lancelot & Mary Granger bur.
Feb. 14 Thomas Shepheard & Jane Wilkinson marr.
Mar. .. Frances wife of Edward Edmunds bur.
Mar. 16 John son of John & Mary Parrie bur.
Mar. 19 Edward Hall bur.
Mar. 20 Roger son of Roger & Katherine Arkinstall bapt.

1664.

Mar. 25 George Antholin, a foundling, bapt.
April 24 William son of Nicholas & Ann Jackson bapt.
April .. William Beale bur.
May 19 Dorothy dau. of Doct[r] John & Dorothy Betts bur.
May 19 [*blank*] dau. of Henry Barton bur.
Aug. 5 Henry Hatley & Hester Whitaker marr.
Aug. 6 Elizabeth dau. of John & Allice Clutterbuck bapt.
Aug. 21 Richard son of Richard & Ann Pue bapt.
Aug. 25 Thomas Hutton & Susanna Webbe marr.
Aug. 30 Anthony son of Anthony & Priscilla Sadler bapt.
Oct. 5 John son of John & Sarah Richmond bapt.
Oct. 6 Daniell Midwinter & Ann King marr.

Oct. 6 Mary dau. of Mathew & Mary Merriton bapt.
Oct. 8 John son of John & Sarah Richmond bur.
Oct. 15 Susanna Chelsam bur.
Oct. 18 Elizabeth dau. of John & Abigall Randoll bapt.
Nov. 20 Paul Carre & Elizabeth Harman marr.
Nov. 24 Mary wife of Mathew Merriton bur.
Nov. 27 The Widow Dean bur.
Jan. 6 [*blank*] Cosford bur.
Jan. 22 M[rs] Hatton, of Bread Street, bur.
Jan. 27 Edward son of Edward & Alice Peachie bur.
Feb. 7 M[rs] Bland, of Fauchurch Street, bur.
Feb. 9 M[rs] Martha Stiles bur.
Feb. 11 Frederick son of Frederick & Mary Clarke bapt.
Feb. 11 Elisha son of George & Barbary Mander bapt.
Feb. 14 Mary Chapline bur.
Feb. 15 Elisha son of George & Barbara Mander bur.
Feb. 16 George son of John & Elizabeth Wright bapt.
Feb. 24 Kempton son of Lancelott & Mary Granger bapt.
Feb. 28 Kempton son of Lancelott & Mary Granger bur.
Mar. 3 Mary Hatchman bur.
Mar. 5 John son of John & Elizabeth Alexander bur.
Mar. 7 Elizabeth dau. of Henry & Sarah Tongue bapt.
Mar. 17 George Griffin bur.

1665.

April 4 Elizabeth dau. of Roger & Katherine Arkinstall bapt.
April 23 Christopher Pearson & Hannah Veares marr.
May 11 James son of John & Mary Parrie bapt.
May 15 Richard son of Thomas & Susanna Whitiker bapt.
May 16 Thomas Heyt & Susanna Bishopp marr.
May 21 William Ince bur.
May 31 Richard son of Thomas & Susanna Whitiker bur.
June 16 Sarah Rogers bur.
July 5 [*blank*] Budd bur.
Aug. 12 Annah Dancer bur.
Aug. 22 Elizabeth Whittaker bur.
Aug. 22 Elizabeth dau. of Francis & Elizabeth Thursfeild bapt.
Aug. 25 Palina Simpson bur.
Aug. 26 Samuel Ledgeinham bur.
Aug. 27 Thomasen Collins bur.
Aug. 29 Sarah Ledgeinham bur.
Aug. 30 Bridgett [*blank*], M[r] Remnant's maid, bur.
Sep. 1 Sarah Pew bur.
Sep. 2 Violett Mormay bur.
Sep. 2 Ann Pew bur.
Sep. 3 Mary Ward bur.
Sep. 4 John Catford bur.
Sep. 4 George Thornley, doct[r], bur.
Sep. 4 Richard Pew bur.
Sep. 4 William Yerberrey bur.
Sep. 5 Mary Ledgeinham bur.
Sep. 13 Frederick Clerke bur.
Sep. 14 George Skuglome bur.
Sep. 14 Thomas Parrett bur.
Sep. 16 Thomas Rowley bur.
Sep. 16 Elizabeth Cox bur.
Sep. 17 Edward Cox bur.

Sep. 19 Elizabeth Perkins bur.
Sep. 19 Ciseley Cox bur.
Sep. 19 Elizabeth Rowley bur.
Sep. 20 Jone Wheeler bur.
Sep. 21 Lyddia Perkins bur.
Sep. 23 Elizabeth wife to Francis Thursfeild bur.
Sep. 23 Francis Bickley bur.
Sep. 25 John Dent bur.
Sep. 27 Jone Oakes bur.
Sep. 28 Sarah Rowley bur.
Sep. 29 William Jackson bur.
Sep. 30 Rebecca Good bur.
Sep. 30 [*blank*] Budd bur.
Oct. 1 Elias Webb bur.
Oct. 2 Robert Hudson, churchwarden, bur.
Oct. 2 Francis son of Francis & Mary Coppinger bapt.
Oct. 7 [*blank*] Vigor bur.
Oct. 13 Ann Price bur.
Oct. 15 John Bulkhole, a Dutchman, bur.
Oct. 18 [*blank*] Budd bur.
Nov. 13 Dorothy dau. of Benjamin & Lucretia Davis bapt.
Nov. 21 Elizabeth How bur.
Dec. 27 Stephen Lock & Ann Cash marr.
Jan. .. Thomas son of Anthony & Hellen Daffye bapt.
Feb. 21 Charles Herbert & Jone Smith marr.
Mar. 13 Lawrence Dread & Margarett Trumper marr.
Mar. 15 Francis Selwood bur.

1666.

April 17 Hannah Pepitt bur.
May 15 William Palmer & Ann Parsons marr.
May 31 James Tompson bur.
June 5 Penellope Antholins bapt.
June 6 Barbarie Woodard bur.
June 14 Abigall dau. of Henry & Sarah Tongue bapt.
June 17 James son of James & Jane Ward bapt.
June 17 John son of Edward & Alice Peachy bapt.
June 18 James Ward bur.
June 21 Samuell Amy & Mary Ingram marr.
June 23 John Oldershaw, M[r] Webb's man, bur.
June 25 Elizabeth Margritts bur.
June 25 Richard Barton bur.
July 6 John son to Richard & Abigaile Mynty bapt.
July 6 Ann dau. to John & Dorothy Betts bapt.
July 7 Barbery Maunder bur.
July 12 Thomas son to Roger & Katherine Arkingstall bapt.
July 22 Winnifry Pew bur.
July 25 Thomas Arkingstall bur.
Aug. 19 Robert Hobbs & Mary Best marr.
Aug. 23 John Sturt & Katharin Williams marr.
Aug. 30 Franses son of Ralph & Sarah Barkor bapt.

THO. SHERMAN, Rector.
JOHN CLUTTERBUCK, Churchwarden.

[*No entries in* 1667.]

1668.

Jan. 4 Mary dau. to Rich. & Ann Willford bapt.
Jan. 6 Mary dau. of Stephen & Elizebeth Cosford bapt.

1669.

Mar. 26 Benjamin son of Peter & Mary Houblune bapt.

1670.

May 15 Sary dau. of Edmund & Sary Rowley bapt.
June 9 Leddia Ryder bur.
Oct. 17 Mr Wilson's child bur.
Oct. 19 Gorge Hoddelow bur.
Oct. 21 Mr John Parrey bur.
Oct. 21 Margrett Fleetwood bur.
Nov. 5 Mary dau. of Richd & Sary Edmonds bapt.
Nov. 15 Mr Webb bur.
Jan. 26 Mr Addams bur.
Feb. 12 Elesibeth dau. of Stephen & Elesibeth Cosford bapt.
Feb. 20 An abortive son of Mr John Randoll bur.
Mar. 6 Mary Chelsam bur.
Mar. 12 Michall son of David Burden bapt.

1671.

April 9 Thomas son of Humprey & Barbrey Barnet bapt.
April 26 Dorkis dau. of John & Mary Parrey bapt.
May 3 Mary wife of Coll. Thomas Neull bur.
May 16 Dorothie dau. of Mr Hoddelo bur.
May 25 A child of Mr Thomas Byfield's bur.
June 4 Elizabeth dau. of William & Susanna Small, born 24 May
June 21 Tryphena dau. of Fras & Mary Hill bapt.
June 29 Michall son of David Burden bur.
July 2 Nathanell Hobson, servt to Mr Tayler, bur.
July 5 Nathanell son to Richard & Ann Willford, born 22 June
July 8 Tryphina dau. of Fras & Mary Hill bur.
July 22 Mary wife of Abraham Williams bur.
Aug. 29 Elizabeth wife of Joseph Trayte bur.
Sep. 21 Thomas son of Richard & Hannah Roberts bapt.
Sep. 30 Hanna dau. of William & Rebeck Barrett bapt.
Oct. 3 Edward son of Edward & Alice Peachy bur.
Oct. 24 Mary wife of John Eburne bur.
Oct. 26 Elizabeth Goodrig bur.
Nov. 5 Thomas son of Richard & Hannah Roberts bur.
Nov. 26 Sary dau. of John Ebourne bur.
Dec. 17 Antholing Stone, a foundling, bapt.
Dec. 17 An abortive son of Robert Glover bur.
Jan. 21 John son of Nicholas & Ann Bell bapt.
Jan. 22 Elizabeth dau. of Willam & Susann Smalle bur.
Feb. 4 Frances Mormy bur.
Feb. 15 Thomas Bruimfeild, Esqr, bur.
Feb. 27 Gorge Mayo, Esqr, bur.
Mar. 24 Roase Beale bur.

1672.

May 14 Mary dau. of Richard & Sary Edmonds bur.
May 31 John son of James & Hannah Lecuse bur.
June 14 An abortive son of Richard Roberts bur.

July 12 A child of Mr Thomas Byfield's bur.
July 14 Sary Antholings, a foundling, bapt.
July 23 Thomas son of Edward & Alice Peachy bur.
July 27 Sary Antholing, a foundling, bur.
Aug. 28 A son of Mr Barker bur.
Sep. 29 Joseph son of Henry & Elezebeath Willson bapt.
Oct. 7 Edward Bridges, serv^t to Mr Rute, bur.
Oct. 23 Mary dau. of Thomas & Martha Haselwood bur.
Nov. 5 Tryphena dau. of Gorge & Tryphena Widdowes bapt.
Nov. 12 Ann dau. of Richard & Ann Willford bapt.
Dec. 3 A stillborn child of Mr Rowley's, the clark, bur.
Dec. 10 Gorge son of Willam & Susanna Small bapt.
Dec. 19 Joane Antholing bur.
Dec. 26 Elezebeth dau. of John & Elezabeth Till bapt.
Jan. 9 Elezebeth dau. of Ralph & Martha Harwood bapt.
Jan. 27 A son of Dr Torlise's bur.
Jan. 28 Francis son of John Beanes bapt.
Jan. 30 Joseph son of Joseph Seers bur.
Feb. 4 Sary dau. of Richard & Sary Edmonds bapt.

1673.

April 23 John Hollis bur.
April 24 A child from Mr Small's bur.
April 29 Ann dau. of Humprey Barnet bapt.
May 21 Sary dau. of Peter & Elezebeth Hublune bur.
May 27 Abigall wife of Mr William Gostling bur.
June 1 A dau. of Mr Willson's bur.
June 14 Joane Tower, a foundling, bapt.
July 29 An abortive son of Richard Robets bur.
Aug. 4 A chrisome child of Mr Eden's bur.
Aug. 14 Elizabeth dau. of John & Elizabeth Adams born & bapt.
Aug. 23 M^rs [*blank*], from Mr Chase's, bur.
Aug. 24 A dau. of Mr Till's bur.
Aug. 24 Wm Horne & Ann Marriott marr.
Sep. 4 Francis son of Francis & Mary Hill born & bapt.
Sep. 11 John son of John & Sary Vernon, born 2 Sep., bapt. 11 Sep.
Sep. 13 Jone Temple, from Mr Seers', bur.
Sep. 18 John son of John & Sary Vernon bur.
Sep. 18 Francis son of Francis & Mary Hill bur.
Oct. 26 Ann Cooper, from Mr Harwood's, bur.
Oct. 26 Gorge son of Mr Gorge Warde bapt.
Nov. 21 William son of Mr William Gostling bur., from Paternoster Row
Nov. 26 John son of John & Mary Tayler bapt.
Dec. 15 Thomas Claton, serv^t to Mr Admas, bur.
Feb. 1 Gorge son of Mr Gorge Ward bur.
Feb. 4 W^m son of Richard & Mary Torlese bapt.
Feb. 19 Elizebeth dau. of Edmond & Sary Rowley bapt.
Mar. 2 Mrs Elezebeth Pamplin bur.
Mar. 14 Susanna dau. of W^m & Rebecca Barret bapt.
Mar. 18 Elizebeth dau. of Joseph & Elizebeth Hill bapt.
Mar. 23 Mark Lambath, foundling, bur.

1674.

Mar. 26 Mrs Flackett bur.
April 22 A child of Mr Eburne's bur.
May 13 Willam son of Willam & Martha Runiell bapt.

June 24 Mr John Otger bur.
July 4 Wm Rallinge, servt to Mr Wilford, bur.
July 10 Elezabeth dau. of Rich. & [*blank*] Chase bapt.
July 16 Mary dau. of John & Hester Raley bapt.
July 18 Elezebeth dau. of Richard Chase bur.
July 28 Margrett & Sary daus. of Tho. & Sary Raymond bapt.
Aug. 4 Edward Kittitt & Anne Bell marr. by lic.
Aug. 5 Gorge son of Mr John Mayo bur.
Aug. 9 Willam son of Timothy & Elenor Chelton bapt.
Aug. 14 John son of Mr John Ince bur.
Aug. 28 Thomas son of Willam & Ann Cox bapt.
Sep. 2 John son of Sampson & Elisabeth Ellicott bapt.
Sep. 4 Mr John Mayo bur. by night
Oct. 11 Mary dau. of Willam & Susanna Small bapt.
Oct. 18 Hanna dau. of John & Elezebeth Till bur.
Oct. 18 Mr [*blank*] Penney bur.
Oct. 18 John 2d son of John & Sary Vernon born at 8 in the morning
Oct. 19 Margret dau. of Mr Pestill bapt.
Oct. 22 Ralph son of Ralph & Martha Harwood bapt.
Oct. 22 Thomas son of Mathew & Elizebeth Raper bapt.
Oct. 28 Elizabeth dau. of Mrs Syers bur. in the new churchyard
Nov. 27 A dau. of Mr Rowse's bur.
Dec. 6 Margrett dau. of Mr Pestell bur.
Dec. 11 Francis son of Mr Gorge Widdowes bur.
Dec. 24 Ann dau. of Stephen & Elizebeth Cosford bapt.
Dec. 26 Benjamyn son of Peter & Mary Hublon bur.
Jan. 4 Mr John Portter bur.
Jan. 19 Capt. Hublon's man bur.
Jan. 24 A dau. of Mr Croney's bur.
Feb. 14 Robertt Preston bur. in the new churchyard
Mar. 17 Mrs Mary Deuew bur.
Mar. 21 Anne dau. of John & Hester Beaues bapt.
Mar. 23 John son of Richard & Sary Edmonds bapt.

1675.

April 29 Mrs Sarah Hawkins bur.
May 1 A son of Mr Syers bur. in new churchyard
May 22 Mr Turner, from Mrs Barner's, bur.
May 27 Mr Barnett bur.
July 6 Robert son of Robert & Elizabeth Preston bapt.
July 21 Elizabeth dau. of Peter & Elizabeth Knowles bapt.
Aug. 6 A child of Dr Torlese bur.
Aug. 9 Mary dau. of Thomas & Mary Rouse bapt.
Aug. 26 Benjamyn Woodrofe, servt to Mr Tayler, bur.
Aug. 29 John Sharp, servt to Mr Eburne, bur.
Sep. 2 A child of Mr Tayler's bur.
Sep. 9 Joseph Marshall, servt to Mr Hotchkis, bur.
Sep. 23 Ceaser son of George & Lucyana Ward bapt.
Sep. 23 James son of Mr Willam Tompson bur.
Sep. 28 Tryphosa Widdowes dau. of Geo. & Tryphena Widdowes bapt., born 11 Sep.
Oct. 19 Paule son of Thomas & Ann Humphreys bapt.
Oct. 21 Paule son of Thomas & Ann Humphreys bur.
Nov. 5 Mrs Hollis bur.
Nov. 11 [*blank*], Mr Dafforne's man, bur.
Nov. 17 Mrs Abigall Hodilow bur.
Nov. 17 Mrs Elizabeth Beale bur.

Jan. 22 Richard son of Francis & Mary Hill bur.
Jan. 24 Humphrey son of Humphrey & [*blank*] Eddy bapt.
Feb. 13 Perregrine son of Theoph. & Sary Raymont bapt.
Feb. 22 Willam son of Tho. & Elizabeth Hastings bapt.
Mar. 16 Thomas son of Sam. & Elizabeth Woodward bapt.
Mar. 22 A child of Mr Syers bur.

1676.

April 6 John Hackshaw & Amabela Harvey marr.
April 26 Elizabeth wife of Mr Samuel Syers bur. in new churchyard
April 26 Dorothy dau. of W^m^ & Ann Cox bapt.
May 9 A dau. of Mr Hall's bur.
May 10 Mrs Elizabeth Davis bur.
May 16 Daniel Fromautle & Joanna Bonnor marr. at ye Tabernacle of St John Baptist
May 18 Mr John Crose & Mrs Elizabeth Blaukson marr. at ye Tabernacle of St John Baptist
May 18 Peter son of John & Sary Vernon born
May 18 W^m^ son of John & Sary Vernon born
May 19 A dau. of Mr Rande's bapt.
May 30 A dau. of Mr Rande's bur.
June 2 John son of John & Sary Vernon bur.
June 2 Mr Elias Pledger bur.
June 28 Stephen Keyes, a foundling, bapt.
July 5 Thomas son of Mathew & Elizabeth Rapper bur.
July 5 Stephen Keyes, a foundling, bur.
July 12 A dau. of Mr Wilford's bur.
July 29 A dau. of Mr Adams bur.
Aug. 1 John son of John & Elizabeth Adams bapt.
Aug. 2 Mr Richard Wilford bur. at Walten
Aug. 17 W^m^ son of W^m^ & Kathrine Tayler bapt.
Aug. 31 Inggrom Dafforne bur.
Sep. 13 Ann dau. of Daniell & Ann Chandler bapt.
Oct. 5 John Randoll, Esq., bur.
Oct. 6 Elizabeth wife of John Till bur.
Oct. 27 Mr Henry Barker bur.
Dec. 13 Francis son of John & Susanna Shepard bapt.
Dec. 15 Francis son of John & Susanna Shepard bur.
Dec. 25 Ann Morney bur.
Jan. 6 Samuell son of W^m^ & Susanna Small bapt.
Jan. 10 Lettis dau. of Petter & Elizabeth Knowels bapt.
Jan. 27 John son of John & Elizabeth Adams bur.
Mar. 1 Charles son of Tobias & Ann Humphereys bapt.
Mar. 2 Sampson son of Sampson & Elizabeth Ellicot bapt.
Mar. 7 George son of Samuell & Constance Hatton bapt.

1677.

Mar. 30 A stillborn child of Mr Cuffler's bur.
April 2 Mr Conyer's man bur.
April 11 John son of Ralph & Martha Harwood bapt.
April 12 John son of Ralph & Martha Harwood bur.
May 28 Martha dau. of Henry & Hannah Goold bapt.
June 15 Lettis dau. of Petter & Elizabeth Knowles bur.
June 17 John son of Lewes & Elizabeth Mordant bapt.
June 21 Mrs Amey bur.
July 5 Thomas son of Samuell & Sarah Fowler bapt.

July 11* Thomas son of Thomas & Mary Rouse bapt.
Aug. 5 Mrs Chelton bur.
Aug. 9 Mr Benjamyn Davis bur.
Aug. 12 Mary dau. of John & Mary Smith bapt.
Aug. 16 Isabella Billinton bur.
Aug. 21 Thomas son of Thomas & Mary Rouse bur.
Aug. 26 Mary dau. of John & Mary Smith bur.
Sep. 5 A child of Dr Torlesse bur.
Sep. 11 Elizabeth dau. of John & Elizabeth Adams bapt.
Sep. 22 Elenor Abbott, Mr Jurion's maid, bur.
Sep. 25 Richard son of Mr John Eburne bur.
Oct. 1 Joseph son of Henry & Elizabeth Wilson bur.
Oct. 9 Robt son of James & Elizabeth Hibbletweite bapt.
Oct. 12 Robt son of James & Elizabeth Hibbletweite bur.
Oct. 21 Thomas son of John & Susanna Stanton bapt.
Oct. 23 Sary dau. of Stephen & Elizabeth Cosford bapt.
Oct. 29 An abortive child of Mr Tayler's bur.
Nov. 26 Mr Eburn's wife bur.
Dec. 9 George son of Humpherey Eddy bapt.
Dec. 11 Mrs Hatton bur.
Dec. 15 Mary Wentworth bur.
Dec. .. John Mordaunt bur.
Jan. 21 Elizabeth dau. of Tobias & Ann Humpherys bapt.
Jan. 22 Richard son of Thomas & Elizabeth Hastings bapt.
Feb. 6 Benjamyn Johnson bur.
Feb. 6 Elizabeth dau. of John & Elizabeth Adams bur.
Feb. 19 Edward son of Edward & Abigall Pennant bapt.
Feb. 24 Elizabeth dau. of Tobias & Ann Humpherys bur.
Mar. 11 A son of Mr Coxe's bur.
Mar. 14 Antholena Dodson, a foundling, bapt.
Mar. 14 Daniell son of Daniel & Alee Gilsmore bapt.
Mar. 16 Abigale Gosling bur.

1678.

Mar. 31 Timothy Chelton bur.
April 19 Theophilus son of Theophilus & Sary Raymont bapt.
May 7 Martha dau. of William & Martha Runiell bapt.
May 10 Hannah dau. of John & Sary Vernon born
May 17 Perregrine son of Theophilus & Sary Raymont bur.
May 17 Charles son of Wm & Susanna Small bapt.
May 19 A child of Mr Harwood's bur.
June 5 Ann dau. of Rich. & Ann Checoll bur.
July 29 Tryphose Widdowes bur.
Aug. 1 George Small bur.
Aug. 2 John Norris bur.
Aug. 17 Charles Small bur.
Aug. 17 Mary Small bur.
Aug. 18 Rose dau. of Paule & Elizabeth Peck bapt.
Aug. 20 Samuell Small bur.
Aug. 27 Thomas Seeres bur. in new churchyard
Aug. 27 Mr Edward Peachy bur.
Aug. 29 Judith dau. of John & Susanna Shepard bapt.
Sep. 5 Martha dau. of Samll & Constance Hatton bapt.
Sep. 16 Elizabeth dau. of Rich. & Sarah Edmonds bapt.
Oct. 4 Katharine Chambers bur.
Oct. 11 Martha wife of Dr Torlesse bur.

* George Thorp, Rector, signs the Register from 1677 to 1679.

Nov. 23 Tryphena wife of Mr George Widdowes bur.
Nov. 24 John son of Joseph & Christian Smith bapt.
Dec. 29 Sary dau. of Lewis & Elizabeth Mordaunt bapt.
Dec. 31 Hugh son of John & Elezabeth Adams bapt.
Jan. 12 Anthony Decosta, a foundling, bapt.
Jan. 12 John Dodson, a foundling, bapt.
Jan. 20 Mrs Johnson bur.
Jan. 21 Sarah dau. of Wm & Sarah Bowen bapt.
Feb. 10 John Antholin Dodson, a foundling, bapt.
Feb. 11 Wm son of Thomas & Mary Harwood bapt.
Feb. 25 Peter Vernon, William Vernon, & Hannah Vernon, sons & dau. of John & Sary Vernon, of St Antholin's, bapt. by me, Geo. Thorp, Rector
Mar. 16 John son of Benjamyn & Hannah Boswell bapt.
Mar. 23 Elizabeth dau. of Thomas & Elizabeth Kirton bapt.

1679.

Mar. 25 Tryphena Hill bur.
April 1 Wm son of Wm & Ann Cox bapt.
April 9 Humphery son of Humphery & [*blank*] Eddy bapt.
April 13 Mordeca Antholin, a foundling, bapt.
April 13 Mary dau. of Rob. & Elizabeth Batts bapt.
April 27 Christian dau. of Jo. Leech bur.
May 4 Samuell son of Samuel & Sarah Fowler bapt.
May 11 Elizabeth dau. of Edward & Ester Leake bapt.
May 15 Daniel Antholing, a foundling, bapt.
June 23 John son of Wm & Susanna Small bapt.
June 29 Hannah dau. of John & Hannah Parrett bapt.
July 9 Hannah dau. of John & Hannah Parrett bur.
July 30 Susanna Stanton bur.
Aug. 7 Mary wife of Mr Wm Attwell bur.
Aug. 10 John Smith bur.
Aug. 12 The Widow Airis bur.

September 1, 1679, Joshua Hotchkis, Clerk, was instituted Rector of this parish, together with St John Baptist's annext, and inducted the 3 of the same mouth.

Sep. 19* A stillborn son of Mr Robert Hill bur.
Oct. 9 John son of Thomas & Elizabeth Hastings bapt.
Oct. 30 Richard Edmonds bur.
Dec. 28 Dorothy Walker, Mr Taylor's maid, bur. in new churchyard
Dec. 30 Cheyre son of Mr John Ince bur.
Dec. 31 Lawrance son of John Chevol bapt.
Dec. 31 Mr John Carpenter bur.
Jan. 2 Lawrance son of Mr John Chevol bur.
Jan. 14 Mr William Raniell bur.
Jan. 28 Mr Richard Hotchkis, of St Mary le Bow, & Mrs Elizabeth Ward, of St Mary Abbchurch, marr.
Jan. 28 Mary dau. of John and Mary Harrison bapt.
Feb. 16 Mrs Sarah Tryst bur.
Feb. 24 John son of Mr John Ince bur.
Feb. 29 Richard son of Wm Taylor bur.
Mar. 6 Elizabeth wife of John Trist bur.

1680.

April 13 John son of John & Elizabeth Briscoe [?]

* Joshua Hotchkis, Rector, signs the Register from 1679 to 1695.

April 14 Rebeccah dau. of Willm & Martha Runiell bapt.
May 13 Isaac Antholin, a foundling, left in ye parish [?]
May 27 John son of John & Elizabeth Adams bapt.
May 28 John Eburne bur.
Aug. 10 Wm son of John Fist bur.
Aug. 24 Mr Wm Rutt bur.
Aug. 29 Thomas Stanaway bur.
Aug. 31 Mary dau. of John & Hannah Parrett bapt.
Sep. 9 Joseph son of John & Elizabeth Taylor bapt.
Sep. 11 Julius Billers bur.
Sep. 23 John Billers bur.
Oct. 5 John son of John & Elizabeth Adams bur.
Oct. 23 Mary dau. of John & Mary Harper bapt.
Nov. 13 Elizabeth dau. of Nathaniel & Margarett Sanders bapt.
Nov. 14 Jane dau. of Tho. & Elizabeth Pennack bapt.
Dec. 4 Sarah dau. of John & Sarah Chevol bapt.
Jan. 2 Jane dau. of Tho. & Elizabeth Pennack bur.
Jan. 16 Hugh son of Tho. & Elizabeth Hastings bapt.
Jan. 20 Hugh son of Tho. & Elizabeth Hastings bur.
Jan. 28 Thomas son of Robert & Ann Hill bapt.
Feb. 10 Mrs Elizabeth Rutt bur.
Feb. 28 George son of Lewis & Elizabeth Mordaunt bapt.
Mar. 18 Sarah dau. of John & Sarah Vernon bapt.

1681.

April 7 Rich. son of Thomas & Elizabeth Hastings bur.
April 10 Edward son of Tho. & Mary Harwood bapt.
April 24 Ann dau. of Wm & Katharine Atwell bapt.
April 27 Ester dau. of Edward & Ester Leake bur.
April 29 Samuell son of Samuell & Sarah Fowler bur.
April 29 Sarah dau. of Samuell & Sarah Fowler bur.
May 18 Mrs Elizabeth Masters bur.
May 19 Hester dau. of Thomas & Hester Alder bapt.
May 23 John Ellis & Mary Greene marr. at ye Tabernacle of St John Baptist
May 24 Phillip Lassells bur.
May 28 Richard Taylor bur.
June 15 Joseph son of Joseph & Christian Smith bapt.
June 28 Elizabeth dau. of Joseph & Ann Vaughan bapt.
July 24 Hannah dau. of John & Martha Rowley bapt.
July 29 Richard son of Robert & Mary Chase bapt.
Aug. 28 Hester Coney bur.
Sep. 8 John Small bur.
Sep. 10 Elizabeth Remington bur. in the new churchyard
Sep. 14 Richard Stephens bur.
Sep. 16 Mary Clark bur.
Sep. 21 John Fist bur.
Sep. 21 Joseph Smith bur.
Oct. 9 John son of Wm & Susanna Small bapt.
Oct. 14 John son of Wm & Susanna Small bur.
Oct. 23 Sarah dau. of John & Mary Lawrance bapt.
Oct. 24 Tryphosa dau. of Francis & Mary Hill bur.
Nov. 12 Ann dau. of Thomas & Elizabeth Pennack bapt.
Nov. 18 Ann dau. of Thomas & Elizabeth Pennack bur.
Dec. 8 Mary Rouse bur.
Dec. 23 Henry Wilson bur.
Dec. 23 Elenor Hooper bur.

Feb. 10 A stillborn child of Mr Brisco's bur.
Mar. 6 Ellenor Meaddowes, widow, bur.
Mar. 20 Ann dau. of Tho. & Ann Price bapt.

1682.

April 2 Elizabeth dau. of James & Elizabeth Child bapt.
April 6 Henry son of John & Elizabeth Boylston bapt.
April 9 Sarah dau. of Samuell & Sarah Fowler bur.
April 24 Ann Lassells bur.
May 9 Thomas son of Francis & Mary Hill bur.
May 23 Speed son of Jonathan & Mary Wilkins bapt.
June 21 Thomas son of Wm & Katharine Atwell bapt.
June 24 Thomas son of Wm & Katharine Atwell bur.
July 3 Elizabeth dau. of Thomas & Hester Hooper bapt.
July 8 Wm Cox bur.
Aug. 1 Susanna Beck bur.
Aug. 20 Elizabeth dau. of Thomas & Hester Alder bapt.
Aug. 25 Samuell son of Samll & Constance Hatton bapt.
Sep. 10 Christopher Torlesse bur.
Sep. 12 Sarah dau. of Thomas & Elizabeth Hastings bapt.
Oct. 2 Elenor dau. of John & Elizabeth Adams bur.
Oct. 6 Sarah dau. of John & Elizabeth Adams bapt.
Nov. 12 Susanna dau. of Robert & Sarah Glover bur.
Nov. 15 Christian wife of Joseph Smith bur.
Nov. 22 Thomas son of Wm & Susanna Small bapt.
Nov. 23 Elizabeth dau. of John & Martha Rowley bapt.
Dec. 3 Earle son of Henry & Ann Rands bapt.
Dec. 21 Ann dau. of John & Hannah Parratt bapt.
Jan. 8 Wm son of Samuell & Sarah Fowler bapt.
Jan. 19 Elizabeth dau. of Joshua & Elenor Richison bapt.
Jan. 28 Mrs Mary Chelsam bur.
Jan. 30 Abraham son of Abraham & Anna Whiteing bapt.
Feb. 1 Henry Boylston bur.
Feb. 14 Elizabeth dau. of Lewis & Elizabeth Mordaunt bapt.
Feb. 24 Thomas Ashworth, Mr Pott's man, bur.
Feb. 25 Martha dau. of John & Mary Harper bur.
Feb. 25 Deborah dau. of Samuell & Deborah Westall bapt.
Mar. 13 Wm son of John & Jane Page bapt.
Mar. 21 Joseph Seers bur.
Mar. 21 John Garrard bur.

1683.

April 6 Pitson son of John & Sarah Vernon bapt.
April 7 Roger Greene bur. in ye new churchyard
April 8 A chrisome son of Mr Atwell's bur.
April 17 Simon Yate & Katharine Jones marr. by lic.
April 18 Honor dau. of Thomas & Honor Lee bapt.
May 3 Ann dau. of John & Sarah Chevoll bapt.
May 5 Honor dau. of Thomas & Honor Lee bur.
May 22 Annah Barton bur.
May 23 Anthony Orson, a foundling, bapt.
June 24 John son of John & Sarah Lawrance bapt.
June 29 John Billers bur.
July 1 Richard Cox bur.
July 7 Joseph son of Andrew & Ann Nettles bapt.
July 9 Edward son of Richard & Bridgett Torlesse bapt.

July 21 Thomas Small bur.
July 25 Edward Torlesse bur.
July 26 Earle Rands bur.
Aug. 21 Thomas son of Wm & Mary Watkins bapt.
Aug. 22 Mr John Anderson bur.
Aug. 22 Joseph Nettles bur.
Sep. 6 Thomas Watkins bur.
Sep. 6 Elizabeth dau. of John & Elizabeth Briscoe bapt.
Sep. 11 John Atkins & Eleanor Sherley marr. by lic.
Sep. 24 Hester Dozel bapt.
Sep. 27 Joseph Wilmot bur.
Oct. 3 John Gosling bur.
Oct. 13 Francis Lassells, a stranger, bur.
Oct. 18 Ann dau. of Nicholas & Ann Jackson bur.
Oct. 28 Joan Draper bur.
Nov. 8 Ame dau. of James & Ame Meacombe bapt.
Nov. 16 Wm son of Phillip & Ann Lassells bapt.
Nov. 30 Phebe dau. of George & Mary Knocker bapt.
Dec. 2 Samuell Hatton bur.
Dec. 7 Mr Robert Jackson & Mrs Elizabeth Wythe marr. by lic.
Dec. 7 Thomas son of Thomas & Hester Hooper bapt.
Dec. 7 Grace Foreden, Capt. Houblon's maid, bur.
Dec. 11 Rebecca Raniell bur.
Dec. 12 Jane dau. of John & Elizabeth Boylston bapt.
Dec. 13 Ann dau. of John & Elizabeth Adams bapt.
Dec. 23 Wm Cawley, of St Dunstan's in ye West, & Elizabeth Rooks, of St Martin's Orgars. marr. by lic.
Jan. 6 Mary dau. of James & Elizabeth Child bapt.
Jan. 9 Wm Norris bur. in ye new churchyard
Feb. 5 Elizabeth Hester bur.
Feb. 14 Mr Nicholas Jackson bur.
Feb. 29 Thomas Theede bur.

1684.

Mar. 27 Wm Hawkins bur.
April 1 Katharine dau. of Wm & Katharine Atwell bapt.
April 6 Mrs Ryder bur.
May 5 Elizabeth Davis bur.
May 12 Edward son of Thomas & Mary Harwood bur.
May 22 Martha dau. of Thomas & Elizabeth Hastings bapt.
June 4 Martha dau. of Tho. & Elizabeth Hastings bur.
June 5 Elizabeth dau. of Tho. & Honnor Lee bapt.
June 19 Mr Ralph Harwood bur.
June 30 Phebe dau. of John & [*blank*] Harper bur.
July 3 Samuell son of Saml & Constance Hatton bapt.
July 18 Ann dau. of Wm & Mary Watkins bapt.
July 26 Samuell son of Joshua & Sarah Hazell bur.
Aug. 18 Thomas son of Thomas & Katharine Hopkins bur.
Aug. 22 Ann Billers bur.
Aug. 27 Foster son of Wm & Hannah Hawkins bur.
Sep. 18 Mr Samuell Hoole, of St Martin's, Ludgate, & Mrs Elizabeth Horton, of Allhallows, Lumber Street, marr. by lic.
Oct. 18 Elizabeth & Mary daus. of John & Sarah Chevoll bapt.
Oct. 21 Christopher son of Richard & Bridgett Torlesse bapt.
Oct. 25 Anna dau. of Abraham & Anna Whiteing bapt.
Oct. 28 Sarah dau. of Christopher & Sarah Dowte bapt.
Oct. 30 Sarah dau. of Christopher & Sarah Dowte bur. in the new churchyard

Nov. 1 Elizabeth & Mary daus. of John & Sarah Chevoll bur.

Nov. 12 Mr Peter Proby bur.

Nov. 13 Elizabeth Wood bur.

Dec. 7 Hester wife of Mr Thomas Tryphuce bur.

Dec. 12 Rebecca Creswell bur.

Jan. 7 John son of John & Hester Sowter bapt.

Jan. 9 Elizabeth Fosdick bur.

Jan. 11 Jonathan Wilkins bur.

Feb. 11 Joseph son of James & Anne Meacombe bapt.

Feb. 16 Ann dau. of Samuell & Deborah Westall bapt.

Mar. 10 John son of Abraham & Elizabeth Cardell bapt.

1685.

Mar. 27 John son of Abraham & Elizabeth Cardell bur.

April 4 Abraham Hastock, servt to Mr Adams, bur.

April 5 Joseph son of Joseph & Ann Hawkins bapt.

April 5 Elizabeth dau. of Thomas & Judith Theede bur.

April 16 Margarett dau. of James Enshe bur. at the new churchyard

April 24 John son of John & Elizabeth Sampson bapt.

April 28 John son of John & Elizabeth Sampson bur.

May 8 Mr Thomas Hastings bur.

May 10 Samuell son of Samuell & Sarah Fowler bapt.

May 14 Wm son of Phillip & Ann Lassells bur.

May 24 Canham son of Daniell & Mary How bur.

June 18 John Godwin & Mary Carter marr. by lic.

June 19 Henry Wakeford, Mr Adams' man, bur.

June 24 Joshua Skinner, a foundling, bapt.

June 25 Joshua Skinner, a foundling, bur. at St John's

July 1 Elizabeth dau. of Brook & Rebeccah Julidah bapt.

July 2 Sarah dau. of John & Elizabeth Adams bur.

July 3 Mathew son of Edward & Frances Stolwortman bapt.

July 12 James Read & Isabella Tongue marr. by lic.

July 23 Josia son of Humphery & Mary Bowyer bapt.

Aug. 21 Ann dau. of Samuell & Deborah Westall bur.

Aug. 23 A stillborn child of Mr Lawrance's bur.

Aug. 30 Josia son of Humphery & Mary Bowyer bur.

Aug. 31 Rebecca dau. of John & Martha Rowley bapt.

Sep. 10 Mary dau. of Thomas & Elizabeth Hastings bapt.

Sep. 15 Rebecca dau. of John & Martha Rowley bur.

Sep. 16 Elizabeth dau. of Henry & Hannah Goold bapt.

Sep. 24 Foster son of Wm & Hannah Hawkins bur.

Oct. 1 Elizabeth dau. of John & Elizabeth Adams bapt.

Oct. 15 Joseph Waldron & Jane Moulton marr.

Oct. 16 Thomas Blamore bur.

Nov. 6 Ann dau. of Wm & Katharine Atwell bur.

Nov. 18 Friswith dau. of George & Mary Knocker bapt.

Nov. 25 Katharine wife of Thomas Hopkins bur.

Nov. 28 Henry son of Wm & Mary Clayton bapt.

Dec. 2 Thomas son of Thomas & Elizabeth Smith bur.

Dec. 12 Joseph Bennett, of St Mary Hill, widr, & Joan Cole, of St Olave, Southwark, widow, marr.

Dec. 17 John Hanbury, of St Clemt Danes, widr, & Ann Bedwell, of ye Old Bayly, spr, marr.

Jan. 3 Elizabeth dau. of John & Sarah Vernon bapt.

Jan. 6 Ann wife of Mordecai Hayward bur.

Jan. 26 Mary dau. of Thomas & Hester Hooper bapt.

Feb. 4 Wm son of Thomas & Elizabeth Aleyn bapt., born 25 Jan.

1686.

Mar. 25 Wm son of Samuell & Constance Hatton bapt.
April 13 Robert Densloe & Elizabeth Mountfort marr.
April 18 Lucy dau. of John & Jane Page bapt.
April 25 Ann dau. of Wm & Katharine Atwell bapt.
May 4 Elizabeth dau. of Saml & Deborah Westall bapt.
May 15 Mary Baylee bur.
June 4 Francis son of Richard & Bridgett Torlesse bapt.
June 5 Thomas son of Thomas Nicolls bur. at ye new churchyard
June 8 Thomas son of John & Elizabeth Briscoe bur.
June 17 Francis son of Richard & Bridgett Torlesse bur.
June 18 Wm son of Thomas Hopkins bur.
June 24 John son of Abraham & Anna W. iteing bapt.
June 26 Wm son of Wm & Mary Watkins bapt.
July 21 Phillip son of Phillip & Ann Lassells bapt.
July 31 Ann dau. of Henry & Elizabeth Dickson bapt.
July 31 Phillip son of Phillip & Ann Lassells bur.
Aug. 3 Abraham son of Abraham & Elizabeth Cardell bapt.
Aug. 21 John son of Samuell & Judith Ryder bapt.
Aug. 26 Wm Colyer, of St Andrew's, Holbourn, gentn, & Katharine Wall, of St Dunstan's in ye West, spr, marr.
Sep. 6 Christian dau. of John & Rachell Hugesson bapt.
Sep. 10 John son of James & Elizabeth Child bapt.
Oct. 7 Mary Antholin, a foundling, bapt.
Oct. 8 Susanna dau. of Thomas & Susanna Nickolls bapt.
Oct. 10 Mary dau. of John & Martha Rowley bapt.
Oct. 12 Samuell son of Wm & Hannah Hawkins bur.
Oct. 20 Nathaniel & John sons of Richard & [*blank*] Hill bapt.
Oct. 28 Thomas son of Thomas & Ann Beadle bapt.
Nov. 10 Hannah dau. of Joshua & Hannah Hotchkis bapt.
Nov. 12 John son of John & Elizabeth Adams bapt.
Nov. 23 John son of Humphery & Mary Bowyer bapt.
Nov. 28 Lucy dau. of John & Jane Page bur.
Nov. 29 Wm son of Henry & Elizabeth Barker bapt.
Dec. 7 Job Convard bur.
Dec. 13 Julius Billers bur.
Dec. 18 Susanna Chalkhill bur.
Jan. 3 Ann wife of Richard Makham bur.
Feb. 1 Richard son of Thomas & Elizabeth Smith bapt.
Feb. 6 John son of Samuell & Judith Ryder bur.
Feb. 17 Gabriel Pennock, of St Dunstan, Stepney, & Hannah Bycott, of this parish, marr. by lic.
Feb. 27 Mary dau. of James & Ame Meakham bapt.
Mar. 3 Thomas Bishop, of Allhallowes, Lumbard Street, & Mary Baber, of St John Baptist, marr. by lic.
Mar. 3 Alice wife of Robert Green bur. at ye new churchyard
Mar. 6 Martha Smith, widow, bur.
Mar. 14 Ann dau. of Mr. John Ince bur.

1687.

April 3 Ann dau. of Daniel & Mary How bur.
May 3 John Ridgley, of St Clement Danes, & Katharine Pinckney, of St Martin in ye Fields, marr. by lic.
May 4 Mrs Hester Dozel bur.
May 10 Mary Hastings bur.
May 13 David Gawthorne bur.
June 1 George son of George & Mary Winfeild bapt.

June 10 Richard son of Thomas & Elizabeth Smith bur.
July 11 Susanna dau. of Thomas & Susanna Nickolls bur. at ye new churchyard
July 14 Humphery Kempton, of St Bridget, widr, & Elizabeth Oliver, of St Andrewe's, Holborn, widow, marr. by lic.
Aug. 7 John son of Samuell & Sarah Fowler bapt.
Aug. 13 Mary dau. of Tho. & Susanna Nicolls bapt.
Aug. 18 Canham son of Daniel & Mary How bur.
Aug. 20 Henry son of Wm & Mary Daldern bur.
Aug. 31 George son of George & Mary Knocker bapt.
Sep. 1 Henry Bonnett bur.
Sep. 1 Michael son of Benjamyn & Alice Baker bapt.
Sep. 12 Elizabeth dau. of Samuell & Constance Hatton bapt.
Sep. 13 George son of Phillip & Ann Lassells bapt.
Sep. 17 George son of Phillip & Ann Lassells bur.
Sep. 26 Mr John Meare bur.
Sep. 27 Thomas son of Francis & Elizabeth Cremer bapt.
Sep. 28 Judith wife of Thomas Theede bur.
Oct. 2 Sarah Oakes bur.
Oct. 5 Wm Gibs, servt to Mr Wilford, bur.
Oct. 8 Sarah dau. of John & Sarah Larrance bur.
Oct. 17 Katharine dau. of John & Elizabeth Smith bapt.
Oct. 22 Mr Wm Blamore bur.
Oct. 23 Mary dau. of Tho. & Dorothy Garrard bapt.
Nov. 10 An abortive male child of Samuell Ryder bur.
Nov. 12 Hannah dau. of John & Martha Rowley bur.
Nov. 16 Thomas Shuckforth, of Clemen's Inn, co. Midd., & Rebeckah Mulso, of St Bridgett, London, marr.
Nov. 17 James son of Wm & Hannah Hawkins bur.
Nov. 21 Edward Dorrell, of St Ann, Westminster, bachr, & Susannah Pennell, of St Martin in the Fields, co. Midd., spr, marr. by lic.
Dec. 13 Wm Smith, of St Botolph, Bishopgate, widr, & Elizabeth Atwell, of this parish, spr, marr. by lic.
Dec. 19 John son of James & Elizabeth Child bapt.
Dec. 23 Hester dau. of Thomas & Hester Hooper bapt.
Dec. 28 Thomas son of John & Elizabeth Adams bapt.
Jan. 1 Samuell son of Samuell & Deborah Westall bapt.
Jan. 5 Samuell son of Samuell & Deborah Westall bur.
Jan. 22 Richard son of Henry & Ann Rands bapt.
Jan. 26 Thomas Higgs, of St Dunstan in the West, bachr, & Mary Hotchkis, of St James, Clerkenwell, spr, marr. by lic.
Feb. 15 Samuell son of Samuell & Sarah Fowler bur.
Feb. 17 Robert Green bur. in ye new churchyard
Feb. 25 John Clark, of St James, Westminster, widr, & Jane Joand, of St Lawrence Poultney, widow, marr. by lic.
Mar. 22 Richard son of Richard & Gartroote Dawson bapt.

1688.

Mar. 25 Elizabeth dau. of Abraham & Elizabeth Cardell bapt.
Mar. 27 Elizabeth Till bur.
April 1 Mary dau. of Wm & Katharine Atwell bapt.
April 17 Ann dau. of Humphery & Mary Bowyer bapt.
April 24 Ann dau. of Humphery & Mary Bowyer bur.
May 22 Lucy dau. of Thomas & Elizabeth Smith bapt.
May 24 Samuell son of Richard & Alice Hill bapt.
July 1 Wm son of Wm & Mary Watkins bapt.
July 5 Robert Smith, of St Clement Danes, widr, & Katharine Smith, of St Antholin's, London, spr, marr. by lic.

July 28 Ann dau. of W^m & Katharine Atwell bur.
Oct. 5 Sarah dau. of Thomas & Sarah Lathwell bapt.
Oct. 24 Mrs Elizabeth Otgar bur.
Nov. 1 John Masey & Margarett Bird marr.
Nov. 27 Lewis Mordaunt bur.
Dec. 16 John son of Henry & Hannah Goold bapt.
Dec. 31 John son of Joshua & Hannah Hotchkis bapt.
Jan. 13 Ann dau. of James & Elizabeth Mead bapt.
Feb. 1 James Story bur.
Feb. 16 Theodocius dau. of Rich. & Bridgett Torlesse bur.

1689.

April 8 Mr Richard Gawthorne bur.
April 8 Benjamin son of Theophilus & Elenor Redding bapt.
April 18 W^m son of Charles & Margarett Hibblethwaite bapt.
April 24 W^m son of W^m & Mary Watkins bur.
April 24 Katharine Keyes, a foundling, bapt.
April 30 Richard Haines, of St Bottolph, Aldersgate, bach^r, & Sara Stanmore, of St Bartholomew ye Less, sp^r, marr. by lic.
May 3 Thomas Cole bur. at ye new churchyard
May 7 John Billers bur.
May 12 John son of Samuell & Sarah Fowler bapt.
July 23 Sarah dau. of John & Sarah Fist bapt.
Aug. 16 Elizabeth dau. of Hump. & Mary Bowyer bapt.
Aug. 20 Katharine Kyes, a foundling, bur.
Aug. 24 Ann dau. of Thomas & Elizabeth Smith bapt.
Sep. 3 Ann dau. of Thomas & Elizabeth Smith bur.
Sep. 3 Elizabeth dau. of Thomas & Susanna Nicolls bur. at the new churchyard
Sep. 20 Thomas Bedford, of St Paul, Covent Garden, wid^r, & Sarah Doble, of Hornsey, co. Midd., widow, marr. by lic.
Oct. 9 John Randall, of St Foster's parish, London, bach^r, & Ann Somner, of Allhallowes, Bread Street, London, sp^r, marr. by lic.
Nov. 4 James Taylor, of St Bartholomew the Great, bach^r, & Mary Bowyer, of the parish of St Anthony, London, marr. by lic.
Nov. 24 Edward son of Michaell & Elizabeth Pym bapt.
Nov. 26 Sarah dau. of Joshua & Hannah Hotchkis bapt.
Dec. 11 Mr George Widdowes bur.
Dec. 15 Mary wife of John Freeman bur.
Feb. 8 Edward son of Phillip & Ann Lassells bur.
Feb. 9 Richard son of Sam^ll & Constance Hatton bapt.
Feb. 9 John son of John & Sarah Lovjoy bapt.
Feb. 9 Elizabeth dau. of Sam^ll & Constance Hatton bur.
Feb. 26 Mordecai Hayward bur.
Mar. 2 Wm Hayward, of St Andrew Undershaft, London, & Elizabeth Peck, of St Dionis Backchurch, London, marr. by lic.
Mar. 4 Mary Legay bur.
Mar. 5 Thomas son of Thomas & Sarah Lathwell bapt.
Mar. 5 Samuell Hayward bur.
Mar. 9 John son of John & Ann Eldridg bapt.
Mar. 16 Joseph son of Christopher & Penelope Moore bapt.

1690.

April 4 Thomas Storer bur.
April 7 Sarah Nuton, Mrs Mears' kinswoman, bur.
April 8 Mr Benjamyn Ducane bur.
May 1 Elizabeth dau. of Robert & Frances Maidston [?]

May 2 John Merriton bur.
May 4 Isaac Stanton son of Nicholas Stanton, dec^d^, bapt.
June 22 Elenor Pym, widow, bur.
June 25 Lucy Maria dau. of Richard & Gartroote Dawson bapt.
July 2 Hannah dau. of Joshua & Hannah Hotchkis bur.
July 9 Wm Pauley bur.
Aug. 26 Robert Vincent, of St Dunstan in the West, & Sarah Hotchkis, of St James, Clerkenwell, marr.
Oct. 11 John son of Thomas & Susanna Nichols, bur. at ye new churchyard
Oct. 19 Thomas Rouse bur.
Oct. 25 John son of Joshua & Hannah Hotchkis bur.
Nov. 1 Richard Corbett, of St Bartholomew the Great, London, wid^r^, & Mary Janes, of St Botolph, Aldersgate, sp^r^, marr.
Nov. 3 Samuell son of Samuell & Mary Pipett bapt.
Nov. 4 Elizabeth Lovell bur.
Nov. 23 John Turner, of St Andrew, Holbourn, & Ann Venables, of St Sepulcher's, marr.
Dec. 4 Tifford son of W^m^ & Katharine Atwell bapt.
Dec. 13 John son of Rich. & Judith Floyd bapt.
Jan. 9 Mrs Ann Pott wife of Mr Wm Pott bur.
Feb. 8 Robert son of Robert & Frances Maidstone bapt.
Feb. 11 Joseph & Thomas sons of John & Margratt Wormlayton bapt.
Feb. 19 W^m^ son of Thomas & Hester Hooper bapt.
Feb. 20 John son of John & Mary James bapt.
Feb. 25 Katharine wife of Mr Atwell bur.
Mar. 1 Phebe dau. of Samuell & Sarah Wilson bapt.
Mar. 12 Daniell son of Daniell & Sarah Bland bapt.

1691.

April 5 Ann dau. of John & Elizabeth Somerstables [*vide* Sep. 25, 1692] bapt.
April 12 Ann dau. of John & Elizabeth Somerstables bur.
April 22 Sarah dau. of Samuell & Sarah Fowler bapt.
May 18 John Ashly son of Wm Ashly, a foundling, was left at Mr Atwell's gate [?]
May 27 Peter King bur.
June 4 Richard Ladds bur.
June 4 Ann dau. of Edmund & Ann Kidby bur.
June 7 Alice dau. of Josh. & Hannah Hotchkis bapt.
July 25 Robert & Wm Russell bur.
July 27 Thomas Smith bur.
Aug. 10 W^m^ son of Edward & Dorothy Taylor bapt., born 29 July
Aug. 11 Elizabeth Alcon bur.
Aug. 13 Thomas son of Theophilus & Elenor Redding bapt.
Aug. 18 Sarah dau. of Richard & Tacy Rowley bur.
Sep. 15 Elizabeth Pell, widow, bur.
Oct. 1 John Pennington, bach^r^, & Susanna Edwards, sp^r^, of St Botolph, Aldersgate, marr.
Oct. 6 Sarah Storer bur.
Oct. 6 Mr Wm Pott bur.
Nov. 24 Robert son of Samuell & Constance Hatton bapt.
Dec. .. Joseph Kilby, of St Giles without Criplegate, wid^r^, & Katharine Barnes, of the same, widow, marr. by lic.
Dec. 22 Thomas Dicken, bach^r^, & Mary Paston, sp^r^, marr. by lic.
Jan. 7 W^m^ son of John & Ann Adams bapt.
Jan. 12 Robert Copley bur.
Jan. 27 Mr Peter Houblon, senior, bur.

Jan. 28 Elizabeth dau. of Thomas & Elizabeth Hopkins bur.
Feb. 8 Daniell son of Daniell & Sarah Bland bur.
Mar. 6 Abigaile dau. of Elias & Abigail Turner bapt., born 1 Mar.

1692.

Mar. 27 Richard son of Georg & Mary Knocker bapt.
Mar. 28 W^m son of John & Margarett Wormlayton bapt.
Mar. 28 Robt son of Rob. & Frances Maidstone bur.
April 2 James son of W^m & Elizabeth Saulsbury bur.
April 4 John Martin, wid^r, & Jane Meek, sp^r, both of Deptford, Kent, marr. by lic.
April 10 Stephen Cosford bur.
April 19 Morris son of Edward & Hope Barrow bapt.
April 29 Anthony Cross, a foundling, bapt.
May 12 Benjamyn Gough, of St Botolph, Aldgate, & Susanna Borroughs, of St Alphage, marr.
May 17 Hannah dau. of Joshua & Hannah Hotchkis bapt.
May 19 Henry Morris, of St Giles, Cripplegate, wid^r, & Susanna Hilliard, of St Mildred, Poultry, marr. by lic.
June 13 Hannah wife of Wm Hawkins bur.
July 19 Ann dau. of W^m & Ann Allin bapt.
July 31 Elizabeth dau. of Phillip & Ann Lascelles born & bapt.
Aug. 2 Mary dau. of John & Mary James bapt.
Aug. 3 Athony Dodson, laid in the parish 30 June, bapt. 3 Aug.
Aug. 3 Anthony Cross, a foundling, bur.
Aug. 6 Mary Goslin bur.
Aug. 11 Henry Cores, of St Dunstant in the West, wid^r, & Sarah Sympson, of Long Acre, Midd., sp^r, marr.
Aug. 18 Elizabeth dau. of W^m & Mary Rawlinson bapt.
Aug. 31 James Antholin, a foundling left in ye parish, bapt.
Sep. 25 John son of John & Elizabeth Sumerscales bapt.
Sep. 27 John son of John & Elizabeth Sumerscales bur.
Oct. 9 John son of Samuell & Sarah Fowler bur.
Nov. 17 John son of Robert & Frances Maidstone bapt.
Nov. 28 John son of Robert & Frances Maidstone bur.
Jan. 15 Henry son of John & Judith Godfrey bapt.
Jan. 26 Charles Jones, of St Giles, Cripplegate, & Mary Calcot, of St Olave, Southwark, marr. by lic.
Jan. 28 Alice dau. of Joshua & Hannah Hotchkis bur.
Feb. 18 Ann dau. of W^m & Mary Dancy bapt.
Feb. 19 Mary dau. of James & Ann Karres bapt.
Feb. 23 John Howard, of St Dunstan's in the West, bach^r, & Sarah Bradgate, of St Gregory's, sp^r, marr. by lic.
Mar. 2 John son of John & Jane Farr bapt.
Mar. 2 Samuell son of Samuell & Constance Hatton bur.
Mar. 3 Sarah Brown bur. at ye new churchyard
Mar. 5 John Howorth bur.
Mar. 13 Anthony Dodson, a foundling, bur.
Mar. 17 Roger son of Thomas & Elizabeth Hopkins bur.
Mar. 20 James Anthony, a foundling, bur.

1693.

Mar. 27 James son of Theophilus & Ellenor Redding bapt.
April 2 Ann dau. of Edward & [*blank*] Rich bur.
April 3 An abortive child of Mr Browne bur.
April 6 Lawrance son of Edward & Hope Barrow bapt.

April 11 John Nicholas, of St Peter's the Poor, bachr, & Elizabeth Hartley, of the same, spr, marr.
April 19 Wm Smith, of St Saviour's, Southwark, co. Surry, bachr, & Rebecca Knight, of St Giles, Cripplegate, widow, marr.
April 29 James Knapton, of St Faith's, bachr, & Hester Rowley, of St Anthony's parish, spr, marr. by lic.
May 3 Mary Anthony, a foundling, bapt.
May 4 Sarah Chaplin bapt.
May 11 Richard son of Sampson & Sarah Chaplin bur.
May 19 Mr Daniell Herringhook bur.
June 12 Mary dau. of Elias & Abigaile Turner bapt., born 20 May
June 18 Anthony son of John & Elizabeth Shellsheere bapt.
June 29 Alice dau. of Joshua & Hannah Hotchkis bapt.
June 29 Mary dau. of Elias & Abigall Turner bur.
July 9 John Muggleton, of St Bottolph's, Aldersgate, bachr, & Hannah Smith, of St Ann, Aldersgate, widow, marr. by lic.
July 16 Martha dau. of John & Sarah Fist bur.
July 17 Thomas son of John & Ann Adams bapt.
July 18 Mary dau. of Samuell & Sarah Fowler bapt.
Sep. 12 Sarah dau. of Elizabeth Mordant bur.
Sep. 15 Eliz. dau. of Wm & Elizabeth Saulsbury bur.
Sep. 28 John son of John & Mary Hawkins bur.
Oct. 17 James Denham, bachr, & Sarah Rowley, spr, both of this parish, marr. by lic.
Oct. 28 Wm son of Wm & Elizabeth Smith bur.
Nov. 2 Samuell Osburn, bachr, & Mary Clark, spr, both of St Giles without Criplegate, marr. by lic.
Nov. 15 Ellen dau. of Robert & Ellen Lankishire bapt.
Nov. 16 Francis August, of St Mary Aldermary, widr, & Rebecca Heming, of St Stephen's, Walbrook, spr, marr. by lic.
Dec. 7 A female child laid in the parish [?]
Dec. 30 Mrs Kathrine Brumfeild bur.
Jan. 3 Edmund Rowley, junior, bur.
Jan. 16 Edward Southwell, of St Andrew's, Holborn, bachr, & Frances Norcliffe, of St Margret, Westminster, spr, marr.
Jan. 16 Mrs Olive Ducane bur.
Feb. 5 Richard son of John & Mary Aris bapt.
Feb. 9 Susanna Tower, a foundling, bapt.
Feb. 24 John son of John & Sarah Fist bapt.
Mar. 13 Francis Hacker bur.
Mar. 18 Margrett dau. of John & Margrett Wormlayton bapt.

1694.

Mar. 27 James Sheildes, of St Vedast *alias* Foster Lane, bachr, & Alice Darrack, of St Ann, Aldersgate, London, marr.
Mar. 31 Edward Story bur.
April 23 Elizabeth dau. of William & Mary Rawlinson bur.
May 24 Francis & Andrew sons of Simon & Jane Beranger bapt.
June 3 Thomas son of John & Ann Adams bur.
June 7 Sarah dau. of Sampson & Sarah Chaplin bapt.
June 9 Ann Nettle bur.
June 12 John son of John & Cassandra Till bapt.
June 15 Mary dau. of Samuell & Deborah Westall bapt.
June 22 William son of William & Mary Rawlison bapt.
June 26 Margrett dau. of Joshua & Hannah Hotchkis bapt.
June 26 Robert Lawson, of Lincoln's Inn, co. Midd., bachr, & Rebecca Farr, of St Dunstan's in the East, spr, marr.

June 26 Phillip Rudsbey, of S[t] James, Westminster, bach[r], & Ailce Rudsbey, of S[t] Bartholomew the Less, sp[r], marr.
July 16 Teroriah dau. of Thomas & [*blank*] Hopkins bur.
July 22 Elizabeth dau. of W[m] & Ailce Saulsbury bur.
July 29 Samuell Fell bur.
Aug. 14 Jane dau. of George & Mary Knocker bapt.
Sep. 1 Mary Ryder bur.
Sep. 26 Thomas son of Henry & Mary Cole bapt.
Oct. 19 Daniell son of Thomas & Sarah Lathwell bapt.
Oct. 20 Rebecca Maidstone bur. at the new churchyard
Oct. 23 William Manning, of Bristoll, wid[r], & Joane Masters, of Bath, wid., marr.
Nov. 12 Mary dau. of Samuell & Mary Fowler bur.
Nov. 13 Hannah dau. of Joshua & Hannah Hotchkis bur.
Dec. 10 Ann dau. of Joseph & Dorythy Willford, born 19 Nov., bapt. 10 Dec.
Dec. 27 Elizabeth Motteux bur.
Jan. 3 Suanna dau. of John & Suanna Edgley bapt.
Jan. 8 Barnett Morris, of S[t] Magnis, bach[r], & Amy Williams, of S[t] Antholin's, sp[r], marr.
Jan. 10 Margrett dau. of Joshua & Hannah Hotchkis bur.
Feb. 24 Mary dau. of John & Elizabeth Rawlison bapt.
Feb. 24 Elizabeth dau. of John & Ann Adams bapt.
Feb. 27 James son of James & Sarah Denham bapt.
Mar. 11 Sarah wife of James Denham bur.
Mar. 12 Dorithy dau. of George & Elizabeth Ashborne bapt., born 5 Mar.
Mar. 17 Sarah dau. of John & Margrett Wormlayton bapt.

1695.

Mar. 31 Elizabeth dau. of Thomas & Mary White bapt.
April 17 Mary Pinfold, of Storrington in Sussex, bapt.
April 17 Anthony Dodson, a foundling, bapt.
April 30 George son of George & Penelope Smith bapt.
May 22 Thomas Fitch, of West Tilbury, Essex, wid[r], & Mary Limpany, of S[t] Botolph, Billingsgate, London, widow, marr. by lic.
June 16 John son of James & Elizabeth Fletcher bapt.
July 14 Richard Seddon, of S[t] Botolph, Aldersgate, bach[r], & Elizabeth Harrison, of S[t] Sepulcher's, London, sp[r], marr.
July 18 William son of John & Jane Farr bapt.
Aug. 9 Charles Anthony, found in the parish, bapt.
Aug. 18 Thomas son of John & Cassandra Till bapt.
Sep. 8 Jane Jaquin bur.
Sep. 19 Suannah dau. of Henry & Mary Cole bapt.
Sep. 21 Phillip son of Phillip & Ann Lassells [?]
Sep. 26 Simon Lawton son of Simon & Jane Beranger bapt., born 31 Aug.
Oct. 26 Henry son of William & Mary Rawlison bapt.
Nov. 1 John son of Joshua & Hannah Hotchkis bapt.
Nov. 13 Thomas Lake bur.
Nov. 21 John son of Samuell & Sarah Fowler bapt.
Nov. 25 Henry son of William & Mary Rawlison bur.
Nov. 26 Elizabeth dau. of Thomas Theed bur.
Dec. 5 Mary dau. of Sampson & Sarah Chaplin bapt.
Dec. 12 William son of Richard & Kathrin Wallett bapt.
Dec. 15 Robert son of Robert & Martha Driver bapt.
Dec. 18 Anthony Tower, a foundling, bapt.
Dec. 24 George Dod, of S[t] Giles in the Feilds, bach[r], & Elizabeth Pendret, of S[t] Martin's in the Feilds, sp[r], marr.
Dec. 24 Margrett dau. of John & Mary Horton bapt.

Dec. 27 Mrs Elizabeth Hills bur.
Jan. 2 John Wearge, of St Thomas the Apostle, bachr, & Jane Bunn, of the parish of Anthony, spr, marr. by lic.
Jan. 12 Mrs Ann Ince bur.
Jan. 12 Martha Driver bur. at ye new churchyard
Jan. 14 John Story, of St John Baptist, bachr, & Elizabeth Bennett, of St Alban, Wood Street, spr, marr. by lic.
Jan. 30 Edward son of Edward & Ellenor Dier bapt.
Feb. 9 Elizabeth dau. of Daniell & Sarah Bland bapt.
Feb. 11 Thomas son of John & Ann Adams bapt.
Feb. 16 Joseph son of Joseph & Suannah Knowles bapt.
Mar. 3 Mary dau. of Edward & Katharine Basden bapt.
Mar. 4 Lenord son of George & Elizabeth Ashborn bapt.
Mar. 12 Mr Isaac Jurion bur.
Mar. 13 Mr Edward Taylor bur.
Mar. 14 James Banfield bur. in ye new churchyard
Mar. 16 William son of John & Jane Farr bur.

1696.

April 5 Mary dau. of Samuel & Mary Stephens bur.
April 16 William Foster, of Lawrence Waltham, co. Berks, bachr, & Constantia Miller, of the same, spr, marr.
May 9 Geo. Sacheverell, of St Bartholomew's the Less, bachr, & Sarah C . . seman, of Friensby, co. Kent, spr, marr.

Robt Lasinby, Clerk, was instituted Rector of St Antholin & St John Baptist the 15th, & inducted the 20th of this month.

May 16* Tho. son of John & Ann Adams bur.
May 29 Daniel Smith, bach., & Sarah Wilson, spr, both of this parish, marr.
June 8 Amey dau. of John & Mary Aris bapt.
June 14 John son of John & Sarah Fist bur.
June 21 John Walker, of Gray's Inn, bach., & Elizabeth Horton, of St Andrew, Holbourn, widow, marr. by lic.
June 23 Richard Sheppard, of St Sepulcher's, bach., & Ann Hotchkis, of St James, Clerkenwell, spr, marr. by lic.
July 1 Mary Earbury bur. at the new churchyard
July 5 Margrett dau. of George & Penellope Smith bapt.
July 9 William Pike, of St Andrew, Holbourn, widr, & Mary Brickhead, of St Martin's the Fields, widow, marr. by lic.
Aug. 4 Antholena Queene, a foundling, bapt.
Aug. 4 Mrs Mary Houblon bur.
Aug. 18 Ann dau. of Edward & Hope Barrow bapt.
Aug. 27 Simon Duncalfe, of St Bartholomew Exchange, bach., & Ann Rogerson, of the same parish, spr, marr.
Sep. 1 Edward Brooks, of St Bottolph, Aldersgate, bach., & Joyce Southerland, of St Leonard, Shordich, spr, marr.
Oct. 9 William son of John & Cassandra Till bapt.
Oct. 11 Joshua Hotchkis bur.
Oct. 25 John Loveday, of St Michaell, Crooked Lane, London, & Margrett Smith, widow, of the same parish, marr.
Nov. 10 Seth Antholings, found in the parish, left the 3 & bapt. the 10
Dec. 10 Thomas Dansie, of Sudbury, co. Suffolk, bach., & Sarah Dansie, of St Edmund the King, London, spr, marr.
Dec. 30 Mary dau. of Henry & Mary Cole bapt.
Jan. 26 James Butterworth, of St Olive, Southwark, bach., & Elizabeth Page, of this parish, spr, marr. by banns

* Robert Lasinby, Rector, signs the Register from 1696 to 1722.

Feb. 5 Ralph son of Simon & Jane Baranger bapt., born 13 Jan.
Feb. 16 George Coply bur.
Feb. 20 Jane dau. of Simon Baranger bur.
Feb. 21 William Hastings bur.
Feb. 26 Ralph son of John & Jane Farr bapt.
Feb. 27 Bennett son of Henry & Kathrine Wallett bapt.
Mar. 5 Mary Chaplin bur.
Mar. 10 Robert son of Robert & Frances Maidston bur.

1697.

Mar. 25 Richard Sanders, of Christ Church, bach., & Mary Baker, of S[t] Lourance Jury, sp[r], marr.
April 6 Edmoud Harrington, of the parish of S[t] Bennett Grace Church, London, Barrowknight, widdower, & Abigall Venor, of the same parish, spinester, marr.
April 20 Jerimiah Myson, of S[t] Martin, Ludgate, London, bach., & Suanna Darlow, of the same, sp[r], marr.
May 13 Mary Antholins, a foundling, bapt.
May 22 Nicholas Bennett, of S[t] Michaell, Wood Street, bach., & Martha Jones, of S[t] Giles, Cripple Gate, London, sp[r], marr.
May 26 Dorothy dau. of Sampson & Sarah Chaplin bapt.
July 5 Rebecca Burford bur.
July 29 William Marwick son of William & Hannah King bapt.
Aug. 1 Bulstrode Barry, of co. Oxford, bach., & Alice Dunn, of S[t] Botolph, Bishopp Glate [*sic*], London, sp[r], marr.
Aug. 11 M[rs] Martha Harwood bur.
Aug. 20 Boyle son of Boyle & Elizabeth Aldworth bapt.
Aug. 27 Thomas Garway, of S[t] Margrett, Wesmister [*sic*], bach., & Ann Manlove, of S[t] Clemon's Deanes, salutas [*sic*], marr. by lic.
Sep. 2 John Story bur.
Sep. 14 Judith Rossellion bur.
Sep. 18 John Stalker, of Christ Church, bach., & Elizabeth Grantham, of S[t] Dunstan the West, sp[r], marr.
Sep. 27 Ann dau. of John & Ann Adams bapt.
Sep. 28 John Carter, bach., & Ann Booth, sp[r], both of S[t] John Baptist, marr.
Oct. 14 Henry son of Richard & Ann Shuett bapt.
Nov. 4 Theophelus Sandford, of S[t] Lawrance Jury, bach., & Ann Bulkley, widow, of the same parish, marr.
Nov. 25 M[rs] Elizabeth Houblone bur.
Nov. 28 A female child left in the parish, bapt. by the name of Margrey Lane
Dec. 8 M[r] Edward Barrow bur.
Dec. 10 Sarah dau. of Daniell & Sarah Bland bapt.
Dec. 25 William son of Joseph & Suanna Knowls bapt.
Dec. 26 M[r] Peter Houblon bur.
Dec. 28 John Bucks, of S[t] Mary Aldermary, bach., & Mary Beard, of this parish, sp[r], marr. by banns
Jan. 4 Thomas Cook, of S[t] Stephen, Coleman Street, bach., & Suanna Thorn, of S[t] Antholin's, sp[r], marr. by lic.
Jan. 8 John Everett, of White Chappel, bach., & Jane Tromaine, of the same, sp[r], marr. by lic.
Jan. 13 Clifford dau. of John & Mary Atkins bapt.
Jan. 28 M[rs] Alborn Mackerraill bur.
Feb. 6 Benjamin Rust, of S[t] Bennett Finck, bach., & Elizabeth Leake, of this parish, sp[r], marr.
Feb. 10 Stephen King, bach., & Mary Barwick, sp[r], both of this parish, marr. by banns

Mar. .. Samuell Smith, of Christ Church, Surry, bach., & Mercy Hallioake, of S[t] Mary, Newington, Surry, sp[r], marr. by lic.
Mar. 13 Mary dau. of John & Elizabeth Cosby bapt.
Mar. 24 Boyle son of Boyle & Elizabeth Aldworth bur.

1698.

May 7 Robert Rich, of the parish Sunning in Barksheir, batcholer, & Mary Walker [? Walter], of Seirden in Oxfordsheir, spinster, were by lycence married
May 7 Grace Cooke bur.
May 12 Lawrance Evans bur.
May 20 Anthony Ball, a foundling, bapt.
June 9 Thomas Boyterton, left in the parish the 9 of June [?]
July 3 Cassandra dau. of John & Cassandra Till bapt.
July 21 Edward son of Edward & Hope Barrow [?]
Aug. .. Joseph Jacob, of Lambeth, bach., & Mary Davis, of S[t] Magnis, London, sp[r], marr. by lic.
Aug. 12 Cladius son of Simon & Jane Berenger bapt.
Aug. 29 Henry White bur.
Oct. 17 Hester Leak bur.
[*blank*] William Taylor, bach., & Ann Gilling, sp[r], both of this parish, marr. by lic.
Nov. 13 M[r] Edward Randall bur.
Nov. 22 John Loveill, of S[t] Peter's the Poore, bach., & Elizabeth Blundall, of S[t] John Baptist, sp[r], marr. by banns
Dec. 3 George Lane, of S[t] Giles, Cripple Gate, bach., & Jane Getting, of S[t] Andrew, Holbourn, widow, marr.
Dec. 17 Thomas Ganning bur.
Dec. 22 Thomas Cobb, of S[t] Saviour's, Southwark, wid[r], & Elizabeth Wood, of S[t] Antholin's, sp[r], marr. by banns
Dec. 25 Samuell son of Samuell & Deborah Westall bapt.
Dec. 27 John Brooks, of S[t] Giles, Cripple Gate, bach., & Mary Charles, of the same parish, sp[r], marr. by lic.
Jan. 20 Daniell son of Daniell & Sarah Bland bapt.
Jan. 22 William Humberson, of S[t] Bennet Grace Church, bach., & Tevera Bird, of S[t] John Baptist, sp[r], marr. by lic.
Feb. 8 Daniell son of Daniell & Sarah Bland bur.
Feb. 20 William Haines, left in the parish [?]
Feb. 21 Henry Stevens, of S[t] Giles, Cripple Gate, bach., & Elizabeth Pearson, of S[t] Austin's, London, sp[r], marr. by lic.
Mar. 19 Mary dau. of Phillip & Elizabeth Dodwell bapt.

1699.

April 2 Thomas son of John & Ailce Spackmon bapt.
April 22 Samuell Stevens bur.
April 28 Mr William Hills bur.
April 30 Jonathan son of Jonathan & Suanna Grew bapt.
May 5 Joseph son of John & Ann Adams bapt.
May 11 Charles Chadwick, of Sewton Coldfeild, co. Warwick, bach., & Dorothy Doleman, of the town of Warwick, solutæ, marr. by lic.
May 12 Mary dau. of Dr Samuell Stevens bur.
May 18 Robert Coleman, of St Botolph, Algate, bach., & Martha Wittingham, of Stewart Street in the Liberty of the Tower, sp[r], marr. by lic.
May 24 Mr John Hublone bur.
May 25 Sarah dau. of Sampson Chaplin bur.
June 3 Mrs Ann Lasselles bur.

June 7 Katharine dau. of White & Mary Woolley bapt.
June 9 James son of John & Jane Farr bapt.
June 14 John Cairnes bur. at St Olive, Hart Street
June 14 Thomas Allen, of Waltham Abby, Essex, barber, bach., & Suanna Walls, of the same, spr, marr. by lic.
July 8 Joseph son of Benjamin Burford bur.
July 16 Thomas son of Thomas & Mary White bapt.
July 19 Mary dau. of Philip Dodwell bur.
July 20 Edward Roper, of Debtford, co. Kent, bach., & Suanna Hayes, of the same, spr, marr. by lic.
July 25 Edmond Prick, of St Mildred, Poultry, bach., & Elizabeth Youres, of St Olive, Jury, spr, marr. by lic.
July 31 Antholena dau. of Henry Ballard bapt.
Aug. 21 Barbary dau. of John & Mary Goodinch bapt.
Aug. 25 Elizabeth dau. of John & Cassandra Till bapt.
Sep. 21 Gabriell John son of Francis & Margrett Bezard bapt.
Sep. 21 John son of Thomas & Kathrine Martin bapt., born 12 Sep.
Oct. 7 Ann dau. of Fredrick Bode bur.
Oct. 20 Henry Nobbs bur.
Oct. 29 Edward son of Abraham Cardell bur.
Nov. 3 Elizabeth dau. of William Waters bur.
Nov. 9 Richard Gould, of St Paul, Shadwell, widr, & Anne Askin, of St Katherin near the Tower, by lic. marr.
Nov. 19 Mr Thomas Jones bur.
Nov. 21 John Lester, of Upminster, co. Essex, bach., & Rebecca Symonds, of Horn Church in the co. aforesd, spr, by lic. marr.
Nov. 21 Judith dau. of Thomas & Judith Truston bapt.
Nov 27 Elizabeth [*blank*], a foundling left in Dodson's Court [?]
Nov. 29 Daniell son of John & Elizabeth Loyd bapt.
Dec. 20 David Martin, of St Bartholomew Exchang, London, bach., & Susanna Rayner, of Hitchin, co. Herts, spr, by lic. marr.
Dec. 21 Mrs Jane Baringer bur.
Jan. 4 Henry son of Henry Figgs bur.
Jan. 16 Elizabeth dau. of Joseph & Elizabeth Ludlow bapt.
Jan. 24 William Scott, of Chipping Barnet, co. Herts, bach., & Ann Stevens, of the same, spr, by lic. marr.
Feb. 6 Mr William Atwell bur.
Feb. 10 John Hunt, of Broxbourne, co. Hertford, bach., & Mary Thomas, of [*blank*], Lumber Street, spr, by lic. marr.
Feb. 13 Kathrine dau. of Daniell & Sarah Bland bapt.
Mar. 17 Edwin son of John & Carola Wills bapt.
Mar. 20 Mrs Martha Hatton bur.

1700.

May 1 James son of John & Jane Farr bur.
May 26 Mary dau. of John & Deborah Scofeild bapt.
May 29 Mr Ambross Devenport bur.
June 5 Mary dau. of Richard & Sarah Torless bapt.
July 14 Susanna wife of Thomas Nicolls, bur. at Bethelem churchyard
Aug. 2 Mr George French bur.
Aug. 8 Edward son of Edward & Sarah Leak bapt.
Aug. 22 Ann dau. of Phillip & Elizabeth Dodwell bapt.
Aug. 24 Paul Lewis, of St Giles in the Fields, bach., mercht, & Claudia Mariot, of St James, Westminster, spr, by lic. marr.
Aug. 24 William son of William Rawlison bur.
Sep. 10 Daniell Wallis bur.
Sep. 11 Ann Sivedall bur.

Oct. 22 Alexander Cosher, of St Sepulcher's, bach., & Sarah Pippiat, of the same, spr, by lic. marr.
Nov. 6 Kathrine wife of Mr Thomas Martin bur.
Nov. 24 Ann dau. of Joseph & Susanna Knowles bapt.
Jan. 4 William Boult, servt to Mr Lassells, bur. at Walbrook
Jan. 20 Mr Robert Spicer bur. at Islington
Feb. 2 Edward Beaumont, in Wheelers Street, Spittle Fields, widr, & Martha Shore, of St Gregory's, widow, by lic. marr.
Feb. 15 Sarah Fist bur.
Feb. 16 Richard son of Thomas & Mary White bapt.
Feb. 26 Edward Fry, of St Mary Aldermanbury, widr, & Ann Ford, of St Martin Vintry, by lic. marr.
Mar. 3 Charles Vale, of St Martin's Vintry, bach., & Sarah Dymes, of the same, spr, by lic. marr.
Mar. 9 Paul son of Paul & Mary d'Aranda bapt., born 26 June 1685
Mar. 11 Thomas Estman, of St Mary Alderman Bury, bach., & Mary Chamberlin, of the same, spr, by lic. marr.
Mar. 18 Lazarus Borden, of St Botolph, Aldersgate, bach., & Eleaner Luff, of the same, widow, by lic. marr.
Mar. 20 Elizabeth dau. of Richard & Martha Fellows bur.

1701.

April 4 Mr Paul Houblon bur.
April 28 Edward son of Joseph & Ann Smith bapt.
April 29 Mary wife of John de Raffou bur.
May 13 John Newnhan, of Marsfield, co. Sussex, Esq., widr, & Edith Norton, of Love Lane, widow, by lic. marr.
May 24 Joseph son of John & Ann Adams bur.
May 31 Isaac Hill, of St Botolph, Aldgate, bach., & Ann Stephenson, of the same, spr, by lic. marr.
June 3 Christopher son of Christopher & Mary Figgs bur.
June 5 Margret Lake, widow, bur.
June 10 Mary dau. of John & Sarah Randall, a poore woman that fell in labour at ye church doore, bapt.
July 21 Mary dau. of John & Ann Adams bapt.
July 24 Ann dau. of Richard & Ann Poulton bapt.
July 30 John Squire, bach., & Sarah Hiller, spr, both of this parish, by lic. marr.
Aug. 3 James Fletcher, of the parish of Andrew, Holborn, bach., & Elizabeth Butterworth, of this parish, by banns marr.
Aug. 17 Mary dau. of Richard & Elizabeth Richards bapt.
Aug. 21 Richard Hay, of St Mary Hill, widr, & Elizabeth Bold, of Hatfield, co. Hertford, solutæ, by lic. marr.
Sep. 6 Ann Maidstone bur. at Tindall's Ground
Sep. 8 Ann dau. of Joseph & Elizabeth Ludlow bapt.
Sep. 11 Sarah dau. of Edward & Sarah Leak bapt.
Sep. 11 Thomas Benbow, of St Sepulcher's, bach., & Sarah Gill, of the same, spr, by lic. marr.
Sep. 24 John Newham, of St Bride's, bach., & Mary Leapidge, of St John Baptist, solutæ, by lic. marr.
Sep. 30 Jonathan Day, of St Saviour in Southwark, bach., & Sarah Leader, of the same, by lic. marr.
Oct. 6 Mrs Sarah Bonnet bur.
Oct. 7 Martha dau. of George & Sarah Hatton bapt.
Dec. 18 William Gough, of St Mary Aldermary, bach., haberdasher of hats, & Martha Stephenson, of this parish, spr, by lic. marr.
Jan. 1 William Kemp, of St Andrew, Holbourn, widr, & Ruth Duncle, of St Antholin's, spr, by banns marr.

Jan. 1 Samuel Smith, of St John Baptist, bach., & Mary Smith, of the Tower of London, sp[r], by lic. marr.
Jan. 13 William Hill, of Shorham, co. Kent, bach., & Rachell Strayherus, of the same, sp[r], by lic. marr.
Feb. 12 Edward Watts, of St John, Wapping, bach., & Suanna Peared, of St Martin, Ludgate, solutæ, by lic. marr.
Feb. 13 Mary Cooledge bur. at the new churchyard
Feb. 15 Rebecca dau. of Thomas & Mary White bapt.
Feb. 17 Richard Metcalfe, of All Saints, city of York, bach., & Barbary Lassells, of St Clement, Eastcheap, London, sp[r], by lic. marr.
Feb. 20 Mrs Elhana Gawthorn bur.
Feb. 21 A child of M[r] White Woolly bur. at Allhallows
Mar. 23 Rodolphus Whittworth, of Stepney, wid[r], & Elizabeth Hall, of S[t] George, Southwark, widow, by lic. marr.

1702.

Mar. 25 Prissilla dau. of Thomas & Judith Truston bapt.
Mar. 28 John Thorowgood, of S[t] Peter, Paul's Wharfe, bach., & Sarah Smith, of the same, sp[r], by lic. marr.
April 5 Hugh Deane, wid[r], & Sarah Moucher, widow, both of this parish, by banns marr.
April 6 William Burtonwood, bach., a weaver, living in courtyard at the upper end of Barnaby Street, in the parish of S[t] Mary Madalen, Bermonsey, & Sarah Watts, of this parish, sp[r], by banns marr.
April 9 Francis Merritt, of Croyden, co. Surrey, bach., & Rebecca Levine, of this parish, sp[r], by lic. marr.
April 17 Ann dau. of Joseph & Elizabeth Ludlow bur.
April 19 Daniell son of David Busanqueste bur.
April 24 M[rs] Ann Heringhook bur.
May 1 Kathrine Jones bur.
May 3 Richard son of Richard & Mary Penn bapt.
May 15 Edmond Rowley, the parish clerke, bur.
May 21 Edward Umfreville, of Farnham Royall, co. Bucks, bach., & Mary Osborn, of S[t] Bridgett, London, marr. by lic.
May 22 James Cutts, of S[t] Paul, Covent Garden, bach., & Honnor Barret, of S[t] Andrew, Holborn, by lic. marr.
May 29 Martha dau. of M[r] Richard Fellows bur.
June 24 A stillborn child of M[r] Till's bur.
July 17 Charles son of John Madston bur.
July 28 M[r] John Hudson bur.
July 30 John son of John Pulinson bapt.
Aug. 27 M[rs] Anne Boneal bur.
Aug. 31 Thomas son of M[r] John Till bur.
Sep. 8 Mary dau. of Edward & Sarah Leak bapt.
Sep. 12 Edmund Carpenter, of S[t] Mary le Savoy, bach., & Margery Holloway, of this parish, by lic. marr.
Sep. 19 John Allen, of the Tower of London, bach., & Mary Lash, of S[t] John, Wapping, marr. by lic.
Sep. 22 John son of Daniel & Sarah Bland bapt.
Sep. 23 Sarah dau. of William & Mary Palmer bur.
Sep. 30 Mary dau. of Richard & Sarah Torlesse bur.
Oct. 15 John Lovejoy bur.
Oct. 25 Phillip Dodwell bur.
Nov. 10 George Butler, of S[t] Giles, Cripplegate, bach., & Anne Debeu (or Debew), of the same, sp[r], by lic. marr.
Nov. 17 Robert son of John & Martha Gilbert bur.

Dec. 3 John Roberts, of Woolwich, co. Kent, wid^{r}, & Anne Cook, of St Paul, Shadwell, widow, marr. by lic.
Dec. 9 Robert son of John & Anne Adams bapt.
Dec. 10 Philip son of Philip & Elizabeth Dodwell bapt.
Dec. 24 Anna Philadelphia Hoppe bur.
Dec. 29 John Barton, of St Mary Abchurch, bach., & Anne Redshaw, of this parish, sp^{r}, marr. by lic.
Jan. 14 Daniel Davis, of St George, Southwark, bach., & Elizabeth Haine, of St Saviour, Southwark, sp^{r}, marr. by lic.
Jan. 26 John Savidge, of St Swithin, London, bach., & Anne Andrew, of [*blank*], Bow in Middlesex, sp^{r}, marr. by lic.
Jan. 27 John Anthony Pheasant, a foundling, bapt.
Feb. 6 Thomas Browne, of St Margaret, Lothbury, London, bach., & Alice Jordan, of this parish, sp^{r}, marr. by banns
Feb. 9 John de Raffau, of St John Baptist, wid^{r}, & Alice Lavie, of the same, sp^{r}, marr. by lic.
Feb. 9 James Page, of St Nicholas Olave, London, bach., & Jane Badly, of St Nicholas Cole Abby, sp^{r}, marr. by lic.
Feb. 9 Charles Turkinton, of St Mary, Savoy, bach., & Sarah Hemming, of St Paul, Covent Garden, sp^{r}, marr. by lic.
Feb. 9 Sarah Annand bur.
Feb. 19 Issachar Spittle, of this parish, bach., & Eliza Rowley, of the same, sp^{r}, marr. by lic.
Feb. 22 William Taylour bur.
Feb. 24 Anne dau. of Rich. & Anne Poulton bapt.
Mar. 2 Elizabeth Semine bur. at Bromley near Bow
Mar. 5 John son of Daniel & Sarah Bland bur.
Mar. 9 Abigail Randal, widow, bur.

1703.

April 7 Hannah dau. of Thomas & Susanah Nicholls bapt.
April 11 William Smith, of St Leonard, Shoreditch, bach., & Susanna Chapman, of St John Baptist, sp^{r}, marr. by lic.
May 30 William Henry son of Paul & Mary d'Aranda, born 20 Dec. 1688, bapt. 30 May 1703.
July 25 Jane dau. of John & Jane Far bapt.
July 25 John son of William & Elizabeth Waters bur.
Aug. 7 Rich^{d} son of Francis & Hannah Holford, bur. at West Ham, Middlesex
Aug. 23 Elizabeth Higginson bur. at Tindall's Ground
Sep. 4 Francis Morris, of St Andrew Hubbard, wid^{r}, & Catherine Shelton, of St Stephen, Coleman Street, sp^{r}, marr. by lic.
Sep. 26 Thomas Cox, of Leigton Buzard, co. Bedford, bach., & Eliz. Walker, of the same place, sp^{r}, marr. by lic.
Sep. 28 Mary dau. of Sam. & Leah Hilliard bur. at Tindall's Ground
Oct. 10 John son of John & Ann Barton bapt.
Oct. 12 Mary dau. of Joseph & Elizabeth Ludlow bapt.
Oct. 21 Mary dau. of Dr George Colebrook & Martha his wife bur.
Nov. 9 Anne dau. of John & Cassandra Till bapt.
Nov. 23 William Allen, of St Antholin, bach., and Mary Goddard, of St Martin le Grand, marr. by lic.
Nov. 30 Mrs Elizabeth Hopkins bur.
Dec. 9 Thomas Pollet, of St Giles in the Fields, bach., & Misericordia Down, of [*blank*], co. Surrey, marr. by lic.
Dec. 16 Holton son of White & Mary Woolley bapt.
Dec. 16 Robert Biggs, of St Antholin, London, bach., & Hester Orton, of the parish of St Michael, Garlick Hith, marr. by lic.
Dec. 26 Anne dau. of [*blank*] & Elizabeth Dodwell bur.

Dec. 30 John Bickerton, of S[t] Nicholas Cole Abbey, bach., & Mary White, of the same parish, marr. by lic.
Dec. 30 Robert Palmer, of S[t] John at Hackney, bach., & Anne Davel, of S[t] Botolph, Bishopsgate, sp[r], marr. by lic.
Jan. 19 Sarah dau. of James & Mary Grey, aged 16 years, bapt.
Jan. 27 George Fairly, of S[t] John, Wapping, bach., & Margaret Redshaw, of the same parish, sp[r], marr. by lic.
Feb. 6 Thomas Robinson, of S[t] Mary Woolnoth, London, bach., & Elizabeth Cossens, of the same parish, sp[r], marr. by lic.
Feb. 11 Hannah Wilson, born in Durham, aged about 29, bapt.
Feb. 14 James Brackstone, of S[t] Botolph, Aldersgate, London, bach., & Martha Morgan, of S[t] Paul, Covent Garden, sp[r], marr. by lic.
Feb. 20 Thomas son of Isaac & Margaret Clerk bur.
Feb. 27 John Aldcock, of S[t] John at Wapping, co. Midd., bach., & Eliza. Gee, of S[t] John Baptist, sp[r], marr. by lic.
Mar. 6 Anne dau. of John & Cassandra Till bur.
Mar. 12 John Vincent, of S[t] Sepulchre, London, bach., & Mary Kynning, of S[t] Dunstan in the East, sp[r], marr. by lic.
Mar. 23 Robert son of Samuel & Constance Hatton bur.

1704.

Mar. 30 Elizabeth dau. of Daniel and Sarah Bland bur.
April 10 William son of Robert & Frances Medstone bur.
April 20 Thomas Hinton, of S[t] Martin, Ludgate, London, bach., & Lucy Hinton, of S[t] Magnus, marr. by lic.
April 22 Gasparo Visconti, of S[t] Andrew, Holborn, bach., & Ebenezar Steffken, of the same parish, sp[r], marr. by lic.
May 2 Antholina Syth, a foundling, bapt.
May 10 James Hotchkis, of North Okendon, co. Essex, bach., & Elizabeth Thickness, of Kelvedon in the same co[y], sp[r], marr. by lic.
May 29 Anne dau. of James & Mary Grey, born at Tring, co. Hertf., aged about 15 years, bapt.
May 31 Rachel dau. of Edward & Sarah Leak bapt.
June 30 Benjamin son of Benjamin & Mary Howell bapt.
Aug. 3 John Dodson, of Deptford, co. Kent, bach., & Elizabeth White, of Dunstan's in the West, sp[r], marr. by lic.
Aug. 3 Richard Allein, of S[t] Botolph, Bishopsgate, bach., & Anne Buttler, of S[t] Leonard, Shoreditch, sp[r], marr. by lic.
Aug. 9 Lawrence Richardson, of S[t] John, Wapping, bach., & Elizabeth Thompson of [this] parish, sp[r], marr. by lic.
Aug. 10 Thomas Homer, of S[t] Martin in the Fields, wid[r], & Anne Sprigmore, of S[t] Dunstan, Stepney, sp[r], marr. by lic.
Aug. 11 Philip son of Francis & Sarah Limborn bur.
Aug. 16 Thomas Bead bur.
Aug. 31 Elizabeth Barnes dau. of Joseph & Elizabeth Bradbury bapt.
Sep. 10 Elizabeth dau. of Thomas & Susannah Nichols bapt.
Sep. 12 Elizabeth Pedder bur.
Sep. 16 Nicholas Carlyon, of St John, Wapping, bach., & Shemuel Blundell, of St Olave, Southwark, sp[r], marr. by lic.
Sep. 28 James Worrel, of St Dunstan, Stepney, co. Midd., bach., & Mary Cruft, of the same parish, sp[r], marr. by lic.
Oct. 8 Peter Joseph son of Francis & Brigetta Andreè bur.
Oct. 10 Hannah dau. of William & Eliza. Waters bur.
Oct. 12 Stephen Ruddock, of St Andrew Undershaft, wid[r], & Sarah Atkinson, of St John Baptist, sp[r], marr. by banns
Oct. 13 Theophilus Rayman bur.
Oct. 18 Francis son of Henry & [*blank*] Procter bur.

Nov. 3 Peter son of Arthur & [*blank*] Cockram bapt.
Nov. 14 Bradford dau. of Rich. & Ann Poulton bapt.
Nov. 22 Bassett son of John & Elizabeth Paran [?]
Dec. 31 James Glascock, of St George, Bottolph Lane, bach., & Mary Lane, of the same parish, sp^r, marr. by lic.
Dec. 31 John Collins, of St Vedast *alias* Foster, bach., & Mary Halloway, of St John Baptist, sp^r, marr. by lic.
Jan. 10 Humphry Ives, of St John at Hackney, bach., & Mary Collins, of St Margaret, New Fish Street, sp^r, marr. by lic.
Jan. 11 Katherine dau. of Joseph & Kath. Lind bur.
Jan. 25 Anne dau. of Jeremiah & Ann Andrews bur.
Feb. 13 John Supply, of St James, Westm^r, bach., & Judeth Wigley, of the same parish, sp^r, marr. by lic.
Feb. 13 George Hall, of St Olave, Southwark, wid^r, and Jane Brandon, of St J^n Baptist, sp^r, marr. by lic.

1705.

Mar. 30 Anne Curtis bur. at St Anne's, Westminster
April 9 Stephen Clerk bur.
April 28 Elizabeth Holton bur. at Allhallows the Great
May 9 Benjamin son of John & Anne Adams bur.
May 10 Thomas Coleborne bur.
May 13 Joseph Syth, a foundling, bapt.
June 3 Sarah dau. of Edward & Sarah Leak bapt.
June 16 Mary Mears bur.
June 30 Jonathan Holmes, of St Leonard, Bromley, co. Midd., bach., & Sarah Salter, of the same parish, sp^r, marr. by lic.
July 3 William Maxey, of St Lawrence Jewry, bach., & Catherine Hotchkis, of St James, Clarkenwell, sp^r, marr. by lic.
July 10 Anne Tifford bur.
July 14 Joseph Slater, of St Paul, Shadwell, bach., & Sarah Thickness, of Kelvedon, Essex, sp^r, marr. by lic.
July 20 John son of John & Mary Jones, born in the street, bapt.
July 31 Thomas Pitts, of Kingston upon Thames, co. Surry, bach., & Eleonor Mugit, of the same place, sp^r, marr. by lic.
Aug. 8 Sarah dau. of William & Mary Austal, born at Ore in Berks 20 Jan. 1686, bapt.
Aug. 26 David Hartley, of Chatham, Kent, wid^r, & Catherine Crosswhite, of St Dunstan in the West, Lond., widow, marr. by lic.
Sep. 29 William Feist bur.
Oct. 7 Sarah dau. of Tho. Yerbury bur. at Tindal's Ground
Oct. 9 William Fletcher, of St John Baptist, bach., & Elizabeth Young, of the same parish, sp^r, marr. by lic.
Nov. 13 Thomas son of Thomas and Susannah Nicholls bapt.
Nov. 18 Jane dau. of George & Hannah Buttler bapt.
Nov. 18 Matthew Wayne, bach., & Barbery Solman, sp^r, both of this parish, marr. by banns
Dec. 3 Sarah d'Costa bur. at Mile End
Dec. 6 Catherine Marks bur.
Dec. 18 John Nutball, of St Paul, Covent Garden, bach., & Elizabeth Ramsey, of the same, marr. by lic.
Dec. 18 Sarah dau. of Joseph & Sarah Lynd bapt.
Dec. 30 Sarah Syth, a foundling, bapt.
Jan. 1 Henry Batchelor, of St Botolph, Bishopsgate, bach., & Sarah Andrews, of Bow in Midd^x, sp^r, marr. by lic.
Jan. 13 Deborah dau. of David Bosanquet bur.
Jan. 23 Anne dau. of John James & Rachel Cæsar bur. [? bapt. ; see 4 Feb.]

Jan. 27 William Thomas bur.
Jan. 30 Paul Mayfield, of St Mary, Lambeth, co. Surrey, bach., & Mary Nicholson, of St Bridget, London, spr, marr. by lic.
Feb. 4 Anne dau. of John James & Rachel Cæsar bur.
Feb. 12 William Coles bur.
Feb. 13 Deborah dau. of Nehemiah & [*blank*] Eastman bur.
Feb. 19 Robert Early, of St Leonard, East Cheap, Lond., bach., & Elenor Davis, of Allhallows, Barkin, marr. by lic.
Mar. 8 Magdalen Wileman bur.
Mar. 20 Stephen Day, of St Giles, Cripplegate, bach., & Elizabeth Bosley, of the same parish, spr, marr. by lic.

1706.

Mar. 30 William Williams, of Lincoln's Inn, gent., & Jane Sandford, of St Giles in the Feilds, spr, marr. by lic.
April 2 Isaac son of Isaac & Margaret Clerk bur.
April 5 Elizabeth Castle, a foundling, bapt.
April 25 Arabella dau. of Rich. & Frances Morton [?]
May 2 Thomas Lynes, of St Bridget, Lond., widr, & Elizabeth Stephens, of the same parish, spr, marr. by lic.
May 13 Susannah dau. of Henry & Mary Figges bur.
May 14 Elias Philpin, of St Bennet Fink, Lond., bach., & Joan North, of St Antholin, spr, marr. by lic.
June 16 Judeth dau. of John & Cassandra Till bapt.
June 16 Thomas Nicholls bur.
June 18 Benjamin son of Benj. & Mary Howell bapt.
June 18 Richard son of Benj. & Mary Howell bapt.
June 24 John Roll, of the Inner Temple, gent., & Isabella Charlotte Walter, of St James, Westminster, spr, marr. by lic.
June 25 Anna dau. of Richard & Anne Poulton bapt.
July 16 Charles Simons, of St James, Westminster, widr, & Priscilla Davis, of the same, spr, marr. by lic.
Aug. 8 William Colnett, of Hambleton, co. Rutland, bach., & Margaret Tylliard, of St Paul, Covent Garden, spr, marr. by lic. by Mr Sparling
Aug. 12 Thomas son of Thomas & Judith Truston bapt.
Aug. 27 John Car (or Care), of St Antholin, bach., & Elizabeth Ariss, of the same parish, spr, marr. by lic.
Aug. 27 Richard son of Cuthbert & Susannah Bland bapt.
Sep. 10 William Munday, of St Botolph, Aldgate, Lond., bach., & Winifrid Palladay, of St George, Southwark, marr. by lic.
Sep. 29 William & Richard sons of Richd & Catherine Bradshaw bapt.
Oct. 22 Elizabeth Castle, a foundling, bapt.
Oct. 23 Thomas Simmerall, of Twickenham, co. Midd., bach., & Mary Gage, of the same parish, by lic. marr.
Nov. 7 A stillborn child of Timothy & Mary Finley bur.
Nov. 9 William James, of St Ann, Blackfryers, Lond., bach., & Sarah Wheeden, of St Giles, Cripplegate, spr, marr. by lic.
Nov. 26 Elizabeth dau. of Charles & Ann Beckingham bapt.
Nov. 28 Daniel son of Daniel & Sarah Bland bapt.
Dec. 1 Robert William Richard son of Lawrence & Mary Nash bapt.
Dec. 4 Baptist Hall, of Richmond, co. Surrey, widr, & Anne Eldridge, of the same parish, spr, marr. by lic.
Dec. 11 Margarett Hallaway bur.
Dec. 15 Stephen Loyn, of St Clement Danes, bach., & Grace Lyn, of the same parish, spr, marr. by lic.
Dec. 26 James Duepree, of St Dunstan, Stepney, widr, & Eleanor Foster, of St Antholin, spr, marr. by lic.

Dec. 26 Ann dau. of John & Mary Archer bapt.
Dec. 26 John Fist bur.
Dec. 26 William Howard, of S[t] Antholin, bach., & Gartrude Cocker, of S[t] Dunstan, Stepney, sp[r], marr. by lic.
Jan. 1 James Ealy, of S[t] Thomas the Apostle, & Sarah Horne, of the same parish, sp[r], marr. by lic.
Jan. 5 Enoch son of Enoch & Elizabeth Warner bur.
Jan. 10 Anthony Street, a foundling, bapt.
Jan. 10 Anthony Street, a foundling, bur.
Jan. 29 Daniel Morat, of Greenwich, Kent, bach., & Frances Green, of the same parish, sp[r], marr. by lic.
Feb. 3 Ezekiel son of John James & Anne Cæsar bapt.
Feb. 5 Sarah dau. of John & Esther Dashwood bapt.
Feb. 11 Christopher Prat, of St Dunstan, Stepney, & Mary Truelove, of St Catherine Creechurch, Lond., sp[r], marr. by lic.
Feb. 13 Robert son of John & Martha Gilbert bur.
Feb. 25 Charles Haynes, of St Giles, Cripplegate, bach., & Mary Hodson, of St Nicolas Colcabby, Lond., sp[r], marr. by lic.
Mar. 8 Isachar Spittle bur.
Mar. 22 Ezekiel son of John James & Anne Cæsar bur.
Mar. 23 William son of Edward & Sarah Leak bapt.

1707.

April 1 Thomas Dafforne bur.
April 6 John Love, of St Gregory, Lond., bach., & Magdalen Roumieu, of St Ann, Blackfryers, widow, marr. by lic.
April 16 John Grout, of St Dunstan, Stepney, bach., & Anne Oakey, of the same parish, sp[r], marr. by lic.
May 9 Mary dau. of Samuel & Mary Smith bapt.
July 12 George Bonnett bur.
July 17 John Londey, of S[t] Giles in the Fields, co. Midd., bach., & Margaret Scot, of Hampstead in the same co[y], sp[r], marr. by lic.
July 25 Mary dau. of Richard & Frances Morton bur.
July 27 Phillip son of John & Anna Gardner bapt.
July 28 Mary dau. of Richard & Frances Morton bur.
July 30 Abraham son of John & Eleanor Williams bur.
Aug. 5 Robert Nicholls, of S[t] Peter, Cornhill, Lond., bach., & Elizabeth Moye, of the same parish, sp[r], marr. by lic.
Aug. 7 Arthur Linton, of S[t] Andrew, Holborn, bach., & Jane Dobson, of this parish, sp[r], marr. by banns
Aug. 30 Thomas Walbank, of East Greenwich, co. Kent, wid[r], & Magdalen Lloyd, of S[t] Andrew, Holborn, sp[r], marr. by lic.
Sep. 2 Elizabeth dau. of Joseph & Sarah Lind bapt.
Sep. 11 Richard Watford, of Ailsbury, co. Bucks, bach., & Sarah Harding, of the same place, sp[r], marr. by lic.
Oct. 6 Samuel Stephens, of Caversham, co. Oxon, bach., & Frances Crockford, of the same parish, sp[r], marr. by lic.
Oct. 14 Samuel Barlow, of S[t] Stephen, Wallbrook, bach., & Mary Newton, of Derby, co. Derby, sp[r], marr. by lic.
Nov. 4 Samuel Evans, of S[t] Dunstan, Stepney, co. Midd., wid[r], & Sarah Johnson, of S[t] John, Wapping, in the same co[y], widow, marr. by lic.
Nov. 21 Mary bastard child of Mary Whitehead bapt.
Dec. 2 Mary bastard child of Mary Whitehead bur.
Dec. 12 Hannah dau. of Susannah Newling bur.
Dec. 20 Esther dau. of John & Esther Dashwood bapt.
Jan. 1 William Woodrofte, of S[t] Catherine near the Tower, Lond., bach., & Grace Church, of S[t] Helen n[r] Bishopsgate, sp[r], marr. by lic.

Jan. 13 Anne dau. of John & Anna Barton bapt.
Jan. 29 Isaac son of James & Elizabeth Craven bapt.
Jan. 31 John son of Charles & Ann Beckingham bapt.
Feb. 3 Isaac son of James & Elizabeth Craven bur.
Feb. 3 Ann dau. of Robert & Ann Davy bapt.
Feb. 3 Anthony Eyland, of St John Baptist, London, bach., & Mary Hutchings, of the same parish, sp^r, marr. by banns
[*blank*] Mary dau. of Edward & Margaret Francis bur.
Feb. 14 Morgen Harbin, of the parish of Trinity, Minories, London, wid^r, & Sarah Wood, of St Mary Abchurch, London, sp^r, marr. by lic.
Feb. 17 Peter Wensley, of Walsoken, co. Norf., bach., & Eleanor Parker, of St Giles without Cripplegate, sp^r, marr. by lic.

1708.

Mar. 29 Job Bearsly, of St Sepulchre, London, bach., & Mary Stevenson, of this parish, singlewoman, marr. by lic.
Mar. 30 Anne dau. of John & Mary Archer bur.
Mar. 31 Mary Sammiwell, a foundling, bur.
April 20 Henry Bradford, of St Sepulchre, London, bach., & Hannah Hill, of Odiham in Hampshire, singlewoman, marr. by lic.
May 28 Gabriel son of Benjamin & Mary Howell bapt.
June 3 William Fowler bur.
June 11 Judith dau. of Thomas & Susannah Newling bapt.
June 19 John Giles, of St Clement Danes, bach., & Elizabeth Cook, of St Gabriel, Fenchurch Street, London, singlewoman, marr. by lic.
June 20 Daniel son of Edward & Sarah Leak bapt.
June 23 Mary dau. of Thomas & Mary Ansell bapt.
June 24 Levi Dalton, of St Dunstan in the West, London, bach., & Mary Griffith, of the same parish, singlewoman, marr. by lic.
June 24 John Humphrys, of St Alhallows, Barkin, London, bach., & Rebeccah Howard, of the same parish, singlewoman, marr. by lic.
July 10 Richard Cook, of St Leonard, Foster Lane, bach., & Martha Blagrave, of the same parish, singlewoman, marr. by lic.
July 21 Mary Carter bur.
Aug. 13 Richard Turner, of St Olave in the Old Jewry, bach., & Eliza. Lawrence, of St James, Garlickhithe, singlewoman, marr. by lic.
Aug. 17 Thomas Tompkins, of St Lawrence, Jewry, bach., & Mary Musgrave, of St Dunstan in the West, singlewoman, marr. by lic.
Sep. 7 Mary dau. of Walter & Mary Yerbury bur.
Sep. 17 Peter Du Bois bur.
Sep. 20 Thomas Robinson, of St Mary at Rotherhith, wid^r, & Sarah Smith, of the same parish, singlewoman, marr. by lic.
Oct. .. Alice Lovee bur.
Nov. 7 James Pickersgill bur.
Nov. 9 Mary dau. of Richard & Assenter [*sic*] Beavis bur.
Dec. 18 Charles Danby, of St Margaret, Westminster, bach., & Anne Russell, of St Dunstan in the East, singlewoman, marr. by lic.
Dec. 18 Samuel son of John & [*blank*] Whittington bapt.
Dec. 19 Catherine dau. of John & [*blank*] Wormlaton bapt.
Jan. 5 John Limb, of Hampstead, co. Midd., bach., & Mary West, of the same place, sp^r, marr. by lic.
Jan. 12 Radman son of Henry & Mary Figges bur.
Jan. 20 William Wareham, of St Giles in the Fields, bach., & Elizabeth Elseworth, of St Dunstan in the East, sp^r, marr. by lic.
Feb. 4 Elizabeth Dafforn bur.
Feb. 14 Elizabeth dau. of John & Mary Barton bapt.
Feb. 15 Elizabeth dau. of Neamiah & [*blank*] Eastman [?]

Feb. 20 Elizabeth Smith bur.
Mar. 3 William Hurrill, of [*blank*], co. Hertford, wid^r^, & Rebecca Smith, of St Botolph, Algate, sp^r^, marr. by lic.
Mar. 3 Richard Page, of St Mary Magdalen, Bermondsey, wid^r^, & Elizabeth Pickering, of St Stephen, Walbrook, sp^r^, marr. by lic.
Mar. 5 Edward Stibbs, of St Clement Danes, bach., & Elizabeth Smith, of Deptford, co. Kent, singlewoman, marr. by lic.

1709.

Mar. 30 Martha dau. of Rich^d^ & Martha Fellows bur.
May 12 Richard Web, of St Giles in the Fields, bach., & Mary Strugnal, of St Botolph, Aldersgate, sp^r^, marr. by lic.
May 20 A stillborn child of Mr Proctor's bur.
May 23 Peter Persehouse, of the Temple, wid^r^, & Barbary Pye, of St Paul, Covent Garden, widow, marr. by lic.
May 25 Honor Harris bur.
June 2 Henry Kindon, of St Bartholomew, London, bach., & Elizabeth Plucknet, of Fulham, co. Midd., sp^r^, marr. by lic.
June 3 William Jordan bur.
July 5 William son of Thomas & Judith Truston bapt.
July 10 Anne Lake bur.
July 14 John Cox, of St Martin in the Fields, bach., & [*blank*] Patterson, of St Dunstan's in the West, sp^r^, marr. by lic.
July 15 William son of Thomas & Judith Truston bur.
July 26 William son of Thomas & Elizabeth Purney bapt.
July 27 Elizabeth dau. of John & Eleanor Williams bur.
Aug. 5 Anne dau. of Thomas & Susanna Newling bapt.
Aug. 11 Thomas Buckly, of Chypping Barnet, co. Hertford, bach., & Frances Cooper, of St Clement Dane, singlewoman, marr. by lic.
Aug. 11 Robert son of Robert & Anne Davy bapt.
Aug. 28 Tevera Humberston bur.
Aug. 28 Sarah dau. of John & Esther Dashwood bapt.
Sep. 18 John & Samuel sons of [*blank*] & Anne Jarris bapt.
Oct. 10 John son of [*blank*] & Anne Jarris bur.
Oct. 12 John Merrey, of St Olave, Hart Street, wid^r^, & Esther Shimmond, of St Botolph, Algate, singlewoman, marr. by lic.
Oct. 14 Anne dau. of William & Mary Morton bapt.
Oct. 16 Robert son of William & Mary Allen bapt.
Oct. 21 William Adams, of St Giles, Criplegate, & Mary Wells, of Allhollows, Bread Street, marr. by lic.
Oct. 27 William Slade, of Allhollows, Barkin, & Grace Walters, of the same parish, marr. by lic.
Nov. 9 Samuel Langford, of St Dunstan in the East, & Hannah Mims, of Wimbleton, co. Surrey, marr. by lic.
Nov. 11 Sarah dau. of Samuel & Mary Trench bapt.
Nov. 17 Robert Penn, of St Lawrence, Jewry, & Jane Hazels, of St Giles, Criplegate, marr. by lic.
Nov. 27 Benjamin son of Thomas & Elizabeth Dickenson bapt.
Nov. 27 Thomas White bur.
Dec. 4 James son of Robert & Elizabeth Wooding bapt.
Dec. 26 Alexander Goodall, of St Martin, Ludgate, bach., & Anne Stockwood, of St Paul's, Covent Garden, marr. by lic.
Dec. 26 William Ball, of St Mary Abchurch, bach., & Mary Pangbourne, of St Mary le Bow, sp^r^, marr. by lic.
Dec. 29 Robert Drury & Rachel Smith, both of Stepney, co. Midd., marr. by lic.
Jan. 29 Rebecca Manwaring bur.
Feb. 8 Elizabeth Wooding bur.

Feb. 14 Lachlane Ross, of Rooding, co. Essex, bach., & Margaret Bayly, of Weale in the same co^{y}, widow, marr by lic.
Feb. 15 John son of John & Mary Archer bapt.
Feb. 24 John son of John & Jane Whittington bapt.
Mar. 7 John son of John & Jane Whittington bur.
Mar. 9 William son of John & Anne Barton bapt.
Mar. 15 Sarah dau. of Simon & Martha Pickersgil bapt.
Mar. 15 Otto David son of John James & Anne Cæsar bur.
Mar. 17 Rachel Babington bur.
Mar. 18 Mary dau. of John & Mary Archer bur.
Mar. 21 Rebeccah Church bur.

1710.

April 13 William Dixson & Mary Hoar, both of St Giles in the Fields, co. Midd., marr. by lic.
April 29 George son of George & Martha Colebrook bur.
April 30 Mary dau. of Nehemiah & [*blank*] Eastman bur.
May 27 Frances Davenant bur.
May 30 William Selby & Sarah Hedgecock, both of Chatham, co. Kent, marr. by lic.
June 12 John son of John & Hannah Wormleyton bapt.
June 22 John Crouch & Anne Disbro, both of St Clement Danes, marr. by lic.
June 27 John son of John & Hannah Wormleyton bur.
July 7 Richard Fellows bur.
July 24 Mary dau. of Clement & Anne Boheme bur.
Aug. 4 William son of Sampson & Anne King bapt.
Aug. 8 John Harvey & Elizabeth Morse, both of the parish of St John at Hackney, co. Midd., marr. by lic.
Sep. 7 Mary dau. of John James & Anne Cæsar bapt.
Oct. 22 William Rayman bur.
Oct. 26 Thomas Rayne, of St Faith, London, bach., & Elizabeth Nash, of Newington Stoke, co. Midd., marr. by lic.
Nov. 15 John Vicary bur.
Nov. 18 Frederick son of Enoch & Elizabeth Warner bapt.
Nov. 23 Philip Hatton, of Stratford upon Avon, co. Warwick, bach., & Grace Woolmer, of St Bartholomew the Great, London, marr. by lic.
Dec. 19 Richard Jones, of St Bridget, London, wid^{r}, & Elizabeth Lewis, of St Martin in the Fields, Midd^{x}, marr. by lic.
Jan. .. Isaac son of Cuthbert & Susanna Bland bapt.
[*blank*] Edward Heyden Peachey bur.
[*blank*] Anne dau. of Robert & Hannah Newling bur.
[*blank*] Charles Inwood, of Allhallows, Lombard Street, bach., & Rebeccah Goodwin, of the same parish, sp^{r}, marr. by lic.
Jan. 30 Thomas Higgins, of St Michael, Crooked Lane, bach., & Diana Snipe, of St Margaret, Westminster, marr. by lic.
Feb. 6 Richard Burrowes, bach., & Elizabeth Hodgkins, sp^{r}, both of this parish, marr. by banns
Feb. 22 Thomas Tott, of St Olave, Southwark, wid^{r}, & Mary Thorner, of St Michael, Crooked Lane, widow, marr. by lic.
Feb. 24 Peter Kingsey, of St Bridget, London, bach., & Anne Amler, of the same parish, sp^{r}, marr. by lic.
Mar. 22 Elizabeth Proctor bur.

1711.

April 3 Peter Goodwin, bach., & Martha Hillier, sp^{r}, both of this parish, marr. by lic.
May 7 Joseph son of Edward & Sarah Leak bapt.
May 16 Elizabeth dau. of Thomas & Catherine Holliday bapt.

May 18 Hannah dau. of John & Hanna Wormlayton bapt.
May 28 Judith Till bur.
May 31 Edmond son of John & Ester Dashwood bapt.
June 5 Richard Croke, of Tinwell, co. Rutland, bach., & Anne Reneu, of St Swithin, London, marr. by lic.
June 29 Antholiah Castle bapt.
July 19 William son of Thomas & Judith Truston bapt.
Aug. 14 John Budgen, of Hackney, co. Midd., bach., & Elizabeth Johuson, of the same parish, sp^r, marr. by lic.
Aug. 30 John Daw, of St Austin, London, wid^r, & Mary Annable, of St Peter's in Cornhill, widow, marr. by lic.
Aug. 30 John son of Clement & Anne Boehm bapt.
Sep. 2 Daniel Bland bur.
Sep. 6 Anne [*blank*], a foundling, bur.
Sep. 14 Robert son of Francis & Mary Cooper bapt.
Sep. 27 William Truston bur.
Oct. 2 Arthur Gilbert, of St Nicholas Coleabby, London, bach., & Anne Chell, of the same parish, sp^r, marr. by lic.
Oct. 9 Thomas Newton, of St Magnus, London, bach., & Elizabeth Preston, of Allhallows the Great, marr. by lic.
Oct. 14 John Cruchley, of St Saviour, Southwark, wid^r, & Rhoda Martyn, of St Antholin, sp^r, marr.
Oct. 26 Mary White bur.
Nov. 5 Margaret Guy bur.
Nov. 24 Charles Walter, of St Martin in the Fields, wid^r, & Theodora [*blank*], of the same parish, marr. by lic.
Dec. 5 Cesar Castle, a foundling, bapt.
Dec. 6 Stephen Whitwell, of St Mary, Whitechappel, bach., & Margaret Smith, of the same parish, sp^r, marr. by lic.
Dec. 13 Ernest Cogislaff Cæsar bur.
Dec. 14 Thomas Nicholas bur.
Dec. 15 Elizabeth Bradburne bur.
Dec. 16 Tho. Sprigmore, of St Dunstan, Stepney, co. Midd., bach., & Elizabeth Wright, of the same parish, sp^r, marr. with lic.
Dec. 28 Frances Williams bur.
Jan. 18 Samuel Skinner son of Sampson & Anne King bapt.
Jan. 22 Anne Sithe, a foundling, bapt.
Feb. 7 Thomas Wright, of St Dunstan, Stepney, co. Midd., bach., & Martha Constable, of St Mary, Whitechappel, in ye same co^y, sp^r, marr. with lic.
Feb. 8 Frances Fegges bur.
Feb. 9 Frederick Warner bur.
Feb. 22 Susanna dau. of Edmond & Lidia Browne bapt.
Mar. 12 John James Claude bur.

1712.

Mar. 26 Richard Syth bur.
[*blank*] Cæsar Castle bur.
May 8 Randal Jones, wid^r, & Mary Hawkes, sp^r, both of this parish, marr. with lic.
June 5 John Dale, of Stoke Newington, co. Midd., bach., & Sarah Chapman, of St Leonard, Shoreditch, sp^r, marr. with lic.
June 8 Philip Lascells bur.
June 11 Elizabeth dau. of John & Hester Dashwood bapt.
July 18 Mary dau. of Benjamin & Sarah Jordan bapt.
July 19 Sarah Jordan bur.
July 20 Thomas Pettit bur.
Aug. 2 Mary Jordan bur.

Aug. 3 Mary dau. of William & Sarah Sparke bapt.
Aug. 8 Thomas Cox, of Bromfeild, co. Essex, bach., & Jane Bruce, of [*blank*], spr, marr. with lic.
Aug. 10 Anne Sith, a foundling, bur.
Aug. 12 Margarett Castle, a foundling, bapt.
Aug. 13 Nathaniel Patten, of St Bennet, Paul's Wharf, bach., & Elizabeth Hockenhull, of St Bride's, spr, marr. with lic.
Sep. 10 William Mosely, of St Dunstan in the East, widower, & Martha Adams, of St Paul at Shadwell, marr. with lic.
Sep. 14 Sarah Rowley bur.
Sep. 19 Elizabeth dau. of John & Elizabeth Hickson bapt.
Sep. 21 Isaac son of Cuthbert & Susan Bland bapt.
Sep. 24 Henry Kendrick, bach., & Catherine Tilbury, spr, both of St Christopher, London, marr. with lic.
Sep. 29 Robert Woollius. bach., & Isabel [*blank*], both of St Anne, Blackfryers, marr. with lic.
Oct. 5 John son of Clement & Anne Boehm bur.
Oct. 28 Margaret Castle bur.
Nov. 1 William Parrot, of St Margaret, Westminster, bach., & Anne Brand, of St Edmond the King, London, marr. by lic.
Nov. 5 Robert Newling bur.
Nov. 16 Elizabeth dau. of John & Eliza. Baynham bapt.
Nov. 16 Lionel Stubbs, of St Paul, Covent Garden, widr, & Elizabeth Maurice, marr. by lic.
Nov. 16 Alexander son of William & Martha Stevenson bapt.
Nov. 20 John son of Michael & Mary Howard bapt.
Dec. 1 Bethiah dau. of George & Prudence Friend bapt.
Dec. 8 Ann dau. of Francis & Mary Cooper bapt.
Dec. 11 Elizabeth Catherine dau. of John James & Rachel Cæsar bapt.
Dec. 11 Bridget Proctor bur.
Dec. 11 Henry Boone, of St Bartholomew the Great, widr, & Bethiah Normansell, of St John at Hackney, marr. by lic.
Dec. 12 Mary Cave bur.
Dec. 16 John Arvolt, of St Andrew Wardrobe, & Ann Pickard, of St Ann in Blackfryers, marr. by lic.
Dec. 28 John Marks bur.
Jan. 27 John Price, of St Ann, Westminster, & Frances Wills, of the same parish, spr, marr. with lic.
Jan. 28 Roger Hunt bur.
Jan. 28 Sarah dau. of Edward & Sarah Leak bapt.
Feb. 10 William son of John & Judith Truston bapt.
Feb. 16 Timothy Cook, of St Giles, Cripplegate, & Mary Nash, of St Michael, Queenhith, marr. by lic.
Feb. 24 Alice Peachey bur.
Mar. 12 Sarah Williams bur.
Mar. 24 Mary Gold bur.

1713.

April 24 Richard son of Richard & Mary Hoar bapt.
April 26 Thomas Henstridge, of Rumford, Essex, bach., & Frances Ludington, of South Mimms in Midd., spr, marr. with lic.
April 26 John Hirons, of Kensington, Middx, widr, & Margaret Loton, of St Dunstan in ye East, London, spr, marr. with lic.
April 30 Sarah Collins bur.
April 30 John Crawley, of St Andrew Undershaft, widr, & Catherine Gerard, of Allhallows on the Wall, spr, marr. with lic.
May 1 Thomas son of John & Hannah Wormleyton bapt.
May 8 Constance dau. of Randal & Mary Jones bapt.

May 21 Samuel Skinner King bur.
May 21 Daniel Stacey, of S[t] John at Hackney, bach., & Judith Jones, of the same parish, sp[r], marr. with lic.
May 26 Robert Jones, of S[t] James, Westminster, bach., & Susan Pulford, of S[t] Martin Orgars, London, sp[r], marr. with lic.
June 3 William Truston bur.
June 6 Daniel Gilbert, of S[t] Botolph, Bishopsgate, bach., & Elizabeth Croxall, of the same parish, sp[r], marr. with lic.
June 7 Martha dau. of Thomas & Eliza. Robinson bapt.
June 15 Bartholomew Greenwood, of S[t] Mary in the Savoy, bach., & Isabel Richally, of the same parish, sp[r], marr. with lic.
June 18 Thomas Wormleyton bur.
July 5 Orlando Brown, of Leisthrop, co. Leic[r], wid[r], & Ann Farmer, of Turlangton in the said co[y], sp[r], marr. with lic.
July 7 Mary dau. of William & Mary Allen bapt.
July 10 Margaret Bosanquet bur.
July 17 John Cotton, of Barking, co. Essex, bach., & Sibilla Shelly, of the same, marr. with lic.
July 19 Susannah dau. of Waldive & Martha Willington bapt.
Aug. 4 Catherine dau. of Robert & Dorithy Manning bapt.
Aug. 6 Prosper Sach, of S[t] George, Southwark, & Ruth Hallford, of the same, marr. with lic.
Aug. 20 Edward Coulson, of S[t] Mary, Whitechappel, & Ann Jackson, of S[t] John Baptist, marr. by banns.
Aug. 27 Anthony Syths, a foundling, bur.
Sep. 8 Philippa Dawling bur.
Sep. 26 William Pettit bur.
Oct. 7 William Haywood, of S[t] Michael Bassishaw, London, bach., & Susannah Ward, of the same, sp[r], marr. with lic.
Nov. 3 Thomas Sparks bapt.
Nov. 3 Mary Houblon bur.
Nov. 7 Elizabeth dau. of John & Mary Hallford bapt.
Nov. 23 Mary Syths, a foundling, bur.
Dec. 7 Elizabeth Cosford bur.
Dec. 10 John Bright, of S[t] James, Westminster, bach., and Arabella Nurse, of the same, sp[r], by lic. marr.
Dec. 20 William son of Richard & Mary Reynolds bapt.
Jan. 1 Joseph Shaw, of S[t] John Baptist, & Phillis Davercourt, of the same, marr. by banns
Jan. 4 Mary dau. of John & Hester Dashwood bapt.
Jan. 10 John Becroft & Elizabeth Game, both of Bishop Storford in Hertfordshire, marr. by lic.
Jan. 13 James Frederick Cesar son of John James & Rachel Cesar bapt.
Jan. 16 George Roffey, of S[t] Saviour, Southwark, bach., & Sarah Walter, of the same, sp[r], marr. with lic.
Jan. 21 Mary Russoe bur.
Jan. 28 Richard son of Clement & Mary Bohem bapt.
Jan. 31 Thomas Grove, of S[t] Mary, Lambeth, wid[r], & Mary Welks, of S[t] Peter Poor, London, marr. with lic.
Feb. 7 Grace dau. of Jasper & Eliza Wilshire bapt.
Mar. 8 Jonathan Painter, of Christ Church, Surry, wid[r], & Ruth Bentham, of S[t] Mary, Wapping, sp[r], marr. with lic.

1714.

April 11 James Frederick Cesar bur.
April 12 Richard Walthaw, of S[t] Andrew, Holbourn, & Mary Shropshire, of Chelsey in Midd[x], sp[r], marr. with lic.

April 16 James & Mary Syths, foundlings, bur.
May 2 Benjamin Wet . . . , of S[t] Botolph, Bishopsgate, & Sarah Robinson, of the same parish, marr. with lic.
May 7 Mary dau. of Richard & Mary Hoar bapt.
May 16 Elizabeth dau. of Thomas & Judith Truston bapt.
May 20 Jemima dau. of John & Mary Archer bapt.
May 20 William Waters bur.
May 27 Thomas Day, of Rickmansworth, Herts, & Dorothy Wankford, of the same place, marr. with lic.
June 1 Anna Clerk bur.
June 15 Jane Holland bur.
June 19 Mary Caffell bur.
July 13 Lawrence Langhorn, of S[t] Clement Danes, bach., & Sarah Compton, of S[t] Dunstan, Stepney, marr. with lic.
July 14 Richard son of Samuel and Ann Clerk [?]
Aug. 20 Susannah Wormlayton bur.
Sep. 8 Mary Eastman bur.
Sep. 27 Peter Houblon bur.
Sep. 27 Ralph Rawlings, of S[t] Dunstan in the East, bach., & Elizabeth Alcox, of Allhallows, Barkin, widow, marr. with lic.
Oct. 20 Prudence dau. of George & Prudence Friend bapt.
Oct. 24 Mary Harris bur.
Oct. 24 Samuel Bird, of S[t] Andrew Undershaft, London, & Elizabeth Reynolds, of the same parish, sp[r], marr. with lic.
Oct. 30 Randal son of Randal & Mary Jones bapt.
Nov. 4 Edward Haynes, of [*blank*], co. Hertford, & Elizabeth Long, of S[t] Olave, Hart Street, London, sp[r], marr. with lic.
Nov. 24 William Harris bur.
Nov. 28 Randal Jones bur.
Dec. 12 John Curtis, of S[t] Saviour's, Southwark, bach., & Susannah Reeves, of the same parish, sp[r], marr. with lic.
Dec. 30 Mary dau. of Patrick & Jane Cane bapt.
Jan. 7 Joyce dau. of Francis & Mary Cooper bapt.
Jan. 9 Catherine dau. of Tho. & Catherine Hollyday bapt.
Jan. 20 Joseph Grillis, of S[t] Giles in the Feilds, co. Midd., & Martha Wellings, of the same, marr. with lic.
Feb. 3 John Downes, of S[t] Andrew Undershaft, London, & Anne Shaw, of S[t] Dunstan in the West, marr. with lic.
Feb. 7 John Slade, of Stepney in Midd., & Anne Haynes, of S[t] Mary Hill, London, marr. with lic.
Feb. 9 Torquel Mackleed, of S[t] Mary Magdalen, Old Fish Street, & Margaret Colt, of the same parish, marr. with lic.
Feb. 17 William Burt bur.
Feb. 17 Mary Hollyday bur.
Mar. 6 Lambert Peachy, of Rotherhith, Surry, & Martha Stanton, of S[t] Michael, Cornhill, marr. with lic.
Mar. 17 Samuel Baker bur.
Mar. 22 Catherine Hollyday bur.

1715.

Mar. 25 John son of William & Sarah Sparks bapt.
April 12 Robert son of Robert & Anne Eden bapt.
April 24 James son of Richard & Mary Reynolds bapt.
April 28 Thomas Warren, of S[t] Bartholomew Exchange, & Elizabeth Hall, of the same, marr. with lic.
May 14 Robert Logan, of S[t] James, Westminster, & Elizabeth Brewer, of the same parish, marr. with lic.

June 9 John Lasoon, of Stepney, Midd., bach., & Sarah Mayne, of Westham, Essex, spr, marr. with lic.
July 2 Sarah Howard bur.
July 28 Sampson Chaplin bur.
July 29 Phillis Williams bur.
July 30 Mountague Lloyd, of Barnwell St Andrew, co. Northampton, bach., & Mary Trenchfield, of St Andrew, Holborn, spr, marr. with lic.
Aug. 8 John son of Bargeriljah & Elizabeth Raymond bapt.
Aug. 20 Hannah dau. of Richard & Mary Hoar bapt.
Aug. 24 Elizabeth Keys bapt.
Sep. 3 John Proden & Sarah Stone, both of this parish, marr. with banns
Sep. 19 Thomas son of Robert & Mary Harrison bapt.
Sep. 20 John Cooper, of [St] Edmond the King, London, bach., & Hannah Skuce, of Chelsey, Midd., spr, marr. with lic.
Sep. 21 Mathew Fletcher, of St Paul at Shadwel, & Anne Hayes, of the same, marr. with lic.
Sep. 26 Robert Terrill, of Greenwich, Kent, & Anne Bates, of the same, marr. with lic.
Sep. 27 Elizabeth Waters bur.
Oct. 16 Mary dau. of Randal & Mary Jones bapt.
Oct. 17 William Syndal, of St Thomas the Apostle, & Mary Morris, of this parish, marr. with lic.
Oct. 23 Jane dau. of John & Hester Dashwood bapt.
Dec. 1 Isaac Finch, of Watford, co. Hertford, bach., & Mary Phillips, of Westham, Essex, marr. with lic.
Dec. 13 Dorothy Empson bur.
Dec. 18 Randal Jones bur.
Jan. 26 John Williams, of St Martin Vintry, London, & Anne Wheeler, of this parish, marr. with banns
Feb. 18 Prudence Friend bur.
Feb. 22 Anna Maria East bur.
Feb. 26 Benjamin Fulsis, of St Martin, Ludgate, widr, & Anne Bishop, of St Mary Magdalen, Old Fish Street, marr. by lic.
Mar. 14 Hester Jones bur.
Mar. 24 Charles Molineer bur.

1716.

April 3 William Richardson, of Allhallows, Barkin, bach., & Anne Dighton, of St Clement, Eastcheap, spr, marr. with lic.
April 4 Thomas Rider, of Reading, Berks, widr, & Sarah Goddard, of St Antho., spr, marr. with lic.
April 17 George Poynter, of St Alphage, widr, & Joan Betteridge, of St Antholin's, spr, marr. with lic.
April 25 John Williams bur.
May 5 Sarah dau. of Wm & Sarah Sparks bapt.
May 8 Robert Cole, of St James, Westminster, bach., & Elizabeth Walter, of the same parish, spr, marr. with lic.
May 12 Peter Carnac, of St Martin in the Feilds, bach., & Adriana Lelonte, of St Leonard, Shoreditch, spr, marr. with lic.
May 14 James son of Thomas & Mary Stevenson bapt.
May 16 Samuel Pendril, of Chelsea, Midd., bach., & Jane Oakey, of the same, spr, marr. with lic.
May 19 Zachariah Bourne, of Newington Butts, Surry, widow, & Elizabeth Miller, of the same place, widow, marr. with lic.
May 22 Thomas Hotchkis, of Botolph, Aldersgate, bach., & Eleanora Day, of Allhallows, Lombard Street, marr. with lic.

June 10 Edmunton Jones, of St Anth., & Mary Jones, of the same parish, widow, marr. with lic.
June 23 Edward Newton, of St Olave in the Old Jewry, bach., & Elizabeth Pindar, of St Stephen, Walbrook, marr. with lic.
June 25 Catherine dau. of Waldive & Martha Willington bapt.
July 15 Anne dau. of Richd & Mary Reynolds bapt.
July 21 John Randal, of St Paul, Covent Garden, bach., & Elizabeth Garnar, of the same parish, widow, marr. with lic.
July 25 John Clark, of Bookham, Surry, bach., & Anne Presey, of Fitcham in the same coy, marr. with lic.
July 30 George Colebrook, Dr of Physick, bur.
Aug. 18 Sarah East bur.
Sep. 5 Thomas Garbrand, of Hackney in Midds, bach., & Anne Nisbett, of the same place, spr, marr. with lic.
Sep. 7 Margaret Theed bur.
Sep. 20 Peter Crabb, of Jetsford, co. Somerset, bach., & Martha Crabb, of the same place, widow, marr. with lic.
Sep. 23 Richard Elsam, of St Margaret, New Fish Street, bach., & Sibyll Ruebridge, of St Bridget, spr, marr. with lic.
Oct. 10 Lucknar son of Richard & Sarah Jones bapt.
Oct. 25 Joshua Shute, of St Andrew, Holbourn, bach., & Elizabeth James, of St Swithin, spr, marr. with lic.
Oct. 25 Mary Wayth bur.
Nov. 11 William Kirby, of Alhallows the Great, & Mary Fresby, of the same parish, marr. with lic.
Nov. 22 Samuel Friend, of St Augustin's, bach., & Dorothy Roberts, of Lambeth, spr, marr. with lic.
Nov. 23 Simon Penn, of St Clement Dane, bach., & Elizabeth Finch, of the same parish, spr, marr. with lic.
Dec. 1 John son of John & Sarah Mountague bapt.
Dec. 21 Charles Claverline bur.
Dec. 23 Arabella Morton bur.
Dec. 25 Jacob Mann, of Cheselhurst in Kent, bach., & Elizabeth Acourt, of the same place, spr, marr. with lic.
Jan. 1 Robert Whitledge, of St Martin, Ludgate, bach., & Mary Cattel, of the same parish, spr, marr. with lic.
Jan. 1 James Latham, of St Clement Dane, & Jennet Held, of St Antholin's, marr. by banns
Jan. 1 George son of George & Prudence Friend bapt.
Jan. 5 William son of Dorothy & Thomas Paine bapt.
Feb. 23 John Wormlayton bur.
Feb. 27 Thomas son of William & Elizabeth Gape bapt.
Mar. 5 Benjamin Thompson, of St Ethelburga, bach., & Mary Phillips, of St Swithin's, London, spr, marr. with lic.
Mar. 16 Thomas Holyday bur.
Mar. 19 Edmunton son of Edmonton & Mary Jones bapt.
Mar. 19 Charles Staples, of St Margaret, Westminster, bach., & Thomasine Morton, of St Paul's, Covent Garden, spr, marr. with lic.
Mar. 20 Susannah Clogie bur.

1717.

April 11 Bargeriljah son of Bargeriljah & Elizabeth Raymond bapt.
April 25 Edmunton Jones bur.
April 25 Bargeriljah Raymond bur.
April 26 Mary Proctor bur.
May 1 William Woolley, of St Ann, Westminster, bach., & Ann Corpes, of the same place, spr. marr.

May 9 Walter Smith, of St George, Southwark, bach., & Mary Elbrey, of the same place, sp^r, marr. with lic.
May 11 John Bosanquet bur.
May 24 Lawrence Andrews, of St Andrew in Holborne, bach., & Sarah Whitehouse, of the same parish, sp^r, marr. with lic.
May 25 Rowland Raymond, of St Bridget, London, bach., & Martha Hill, of St Botolph, Aldersgate, marr. with lic.
May 31 Mary dau. of Waldive & Martha Willington bapt.
June 18 James son of James & Martha Prince bapt.
June .. Thomas son of Ellis & Susannah Wright bapt.
June .. Robert Allen bur.
July 3 Matthew Kitchener, of St Botolph, Aldersgate, bach., & Martha Worden, of St Lawrence, Jewry, sp^r, marr. with lic.
July 6 John son of Thomas & Catherine Hollyday bapt.
July 19 John son of John & Mary Clerk bapt.
Aug. 8 Ralf Oulsman, of Epsom, Surry, bach., & Martha Sanders, of the same place, widow, marr. with lic.
Aug. 15 William Ellis, of St Martin, Ludgate, bach., & Selena Goss, of Hackney, co. Midd., sp^r, marr. with lic.
Aug. 18 Thomas son of Thomas & Ann Janeway bapt.
Aug. 25 Thomas son of Rich^d & Mary Hutt bapt.
Aug. 26 John Beaufills bur.
Oct. 2 William Peachy, Esq., bur.
Oct. 13 John Eastman, of St Botolph, Aldersgate, bach., & Elizabeth Goodwin, of the same parish, sp^r, marr. with lic.
Oct. 29 William son of Richard & Mary Hoar bapt.
Nov. 2 Mordecai Abbot, of St Martin in the Feilds, bach., & Isabella Molyneux, of the same parish, sp^r, marr. with lic.
Nov. 10 Samuel Walford, of Newington Butts, co. Surry, bach., & Mary Eades, of the same place, sp^r, marr. with lic.
Nov. 17 John Dennis, of Stepney, co. Midd., bach., & Mary de la Mare, of the same place, sp^r, marr. with lic.
Nov. 26 William Courcey, of St. Dunstan in the West, wid^r, & Martha Coxall, of the same parish, sp^r, marr. with lic.
Dec. 26 Hugh Smithson, Esq., of Tottenham in the county of Middlesex, widower, & the Honourable Constantia Hare, of the same place, with licence marr.
Dec. 27 Mertilla dau. of Thomas & Dorothy Pain bapt.
Dec. 30 William Newton bur.
Jan. 2 John Ince bur.
Jan. 14 Mary Anderson bur.
Jan. 17 Samuel Hotchkis bur.
Jan. .. John son of Henry & Mary Ellis bapt.
Feb. 9 Elizabeth Smith bur.
Feb. 13 Thomas Proctor, of St Mary Abchurch, bach., & Susannah Chapman, of the same parish, sp^r, marr. by lic.
Feb. 20 Dorcas Howard bur.
Feb. 20 Robert Bryan, of St Peter, Paul's Wharf, bach., & Sarah Hildeck, of St Margaret, Lothbury, sp^r, marr. by lic.
Feb. 20 Peter Normansel, of St Michael Bassishaw, bach., & Hester Northey, of St John at Hackney, sp^r, marr. by lic.
Feb. 21 Wm Furnish, of Chigwel in Essex, bach., & Sarah Sagurs, of the same place, sp^r, marr. with lic.
Feb. 25 Robt Cock, of Wandsworth in Surry, wid^r, & Margaret Cole, of the same place, sp^r, marr. by lic.
Mar. 1 Elizabeth Wilson bur.
Mar. 17 Wm Sherwood, of St Dunstan in the East, bach., & Jane Bradshaw, of the same, sp^r, marr. by lic.

Mar. 30 Abraham Lincoln, of S[t] Dunstan at Stepney, & Hannah Bradford, of S[t] Helen near Bishopsgate, marr. by lic.
April 17 Julius Deeds, of Hush, co. Kent, bach., & Elizabeth Drake, of Blechinly, co. Surry, sp[r], marr. by lic.
April 24 George Rose, of Great Gadden [? Gaddesden], co. Hertf., bach., & Ann Graves, of S[t] Alban's in the same co[y], widow, marr. by lic.
April 29 W[m] Presland, of Chigwell, Essex, wid[r], & Cornelia Symonds, of S[t] Botolph, Bishopsgate, sp[r], marr. by lic.
April .. W[m] Halstead, of S[t] Clement's Danes, bach., & Jane Chaliner, of the same parish, sp[r], marr. by lic.
May 2 John Wild, of S[t] Botolph, Aldersgate, wid[r], & Alice Hotchkis, of the same parish, sp[r], marr. by lic.
May 4 W[m] Dangerfield, of S[t] Peter's near Paul's Wharf, bach., & Mary Gaspey, of the same parish, sp[r], marr. by lic.
June 16 Grace dau. of Edward & Mary Jones bapt.
June 16 John son of James & Martha Prince bapt.
June 27 Robert Gary, of S[t] James, Garlick Hith, bach., & Elizabeth Collins, of S[t] John's at Hackney, sp[r], marr. by lic.
June 29 Augustin son of Augustin & Elizabeth Bryan bapt.
July 5 James son of James & Joan Harvey bapt.
Aug. 1 John son of John & Anne Gold bapt.
Aug. 4 Thomas son of Thomas & Elizabeth Dixson bapt.
Aug. 21 Thomas Howard bur.
Sep. 17 W[m] Carr, of S[t] Andrew, Holborn, bach., & Margaret Scofeild, of the same parish, sp[r], marr. by lic.
Sep. 20 John Champion, of S[t] James, Clarkenwell, bach., & Elizabeth Hubbard, of the same parish, sp[r], marr. by lic.
Sep. 28 James Wood, in the Liberty of the Tower, wid[r], & Margaret Lackey, of S[t] Nicholas Colcabby, sp[r], marr. by lic.
Oct. 5 Thomas Williams, of S[t] Clement Danes, bach., & Anne Nokes, of S[t] Andrew, Holborn, sp[r], marr. by lic.
Oct. 7 Ralf Bickerton, of S[t] Mary le Bow, London, wid[r], & Elizabeth Smith, of Hackney in Midd., sp[r], marr. by lic.
Oct. 11 Anne dau. of Mary & John Joy bapt.
Oct. 22 William son of Elizabeth & W[m] Gape bapt.
Oct. 23 Antholina Pig, a foundling, bapt.
Oct. 26 James Penncard, of S[t] James, Garlick Hyth, London, bach., & Mary Bollard, of S[t] Botolph, Aldgate, sp[r], marr. by lic.
Oct. 27 Constantia Eastman bur.
Nov. 4 Mary dau. of Lancelot & Priscilla Bromicham bapt.
Nov. 6 John Reed, of S[t] John, Wapping, wid[r], & Isabella Bird, of the same place, sp[r], marr. by lic.
Nov. 14 Mary dau. of Sam[l] & Anne Clerk [?]
Nov. 17 Prudence dau. of George & Prudence Friend bapt.
Nov. 19 Susanna Wright bur.
Nov. 30 Thomas Leamon, of S[t] Alphage, London, bach., & Mary Mills, of Low Layton, Midd. [Essex], sp[r], marr. by lic.
Dec. 2 John Hodsdon, of Harrow on the Hill, co. Midd., wid[r], & Norris Lee, of the same place, sp[r], marr. by lic.
Dec. 8 Thomas son of John & Mary Clerk bapt.
Dec. 20 Edward King, of S[t] Bridget, London, bach., & Elizabeth Brown, of the same parish, widow, marr. by lic.
Dec. 25 Elizabeth Eastman bur.
Jan. 11 John son of John & Hester Dashwood bapt.
Jan. 23 Mary dau. of Edw[d] & Sarah Betteridge bapt.
Jan. 29 Mary Betteridge bur.

Feb. 1 Thomas Godber, of St Martin's in the Fields, bach., & Anne Wepsbot, of St Margaret, Westminster, sp^r^, marr. with lic.
Feb. 5 John Brown, of St Swithin, London, bach., & Sarah Pitfeild, of Clapham in Surrey, widow, marr. with lic.
Feb. 5 Jacob Watson, of Eltham in Kent, bach., & Susannah Smith, of St Andrew's, Holborn, sp^r^, marr. with lic.
Feb. 18 Prudence Friend bur.
Feb. 22 Susannah Booth bur.

1719.

Mar. 31 Andrew Quelch, of St Dunstan's, Stepney, bach., & Sarah James, of the same parish, sp^r^, marr. by lic.
April 4 William Ridge, of St Andrew Undershaft, London, bach., & Ann Nash, of St Peter's, Cornhill, sp^r^, marr. with lic.
April 8 John Till bur.
April 12 Maria dau. of Josiah & Mary Odams bapt.
May 3 Ann dau. of Stephen & Mary Marshal bapt.
May 17 John Braudhurst & Mary his wife bur.
May 20 Thomas Young, of Westham in Essex, bach., & Agnet Reditt, of St Laurence Pountney, London, sp^r^, marr. with lic.
May 20 Robert Cox, of St Michael in Wood Street, wid^r^, & Mary Ellaby, of St Alban, Wood Street, sp^r^, marr. with lic.
June 2 Richard Jones, of St Leonard, Shoreditch, bach., & Mary Bravinder, of St Gregory's, London, sp^r^, marr. with lic.
June 4 Samuel son of Samuel & Mary Smith bapt.
June 9 Thomas Savill, of St Lawrence, Jewry, bach., & Elizabeth Russell, of North Okindon, co. Essex, sp^r^, marr. with lic.
June 12 Martha, dau. of Waldive & Martha Willington bapt.
June 18 Thomas Thistleton, of St Giles in the Fields, wid^r^, & Sophia Lennard, of St Giles, Cripplegate, sp^r^, marr. with lic.
July 2 Mary St John, a foundling, bapt.
July 4 James Molineer bur.
July 8 Thomas Church, of Hendon in Midd^x^, bach., & Sarah Caper, of the same place, sp^r^, marr. with lic.
July 22 Samuel son of Samuel & Mary Jones bapt.
July 27 Samuel Jones bur.
Aug. 14 Elizabeth Procter bur.
Aug. 15 Caleb Lambert, of St Saviour's, Southwark, widow^r^, & Sarah Cosford, of this parish, sp^r^, marr. with lic.
Aug. 28 Mary dau. of Thomas & Elizabeth Smith bapt.
Sep. 27 Sarah dau. of Augustin & Elizabeth Bryan bapt.
Oct. 8 Richard Davis, of St Martin, Ironmonger Lane, bach., & Mary Cooper, of St John at Hackney, sp^r^, marr. with lic.
Oct. 18 Mary dau. of Henry & Judith Grover bapt.
Nov. 14 John Whetstone, of St Paul's, Shadwell, wid^r^, & Jane Price, of the same parish, sp^r^, marr. with lic.
Nov. 15 John Sandishstreet, son of a poor woman who fell into labour in the street, bapt.
Nov. 29 John Prince bur.
Nov. 30 John Watts, of Lincoln's Inn, bach., & Mary Mosely, of St John's parish, sp^r^, marr. with lic.
Dec. 3 Rachel widow of Dr James Cæsar bur.
Dec. 3 George Green, of St Saviour's, Southwark, bach., & Elizabeth Charles, of St Botolph, Bishopsgate, sp^r^, marr. with lic.
Feb. 2 William Matthews, of St John at Wapping, bach., & Anne Stone, of the same parish, sp^r^, marr. with lic.
Feb. 8 Prudence dau. of George & Prudence Friend bapt.

Feb. 9 Thomas Peirce, of Yarmouth, co. Norfolk, bach., & Elizabeth Hatt, of St Mary Colechurch, London, spr, marr. with lic.
Feb. 25 John Tovey, of St Martin in the Fields, co. Midd., bach., & Elizabeth Brigham, of St Paul, Covent Garden in the same coy, spr, marr. with lic.
Feb. 27 Daniel Blackwell, of St James, Clarkenwell, co. Midd., widr, & Jane Benwell, of St Gregory's, London, widow, marr. with lic.
Feb. 28 William Burkett, of St Botolph, Aldersgate, bach., & Susannah Tinker, of St Bride's, London, spr, marr. with lic.
Mar. 1 John Dod & Elizabeth Finch, both [*blank*], marr.
Mar. 6 Constantia Hatton bur.
Mar. 6 James Peter son of James & Jane Mentell bapt.
Mar. 10 Jane dau. of James & Martha Prince bapt.
Mar. 20 Susannah Henley bur.

1720.

April 15 Honner Olde bur.
April 17 Thomas Dade, of St Michael, Queenhith, London, bach., & Sarah Andrews, of the same parish, widow, marr. with lic.
April 18 John Woodruffe, of Alhallows, Barking, London, bach., & Margaret Davison, of St John at Wapping, widow, marr. with lic.
April 20 William Oswin, of St Martin in the Fields, bach., & Mary Brigham, of St Paul, Covent Garden, spr, marr. with lic.
April 22 Edward Wilson, of Alhallows, Barking, London, bach., & Elizabeth Stevenson, of the same parish, spr, marr. with lic.
April 25 Elizabeth Haler bur.
May 7 Waldive son of Waldive & Martha Willington bapt.
May 8 James Stevenson, of Deptford, co. Kent, bach., & Elizabeth Gibson, of the same place, spr, marr. with lic.
May 12 Thomas Keat, of St Olave, Hart Street, London, bach., & Elizabeth Hawkes, of this parish, spr, marr. with lic.
June 16 Jane dau. of Robert & Dorothy Manning bapt.
June 29 William Walker, of St Mary Abchurch, London, bach., & Mary Baily, of St Laurence, Jewry, spr, marr. with lic.
June 30 Joseph Macock, of Great Okley, co. Northampton, bach., & Elizabeth Sergean, of St Mary Hill, London, spr, marr. with lic.
July 19 William Brown, of St Olave, Southwark, widr, & Anne Reading, of the same parish, spr, marr. with lic.
July 27 Ambrose Clemens, of Plymouth, co. Devon, bach., & Elizabeth Nicholls, of St Mary, Whitechapel, co. Midd., spr, marr. with lic.
July 31 James son of James & Anne Joy bapt.
Aug. 19 Joseph Poynter, of Alhallows the Great, London, bach., & Mary Tharpe, of the same parish, spr, marr. with lic.
Aug. 22 William Andrews, of St John Baptist, London, bach., & Rebeccah Cooper, of the same parish, spr, marr. with lic.
Aug. 23 Nathaniel Pippin, of St Clement Danes, co. Midd., bach., & Sarah Goody, of St Botolph, Bishopsgate, London, spr, marr. with lic.
Aug. 30 William son of Thomas & Elizabeth Holmes bapt.
Aug. 31 Mary Allen bur.
Sep. 4 Samuel Eastman bur.
Sep. 15 William Barrow, of St Martin in the Fields, co. Midd., & Mary Roe, of St Margaret, Westminster, spr, marr. with lic.
Sep. 26 George Jackson, of St Mary, Whitechapel, co. Midd., bach., & Susannah Harrison, of St James, Clerkenwell in the same coy, spr, marr. with lic.
Sep. 28 James Arnold bur.
Oct. 15 [*blank*] Burdet, a pentioner's child. bur.

Nov. 12 Edward Sanders, of S[t] Martin's le Grand, London, wid[r], & Anne Abbitt, of S[t] Dunstan in the East, London, sp[r], marr. with lic.
Nov. 22 Allen Webb, of S[t] Mary le Bow, London, bach., & Sarah Webb, of S[t] John at Hackney, co. Midd., sp[r], marr. with lic.
Nov. 22 Peter Warren bapt.
Nov. 26 Joseph Cooper, of S[t] Dunstan at Stepney, co. Midd., bach., & Mary Rix, of S[t] Mary, Whitechappel in the same co[y], sp[r], marr. with lic.
Nov. 29 William Land, of S[t] Peter Poor, London, bach., & Mary Brooks, of the same parish, sp[r], marr. with lic.
Dec. 9 Mary Storke bur.
Dec. 16 Aaron Westerband, of S[t] Botolph, Aldgate, co. Midd., bach., & Sarah Hoult, of S[t] Dunstan at Stepney in the same co[y], widow, marr. with lic.
Dec. 22 Sarah dau. of Henry & Judith Grover bapt.
Dec. 24 Thomas Wharton, of Watford, co. Herts, wid[r], & Mary King, of the same place, sp[r], marr. with lic.
Jan. 3 Elizabeth, dau. of George & Elizabeth Chebsey bapt.
Jan. 4 Thomas Fowler bur.
Jan. 6 Sarah Burdit bapt.
Jan. 6 Marmaduke Castle bapt.
Jan. 6 William Lowder, of S[t] Mary Hill, London, bach., & Mary Strowd, of S[t] Paul, Shadwell, co. Midd., sp[r], marr. with lic.
Jan. 8 Isaac Skinner, of S[t] Leonard, Foster Lane, London, bach., & Susanna Lloyd, of S[t] Edmond the King, sp[r], marr. with lic.
Jan. 8 Hester Davison bur.
Jan. 12 Sarah Wignall bur.
Jan. 15 Ann dau. of Robert John & Mary Little bapt.
Jan. 22 Thomas son of Edmond & Mary Jones bapt.
Feb. 2 Daniell Bott, of S[t] Paul, Shadwell, co. Midd., wid[r], & Anne Newland, of S[t] Michael, Queenhith, London, sp[r], marr. with lic.
Feb. 2 Anthony Peircey, of S[t] Clement Danes, co. Midd., wid[r], & Avicia Bilbey, of S[t] Mary le Bone in the same co[y], widow, marr. with lic.
Feb. 9 James Austin, of S[t] Bride's, London, bach., & Hope Read, of S[t] Ann, Blackfryers, London, sp[r], marr. with lic.
Feb. 10 Elizabeth dau. of Samuel & Ann Clerk bapt.
Feb. 19 William Cooks bur.
Feb. 21 Peter Hull, of S[t] Giles in the Fields, co. Midd., bach., & Anne Beevas, of the same parish, sp[r], marr. with lic.
Feb. 21 William Mason, of S[t] Mary, Whitechappel, co. Midd., wid[r], & Catherine Elliston, of Yealing in the same co[y], widow, marr. with lic.
Mar. 1 Frances Cox bur.
Mar. 1 John son of John & Mary Watts bapt.
Mar. 9 Catherina Mary de Putter bur.

1721.

April 11 William Bratcher, of Hammersmith, co. Midd., bach., & Anne Abbett, of the same place, sp[r], marr. with lic.
April 14 James Storke bur.
April 27 Thomas Roman, of Long Ditton, co. Surrey, bach., & Anne Bartlet, of Malden in the same co[y], sp[r], marr. with lic.
April 28 John Warde bur.
May 2 Sarah Milborn bur.
May 7 Stephen Lockington bur.
May 30 Philip Miller, of S[t] George, Southwark, Surrey, bach., & Mary Kennel, of [S[t]] Olave, Southwark, sp[r], with lic. marr.

June 1 Richard Rawlins, of St George, Southwark, Surrey, bach., & Mary Rayner, of St Anne's, Aldersgate, London, spr, marr. with lic.
June 6 John Woodhouse, of St Mildred in the Poultry, bach., & Elizabeth Weeden, of St John at Hackney, widow, marr. with lic.
June 16 Ephraim Clarke, of Camberwell, Surrey, & Susannah Grafton, of the same parish, spr, marr. with lic.
June 21 Thomas Witham, of St Michael, Queenhith, London, widowr, & Hester Bell, of the same parish, spr, marr. with lic.
June 22 Joseph Gilbert bur.
June 27 John Artis, of Ipswich, co. Suff., bach., & Mary Collingwood, of St John at Wapping, spr, marr. with lic.
June 29 Thomas Alderman, of [*blank*], & Dorothy Hutchel, of St John Baptist, marr. by banns
July 1 Charles Calabar, of St John at Wapping, co. Midd., widr, & Mary Morris, of St Christopher's, London, spr, marr. with lic.
July 8 Edmond Allen, of the Middle Temple, London, bach., & Elizabeth Bowen, of St Mary le Savoy, Middx, spr, marr. by lic.
July 9 Robert Weekes, of St Mary le Bow, London, bach., & Elizabeth Ross, of the same parish, spr, marr. with lic.
July 15 John Leavett, of Morden, co. Surrey, widr, & Jane Roffey, of Chipstead in the same coy, spr, marr. with lic.
July 17 Thomas Anthony, a foundling, bur.
July 18 Benjamin Woolston, of St Peter in Cheapside, London, widr, & Elizabeth Rymill, of St Michael, Queenhith, London, spr, marr. by lic.
July 26 Ann dau. of Caleb & Sarah Lambert bapt.
July 30 Matthew Hanscombe, of Redburne, co. Hertf., widr, & Catherine Edde, of Caple, co. Surrey, widow, marr. with lic.
Aug. 21 Penelope dau. of Augustin & Elizabeth Bryan bapt.
Aug. 27 Abraham le Febure, of the Hamletts of the Tower of London, bach., & Magdalen Carante, of St Dunstan at Stepney, co. Midd., spr, marr. with lic.
Sep. 26 Thomas Church, of St Andrew, Holborn, widr, & Love Alesbury, of St George, Southwark, marr. with lic.
Sep. 28 John Mason, of Barking, Essex, bach., & Jane Wilkinson, of the same place, spr, marr. with lic.
Sep. 28 John Wicks, of this parish, bach., & Thomasine Stubbs, of St Sepulchre's, London, spr, marr. by banns
Oct. 26 William Adams, of Enfield, co. Midd., bach., & Mary Ellton, of the same parish, spr, marr. with lic.
Oct. 26 Joseph Kent, of Hornsey, co. Midd., bach., & Hester Hobbard, of St Sepulchre's, London, spr, marr. with lic.
Nov. 1 Sarah Snowden bur.
Nov. 5 Anne, a foundling, bur.
Nov. 16 Robert Arrold, of St Giles in the Feilds, co. Midd., & Anne Cholmondely, of the same parish, widow, marr. with lic.
Nov. 16 John son of John & Mirabella Rogers bapt.
Nov. 21 Anthony King, of St Clement Danes, widr, & Frances Hughes, of St Mary le Savoy, spr, marr. with lic.
Nov. 28 William Fairchild, of St Andrew, Holborn, co. Midd., spr [*sic*], & Elizabeth Sayer, of St Clement Danes in the same coy, spr, marr. with lic.
Nov. 30 Isaac Tarlton, of St Martin in the Feilds, co. Midd., bach., & Jane Dowson, of this parish, spr, marr. by lic.
Dec. 1 Isaac Clarke bur.
Dec. 6 Richard Fellowes bur.
Dec. 10 William Yate, of St Bartholomew the Less, London, & Mary Clarke, of St Sepulchre's, London, spr, marr. with lic

Dec. 26 Edward Hait, of Rochester, co. Kent, bach., & Frances Eason, of the same place, sp[r], marr. with lic.
Dec. 26 John Dawkins, of S[t] Botolph, Aldersgate, London, bach., & Ann Ellis, of this parish, sp[r], marr. by banns.
Jan. 13 William son of Waldive & Martha Willington bapt.
Jan. 25 Abraham Price, of S[t] Bridget *vulgo* S[t] Bride's, London, & Hester Faulkner, of the same parish, sp[r], marr. by lic.
Jan. 29 William Barker, of S[t] Clement Danes, co. Midd., bach., & Margaret Samworth, of the same parish, sp[r], marr. by lic.
Jan. 31 Carrol Friend dau. of George & Prudence bapt.
Feb. 1 Erasmus Hopffer, of S[t] Dunstan in the East, bach., & Theodosia Boehm, of this parish, sp[r], marr. with lic.
Feb. 15 Anne Queen, a foundling, bur.
Feb. 23 Carrol Friend bur.
Feb. 24 Richard son of Rob[t] & [*blank*] Kerrington bapt.
Mar. 7 John Merry, of S[t] Michael, Crooked Lane, London, bach., & Elizabeth Jeamineau, of Lee, co. Kent, sp[r], marr. by lic.
Mar. 23 Margaret Antholin, a foundling, bapt.

1722.

Mar. 29 Thomas Wilson, of S[t] Mary Hill, London, bach., & Jane Cooper, of the same parish, sp[r], marr. by lic.
April 10 Silas Jennings, of this parish, bach., & Susannah Wilkins, of S[t] Mary le Bow, sp[r], marr. by lic.
April 11 John Thorp, of S[t] Swithin, London, bach., & Dorothy Worgin, of S[t] Dunstan at Stepney, co. Midd., sp[r], marr. by lic.
April 13 Giles Dance, of S[t] Giles, Cripplegate, wid[r], & Sarah Brett, of Carshalton, Surry, marr. by lic.
April 13 John Arnold bur.
April 30 Anne Boehm bur.
May 5 Edward Satchwell, of S[t] Margaret, Lothbury, London, bach., & Mary Godbor, of S[t] Stephen, Coleman Street, London, sp[r], marr. by lic.
May 19 Charles Killigrew, of S[t] Mary, Whitechapel, Midd[x], bach., & Elizabeth Vaughan, of the same parish, sp[r], marr. by lic.
May 30 Grace dau. of Edmond & Mary Jones bapt.
June 2 Henry Southouse, of S[t] Giles, Cripplegate, London, bach., & Mary Kynaston, of S[t] Paul, Covent Garden, co. Midd., sp[r], marr. by lic.
June 3 Catherine Hotchkis bur.
June 5 John son of John & Mary Arnold bapt.
June 12 Joseph Webster, of S[t] Saviour, Southwark, Surry, bach., & Mary Johnson, of S[t] Leonard, Shoreditch, co. Midd., sp[r], marr. by lic.
June 24 Robert Pool & Mary Piat, of S[t] Antholin's, marr. by banns
June 30 Joseph Sodeen, of S[t] Botolph, Aldersgate, London, wid[r], & Mary Bull, of S[t] Bartholomew near the Exchange, London, sp[r], marr. by lic.
Aug. 2 Joseph Williams, of S[t] George's, Southwark, Surry, bach., & Elizabeth Cooper, of S[t] Olave, Silver Street, London, sp[r], marr. by banns
Aug. 23 Ambrose Fellow, of S[t] Michael's, Crooked Lane, London, bach., & Mary Mills, of S[t] Mary at Lambeth, Surry, sp[r], marr. by lic.
Aug. 26 Thomas Teasdall, of S[t] Bridget *vulgo* S[t] Bride's, London, bach., & Martha Green, of the same parish, sp[r], marr. by lic.
Aug. 30 John Barlow, of S[t] Mary Aldermary, London, & Mary Ram, of the same parish, sp[r], marr. by lic.
Sep. 4 Anthony Rodney Buckeridge, of S[t] Bridget *vulgo* S[t] Bride's, London, & Anne Lewis, of S[t] Margaret, Westminster, co. Midd., sp[r], marr. by lic.

Sep. 18 Richard Parkes, of St Saviour, Southwark, Surry, bach., & Elizabeth Bassett, of the same parish, spr, marr. by lic.
Sep. 25 Joseph Nursey, of St Dunstan in the West, London, & Margaret Jones, of the same parish, spr, marr. by lic.
Sep. 26 John Burrows, of St Catherine near the Tower, London, bach., & Ann Cowper, of St Dunstan at Stepney, co. Midd., spr, marr. by lic.
Sep. 28 Mary Whitfeild bur.
Oct. 9 Thomas Brook, of Malden, Essex, bach., & Susannah Bourman, of the same place, spr, marr. by lic.
Oct. 13 Richard Chapman, of St Peter Poor, London, bach., & Elizabeth Masham, of St Olave's, Hart Street, London, spr, marr. by lic.
Oct. 23 John Duffell, of St Leonard, Shoreditch, co. Midd., widr, & Elizabeth Barker, of St Dunstan, Stepney, Middx, widow, marr. by lic.
Nov. 8 Elizabeth Stiles bur.
Nov. 15 Thomas Hends, of St Margaret, Lothbury, London, bach., & Anne Low, of the same parish, widow, marr. by lic.
Nov. 19 Henry Cooper, of St John Baptist, London, widr, & Elizabeth Woodcock, of St Leonard, Shoreditch, widow, marr. by lic.
Nov. 27 John Mills & Mary Clorybus, both of St John Baptist, London, marr. by banns
Dec. 2 John Baxter son of Edward & Elizabeth Treyloe bapt.
Dec. 4 John Jones, of St Mary Staining, London, bach., & Sarah Layton, of the precinct of Bridewell, London, spr, marr. by lic.
Dec. 11 John Batty, of St John at Wapping, co. Midd., bach., & Elizabeth [*blank*], of the same parish, spr, marr. by lic.
Dec. 13 Edward Limby, of St Clement, Eastcheap, London, bach., & Anne Long, of the same parish, spr, marr.
Jan. 3 John Angil, of St Margaret, Westminster, co. Midd., bach., & Elizabeth Beale, of St Andrew Hubbard, London, spr, marr. by lic.
Jan. 10 Joseph Lane, of this parish, bach., & Elizabeth Paul, of this parish, spr, marr. by banns
Jan. 13 Penelope Bryan bur.
Jan. 30 Joseph Ludlow bur.
Jan. 31 Thomas Newton, of St Paul, Covent Garden, co. Midd., bach., & Frances Record, of St Dunstan in the West, widow, marr. by lic.
Feb. 3 Carrol son of George & Prudence Friend bapt.
Feb. 5 John Manship, of St Michael, Cornhill, bach., & Elizabeth Garbrand, of St John's at Hackney, co. Midd., spr, marr. by lic.
Feb. 10 Arthur Yeo, of St Mary le Savoy, co. Midd., widr, & Mary Dowling, of this parish, spr, marr. by lic.
Feb. 23 Thomas King, bach., & Anne Daniel, spr, both of St Botolph, Aldgate, London, marr. by lic.
Feb. 27 John Wharton, of Peterspool, co. Hertf., widr, & Elizabeth White, of St Matthew, Fryday Street, London, spr, marr. by lic.
Mar. 14 Margaret Boehm bur.

1723.

April 2 Benjamin Manning, of St Mary Woolnorth, London, bach., & Mary Harwell, of St John at Wapping, Middx, spr, marr. by lic.
April 5 Mary dau. of John & Mirabella Rogers bapt.
April 13 Richard Carpender, of St Bennet Finck, London, bach., & Anne Hambridge, of St Thomas the Apostle, London, spr, marr. by lic.
April 14 Francis Ponthieu, bach., & Elizabeth Fielding, spr, both of St Swithin, London, marr. by lic.
April 18 William Giles, of Beckingham, co. Kent, bach., & Elizabeth Upton, of Croyden in Surrey, spr, marr. by lic.

May 2 Margaret dau. of Samuel & Mary Clerk bapt.
May 22 Mary dau. of John & Mary Walton bapt.
June 3 Anne dau. of John & Martha Wilson bapt.
June 4 Francis Cook, of Rumford, co. Essex, bach., & Elizabeth Love, of this parish, spr, marr. by lic.
June 5 Mary dau. of John & Elizabeth Smith bapt.
June 11 Anne Baines bur.
June 30 Elizabeth dau. of John & Joyce Bell bapt.
July 5 Massey Stork bur.
July 10 Elizabeth Bell bur.
July 13 John Storey, bach., & Elizabeth Noble, spr, both of St Clement Danes, co. Midd., marr. by lic.
Aug. 11 Mary Smith bur.
Aug. 13 Thomas Hitchcott, of St Mildred, Bread Street, London, bach., & Joan Chessum, of St Olave, Old Jewry, London, spr, marr. by lic.
Aug. 18 Peter son of John & Mary Clarke bapt.
Aug. 21 Mary Starling bur.
Sep. 15 Judith dau. of Henry & Judith Grover bapt.
Sep. 16 Edmond son of Edmond & Mary Jones bapt.
Sep. 18 Elizabeth dau. of Peter & Elizabeth Hawkins bapt.
Sep. 25 Mary Jones & Edmond her son both bur.
Sep. 27 Elizabeth Hawkins bur.
Sep. 29 John Bath, of St Sepulchre, London, bach., & Sarah Meakin, of St Mary, Islington, co. Midd., spr, marr. by lic.
Oct. 28 Martha dau. of Waldive & Martha Willington bapt.
Nov. 28 Robert Smith, of this parish, bach., & Anne Smith, of St Andrew, Holborn, co. Midd., spr, marr. by lic.
Nov. 30 Penelope dau. of Augustin & Elizabeth Briant bapt.
Dec. 11 Samuel Houblon bur.
Jan. 2 Randolph Fernley bur.
Jan. 5 Augustin Seaton, of St Margaret, Lothbury, London, bach., & Elizabeth Snow, of this parish, spr, marr. by lic.
Jan. 9 Richard Clarke, of Enfield, co. Midd., bach., & Elizabeth Pitsom, of St Mary Hill, London, spr, marr. by lic.
Jan. 16 Samuel Nichols bur.
Jan. 16 Anne Clarke bur.
Feb. 10 Samuel Follet, of St Mildred, Poultry, widr, & Anne Young, of St John Baptist, London, marr. by lic.
Feb. 18 Thomas Brown, of Dean, co. Lancr, bach., & Susannah Robinson, of St Bennet Fink, London, marr. by lic.
Mar. 1 Thomas Tickner, of Christ Church, London, bach., & Assell Hill, of St Gregory's, London, spr, marr. by lic.
Mar. 3 Martha dau. of Thomas & Elizabeth Ballard [?]

1724.

April 2 Henry Harison, of St Anthony, Gravesend, co. Kent, widr, & Mary Arundel, of St Peter nr Paul's Wharf, widow, marr. by lic.
April 9 Richard Price, of Debptford, co. Kent, bach., & Sarah Robinson, of Greenwich in the same coy, spr, marr. by lic.
April 10 Charles Cove . . ., of St Andrew, Holborn, co. Midd., bach., & Margaret Durrett, of All Hallows, Barking, London, spr, marr. by lic.
April 18 John Ridgley bur.
April 18 Ferdinando Burdet bur.
April 20 Elizabeth Crips bur.
May 13 John Skinner, of St Martin Vintry, London, bach., & Catherine Pennard, of St James, Garlickhith, London, spr, marr. by lic.
May 22 Roger Baines bur.

June 17 John Elliot, of St Botolph, Bishopsgate, bach., & Elizabeth Anderson, of St Mary at Newington, co. Surry, spr, marr. by lic.
June 23 Josias Spearman, of Westham, co. Essex, bach., & Mary Staples, of St Andrew, Holborn, co. Midd., spr, marr by lic.
July 2 Samuel Stanfield, of St Catherine Cree Church, London, widr, & Jane Hallen, of the same parish, spr, marr. by lic.
July 16 John Makay, of St Lawrence Pountney, London, widr, & Mary Bradford, of the same parish, spr, marr.
July 18 William Henman, of Maidstone, co. Kent, bach., & Mary Poole, of Charing in the same coy, spr, marr. by lic.
July 19 Mary Starling bur.
July 21 Henry Clarke bur.
Aug. 4 John Walton, of St Bartholomew the Less, London, bach., & Phebe Garbrand, of Hackney, co. Midd., spr, marr. by lic.
Aug. 22 Elizabeth Storke bur.
Oct. 1 Andrew Hunter, of Wapping, co. Midd., bach., & Mary Brown, of the same, spr, marr. by lic.
Oct. 11 Mary dau. of George & Elizabeth Chebsey bapt.
Oct. 11 George son of George & Sarah Peal bapt.
Oct. 12 Josias Lambert, of St John Baptist, London, bach., & Elizabeth Penner, of the same parish, spr, marr.
Oct. 18 William son of Thomas & Catherine Horabim bapt.
Nov. 8 Thomas Jones bur.

Mem.: From this time all Births & Burials belonging to St John's Baptist parish are registred in ye proper Register of that parish.

MARRIAGES.

1724.

Nov. 24 Thomas Kidd, of St Mary Aldermanbury, London, bach., & Margaret Ware, of St Bennett Grace Church, London, spr, marr. by lic.
[Dec.]11 William Pennard, of St Peter, Cornhill, London, bach., & Elizabeth Ford, of the same parish, spr, marr. by lic.
[Dec.]24 Eelgate Sandwell, of this parish, bach., & Frances Lockton, of St Mildred, Poultry, spr, marr. by lic.
Jan. 5 Nathaniel Sanderson, of St Botolph, Allgate, London, bach., & Ann Collins, of St John at Hackney, co. Midd., spr, marr. by lic.
Jan. 10 Richard Ayars, of St Alpage, London, bach., & Ann Cole, of St Andrew, Holborn, spr, marr. by lic.
Jan. 31 Thomas Blest, of St Ann, Westminster, co. Midd., bach., & Sarah Rowley, of the same parish, spr, marr. by lic.
Feb. 5 John Nunn, of Chigwell, co. Essex, widr, & Sarah West, of this parish, spr, marr. by lic.

1725.

Mar. 29 Richard Day, of St Michael, Queenhith, London, bach., & Mary Newland, of the same parish, spr, marr. by lic.
April 17 William Andrews, of St Andrew, Holborn, London, bach., & Sarah Griffin, of the same parish, spr, marr. by lic.
May 2 Joshua Crewdon, of St Mary, Whitechappel, co. Midd., bach., & Phillis Rich ., of the same parish, spr, marr. by lic.

May 13 William Munyard, of S[t] Andrew, Holborn, London, bach., & Rebecca Humphreys, of the same parish, sp[r], marr. by lic.
May 22 Stephen Piermont, of Fullham, co. Midd., bach., & Elizabeth Harsnett, of S[t] Marg., Westminster, sp[r], marr. by lic.
June 1 John Ball, of Allhallows Staining, London, bach., & Cathrine Burford, of S[t] Cathrine Coleman, London, marr. by lic.
July 15 William Flight, of this parish, bach., & Mary Stone, of this parish, sp[r], marr. by lic.
Aug. 5 Thomas Mathews, of this parish, bach., & Elizabeth Lasinby, of this parish, sp[r], marr. by lic.
Sep. 12 Stephen March, of Poplow [*sic*], co. Midd., bach., & Sarah Pleasant, of the same parish, sp[r], marr. by lic.
Sep. 26 Daniel Adams, of S[t] Mary Abchurch, London, bach., & Elizabeth Perry, of the same parish, sp[r], marr. by lic.
Sep. 30 John Pane, of Cheshunt, co. Hertf., bach., & Ann Adams, of Endfield in the same co[y], sp[r], marr. by lic.
Oct. 7 Henry Hanson, of S[t] Kerthrine Cree, London, bach., & Elizabeth Hickas, of the same parish, marr. by lic.
Oct. 14 Roger Ryland, of Christ Church, London, bach., & Mary Willmore, of S[t] Hellen's, London, sp[r], marr. by lic.
Nov. 3 John Harwood, of Barnes, co. Surry, bach., & Mary Tomlinson, of the same parish, sp[r], marr. by banns
Nov. 18 John Cox, of S[t] John at Hackney, co. Midd., wid[r], & Mary Crutchfield, of S[t] Alband's, Wood Street, London, sp[r], marr. by lic.
Nov. 25 Samuel Rodham, of S[t] John, Wapping, co. Midd., wid[r], & Dorothy Hale, of the same parish, widow, marr. by lic.
Dec. 4 Samuel Rodham, of S[t] John, Wapping, co. Midd., bach., & Isabellah Robinson, of the same parish, widow, marr. by lic.
Dec. 14 John Wilkes, of the parish of Peter's Poor, London, bach., & Mary Stocker, of Ash, co. Kent, sp[r], marr. by lic.
Dec. 14 Scipio Godard, of S[t] Margarett Patton, London, bach., & Jane Gidings, of S[t] Dunstan's, London, widow, marr. by lic.
Dec. 21 John Herd, of S[t] Margaret Patton's, London, bach., & Ann More, of S[t] Mary Mounthaw, London, sp[r], marr. by lic.
Dec. 24 The Right Hon[ble] Frances Joseph Ignatious [*sic*], Barron D'Ongnyes, of the parish of S[t] Martin's in the Fields, London, cœlebs, & the Hon[ble] the Lady Ann Cole, of the parish of S[t] James, Westminster, in the county of Mid-six, vidua. Lic.
Feb. 3 William Horabin, of S[t] Botolph, Bishopsgate, co. Midd., bach., & Elizabeth King, of S[t] Dunstan, Stepney, widow, marr. by lic.
Feb. 19 Thomas Howill, of S[t] Swithin's, London, bach., & Elizabeth Cosford, of the same parish, sp[r], marr. by lic.
Mar. 14 John Farrey, of Woburn, co. Bedf., wid[r], & Mary Speake, of the [same] parish, marr. by banns
Mar. 15 Joseph Lewendon, of S[t] Dunstan's in the West, London, bach., & Sarah Richardson, of S[t] Antholin's, sp[r], marr. by lic.

1726.

April 2 William Leverland, of S[t] Paul's, Covent Garden, co. Midd., bach., & Martha Lee, of Lincoln's Inn in the same co[y], sp[r], marr. by lic.
April 10 Henry Chettey, of S[t] Stephen, Wallbrook, London, bach., & Sarah Brookes, of S[t] Swithin's, London, sp[r], marr. by lic.
April 12 George Coleborn, of S[t] Mary Magdalen, Old Fish Street, London, bach., & Lucy Fibbas, of the same parish, sp[r], marr. by lic.
May 19 Edward Atkins, of S[t] Dunstan's, Stepney, co. Midd., wid[r], & Jane Fox, of the same parish, sp[r], marr. by lic.

July 5 Peter Kolls, of St Andrew, Holborn, co. Midd., bach., & Love Church, of St George's, Southwark, Surry, widow, marr. by lic.

July 16 Thomas Savory, of Earith in Kent, bach., & Priscilla Baxter, of St Anne's, Black Fryers, London, spr, marr. by lic.

July 28 George Bedells, of St Mary Magdalen, Bermondsey, Surry, bach., & Martha Wall, of ye same parish, spr, marr. by lic.

Aug. 25 James Markendle, of St Martin Outwich, London, bach., & Mary Thomas, of this parish, spr, marr. by banns

Sep. 7 John Paschall, of Sandon, co. Essex, bach., & Sarah Skingle, of the same parish, spr, marr. by lic.

Oct. 18 Thomas Brookes, of St Olive, Southwark, Surrey, bach., & Ann Williams, of St Magnes ye Martyr, London, spr, marr. by lic.

Nov. 10 John Dawson, of Croydon, co. Surrey, bach., & Elizabeth Collins, of St Michael, Cornhill, London, spr, marr. by lic.

Nov. 17 William Careloss, of St Botolph, Alldersgate, London, widr, & Ester Gibson, of St James, Clarkenwell, co. Midd., widow, marr. by lic.

Nov. 29 Thomas Saunders, of Wansworth, Surrey, bach., & Sarah Lord, of ye same parish, spr, marr. by lic.

Dec. 14 William Wills, of St Sepulchre's, London, bach., & Honor Kemp, of the same parish, spr, marr. by lic.

Jan. 5 [*blank*] Pickett, of Stretham, co. Surrey, bach., & Ann Godard, of the same parish, marr. by lic.

Mar. 9 Jacob Blizard, of Lambeth, co. Surrey, bach., & Elizabeth Wilson, of St Dunstan in ye West, widow, marr. by lic.

1727.

April 14 Jacob Hoare, of St Lenard in Foster Lane, London, bach., & Elizabeth Ham, of St Dunstan's [*blank*], London, spr, marr. by lic.

April 15 Samuel Deport, of St Andrew, Holborn, co. Midd., bach., & Sarah Stroude, of ye same parish, spr, marr. by lic.

April 18 John Hambleton, of St Olive, Southwark, Surrey, bach., & Alce Ives, of ye same parish, widow, marr. by lic.

May 3 Joshua Nunn, of Wansworth, Surrey, bach., & Ann Salter, of Barnes in ye same coy, spr, by lic.

May 20 John Agar, Esq., of the Middle Temple, widr, & Margarett Pugh, of St Clement Danes, co. Midd., spr, by lic.

June 13 James Cooke, of Ashstead, co. Surrey, bach., & Ann Skrine, of Clarverton, co. Somerset, widow, by lic.

June 24 Richard Morley, of Grase in [? Gray's Inn], co. Midd., bach., & Mary Dorrington, of St Andrew, Holborn, London, spr, by lic.

July 14 Edward White, of St Mary Magdaline, Bermondsey, London [*sic*], bach., & Sarah Pyne, of ye same parish, spr, by lic.

Aug. 20 William Paine, of Allhalows, London Wall, bach., & Cæliæ [*sic*] Owen, of ye same parish, widow, by lic.

Aug. 20 Edward Watson, of St Bartholomue Major, London, bach., & Mary Coleman, of the same parish, spr, by lic.

Aug. 30 Richard Rice, of St James, Westminster, co. Midd., widr, & Isabella Vary, of St Magnis Marter, London, spr, by lic.

Aug. 30 Thomas Lutton, of St George, Southwark, Surrey, widr, & Ann Morris, of ye same parish, widow, by lic.

Sep. 17 Isaac Stephens, of this parish, bach., & Jane Lowder, of St. Olive's, Southwark, by banns

Oct. 9 Samuel King, of Quenhoe in co. Essex, widr, & Mary Brougton, of Cranbrook in co. [*blank*], spr, marr.

Dec. 14 John Comins, of ye Inner Temple, London, bach., & Bell Wright, of St Andrew, Holborn, London, spr, by lic.

Jan. 11 William Bincks, of S[t] George, Botolph Lane, London, bach., & Deborah Wrench, of S[t] Magnis y[e] Marter, London, sp[r], by lic.
Feb. 3 John Brombey, of S[t] Lenord, Foster Lane, London, bach., & Judith Davis, of S[t] Bride's, London, sp[r], by lic.
Feb. 6 John Chantrell, of S[t] Giles, Cripplegate, co. Midd., bach., & Mary Jackman, of S[t] John Baptist, London, sp[r], by lic.
Feb. 8 William Barcroft, of Deffairsded [*sic*] in co. Essex, bach., & Elizabeth Smithies, of S[t] Martin's in y[e] Fields, Midd., sp[r], by lic.
Feb. 25 John Ballwin, of S[t] Olive's, Southwark, bach., & Elizabeth Laurance, of this parish, sp[r], by banns
Feb. 28 Thomas Brookes, of Lambeth, co. Surrey, bach., & Elizabeth Gould, of the same parish, sp[r], by lic.
Mar. 1 John Tompson, of y[e] parish of Bread Street, London, wid[r], & Ann Ghiselin, of S[t] Leonard's, Shoreditch, co. Midd., widow, by lic.

1728.

April 2 Daniel Walter, of S[t] Andrew, Holborn, co. Midd, bach., & Mary Denton, of S[t] Auston, London, sp[r], by lic.
May 1 Thomas Swallow, of Writtle, co. Essex, bach., & Elizabeth Lloyd, of the same parish, sp[r], by lic.
May 15 Richard Coxall, of Twickenham, co. Surrey, wid[r], & Ann Hill, of y[e] same parish, sp[r], by lic.
Aug. 20 Thomas Bankes, of S[t] Botolph, Billingsgate, London, bach., & Ann Person, of the same parish, sp[r], by lic.
Sep. 21 Gilbert Crockett, of S[t] Martin, Ludgate, London, bach., & Francies Clarke, of Walthamstow, co. Essex, sp[r], by lic.
Sep. 22 William Holdway, of S[t] Olive's, Southwark, co. Surrey, bach., & Elizabeth Hadds, of y[e] same parish, widow, marr. by lic. by M[r] Parry, curate*
Oct. 3 Allin Cooper, of S[t] Mary, White Chapple, co. Midd., wid[r], & Hannah Hawes, of Farnburough, co. Kent, widow, by lic.
Oct. 14 Ebenezer Brathwait, of S[t] Michael, Cornhill, London, bach., & Phebe Stanton, of S[t] John at Hackney, co. Midd., sp[r], by lic.
Oct. 24 Robert Wilson, of S[t] Michael, Cornhill, London, bach., & Mary Cullen, of Richmond, Surrey, sp[r], by lic.
Nov. 6 Henry Godde, of S[t] Martin's in the Fields, co. Midd., bach., & Elizabeth Beaufields, of this parish, sp[r], by lic.
Nov. 15 John Cleland, of S[t] Peter's Poor, London, bach., & Mary Perrie, of S[t] George's, London, sp[r], by lic.
Nov. 25 Harding Tomkins, of S[t] Edmond y[e] King, London, bach., & Hannah Prine, of S[t] Peter's, Cornhill, London, sp[r], by lic.
Feb. 6 Thomas Howard, of S[t] James, Clarkenwell, Midd[x], bach, & Sarah Inskip, of S[t] Olive's, Southwark, Surry, widow, by lic.
Feb. 17 John Ellicott, of Allhollows, London Wall, London, bach., & Deborah Saunderson, of S[t] John, Hackney, co. Midd., sp[r], by lic.

1729.

April 3 William Smith, of Lincoln's Inn, co. Midd., bach., & Ann Fox, of S[t] Mary Aldermary, London, sp[r], by lic.
April 8 Richard Robinson, of S[t] Mildred in y[e] Poultrey, London, wid[r], & Sarah Franklin, of S[t] Bottolph, Bishopsgate, London, sp[r], by lic.
April 10 Francies Stinton, of [S[t]] Giles, Cripplegate, bach., & Mary Sarratt, of this parish, sp[r], by banns
April 19 Henry Bartholomew, of S[t] Andrew, Holborn, London, wid[r], & Mary Simms, of Chesham, co. Bucks, sp[r], by lic.

* This entry is inserted on a slip of paper.

April 24 William Franklin, of Maidstone, co. Kent, wid^{r}, & Jane Junes, of ye same parish, by lic.

May 25 James Ridgway, of St John Baptist, London, bach., & Elizabeth Harrison, of ye same parish, by lic.

June 29 William Wayto, of Holy Trinity, London, wid^{r}, & Joyce Millner, of [S^{t}] Mary Aldermary, London, sp^{r}, by lic.

July 6 Thomas Frankling, of St Botolph without Aldgate, London, bach., & Ann Green, of this parish, by banns

Aug. 23 Thomas Whinyard, of Christ Church, Spittlefields, co. Midd., wid^{r}, & Eliz. Larcomb, of St Mildred in the Poultrey, London, widow, by lic.

Aug. 26 Joseph Shelton, of Northamton, bach., & Mary Tingey, of St Andrew, Holborn, London, sp^{r}, by lic.

Sep. 4 Charles Kinsey, of Mortlate [*sic*], co. Surrey, bach., & Kerthrine Rever, of Putney in ye same co^{y}, sp^{r}, by lic.

Sep. 28 Richard Hall, of Woolrich [*sic*], co. Kent, bach., & Ann Henstridge, of Eltham in ye same co., sp^{r}, by lic.

Oct. 5 Roger Gething, of Bridwell, London, bach., & Ann Berkley, of [S^{t}] Bride's, London, widow, by lic.

Oct. 7 John Simmonds, of Christ Church, Surrey, bach., & Phebe White, of St Saviour's, Southwark, in ye same co., sp^{r}, by lic.

Oct. 10 Joseph Pigg, of Hillingdon, co. Midd., bach., & Rebecca Yenell, of ye same parish, sp^{r}, by lic.

Oct. 27 Samuel Wells, of St Michael's, Cornhill, London, bach., & Elizabeth Browne, of St Mary Magdaline, Bermondsey, co. Surrey, sp^{r}, by lic.

Nov. 27 Abraham Cambridge, of this parish, bach., & Millicant Tidman, of this parish, by banns

Dec. 11 Edward Cox, of Rotherhith, co. Surrey, bach., & Elizabeth Goodwin, of this parish, sp^{r}, by lic.

Jan. 15 James Mathews, of St Alphago, London, bach., & Mary Rust, of ye same parish, sp^{r}, by lic.

Feb. 1 Charles Welbeloved, of Thorpe, co. Surrey, & Margaret Chapman, of Lambeth in ye same co., sp^{r}, by lic.

Feb. 2 John Matts, of St George's in the East, co. Midd., bach., & Sarah Pickett, of the same parish, sp^{r}, marr. by lic. by Mr Parry

1730.

April 9 John Silk, of Nutshelling, co. Southamton, bach., & Mary Tull, of ye same parish, sp^{r}, marr. by lic. by Mr Parry

April 15 John Brasscup, of St Mildred, Bred Street, London, wid^{r}, & Jane Thatcher, of St Swithin's, London, sp^{r}, marr. by lic. by Mr Berryman

April 17 Richard Roy, of Chittesster [*sic*], co. Sussex, bach., & Ann Butler, of ye same parish, sp^{r}, marr. by lic. by Mr Bayley

April 23 Jeffry Meggs, of Stradford, co. Essex, bach., & Dorithy Bond, of Popler, co. Midd., sp^{r}, marr. by lic. by Mr Parry

May 7 Abraham Winterbottom, of St Mary Aldermary, London, bach., & Eliz. Whitaker, of St James, Garlick Hith, London, sp^{r}, marr. by lic. by Mr Venn

May 17 Edward Hodgkins, of St Mildred, Bred Street, London, bach., & Elizabeth Lambert, of this parish, widow, marr. by lic. by Mr Parry

May 20 John Tomkins, of St Margaret, Westminster, co. Midd., bach., & Alce Parker, of ye same parish, sp^{r}, marr. by lic. by Dr Oliver

May 26 Percival Deane, of St James, Westminster, wid^{r}, & Eliz. Phillip, of St Mary le Bowe, London, widow, marr. by lic. by Mr Parry

May 26 Samuel Thomson, of St Martin, Ludgate, London, widr, & Hannah Cooper, of Hackney, co. Midd., wid., marr. by lic. by Mr Newcome
June 13 William Leigh, of St George's, Botolph Lane, London, bach., & Eden Briggs, of St Savour's, Southwark, Surrey, wid., marr. by lic. by Mr Parry
June 23 Blunt Rogers, of St Peter le Poor, London, bach., & Ann Berry, of St Mary, Islington, co. Midd., spr, marr. by lic. by Mr Wood
June 24 William Wasey, of St Martin in ye Fields, co. Midd., bach., & Margaret Spearman, of St John Baptist, London, spr, marr. by lic. by Mr Venn
Aug. 24 Thomas Smith, of St Mary Monthaw, London, widr, & Jane Blake, of ye same parish, spr, marr. by lic. by Mr Perry
Aug. 27 James Whittle, of St Giles in the Fields, co. Midd., bach., & Ann Homer, of St Martin in ye Fields in the same co., spr, marr. by lic. by Mr Parry
Oct. 13 Peter Mason, of Edminton, co. Midd., bach., & Mary Penson, of the same parish, spr, marr. by lic. by Mr Parry
Nov. 26 Robert Mackmorran, of this parish, bach., & Mary Anderson, of this parish, spr, marr. by lic. by Mr Creyk
Feb. 24 Even Jones, of St Botolph, Bishopsgate, London, bach., & Carthrine Thomas, of Fenchurch, London, spr, marr. by lic. by Mr Lucey

1731.

May 2 Josep Thursby, of St Stephen, Wallbrook, London, bach., & Ellaner Smith, of this parish, spr, marr. by lic. by Mr Wood
May 25 Richard Wootton, of Hackney, co. Midd., bach., & Ann Lant, of the same parish, spr, marr. by lic. by Mr Newcome
June 3 Samuel Dennitt, of Lambeth, Surrey, bach., & Lucza Sheakle, of St John Baptist, London, spr, marr. by banns by Mr Parry
June 27 John Raymond, of Christ Ch., Spittlefields, co. Midd., bach., & Elizabeth Allaway, of Hockley, co. Bedf., spr, marr. by lic. by Mr Wood
July 10 Nathaniel Geary, of Hackney, co. Midd., widr, & Emma Kilgoner, of the same parish, wid., marr. by lic. by Mr Newcome
July 27 James Peters, of Great St Helen's, London, & Ellizabeth Stump, of St John Baptist, London, spr, marr. by banns
Aug. 1 Richard Gutteridge, of St Giles, Cripplegate, co. Midd., bach., & Lydia Birkitt, of the same parish, spr, marr. by lic. by Mr Parry
Aug. 12 Gualtiro Riddell, of St Clement's Danes, co. Midd., bach., & Jane Woolkinson, of the same parish, marr. by lic. by Mr Parry
Sep. 16 Austin Weddell, of St Martin, Ludgate, London, bach., & Sary Knowls, of St Martin in ye Fields, co. Midd., by lic.
Sep. 23 John Feildall, of Debtford, co. Kent, widr, & Ellizabeth Harding, of the same parish, wid., by lic.
Sep. 25 Henry Ward, of Bromley in Kent, widr, & Dorcas Johnson, of the same parish, by lic.
Nov. 2 John Burton, of St Lennard, Shorditch, co. Midd., bach., & Rebecca Heasey, of Hackney in ye same co., by lic.
Nov. 28 John Blake, of St Botolph, Algate, London, widr, & Ann Maria Brimmer, of the same parish, by lic.
Dec. 11 Ezekiel George, of St Savour's, Southwark, Surrey, bach., & Frances Burton, of St Leannard, Eastchip, London, wid., by lic.
Jan. 25 William Kirby, of St Botolph, Bishopsgate, London, bach., & Ann Hill, of this parish, spr, by banns
Feb. 11 Thomas Savage, of Clapham, co. Surry, bach., & Ann Cotton, of Peckam in the same co., spr, by lic.

Feb. 13 Benj. Roads, of St Sepulcher's, London, bach., & Elliz. Ash, of ye same parish, by lic.

Feb. 18 William Cogdell, of this parish, bach., & Judith Hunt, of this parish, sp^r, by lic.

Feb. 19 John Atwood, of St Andrew, Holborn, co. Midd., bach., & Ann Rawson, of St James, Westminster, co. Midd., wid., by lic.

Feb. 27 Jervis Staverton, of St Mary, White Chapple, co. Midd., bach., & Ann Mary Colby, of St Dunstan's, Stepney, in ye same co., by lic.

1732.

April .. Peter Walker, of St Mary in Dover, co. Kent, wid^r, & Dorithy Sexton, of St Michael Royal, London, wid., marr. by lic. by Mr Land

April 25 Edwd Cooper, of St Ann, Westm^r, co. Midd., wid^r, & Mary Collins, of St John's, Hackney, in the same co., sp^r, marr. by lic. by Mr Newcome

June 1 Thomas Chesson, of Allsainst [*sic*], Bread Street, London, bach., & Elizabeth Newman, of S^t [*blank*], Westminster, co. Midd., sp^r, marr. by lic. by Mr Abbit

June 25 Samuel Sharpe, of St Albon's, Wood Street, London, wid^r, & Kerth. Price, of St James, Garlickhith, London, sp^r, marr. by lic. by Mr Land

July 5 Sotherton Barker, of St Giles, Cripplegate, London, bach., & Ann Ashley, of St Olive Jewry, London, sp^r, marr. by lic. by Mr Land

Sep. 3 Samuel Woodfield, of Hackney, co. Midd., bach., & Elizabeth Fifield, of Romford in Essex, sp^r, marr. by lic. by Mr Newcom

Sep. 10 Charles Smith, of St Mary Magdalen, Milk Street, London, bach., & Ann Whiteing, of Thames Street, London, sp^r, marr. by lic. by Mr Land

Sep. 13 George Hardy, of Raisborough, co. Bucks, bach., & Jane Brownsord, of St John Baptist, London, sp^r, marr. by lic. by Mr Land

Oct. 5 Samuel Freeman, of St Giles, Cripplegate, co. Midd., wid^r, & Mary Wells, of this parish, sp^r, marr. by lic. by Mr Pantir

Oct. 12 George Easman, of Bickington, co. Somerset, wid^r, & Mary Welsh, of St Mary Magdalen, Milk Street, London, sp^r, marr. by lic. by Mr Rider

Oct. 25 William Waller, of Deptford, co. Kent, wid^r, & Ann Fann, of St Swithin's, London, wid., marr. by lic. by Mr John Berryman

Dec. 7 Charles Far, of St Laurance Jury, London, bach., & Ann Noss, of St Mary le Bow, London, sp^r, marr. by lic. by Mr Burn

Dec. .. John Basson, of Coleman Street, London, wid^r, & Elizabeth Bayley, of Allhollows, London Wall, sp^r, marr. by lic. by Mr Panton

1733.

Mar. 27 Joseph Barber, of St Mich., Crooked Lane, London, bach., & Mary Hill, of St Bartholomew the Great, London, sp^r, marr. by lic. by Mr Panton

April 5 Thomas Noone, of St Mich., Wood Street, London, bach., & Ann Woodhouse, of St Giles, Cripplegate, co. Midd., sp^r, marr. by lic. by Mr Abbott

April 7 William Bull, of St Peter le Poor, London, bach., & Susannah Pinkcott, of St Foster otherwise Vedast, London, sp^r, marr. by lic. by Mr Dubardieu

May 10 Ralph Rose, of Little Marlow, co. Barks [*sic*], bach., & Mary Lattermer, of Great Marlow in the same co., marr. by lic. by Mr Bayley

July 8 Benjamin Hawes, of St Bride's, London, bach., & Elizabeth Fore, of the same parish, marr. by lic. by Mr Panton

July 26 John Wood, of St Dunstan's in the West, bach., & Frances Plizzard, of St Savour's, Southwork, Surrey, spr, marr. by lic. by Mr Browne
July 30 Richard Brice, of St Ann's, Aldersgate, London, bach., & Jane Evans, of St Antholin's, London, spr, marr. by banns by Mr Panton
Sep. 7 Edward Humphreys, of St James's, Westminster, co. Midd., bach., & Eleanor Towers, of St Martin's, Ironmonger Lane, London, marr. by lic. by Mr Panton
Oct. 8 William Pigg, of St John Baptist, London, widr, & Mary Morris, Alhollows the Less, London, wid., marr. by lic. by Mr Panton
Dec. 15 John Fuzly, of St Botolph, Bishopsgate, London, bach., & Mary Bowly, of the same parish, wid., marr. by lic. by Mr Venn
Jan. 1 John Rogers, of St Mary Sommerst, London, bach., & Ann Wilkinson, of St Mary Aldermary, London, spr, marr. by lic. by Mr Panton
Feb. 14 Andrew Mills, of St Paul's, Covent Garden, co. Midd., bach., & Ann Bignell, of St Mary Axe, London, spr, marr. by lic. by Mr Venn
Feb. 21 Henry Branson, of St Mary Magdalen, Old Fish Street, London, bach., & Eliz. Wilkins, of St George, Buttolph Lane, London, spr, marr. by lic. by Mr Sherlock
Mar. 14 William Walter, of St Clement, Eastcheape, London, bach., & Elizabeth Charr, of Putney, co. Surrey, spr, marr. by lic. by Mr Venn

1734.

April 30 Isaac Knibbs, of Great Oakley, co. Northampton, bach., & Elizabeth Hawkins, of St Swithin's, wid., marr. by lic. by Mr Venn
May 11 Charles Johnson, of St Leonard, Shoreditch, co. Midd., bach., & Elizabeth Garratt, of this parish, spr, marr. by lic. by Mr Venn
July 21 William Lipyeat, of Queenbith, London, bach., & Mary Jefferys, of the same parish, wid., marr. by lic. by Mr Panton
July 23 Daniel Bayes, of Market Harborough, co. Leic., widr, & Eliz. Watts, of St John, Hackney, co. Midd., wid., marr. by lic. by Mr Newcom
Sep. 16 William Tovery, of Staines, co. Midd., widr, & Martha Smith, of the same place, spr, marr. by lic. by Mr Panton
Sep. 17 Thomas Frankham, of Trinity in the Minories, in the Liberty of the Tower, widr, & Susannah Banwell, of St Antholin's, London, spr, marr. by lic. by Mr Roberts
Nov. 9 Samuel Rowley, of St Sepulcher's, co. Midd., bach., & Martha Crawley, of St Botolph, Allgate, London, spr, marr. by lic. by Mr Duburdieu
Nov. 21 Phillip James, of Christ Church, London, bach., & Carthrine Byland, of St Giles, Cripplegate, London, spr, marr. by lic. by Mr Seagrave
Dec. 17 Mountagu Powell, of Christ Church, Spittlefields, co. Midd., bach., & Sarah Harrison, of St Mary, Whitechapple, co. Midd., spr, marr. by lic. by Mr Venn
Dec. 21 Jacob Yellely, of St Clement Danes, co. Midd., widr, & Ann Gibbson, of the same parish, marr. by lic. by Mr Venn
Dec. 26 Henry Fisher, of St Margarett, Lothbury, London, [*blank*], & Elizabeth Walicourt, of St Antholin's, London, wid., marr. by lic. by Mr Venn
Mar. 18 John Semethurst, of St Andrew, Holborn, London, widr, & Mary Lewen, of St George, Southwark, Surrey, spr, marr. by lic. by Mr Panton

1735.

Mar. 26 Henry Driver, of Putney, co. Surrey, widr, & Mary Rice, of the same parish, spr, marr. with lic. by Mr Venn

June 30 Thomas Dicker, of Putney, co. Surrey, bach., & Mary Lucas, of St Mary Magdalen, Milk Street, London, marr. by lic. by Mr Seagrave

Aug. 19 Benjamin Blackden, of St Bartholomew the Less, London, bach., & Mary Brisgeman, of St Mary Aldermanbury, London, spr, marr. by lic. by Mr Seagrave

Sep. 20 The Revd Peter Smith, of Barnes, co. Surrey, bach., & Elizabeth Baldwin, of Putney in the same co., wid., marr. by lic. by Mr Duberdieu

Nov. 2 Edward Parr, of St Leonard, Shoreditch, co. Midd., widr, & Margaret May, of the same parish, marr. by lic. by Mr Venn

Nov. 20 John Raymond, of St Ann, Limehouse, co. Midd., bach., & Britania Lambe, of St John, Hackney, spr, marr. by lic. by Mr Newcome

Dec. 1 Robert Eyles, of Halsted, co. Kent, bach., & Diana Dyer, of Kensington, co. Midd., spr, marr. by lic. by Mr Venn

Dec. 25 Laurance Garner, of Chatham, co. Kent, bach., & Elizabeth Clarke, of Rochester in the same co., marr. by lic. by Mr Panton

Jan. 14 Henry Batton, of St Savour's, Southwark, Surrey, widr, & Mary Stevents, of St Thomas, Southwark, wid., marr. by lic. by Mr Berryman

Feb. 19 Edward York, of [St] Michael, Wood Street, London, bach., & Elizabeth Maria Lloyd, of the same parish, spr, marr. by lic. by Mr Abbot

Mar. 7 Thomas Baldwin, of Alhollows the Great, London, widr, & Chrisan [*sic*] Holbert, of St George, Bloomsbury, co. Midd., spr, marr. by lic. by Mr Panton

1736.

Mar. 29 Thomas Benbridge, of St John Baptist, London, bach., & Martha Stoott, of the same parish, spr, marr. by lic. by Mr Venn

April 28 William Moore, of Foots Cray, co. Kent, bach., & Sarah Brooker, of Chislehurst in the same co., spr, marr. by lic. by Mr Panton

May 4 Absolom Robinson, of St John Baptist, London, bach., & Elizabeth Chesman, of the same parish, spr, marr. by banns by Mr Panton

June 6 John Reefen, of London, mercht, bach., & Mary Van Fleet, of St John Baptist, London, spr, marr. by banns by Mr Panton

June 15 Johnathan Darke, of St Thomas Apostle, London, widr, & Mary Wotton, of St Andrew, Holborn, London, wid., marr. by lic. by Mr Panton

July 1 Samuel Harwood, of St George, co. Midd., bach., & Sarah Bamber, of the same parish, spr, marr. by lic. by Mr Panton

July 6 Henry Mussitt, mariner, bach., & Catherine Frainingham, of St John Baptist, marr. by banns by Mr Panton

July 27 Thomas Kinnard, of [St] Paul, Covent Garden, co. Midd., bach., & Mary Lamb, of Battersea, co. Surrey, widow, marr. by lic. by Mr Panton

Aug. 19 John Ledwell, of St Michael, Queen Hith, London, widr, & Ann Bolt, of St Paul, Shadwell, co. Midd., wid., marr. by lic. by Mr Wm Daws

Aug. 22 Thomas Davis, of St Mary, White Chapple, co. Midd., bach., & Prissilla George, of the same parish, wid., marr. by lic. by Mr Panton

Sep. 4 Thomas Hammond, of Beddington, co. Surrey, bach., & Ann Askinson, of the same parish, wid., marr. by lic. by Mr Dubordieu

Oct. 23 Arthur Allen, of Harrow on the Hill, co. Midd., bach., & Sarah Spenson, of St Martin's in the Fields in the same co., spr, marr. with lic. by Mr Panton

Nov. 9 Joseph Nash, of St George's, Southwark, co. Surry, bach., & Eliz. Parrot, of the same parish, spr, marr. by lic. by Wm Jackson

Nov. 14 Francis Hall, of St Martin, Ludgate, London, bach., & Susanna Johnson, of St Michael, Crooked Lane, London, spr, marr. with lic. by Mr Panton

Nov. 30 Edward Prior, of St Martin Vintry, London, widr, & Pheabe Squier, of St Antholin's, spr, marr. by lic. by Mr Jackson

Jan. 1 William Court, of St Gregory's, London, bach., & Jane Booth, of St Botolph, Aldgate, London, spr, marr. by lic. by Mr Dubordieu

Jan. 4 Thos Millington, of this parish, bach., & Mary Hunt, of this parish, spr, marr. by lic. by Mr Weathers

Feb. 19 John Langmore, of St Edmund the King, London, bach., & Elizabeth Budgen, of St Bride's, London, spr, marr. by lic. by Wm Reading

Feb. 20 Francis Baker, of St Seven [*sic*], Coleman Street, London, widr, & Frances Stokes, of St Botolph, Bishopsgate, London, wid., marr. by lic. by Dr Hayes

Mar. 1 Clendon Daukes, of St Saviour's, Southwarke, co. Surrey, bach., & Sarah Bright, of St Mary, Whitechapple, co. Midd., spr, marr. by lic. by Mr Seagrave

1737.

May 12 Thomas Wright, of St Botolph, Aldgate, co. Midd., widr, & Mary Sprickly, of St Antholin's, London, spr, marr. by lic. by Mr Panton

July 1 John Hunt, of this parish, bach., & Lucy Farrow, of St Stephen, Coleman Street, London, spr, marr. by lic. by Mr Segrave

July 4 John Cock, of St John Baptist, London, widr, & Martha Wooding, of St Nicholas Acons, London, spr, marr. by lic. by Mr Panton

Aug. 8 John Barnard, of Kinsington, co. Midd., widr, & Elizabeth Sheppard, of Richmond, co. Surrey, spr, marr. by lic. by Mr Lloyd

Aug. 21 John Bates, of Allhallows, Barking, London, bach., & Mary Hall, of the same parish, spr, marr. by lic. by Mr Panton

Oct. 6 Charles Humphreys, of [St] Botolph, Bishopsgate, London, bach., & Jane Daze, of St Leonard, Shorditch, co. Midd., spr, marr. by lic. by Mr Panton

Oct. 13 Nicholis Trice, of St Martin in the Fields, co. Midd., bach., & Mary Wright, of St George the Martyr in sd coy, spr, marr. by lic. by Mr Panton

Oct. 27 James Millet, of this parish, bach., & Mary Segry, of St Luke, co. Midd., spr, marr. by lic. by Mr Panton

Nov. 12 John Terrey, of Newing [*sic*] Butts, co. Surry, bach., & Elizabeth Monk, of St Benedict near Paul's Wharfe, London, spr, marr. by lic. by Mr Venn

Nov. 13 William Simpson, of Southwell, co. Nott., bach., & Sarah Pilgrim, of St Luke, co. Midd., spr, marr. by lic. by Mr Seagrave

Nov. 29 Elias Lock, of St Dunstan in the East, London, widr, & Goodeth Jeys, of St Luke, co. Midd., wid., marr. by lic. by Mr Seagrave

Nov. 29 William Jeys, of St Clement Danes, co. Midd., bach., & Jane Love, of the same parish, spr, marr. by lic. by Mr Seagrave

Feb. 12 John Hippisley, of Lambourne, co. Berks, bach., & Maria Odams, of this parish, spr, marr. by lic. by Mr Venn

Feb. 13 Zacchias Holliday, of St Oliev, Silver Street, London, widr, & Mary Edlin, of the same parish, wid., marr. by lic. by Mr Seagrave

Mar. 23 George Turner, of St Leonard, Shorditch, co. Midd., bach., & Elizabeth Cartlitch, of Hornett, co. Herts, wid., marr. by lic. by Mr Seagrave

1738.

April 8 Joshua Broughton, of Allhollows the Less, London, wid^r^, & Ann Cox, of the same parish, wid., marr. by lic. by Mr Panton

May 11 The Right Honble Henry, Lord Viscount Palmerston, widower, & Dame Isabella Fryer, of the parish of St Andrew, Holbourn, in the county of Middlesix, widow, marr. by licence by Mr John Laurance

May 20 Joseph Steevenson, of St George, Bloomsbury, co. Midd., bach., & Anne Pakenran, of the same parish, sp^r^, marr. by lic. by Dr Watkenson

May 23 John Maccartney, of St Giles, Cripplegate, London, bach., & Eliz^th^ Winter, of the same parish, sp^r^, marr. by lic. by Dr Watkinson

June 8 Thomas Rogers, of Stretthain, co. Surrey, wid^r^, & Elizabeth Leopard, of the same parish, sp^r^, marr. by lic. by Mr Panton

June 15 Claude Fonnereau, of St Antholin's, London, wid^r^, & Ann Boehme, of the same parish, sp^r^, marr. by lic. by Mr Venn

June 17 Henry Simon, of the Inner Temple, London, bach., & Mary Jones, of St Clement Danes, co. Midd., sp^r^, marr. by lic. by Mr Panton

July 7 Knolles Gosnell, of Allhallows, Bread Street, London, bach., & Jane Payton, of the same parish, sp^r^, marr. by lic. by Mr Seagrave

Sep. 12 The Honble Henry Temple, Esqr, of East Sheen, in the county of Surrey, widower, & Jane Barnard, of Mincing Lane, London, spinster, marr. by licence by Mr Venn

Oct. 13 Samuel Brooks, of Woolverstill Hall, in parish of Bulkinton, co. Warw., wid^r^, & Mary Saunders, of Denton, co. Norf., sp^r^, marr. by lic. by Mr Seagrave

Nov. 11 William Foreman, of St Mary, Rotherhith, co. Surry, bach., & Mary Foster, of the same parish, sp^r^, marr. by lic. by Thos Curling

Dec. 10 William Noble, of St Clement Danes, co. Midd., bach., & Elizabeth Cooke, of White Fryers, sp^r^, marr. by lic. by Mr Land

Dec. 15 Thomas Creed, of St Bottolph, Bishopsgate, London, wid^r^, & Ann Andrews, of Tottenham, co. Midd., sp^r^, marr. by lic. by Mr Panton

Dec. 20 William Lewis, of St Giles in the Fields, wid^r^, & Hester Haris, of St Clement Danes, co. Midd., sp^r^, marr. by lic. by Mr Panton

Jan. 20 Thomas Hodges, of St Mildred in Poultrey, London, bach., & Mary Bourne, of St Mary Colechurch, wid., marr. by lic. by Mr Fayton

Feb. 2 Thomas Hawes, of St George, co. Midd., wid^r^, & Elizabeth Rodway, of St Michael, Wood Street, marr. by lic. by Mr Richd Seargrave

Feb. 10 Thomas Hudson, of St Laurance Jury, London, bach., & Sarah Stevens, of the same parish, sp^r^, marr. by lic. by T. Keighly

Feb. 11 Henry Singleton, of St Michael, Wood Strett, London, bach., & Susanah Forster, of the same parish, sp^r^, marr. by lic. by Mr Abbott

Mar. 2 John Bullpitt, of St Ann & Agnes, London, bach., & Mary Watts, of the same parish, sp^r^, marr. by lic. by Mr Seagrave

Mar. 12 Goodyer St John, of the city of Oxford, bach., & Anne Parry, of St Clement Danes, co. Midd., sp^r^, marr. by lic. by Mr John Dubordieu

1739.

July 14 John Flavill, of St Ann, Blackfryers, London, bach., & Sarah Purser, of the same parish, sp^r^, marr. by lic. by the Rev. Mr David Capon

Aug. 25 Samuel Clarke, of St Mary, Rotherhith, co. Surry, bach., & Elizabeth Hoddilow, of St Michael, Crooked Lane, London, sp^r^, marr. by lic. by Mr Leo^d^ Howard

Sep. 8 Edward Say, of St Michael, Queen Hith, London, widr, & Alce Brookes, of St Olave, Southwark, Surrey, marr. by lic. by Mr Comarque

Sep. 22 David Mathews, of St Mary Magdlen, Bermonsey, co. Surrey, widr, & Mary Harris, of St George, Southwork, in the same co., spr, marr. by lic. by Mr Robt Seagrave

Oct. 14 Arthur Lewis, of St Saviour, Southwork, Surry, bach., & Hannah Sharpe, of Newington in the same co., spr, marr. by lic. by Mr Seagrave

Oct. 30 Benjamin Figgins, of Reading, co. Berks, bach., & Jane Huckle, of the same town, spr, marr. by lic. by Mr Seagrave

Nov. 20 William Shephard, of St Catherine Cree Church, London, bach., & Elizabeth Blake, of St Botolph, Aldgate, London, spr, marr. by lic. by Mr Wm Nowell

Feb. 7 John Orowder [? Crowder], of the Liberty of Norton Falgate, co. Midd., widr, & Martha Vernet, of St Martin in the Fields in the sd co., widow, marr. with lic. by Mr Samuel Hilliard

Feb. 10 Mr Edward Kite, of St Giles, Cripplegate, London, widr, & Phebe Jefferys, of the same parish, widow, marr. by lic. by Mr Cooksey

1740.

May 29 Thomas Sheppard, of St Andrew, Holborn, London, bach., & Sarah Mills, of St James, Garlick Hith, London, spr, marr. by lic. by Tristam Land

June 5 Joseph Smith, of Queen's College, Univy of Oxford, bach., & Lydia Barney, of St Dionis Back Church, London, spr, marr. by Dr Smith, Rector of the above church

Aug. 14 Bathold Christopher Lutyens, of St Antholin's, London, bach., & Ann Boehm, of the same parish, spr, marr. by lic. by Mr Kippax, Curate of this parish

Sep. 3 John Lyde, of St Botolph, Aldersgate, London, widr, & Anna Maria Aprice, of St Mary, White Chapple, co. Midd., widow, marr. by lic. by Mr Seagrave

Sep. 4 Richard Gibbs, of St Leonard, Shorditch, co. Midd., bach., & Anna Cason, of the same parish, spr, marr. by lic. by Mr Browne

Oct. 1 Henry Butler, of St John, Southwarke, Surrey, widr, & Mary Knowls, of St Botolph, Aldersgate, London, spr, marr. by lic. by Mr Howard

Oct. 26 Charles Walker, of St John Baptist, London, bach., & Elizabeth Jones, of St Martin in the Feilds, co. Midd., widow, marr. by lic. by Mr Kippax

Nov. 15 Thomas Gwilling, of Wendver, co. Bucks, bach., & Mary Coles, of St Bride's, London, spr, marr. by lic. by Mr Seagrave

Nov. 24 Edward Whitaker, of St Paul's, Shadwell, co. Midd., bach., & Elizabeth Winkworth, of the [same] parish, spr, marr. by lic. by Mr Seagrave

Dec. 1 Stafford Crane, of St Bridget otherwise Bride's, London, bach., & Phebe Blundell Freke, of the same parish, spr, marr. by lic. by Dr Roper

Jan. 29 Edward Durnford, of Christ Church, co. Hants, bach., & Mary Higgins, of Reading, co. Berks, spr, marr. by lic. by Mr Seagrave

Feb. 5 Charles Newsham Pigot, of Wimbleton, co. Surrey, widr, & Elizabeth Weeble, of the same parish, marr. by lic. by Mr Cooksey

Feb. 5 Henry Wood, of Queen Hith, London, bach., & Anna Maria Hirons, of Kinsington, co. Midd., spr, by lic. by Mr Bailey

Mar. 17 James Turlis, of St Sepulchre, London, bach., & Martha Jones, of the same parish, spr, by lic. by J. Waring, Curate

1741.

May 4 Joseph Maylin, of St Ann's, co. Midd., bach., & Sarah Leavesley, of St Mary Magdalen, Bermondsey, co. Surry, spr, by lic. by Mr Seagrave

May 29 Charles Sandys, of St Giles in the Fields, co. Midd., bach., & Mary Brooker, of St Stephen, Walbrook, spr, by lic. by Mr Seagrave

July 26 Philip Bovinton, of [St] Andrew, Holborn, co. Midd., bach., & Mary Goodwin, of St Giles in the Fields, co. Midd., widow, by lic. by Dr Watkinson

Aug. 14 Francis Spencer, of Ashby Delazoch, co. Leic., bach., & Mary Mitchell, of St George, Hannover Square, co. Midd., spr, by lic. by Mr Waring, Curate

Sep. 7 George Dickison, of St Martin's in the Fields, co. Midd., & Elizabeth Eiling, of this parish, by banns

Sep. 13 William Danger, of St Mary, White Chapel, co. Midd., widr, & Ann Marchant, of St Bottolph, Bishopsgate, London, spr, by lic. by Mr Robt Seagrave

Oct. 14 John Addams, of Epsom, Surry, bach., & Sarah Borer, of Christ Church, London, spr, with lic. by Mr Waring

Nov. 24 William Freman, of St Giles, Criplegate, London, bach., & Mary Cooke, of St Bartholomew by the Royal Exchange, London, spr, by lic. by Mr Cooksey

Dec. 17 George Pope, of Christ Church, London, bach., & Martha Forster, of the same parish, spr, by lic. by Mr Edwd Lloyd

Jan. 1 John Angell, of St Savjour, Southwark, Surrey, bach., & Ann Gutridge, of the same parish, spr, by lic. by Mr L. Howard

Jan. 17 William Worgan, of St Mary, Rothorhith, Surry, bach., & Elizabeth Hide, of St Leonard, Shoreditch, co. Midd., spr, by lic. by Mr Land

Jan. 20 Swift Kirby, of Wimbleton, co. Surrey, widr, & Elizabeth Bicknall, of the same parish, spr, by lic. by Mr Cooksey

Feb. 18 Michael Purton, of St James, Garlick Hythe, London, bach., & Ann Wilkins, of St Margarett, Lothbury, London, spr, by lic. by Mr Cooksey

1742.

April 21 Thomas Davies, of St Luke, co. Midd., widr, & Jane Stalker, of St Magnus the Martyr on London Bridge, spr, by lic. by Mr L. Howard

May 13 Richard Tootal, of St Bridget *alias* Bride, London, bach., & Elizabeth Briers, of St John Baptist, London, spr, by banns by Mr Waring, Curate

July 8 Henry Hohling [? Hobling], of St Andrew near the Tower of London, & Mary Mason, of St Mary, Whitechaple, co. Midd., spr, by lic. by Mr L. Howard

Sep. 16 Samuel Wynn, of St George in the East, co. Midd., bach., & Ann Grigg, of the same parish, spr, by lic., by Mr Augustian Bryan

Oct. 16 John Seaman, of St Saviour, Southwark, co. Surry, bach., & Mary Colbatch, of Hereford, spr, with lic. by Mr Lloy of St Paul's

Oct. 24 Mathew Blest, of St Antholin, London, bach., and [*blank*] Kingstone, of St Margaret, Westminster, co. Midd., spr, with lic. by Mr Cooksey

Oct. 25 Joseph Bayley, of Wotton, co. Warw., bach., & Lucy Grissel, of St Antholin, London, spr, with lic. by Mr Cooksey

Nov. 25 George Sales, of Eltham, co. Kent, bach., & Mary Savage, of East Greenwich in the same coy, spr, by lic. by Mr Cooksey

Jan. 27 John Horton, of Yealing, co. Midd., widr, & Mary Brookes, of the same place, widow, by lic. by Mr Cooksey

1743.

April .. William Houson, of S[t] Marg[t], Westmins[r], co. Midd., bach., & Elizabeth Webb, of the same parish, sp[r], with lic. by M[r] Cooksey

April 26 Humphrey Barton, of S[t] George, Southwark, Surry, wid[r], & Elizabeth Craggs, of the same parish, wid., with lic. by M[r] John Cooksey, Rector

May 28 Hill Burton, of Low Layton, Essex, wid[r], & Susan Pindar, of S[t] Savior, Southwark, co. Surry, wid., with lic. by M[r] Duberdieu

June 21 Thomas Milles, of S[t] Nicholas Acon, London, bach., & Mary Goodyear, of the same parish, sp[r], with lic. by M[r] Wilson

July 26 George Fern, of S[t] Dunstan in the East, London, bach., & Maria Margaretta Symonds, of Allhollows the Great, London, sp[r], with lic. by M[r] Worlich

July 28 John Bricker, of S[t] Botolph, Aldgate, London, bach., & Ann Swannell, of the same parish, sp[r], with lic. by M[r] A. Hotblack

Aug. 17 John Warrington, of S[t] Mary, Newington, Surry, wid[r], & Elizabeth Lightfoot, of the same parish, sp[r], with lic. by M[r] Waring, Curate

Sep. 7 John Harris, of S[t] Martin's in the Fields, co. Midd., bach., & Ann Holdship, of the same parish, sp[r], with lic. by M[r] Waring, Curate

Sep. 11 Caleb Nicholetts, of S[t] George, Bottolph Lane, London, bach., & Sarah Darby, of the same parish, sp[r], with lic. by M[r] Waring

Oct. 2 Richard Elmer, of Farnham, co. Surry, bach., & Emm Pigg, of S[t] Antholin's, London, sp[r], with lic. by M[r] A. Hotblack

Oct. 23 Henry Shephard, of S[t] Ann, Aldersgate, London, bach., & Mary Godhelp, of S[t] Edmund the King, London, sp[r], with lic. by M[r] Panton

Oct. 27 James Berry, of S[t] Andrew, Holborn, co. Midd., wid[r], & Jane Biggs, of the same parish, sp[r], with lic. by M[r] Waring

Nov. 10 Edward Billington, of Allhollows, Lombard Street, London, wid[r], & Mary Marvin, of S[t] Laurance Jewry, London, sp[r], by lic. by M[r] Browne

Nov. 25 Joseph Mason, of [S[t]] Gregory, London, bach., & Ann Kennett, of S[t] John, Hackney, co. Midd., sp[r], with lic. by M[r] Augustin Bryan

Dec. 8 William Coster, of Chinkford, Essex, wid[r], & Hannah Liddall, of S[t] Andrew Undershaft, sp[r], with lic. by M[r] Bryan

Dec. 11 Joseph Fish, of S[t] Dunstan in the East, London, bach., & Sarah Pownall, of S[t] Olave, Old Jewry, London, sp[r], by lic. by M[r] Cooksey

1744.

June 30 John Crowder, of S[t] James, Clarkenwell, co. Midd., wid[r], & Sarah Whiting, of S[t] Antholin's, London, sp[r], by lic. by M[r] Jn[o] Waring

Aug. .. Noah Roome, of Acton, co. Midd., wid[r], & Mary Miller, of S[t] Michael Royal, London, sp[r], by lic. by M[r] John Negus

Sep. 9 James Theobald, of Wandsworth, Surry, bach., & Mary Theobalds, of S[t] Sepulcher's, London, wid., by lic. by M[r] Warring

Oct. 9 Edward Newsham, of S[t] Dunstan in the East, London, bach., & Jane Phipps, of S[t] Antholin's, London, wid., by lic. by M[r] John Negus

Dec. 18 George Cole, of S[t] Margaret, Westminster, co. Midd., bach., & Elizabeth Anderson, of the same parish, sp[r], by lic. by the Rev. John Lloyd of S[t] Paul's, London

Dec. 23 George Power, of S[t] Clement Danes, co. Midd., bach., & Elizabeth Story, of the same parish, sp[r], by lic. by M[r] Waring

Mar. 22 William Smith, of S[t] Mary at Hill, London, wid[r], & Ellin Martin, of the same parish, sp[r], by lic. by M[r] Waring

1745.

Mar. 30 David Cheriton, of St John the Evangelist, Westminster, co. Midd., wid^r, & Elizabeth Sill, of St Paul, Covent Garden, in the same co^y, sp^r, by lic. by Mr Edward Lloyd

April 25 Robert Browne, jun^r, of St John Baptist, bach., & Elizabeth Ennis, of the same parish, sp^r, by lic. by Mr Cooksey

May 4 William Skelton, of Brentford in the parish of Yealing, co. Midd., bach., & Elizabeth Peters, of Chiswick in the same co^y, sp^r, by lic. by Mr Welles

Aug. 17 Edward Mounteney, of St James, Garlick Hith, London, & Cartherine Capen, of the same parish, by lic. by Mr Browne

Oct. 11 Thomas Philibrowne, of St Botolph, Bishopsgate, London, wid^r, & Elizabeth Shephard, of St Dionis Backchurch, London, wid., by lic. by Mr Nowell

Jan. 5 Samuel Major, of Harlington, bach., & Ann Glover, of this parish, sp^r, by banns by Mr Waring

Feb. 4 George Campbell, of St Margaret, Westminster, co. Midd., wid^r, & Margaret Bishop, of the same parish, wid., by lic. by Mr Waring

Feb. 11 William Young, of St Luke, co. Midd., wid^r, & Christian Walker, of St Swithin, London Stone, by lic. by Mr Waring

1746.

Mar. 30 Thomas Caldecott, of St Gregory's, London, bach., & Mary Cardall, of St Andrew's, Holborn, London, sp^r, by lic. by M^r Ed. Lloyd

April 8 William Garnham, of St Giles, Cripplegate, London, bach., & Sarah Noss, of Allhollows, Honny Lane, London, sp^r, by lic. by Mr Jno Downes

June 30 John Laurance, of Heybridge, Essex, wid^r, & Martha Beadle, of St Peter's in the same parish, wid., by lic. by Mr Anthony Hotblack

July 8 The Revd Mr Thomas Locker, of Soley Northfield, co. Worc., clerk, a bach., & Elizabeth James, of Ightham, co. Kent, sp^r, by lic. by William Halford

July 10 Martin Bockett, of Christ Church, Surrey, wid^r, & Martha Wooffendall, of the same parish, sp^r, by lic. by Mr Cooksey

Aug. 29 Abraham Andrews, of St Martin Outwich, London, bach., & Phanny Jackson, of the same parish, sp^r, with lic. by Mr Waring

Oct. 2 Edward Powell, of St Mary, Rotherhith, Surry, bach., & Mary Lamper, of St Mary Aldermanbury, London, sp^r, by lic. by Mr Richardon

Nov. 10 John Thornton, of Norton Forgate, London, bach., & Cathrine Cotteby, of the same place, sp^r, by lic. by Mr Dubordieu

Nov. 30 John Mills, of St John Baptist, London, wid^r, & Sarah Monger, of St Martin in the Fields, Midd^x, wid., by lic. by Mr Cooksey

Dec. 10 John Achison, of Walthamstowe, Essex, wid^r, & Eleanor Steel, of Waltham Abby in the co^y afs^d, sp^r, by lic. by Mr Cunningham

Dec. 26 James Rogers, of St John Baptist, London, bach., & Mary Futrell, of St Mary, Whit Chapple, (a minor), with the consent of Henry Futrell her father, with lic. by Mr Bryan

Jan. 28 John Kyte, of St Michael, Cornhill, London, bach., & Sarah Smith, of St Botolph, Aldgate, London, sp^r, by lic. by Mr Cooksey

Feb. 8 William Sheen, of St Giles, Cripplegate, London, bach., & Mary Ann West, of the same parish, sp^r, by lic. by Wm Sandford

Feb. 24 Francis Robins, of St John Baptist, wid^r, & Sarah Hutchenson, of the [*sic*] parish, widow, with lic. by Mr Waring

1747.

May 5 The Revd Charles Jackson, Bach. in Divinity, of Emanuel Colledge, Cambridge, & Margaretter Bridges, of Kettering, co. Northampton, a widow, by lic. by Joshua Tillottson

May 8 James Colebrook, of St Botolph's, Bishopsgate, London, bach., & Mary Skyner, of Low Laton, co. Essex, sp^r, with lic. by Mr Cooksey

June 11 Moses Dore, of St Mary Aldermanbury, London, bach., & Rebeccah Rideant, of the same parish, sp^r, by lic. by John Welles

July 30 John Steward, of St Michael, Queenhith, London, bach., & Ann Highmore, of St James, Garlickhith, London, sp^r, with lic. by Rev. Jno Moore

Oct. .. John Oliver, of Westham, Essex, bach., & Ann Eades, of the same parish, sp^r, with lic. by Mr Tillotson

Oct. 12 William Baker, of St James, Garlickhith, London, bach., & Charlotte Jackson, of Rushton, co. Northampton, sp^r, with lic. by Chas Jackson

Feb. 18 Mathias Huntley, of St Peter's, Cornhill, London, wid^r, & Anna Maria Pike, of St John, Hackney, co. Midd., sp^r, with lic. by Mr John Duburdieu

Feb. 23 John Roe, of Putney, co. Surrey, bach., & Carthrine Frances de Derpore, of Barnes in the same co^y, sp^r, with lic. by E. Jackson

1748.

April 10 Richard Holden, of St Marga^t, Lothbury, London, bach., & Sarah Stanefeld, of Hallifax, co. York, sp^r, with lic. by Mr Tillotson

April 14 James Jorrett, of Camberwell, co. Surry, bach., & Ann Barkett, of St Mary, Lambeth, in the same co^y, sp^r, with lic. by Mr Tillotson

Oct. 8 Henry Hawthorn, of Walthamstow, Essex, bach., & Mary Batsford, of Wansted in the same co^y, sp^r, by lic. by Mr Cunningham

Oct. 14 Job Pearson, of Clapham, Surrey, wid^r, & Eleanor Bends, of the same parish, sp^r, by lic. by Mr Pollen

Oct. 20 Strickland Hudson, of St George the Marter, Southwork, co. Surrey, wid^r, & Catherine Clark, of the same parish, widow, by lic. by Mr Negus

Jan. 31 Joseph Everard, of St Andrew, Holborn, Midd^x, wid^r, & Martha Goodwin, of St Botolph, Bishopsgate, London, sp^r, with lic. by Mr Pollin

1749.

Mar. 27 Benjamin Webb, of St Stephen, Wallbrook, London, wid^r, & Mary Girl, of St Giles, Cripplegate, London, sp^r, with lic. by Mr Cooksey

April 8 William Smith, of Christ Church, London, bach., & Isabella Haynes, of the same parish, sp^r, by lic. by Edward Fisher

April 18 John Simco, of St Geo., co. Surry, wid^r, & Susannah Neale, of St Olave, Southwark, Surry, sp^r, by lic. by Mr Pallin, Curate

April 25 Edward Brindfield, of St Mary le Strand, co. Midd., wid^r, & Margaret Willock, of St Antholin's, London, sp^r, with lic. by Mr Waring

May 11 The Revd George Morrison, clerk, of Eastwood, co. Essex, bach., & Sarah Case, of Prittlewell in the co^y afs^d, sp^r, with lic. by Edwd Lloyd

May 21 William Tate, of St Antholin's, London, bach., & Rebecca Smith, of the same parish, sp^r, with lic. by Mr Pollin

July 10 Michael Smyth, of Croydon, Surrey, bach., & Jane Hill, of the same parish, sp^r, with lic. by Rev. Tho. Pollin, Curate of this parish

Sep. 30 John Brewer, of St John, Wappin, Midd^x^, bach., & Judeath Frydingbarg, of St Lawrence Jury, London, sp^r^, with lic. by Augus. Bryan

Jan. 12 Stephen Pett, of St John, Wappin, co. Midd., wid^r^, & Elizabeth Haynes, of the same parish, wid., with lic. by Augustian Bryan

Feb. 20 William Wright, of St Botolph, Aldgate, Midd., bach., & Judith Love, of St Michael, Cornhill, London, sp^r^, by lic. by Mr Pallin, Curate

Mar. 8 Robert Cookson, of St Michael, Queenhith, bach., & Martha Warner, of Hadley, co. Midd., sp^r^, by lic. by Mr Pallin, Curate

1750.

July 12 William Jarvis Ellworthy, of St Stephen, Coleman Street, London, bach., & Patience Stone, of St Margaret, Westminster, Midd^x^, sp^r^, by lic. by Mr Pallin

July 26 Richard Munday, of St Botolph, Bishopsgate, London, bach., & Hannah Brant, of the same parish, sp^r^, by lic. by Mr Territt

Aug. 30 George Gardner, of St John the Evangelist, Westminster, Midd., wid^r^, & Elizabeth Roberts, of the same parish, wid., by lic. by B. Heckstall

Oct. 2 Thomas Thomas, of the city of Worcester, bach., & Mary Cookesey, of Claines in the same co^y^, sp^r^, by lic. by Mr Cookesey

Oct. 9 John Paterson, of Wimbleton, Surrey, wid^r^, & Ann Lamb, of Acton, co. Midd., sp^r^, by lic. by Mr Cooksey

Oct. 30 John Willson, of Cheshunt, Herts, bach., & Ann Slater, of St John Baptist, London, sp^r^, by lic. by Mr John Waring

Nov. 13 William Story, of St Clement Danes, Midd^x^, bach., & Mary Newman, of Obbisham otherwise Epsom, Surry, sp^r^, by lic. by Mr Pallin

Nov. 14 John Allsop, of Newcastle under Line, co. Staff., wid^r^, & Sarah Nicholas, of St Michael Bassishaw, London, sp^r^, by lic. by Mr Pallin

Nov. 26 Levey Perry, of St Michel, Queenhith, London, wid^r^, & Philepia Stacey, of St Antholin's, London, wid., by lic. by Mr Pallin

Feb. 3 Henry Wardman, of St Laurance Pountney, London, bach., & Elizabeth Mulenex, of St Michael, Wood Street, London, sp^r^, with lic. by Mr Pallin

Feb. 7 John Jordain, of Christ Church, London, bach., & Margaretta Downing, of the same parish, sp^r^, with lic. by William Sclater

Mar. 7 Henry Bennett, of St James, Clerkenwell, Midd^x^, wid^r^, & Elizabeth Downing, of Christ Church, London, wid., with lic. by Mr Sclater

1751.

May 30 George Hoare, of Rigate, Surry, wid^r^, & Mary Lyfe, of the same parish, sp^r^, by lic. by Mr Browne

July 4 John Jarman, of St George, Southwark, Surrey, bach., & Sarah Braceegirdle, of the same parish, sp^r^, by lic. by Mr Pallin

July 6 Samuel Maut, of St Mary Magdalen, Bermondsey, Surrey, bach., & Mary Hulls, of St Leonard, Shorditch, Midd^x^, sp^r^, by lic. by Mr Cunningham

July 7 Benjaman Sect, of St Saviour's, Southwark, Surrey, bach., & Mary Glover, of St Antholin's, London, sp^r^, by lic. by Mr Pallin

July 15 William Butler, of St Andrew Undershaft, London, bach., & Mary Linsell, of the same parish, sp^r^, by lic. by Mr Aug. Bryan

July 19 Thomas Edwards, of St Faith, London, bach., & Martha Holt, of St Laurence Jewry, London, sp^r^, by lic. by Mr Pallin

Aug. 15 Jasper Mandint [? Manduit], of St Dionis Backchurch, London, bach., & Elizabeth Thody, of St John, Southwark, Surrey, sp^r^, by lic. by Rev. Mr Nowell

Aug. 24 William Allister & Ann Funnell, both of St John Baptist, by banns by Mr Pallin

Nov. 11 Thomas Yerbury, of Bedford, co. Wilts, bach., & Ann Tatlor, of St John, Wapping, Midd^x, sp^r, by lic. by Mr Bryan

1752.

Jan. 28 Dennis Maccarthey, of Chelseie, co. Midd., bach., & Ann Gordon, of St Andrew, Holborn, London, sp^r, by lic. by Mr Pallin

Feb. 22 William Randell, of St Michael, Queenhith, London, wid^r, & Martha Smith, of St Thomas Apostle, London, sp^r, by lic. by Mr Pallin

April 16 Atkins Spencer, of St Mary Magdalen, Bermondsey, Surrey, wid^r, & Elizabeth Wadham, of the same parish, sp^r, by lic. by Mr Pallin

May 9 Thomas Coleman, of Markett Harborough, co. Leic., bach., & Phebe Brathwait, of St John, Hackney, Midd^x, sp^r, by lic. by Mr Pallin

July 16 Richard Pullen, of St Andrew, Holborn, Midd^x, bach., & Mary Fuller, of St Botolph, Bishopsgate, sp^r, by lic. by Mr Pallin

Aug. 8 Joseph Richards, of Lambeth, Surrey, bach., & Ann Crossby, of the same parish, sp^r, by lic. by [*blank*]

Oct. 1 Edward Wilmot, of Manchester, co. Lanc., bach., & Elizabeth Wilmot, of St Bartholomew the Great, London, sp^r, by lic. by Ri^d Wilmot

Oct. 15 Robert Cowdall, of All Saints, co. Leic., bach., & Mary Lowe, of St John, Wapping, Midd^x, sp^r, by lic. by Augustine Bryan

Oct. 19 Richard Huntly, of St Magnus the Martyr, London, wid^r, & Penelope Bryan, of St Gregory, London, sp^r, by lic. by Augustine Bryan

Oct. 31 Edward Tymbs, of Uxbridge, co. Midd., bach., & Heneretta Maria Smith, of St Bottolph, Bishopsgate, London, sp^r, by lic. by Mr Sharpe

Nov. 9 William Warren, of St Leonard, Shoreditch, Midd^x, wid^r, & Mary Bulliford, of the same parish, sp^r, by lic. by Mr Wheatley

1753.

Feb. 20 Philip Bow, of St Edmund the King, London, bach., & Sarah Castell, of Clapham, Surry, sp^r, by lic. by Wm Nowell

Mar. 17 William Reynolds *alias* Highmore, of St James, Garlick Hith, London, bach., & Rachael Spellerberg, of St Leonard, Eastcheap, London, sp^r, a minor, with lic. by John Moore

Aug. 21 Johnathan Lawson, of St Mary, Rotherhith, Surry, wid^r, & Elizabeth Jaques, of St John, Southwark, in the same co^y, sp^r, by lic. by Mr Falconer

Nov. 2 Benjamin Lutkins, of Allhallows the Great, London, bach., & Salome Well, of St Antholin's, London, sp^r, by lic. by Robert Aylmer, Vicar of Camberwell, Surrey

Nov. 2 Jervase Adams, of St Mildred, Bread Street, London, wid^r, & Mary Williams, of the parish of St Peter, Cornhill, London, sp^r, by lic. by Aug^n Bryan

Nov. 8 John Chard, of St Saviour, Southwark, Surry, wid^r, & Elizabeth Holton, of the same parish, sp^r, by lic. by Rev. Jno Browne

Dec. 9 Sacheverell Hellyer, of Walthamstow, Essex, wid^r, & Jane Huntington, of St Bottolph, Aldgate, London, widow, by lic. by A. Cunningham

1754.

Mar. 17 William West, of S[t] Vedest otherwise Foster, London, bach., & Elizabeth Brewer, of S[t] Bennet Fink, London, sp[r], by lic. by M[r] Falconer

Mar. 23 John Venable, of S[t] Mary, Whitechappel, Midd[x], wid[r], & Ann Hellyer, of Walthamstow, Essex, sp[r], with lic. by A. Cuningham

---

BIRTHS AND BURIALS.*

1724.

Nov. 13 Thomas Hopkins bur.
Nov. 27 Ann Eastman bur.
Dec. 1 Mary Smith, a pentioner, bur.
Dec. 20 Susanna dau. of James & Susanna Warter bapt.
Dec. 20 Elizabeth dau. of Henry & Judith Grover bapt.
Jan. 8 John Archer bur.
Jan. 9 Rebeccah Williams bur.
Jan. 29 Thomas son of George & Mary Harris bapt.
Feb. 14 John son of a poor woman delivered in the street bapt.
Feb. 19 John ditto [*sic*] bur.

1725.

Mar. 31 John & Mary Dickinson bur.
April 4 Anthony Cross, a foundling, bapt.
April 11 Thomas son of William & Ann Sparkes bapt.
April 15 Rachael Mallertey bur.
April 22 John Mallertey bur.
May 29 Richard son of Josias & Elizabeth Lambert bapt.
June 6 James Hunt bur.
June 13 Anthony Cross bur.
June 22 W[m] son of Peter & Elizab[h] Hawkins bapt.
Aug. 24 George son of Auguston & Elizabeth Bryan bapt.
Aug. 29 Thomas son of Thomas & Margaret Craggs bapt.
Sep. 10 William son of John Van Rixtill bapt.
Sep. 19 Rebecca Storke bur.
Sep. 27 William Henderson bur.
Oct. 23 Jacob Fredric Jordis bur.
Nov. 14 John son of William & Sarah Barksdale bapt.
Dec. 12 Mary dau. of Henry & Judith Grover bapt.
Dec. 19 Thomas son of Thomas & Cathrine Horabin bapt.
Mar. 3 Samuel son of Samuel & Alce Wheat bapt.
Mar. 18 Jane Palmer bur.

1726.

Mar. 25 Anthony, a foundling, bapt.
Mar. 28 Mary, a foundling, bur.
Mar. 28 Anthony, a foundling, bur.
April 13 Augustion Bryan bur.
May 7 John Ghiselin son of Sezer & Mary bapt.
May 11 Thomas son of Thomas & Mary March bapt.
June 7 A foundling bur.

* These are continued from p. 139.

July 11 Peter son of George & Elizabeth Michael bur.
July 14 Peter son of Peter & Elizabeth Hawkins bapt.
July 19 Elizabeth dau. of Josias & Eliz. Lambert bapt.
Aug. 3 Mary dau. of James & Elizabeth Burdict bapt.
Aug. 26 Ellis Brownsword bur.
Sep. 7 Elizabeth Ludlow bur.
Sep. 14 Elizabeth Prockter bur.
Sep. 16 Peter son of Peter & Hannah Beyard bapt.
Oct. 3 Daniel Prockter bur.
Oct. 23 Baron Booth bur.
Dec. 21 Elizabeth Hale bur.
Jan. 3 Mary dau. of Thos & Elizabeth Knight bapt.
Jan. 5 Sarah Prockter bur.
Jan. 12 Elizabeth Gape bur.
Jan. 25 William son of George & Elizabeth Chebsey bapt.
Feb. 5 Ann dau. of George & Elizabeth Haris bapt.

1727.

Mar. 26 Martilda Coleman, an adult, bapt.
April 13 Robert Spencer bur.
April 16 William son of Edwd & Lidia Reeves bapt.
April 27 Henry Martin bur.
May 1 Sarah dau. of Charles Fisher bapt.
May 18 John son of John & Mary Van Rixtel bapt.
June 11 Thomas son of Thos & Cathrine Horabin bapt.
June 30 Mary Barrett bur.
July 2 Sarah Fisher bur.
Aug. 12 Frances Maidstone bur.
Aug. 31 Sarah dau. of Edwd & Sarah Laurance bapt.
Sep. 13 Samuel Toran bur.
Sep. 14 Judith Truston bur.
Oct. 9 Mary dau. of Elizabeth & Peter Hawkins bapt.
Oct. 19 Thomas son of John & Hannah Jerratt bapt.
Nov. 5 William son of John & Sarah Booth bapt.
Nov. 12 Sarah dau. of John & Deborah Harris bapt.
Dec. 17 Mary dau. of Thomas & Mary Smith bapt.
Dec. 24 Robert son of Robert & Ann Berry bapt.
Jan. 14 Mary Smith bur.
Jan. 14 Anthony Joseph son of Isaac & Mary Hunter bapt.

1728.

April 17 Ann dau. of George & Elizabeth Bradshaw bapt.
April 19 Hannah dau. of Josias & Elizabeth Lambert bapt.
May 15 Daniel son of John & Mary Van Rixtel bapt.
May 26 Edward Milles bur.
June 10 Samuel Fowler bur.
June 14 Ann, a foundling, bapt.
Aug. 6 John son of Thomas & Cathrine Horabin bapt.
Aug. 11 Eliz. & Ann daus. of Thomas & Ann Baker bapt.
Sep. 7 Elizabeth Bristow bur.
Sep. 29 Elizabeth dau. of Eliz. & Thomas Knight bapt.
Nov. 15 Sarah dau. of John & Sarah Booth bapt.
Dec. 1 Catherine Wormleigton bur.
Jan. 15 Sarah Booth bur.
Feb. 26 Jemima dau. of Edward & Mary Rimington bapt.
Mar. 23 John son of John & Ann Jerratt bapt.

1729.

Mar. 28 Charles Milbourn, Esq., bur.
April 6 John Wormlayton bur.
April 20 Mary dau. of John & Mary Clarke bapt.
May 24 Sarah Fowler bur.
May 24 Elizabeth Pulkin bur.
June 9 Mary dau. of Edward & Sarah Laurance bapt.
July 5 Thomas son of Thomas & Mary Smith bapt.
July 13 John son of Stephen & Jane Bradshaw bapt.
Aug. 25 Thomas Smith bur.
Sep. 23 Josias son of Josias & Elizabeth Lambert bapt.
Oct. 3 John son of Rich[d] & Elizabeth Osborn bapt.
Oct. 13 Josias Lambert bur.
Nov. 15 Dorothy Manning bur.
Nov. 28 Henry Prockter bur.
Dec. 24 James Williams bur.
Jan. 7 John son of John & Elizabeth Ridges bapt.
Jan. 9 John son of Francies & Margaret Grizell bapt.
Feb. 2 Ann Deponticue bapt.
Feb. 6 Wallter son of John & Sarah Barnes bapt.
Mar. 6 Mary Storke bur.

1730.

Mar. 25 William son of Thomas & Carthrine Horabin bapt.
Mar. 29 Thomas Parry bur.
April 3 Robert Brisco bur.
May 31 Ann Eastman bur.
June 17 Beata dau. of William & Ester Hobbs bapt.
June 19 Carthrine dau. of Edw[d] & Sarah Laurance bapt.
Aug. 30 Tho[s] son of Tho[s] & Mary Smith bapt.
Sep. 2 Mary & Tho[s] Smith bur.
Sep. 9 Ann dau. of John & Deborah Haris bapt.
Sep. 24 Esster dau. of John & Sarah Buried [*sic*] bur.
Oct. 6 John Stephens Facer bur.
Nov. 3 Thomas son of Tho[s] & Doratha Chance bapt.
Nov. 13 James son of George & Elizabeth Bradshaw bapt.
Nov. 20 Robert Whitfield bur.
Jan. 27 James son of John & Mary Clarke bapt.
Feb. 5 John Boddel bur.
Feb. 10 Samuel Burean bur.
Mar. 11 Mary dau. of Edw[d] & Elizabeth Hodgkins bapt

1731.

May 10 The Rev[d] M[r] Jn[o] Holland bur.
May 14 Elizabeth dau. of Tho[s] & Ann Townsend bur.
May 18 Ester Judith Gambier bur.
June 21 Ester Booth bur.
June 23 Anthony Joseph Hunter bur.
July 2 Nehemiah Eastman bur.
July 6 John son of John & Hannah Jarratt bapt.
July 8 William Booth bur.
July 13 Hennerritter Mary Ann dau. of Henry & Judith Gambier bapt.
July 25 Elizabeth dau. of Tho[s] & Jane Holmes bur.
Oct. 14 John son of John & Jane Horton bur.
Oct. 17 Ann dau. of John & Ann Bennitt bapt.

Oct. 25 Thomas Chance bur.
Nov. 14 Thomas son of Tho[s] & Kerthrine Horabin bapt.
Dec. 10 Edward son of Edw[d] & Eleaner Tayler bapt.
Dec. 16 Kerthrine East bur.
Jan. 12 Ann, a foundling, bapt.
Jan. 24 Ann Mace, a pen[r], bur.
Jan. 25 Josias Deponthieu bur.
Feb. 1 Edw[d] son of Edw[d] & Elizabeth Hodgkins bapt.
Feb. 9 Mary Tayler bur.

1732.

May 29 Thomas son of Tho[s] & Jane Groves bapt.
July 20 Ann, a foundling, bur.
Aug. 4 Edward Maried [*sic*] bur.
Aug. 13 John Pantin bur.
Sep. 11 Edmond Tayler bur.
Sep. 29 Robert, a bastard child, bur.
Oct. 5 Thomas Wright bur.
Oct. 8 Jane Elinor Le Roux bur.
Nov. 3 Sarah Bland bur.
Nov. 14 Cassandra Till bur.
Nov. 16 Mary dau. of George & Elizabeth Bradshaw bur.
Nov. 24 Eliz. Mallertie bur.
Nov. 26 Samuel Hatton bur.
Dec. 11 Mary Archer bur.
Jan. 23 John Holland bur.
Jan. 28 Gabriel Resoue bur.
Feb. 8 Ann Ierland bur.
Feb. 22 Henrietta Thomas bur.
Mar. 3 [*blank*] Gizeling bur.

1733.

April 7 Hannah Wormlayton bur.
May 26 John son of Edw[d] & Elizabeth Hodgkins bur.
June 6 Mary dau. of Frances & Marg. Grizell [?]
June 7 Mary dau. of Tho[s] & Dorithy Chance bapt.
June 29 Mary Chance bur.
July 6 Kerthrine dau. of y[e] woman deliver'd in the church bapt.
July 10 Temperance dau. of Thomas & Jane Groves [?]
Aug. 26 Ann dau. of David & Mary Tayler bapt.
Sep. 21 Elizabeth Ackland bur.
Oct. 12 John, a foundling, bapt.
Dec. 21 Robert son of William & Jane Seagrave bapt.
Jan. 3 Prudence dau. of Henry & Mary Wootton bapt.
Jan. 3 Mary Cutler bur.
Jan. 4 Sarah, a child born in the street, bapt.
Jan. 23 Samuel Drake & Robert sons of John & Hannah Jarratt bapt.
Feb. 27 Mary dau. of Will[m] & Hester Slayter bapt.
Mar. 7 William East bur.
Mar. 8 Ann De Ponthieu bur.

1734.

June 12 Thomas son of Edw[d] & Eliz. Hodgkins bapt.
June 20 Clement Boehm bur.
Aug. 7 Thomas son of Tho[s] & Dorithy Chance bapt.
Sep. 10 Henneretta Maria Ann Gambier bur.

Sep. 20 Thomas son of Thomas & Sarah Walker bapt.
Sep. 20 Ann Harper bur.
Sep. 29 Henry son of John & Jenuitt Mathews bapt.
Sep. .. Mary Hodgkins bur.
Jan. 10 John Pantin bur.
Jan. 12 John son of Jasper & Eliz. Pane bapt.
Feb. 2 James son of John & Dorithy Van Rixtell [?]

1735.

April 5 Henry Milbourn bur.
April 10 John Warneck bur.
April 18 Tabitha Boorne wife of Joseph Boorne, an adult person, bapt.
April 30 Eliz. Fonnereau bur.
May 2 Esabella Tantlen bur.
May 23 James son of Rich[d] & Martha Giles bapt.
July 10 Eliz. Martin bur.
Aug. 27 Mary dau. of William & Jane Seagrave bapt.
Aug. 31 Andrew son of Andrew & Mary Dixon bapt.
Sep. 2 Andrew Dixon bur.
Nov. 2 Ann dau. of David & Mary Tayler bapt.
Nov. 28 Thomas son of Thomas & Johannah Warmsley bapt.
Dec. 5 John son of John & Deborah Haris bapt.
Dec. 9 Jane dau. of John & Temperance Goulding bapt.
Dec. 17 James Morton bur.
Feb. 5 Ann Simson bur.
Feb. 10 Mary dau. of John & Mary Clarke bapt.
Feb. 24 Eliz. dau. of Ralph & Martha Grigge bapt.
Mar. 3 Francis & William sons of Francis & Mary Grizel bapt.
Mar. 22 Eliz. Woolf bur.

1736.

April 26 Emma Susanna dau. of Edmond & Martha Boehm bapt.
April 27 Richard Arnold bur.
May 20 Ralph Ford bur.
June 2 Sarah dau. of William & Ann Vickers bapt.
June 2 William son of William & Eelizabeth Edwards bapt.
June 23 Josina dau. of John & Doritha Van Rixtel bapt.
Aug. 1 John son of John & Jennett Matthews bapt.
Aug. 3 Timothy son of Tho. & Dorithy Chance bapt.
Aug. 21 Timothy Chance bur.
Aug. 26 Elizabeth dau. of Edw[d] & Elizabeth Hodghkins bapt.
Nov. 5 Mary dau. of Benj[n] & Ann Banks bapt.
Dec. 29 James Mallortie bur.
Dec. 30 Josiah Boddell bur.
Jan. 6 John son of John & Lois Gibson bapt.
Feb. 16 Timothy Whitting son of Thomas & Liddia Moore bapt.

1737.

Mar. 29 Walter son of Peter & Elizabeth Yerbury bapt.
April 20 Hannah Cock, an adult person, aged ab[t] 27, bapt.
May 11 Mas[r] Isaac Hunter bur.
Aug. 10 James son of Thomas & Dorothy Aish bapt.
Aug. 18 Jane Nash bur.
Sep. 2 Mary Berdit bur.
Sep. 15 Roger son of Edmond & Martha Boehm bapt.
Sep. 21 Temperance dau. of John & Temperance Goulding bapt.

Oct. 28 Mary dau. of David & Mary Crawford bapt.
Nov. 8 Elizabeth dau. of George Arther & Eliz. Ellard bapt.
Feb. 8 Catherine Judith, a foundling, bapt.
Mar. 8 Edw[d] Newton bur.
Mar. 15 Vollintine son of Benj[n] & Ann Bankes bapt.
Mar. 20 Roger M[c]Carmick bur.

1738.

April 12 Elizabeth Warrin bur.
June 23 Ann Tayler bur.
June 27 William son of John & Lucey Hunt bapt.
June 28 Samuel son of Ralph & Martha Grigg bapt.
July 30 William Hunt bur.
Aug. 16 James Ridgway bur.
Aug. 16 Christiana Walker bur.
Sep. 1 Mary dau. of James & Mary Millet bapt.
Sep. 11 Isaac Besils bur.
Sep. 15 Mas[r] Clement Hopffer bur.
Sep. 20 Robert son of Thomas & Liddia Moore bapt.
Oct. 12 Elizabeth Vincent bur.
Oct. 27 John son of John & Mary Wright bapt.
Dec. 5 Thomas son of Luke & Elizabeth Dowley bapt.
Dec. 10 Thomas Dowley bur.
Jan. 31 Ann dau. of Edw[d] & Elizabeth Hodgkins bapt.
Feb. 20 The Rev[d] M[r] Rich[d] Venn bur.
Feb. 24 Eliz. Empson bur.
Feb. 28 Elizabeth dau. of Tho[s] & Joanna Walmsley bapt.
Mar. 2 Mary Arnold bur.

1739.

Mar. 30 Elizabeth Dodwell bur.
Mar. 31 Francies dau. of Francies & Mary Driver bapt.
April 8 Carthrine dau. of John & Jennitt Mathews bapt.
May 6 Richard son of William & Hester Hobbs bapt.
June 6 Margery Witfeild bur.
June 8 Francies Moreton bur.
June 27 Phillip son of Phillip & Margarett Fonnereau bapt.
July 15 John son of John & Elizabeth Smith bapt.
Aug. 5 John Smith bur.
Aug. 11 Elizabeth dau. of John & Elizabeth Wilkson bapt.
Sep. 5 Lucey dau. of John & Lucey Hunt bapt.
Sep. 20 John Fredrick son of William John & Kerthrin Hester Andrews bapt.
Oct. 24 Margarett Allix bur.
Nov. 30 Marg[t] dau. of David & Mary Crawford bapt.
Dec. 7 William son of William & Elizabeth Milles bapt.
Dec. 28 Benjaman Mace bur.
Jan. 21 Ann dau. of Edmond & Martha Boehm bapt.
Feb. 6 James son of Thomas & Liddia Moore bapt.
Feb. 13 Richard Arnold bur.
Feb. 14 Marg[t] Panton bur.
Feb. 19 Mary Ann Dobson bur.
Mar. 11 John Mace bur.

1740.

Mar. 30 William son of Abraham & Elizabeth Winterbottom bapt.
April 3 Frances Martin bur.
April 16 Claude Fonnereau, Esq., bur.

April 18 Elizabeth Elter bur.
May 2 John son of Joseph & Ann Martin bapt.; born in the parish workhouse
May 14 Frances dau. of Giles & Frances Rooke bapt.
June 29 James son of James & Mary Millett bapt.
July 10 Ann Boehm bur.
July 11 Ann Beata dau. of William & Hester Hobbs bapt.
Dec. 10 Sarah dau. of Thomas & Frances Saunders bapt.
Dec. 10 Mary, a foundling, bapt.
Dec. 20 Fredrick William son of John & Kerthrine Andrews bapt.
Dec. 20 Kerthrine dau. of David & Francis Falconer bapt.
Jan. 9 John Withers bur.
Mar. 24 Eliz. Jones bur.
Mar. 24 Cathrine Lane bur.

1741.

Mar. 26 Martyn son of Phillip & Margarett Fonnereau bapt.
April 17 Nicholis Lewis Well bur.
May 2 Edmond son of Edmond & Martha Boehm, & Theodosia dau. of Edmond & Martha Boehm, bapt.
May 24 Liddia Anna dau. of Thomas & Liddia Moore bapt.
June 3 Susannah dau. of William & Mary Saward bapt.
June 17 Mrs Mary Demaretz bur.
Aug. 30 Elizabeth dau. of John & Elizabeth Wilkinson bapt.
Aug. 31 Ann Croson bur.
Sep. 6 John, a foundling, bapt.
Sep. 24 Ann Coleman bur.
Oct. 14 Joseph son of John & Lucey Hunt bapt.
Oct. 21 Ann dau. of John & Ann Smallpiece bapt.
Oct. 23 Mary Allen bur.
Nov. 30 George Friend bur.
Dec. 8 Ann Griszell bur.
Jan. 15 Sarah Williams bur.
Jan. 22 Elizabeth Lascelles bur.
Jan. 31 Elizabeth dau. of John & Ann Cowper bapt.
Feb. 9 Charlotte dau. of Phillip & Margarett Fonnereau bapt.

1742.

Mar. 26 Frances dau. of David & Mary Crawford bapt.
April .. Dorothy Mariah dau. of John & Dorothy Van Rixtell bapt.
May 9 Joshua Odams bur.
May 26 Phillip Rouseau bur.
June 9 John son of James & Mary Millett bapt.
June 18 Daniel son of Josias & Elizabeth Hodgkins bapt.
June 30 Richd son of Wm & Ann Gee bapt.
July 25 Elizabeth dau. of Samuel & Elizabeth Whiting bapt.
Oct. 5 Miles Peter son of William John & Kerthrine Andrews bapt.
Nov. 1 Theodosia Boehm bur.
Nov. 9 Frances dau. of David & Frances Falconer bapt.
Nov. 17 Thomas son of Thomas & Mary Ann Norris bapt.
Jan. 7 Mary Roe, a foundling, bapt.
Jan. 19 Thomas son of Phillip & Margarett Fonnereau bapt.
Feb. 13 Thomas Fonnereau bur.
Feb. 26 Fillis Devenport bapt.

1743.

April 3 Mary Allen bur.
April 17 Martha dau. of John & Sarah Mitchael bapt.
May 11 Ann dau. of John & Hannah Wood bapt.

May 24 Mary Godwin bur.
June 8 John son of John & Ann Smallpiece bapt.
July 8 Jane dau. of Josiah & Jane Cottin bapt.
Aug. 3 Thomas son of Thomas & Mary Martin bapt.
Oct. 21 Peter Fonnereau bur.
Oct. 23 Mary dau. of Rich[d] & Ann Walter bapt.
Oct. 31 Martha Fellows bur.
Dec. 13 Jane dau. of David & Frances Falconer bapt.
Dec. 23 Jane Falconer bur.
Jan. 1 George son of George & Ann Reynolds bapt.
Jan. 1 Elizabeth dau. of David & Mary Crawford [?]
Jan. 13 William Jones bur.
Jan. 13 Fanny dau. of Phillip & Margarett Fonnereau bapt.

1744.

Mar. 25 Mary dau. of John & Lucey Hunt bapt.
Mar. 27 Elizabeth dau. of Samuel & Eliz. Whiting bapt.
April 1 Richard son of Thomas and Lidia Phinchback bapt.
June 13 Avis dau. of James & Mary Millet bapt.
July .. Hannah dau. of Benitt & Sarah Scott bapt.
July 13 Isaac son of Isaac & Sarah Hooper bapt.
Aug. 24 Stephen Frederick son of William John & Kerthrine Andrews bapt.
Jan. 20 Mary Ann dau. of Tho[s] & Eliz. Hall bapt.
Jan. 31 Elizabeth Bryan bur.
Mar. 4 Elizabeth Hale bur.

1745.

May 7 Elizabeth Dupuy bur.
May 8 Ann dau. of Anthony & Ann Bond bapt.
May 21 Alexander son of Josiah & Jane Cottin bapt.
May 25 David son of David & Frances Falconer bapt.
July 2 James son of Isaac & Sarah Hooper bapt.
Sep. 13 James son of James & Mary Guy bapt.
Oct. 25 Sarah dau. of William & Elizabeth Gobble, a pentioner, bapt.
Oct. 30 Margaretta Well bur.
Nov. 5 Katherne Elizabeth dau. of William John & Katherne Andrews bapt.
Nov. 29 Mary dau. of James & Elizabeth Clarke bapt.
Dec. 21 Mary Pennard bur.
Dec. 21 Richard son of William & Elizabeth Winn bapt.
Dec. 30 Carthrine dau. of John & Hannah Wood bapt.
Jan. 23 Judith Theoroude bur.
Jan. 26 Edward Thomas son of Tho[s] & Elizabeth Hall bapt.
Jan. 29 Charles son of Joseph & Ester Garrard bapt.
Jan. 30 Thomas son of Phillip & Margaret Fonnereau bapt.
Feb. 16 Carthrine Elizabeth Andrews bur.

1746.

April 9 Mary Cambridge Storke bur.
April 30 Miss Martha Boehm bur.
May 1 Thomas son of Thomas & Lidia Pinchback bapt.
May 7 William son of William & Hannah Jobbins bapt.
May 28 Richard Pigg son of Richard & Emm Elmer bapt.
July 20 Mary dau. of Robert & Elizabeth Anderson bapt.
Aug. 20 Deborah dau. of John & Susannah Haynes bapt.
Nov. 11 Teresia dau. of David & Frances Falconer bapt.
Nov. 17 William Lake son of Lake & Hannah Young bapt.
Jan. 16 Ann dau. of William & Sarah Young bapt

Feb. 10 Thomas son of Thomas & Ann Price bapt.
Mar. 11 Harry son of Phillip & Margaret Fonnereau bapt.

1747.

April . . Isaac son of Isaac & Sarah Hooper bapt.
April 30 Ann dau. of Joseph & Mary Magdalin Fisher bapt.
Aug. 12 Elizabeth dau. of John Blake & Elizabeth Grover bapt.
Aug. 24 Robert son of Christopher & Ann Hartwell bapt.
Aug. 29 Henry son of Henry & Ann Lindsay bapt.
Sep. 11 John son of Josiah & Jane Cottin bapt.
Oct. 19 Elizabeth Prockter bur.
Nov. 1 Elliner dau. of James & Margaret Steward bapt.
Nov. 8 Thomas Price bur.
Nov. 22 Charles Henry son of Thos & Elizabeth Hall bapt.
Nov. 29 William son of Thomas & Lidia Pinchback bapt.
Dec. 31 John & William sons of John & Catherine Wood bapt.
Jan. 9 Elizabeth dau. of David & Frances Falconer bapt.
Feb. 6 Sarah Fowler bur.
Feb. 12 Frances dau. of Richard & Emm Elmer, bapt.
Feb. 19 James Cox son of William John & Kerthrine Andrews bapt.
Feb. 23 Mary Munorett bur.
Feb. 24 James Cox Andrews bur.
Mar. 13 Ann dau. of late Thos & Ann Price bapt.
Mar. 14 Martha Colebrooke bur.

1748.

April . . Elizabeth Storke bur.
May 11 Isaac son of Mark & Alce Graves bapt.
May 18 Thomas son of William & Sarah Young bapt.
May 20 Samuel son of William Hampleto & Ann Squire bapt.
May 27 Joseph son of John & Martha Bonner bapt.
June 12 Elizabeth dau. of William & Ann Walne bapt.
Aug. 19 Richard son of Edward & Anna Margaretter Davies bapt.
Aug. 29 Erasmus Hopffer bur.
Sep. 4 Robert Coleman bur.
Sep. 16 Cary dau. of Phillip & Margaret Fonnereau bapt.
Sep. 18 John son of John & Elizabeth Snowdon bapt.
Jan. 28 Isabelah dau. of Henry & Isabelah Williams bapt.
Mar. 1 Jane dau. of Robert & Elizabeth Anderson bapt.

1749.

April 9 Elizabeth dau. of Elizabeth & Thomas Hall bapt.
April 9 Elizabeth dau. of Isaac & Sarah Hooper bapt.
April . . Charles Summers son of Thomas & Elizabeth Sanderson bapt.
June 4 Mary Vickers bur.
July 12 Elizabeth Crouch bur.
Aug. 10 James Cox son of William John & Kerthrine Andrews bapt.
Sep. 8 James Cox Andrews bur.
Oct. 1 William son of Richard & Emm Elmer bapt.
Oct. 10 Charles son of David & Frances Falconer bapt.
Oct. 12 Elizabeth Streatfield [?]
Nov. 18 George son of Phillip & Margarett Fonnereau bapt.
Nov. 21 George Fonnereau bur.
Nov. 24 Mary dau. of John & Carthrine Wood bapt.
Jan. 3 Carthrine Hester Andrews bur.
Mar. 12 Thomas Follintine son of Solloman & Eliz. Goldsmith bapt.

1750.

May 27 Daniel Russel bur.
June 13 John son of William & Mary Cornelus bapt.
Aug. 16 Richard Peter son of Peter & Mary Maritte bapt.
Oct. 24 Samuel Parratt bur.
Oct. 31 Frances dau. of David & Frances Falconer bapt.
Nov. 2 Mary dau. of Benj[n] & Elizabeth Marshall bapt.
Dec. 4 George son of Phillip & Margaret Fonnereau bapt.
Jan. 21 D[r] William Ince bur.
Jan. 23 Thomas son of James & Elizabeth Holmes bapt.
Jan. 24 Margaret Rebeccah dau. of William & Judith Adkins bapt.
Mar. 6 Elizabeth Storke bur.
Mar. 22 Benjaman son of James & Mary Frost bapt.

1751.

Mar. 29 Anna Margaretter dau. of Edward & Anna Davis bapt.
April 22 Mary Palmer bur.
May 22 Samuel Storke bur.
May 31 William son of Solloman & Elizabeth Goldsmith bapt.
July 26 James son of James & Sarah Laman bapt.
July 26 Mary Croson bur.
Aug. 4 Sarah dau. of Isaac & Sarah Hooper bapt.
Oct. 1 Ellin dau. of Thomas & Susannah Bull bapt.

1752.

Jan. .. Benjaman son of Benjaman & Elizabeth Marshall bapt.
Mar. 13 George son of James & Elizabeth Holmes bapt.
Mar. 30 Jane Hannah dau. of the late Rev. James & Mary Hotchkins bapt.
Mar. 30 Mary Constant Charity dau. of George Daniel & Elizabeth Feissier bapt.
June 12 Mary Hotchkins bur.
June 28 Samuel son of Solloman & Elizabeth Goldsmith bapt.
July 9 Claude Fonnereau son of Phillip & Margaret Fonnereau bapt.
Nov. 14 Robert Manning bur.

1753.

Jan. .. John son of David & Frances Falconer bapt.
Feb. 4 Ester Dufour bur.
Feb. 4 William son of Benjaman & Elizabeth Marshall bapt.
April 8 Jonas son of Thomas & Susannah Bull bapt.
April 20 William son of Richard & Elizabeth Bradley bapt.
May 29 John Palmer bur.
June 3 Stephen son of Richard & Emm Elmer bapt.
Sep. 16 Ann dau. of Edward & Mary Lee bapt.
Oct. 15 Joanna dau. of Dorothy Sims, widow, bapt.
Nov. 7 Abel son of Phillip & Margaret Fonnereau bapt.
Nov. 25 Susanah dau. of Bosswell & Susanah Jenkins bapt.
Dec. 7 Joseph son of Solloman & Eliz. Goldsmith bapt.
Dec. 7 Frances Jenks bur.

1754.

Jan. .. Mary dau. of Isaac & Sarah Hooper bapt.
Jan. 29 Elizabeth Rix bur.
Feb. 27 Elizabeth dau. of William & Elizabeth Marsham bapt.
June 18 Seline dau. of William & Jane Mary Brooke bapt.

St. John Baptist on Wallbrook.

Register of Baptisms and Burials.

REGISTER OF BAPTISMS FROM NOV. 5, 1682.

1682.

Nov. 5 James Edwards son of Nathaniell & Jane Edwards; born 26 Oct.

[*No other entry until* 1686.]

1686.

April 4 John Edwards son of Nathaniell & Jane Edwards; born 31 March
June 15 Ann dau. of Daniell & Mary Howe
June 22 Susanna dau. of Wm & Elizabeth Dickason
Sep. 30 Samuell son of William & Hanna Hawkins
Oct. 1 Ruth dau. of Roberte & Elizabeth Radford
Oct. 3 Hannah dau. of Eliezer & Hannah Potts
Nov. 4 Richarde Maninge son of Richarde & Marey Maninge
Nov. 22 Henerey son of Mathwiu & Barbery Berrisfeilde
Jan. 10 Leiwis son of Benjamin & Marey Fouke
Mar. 23 Anne & Marey daus. of Ralph & Margerett Benton

1687.

Mar. 27 Jerimiah son of Jeriminh & Victoria Wrighte
Mar. 28 Elizabeth dau. of Peter & Elizabeth Tonby
April 13 Samuell son of Joshua & Sarah Hazell
April 24 Abel son of Wm & Alice Saulsbury
May 9 Elizabeth dau. of Wm & [*blank*] Winter
July 3 Wm & Henry sons of Wm & Mary Daldern
Aug. 12 Mary dau. of Samuell & Mary Howard
Aug. 14 Canham son of Daniel & Mary How
Sep. 11 Sarah dau. of John & Hannah Horne
Oct. 2 Edith dau. of John & Agnes Loyd
Oct. 16 Anne dau. of Gilbert & Jane Brandon
Oct. 16 Thomas son of Wm & Hannah Batson
Nov. 6 Mary dau. of Thomas & Mary Bell
Nov. 7 James son of Wm & Hannah Hawkins
Dec. 4 Mary dau. of John & Ann Orsburn
Dec. 12 Wm son of Edward & Edith Lawrance
Dec. 18 Thomas son of Thomas & Elizabeth Hopkins
Dec. 29 Hannah dau. of Wm & Elizabeth Dickson
Feb. 5 Thomas son of William & Elizabeth Kemp
Mar. 23 William son of William & Sarah Reeve

1688.

Mar. 27 Isaac son of Daniel & Mary Withers
April 15 Easter dau. of Eleazer & Hannah Potts
July 20 Elizabeth dau. of Jeremiah & Victory Wright
Aug. 18 Ruben son of Robert & Elizabeth Radford
Aug. 20 George son of Richard & Elizabeth Elliott

Oct. 28 Martha dau. of Ralph & Margarett Benton
Oct. 31 Thomas son of Samuell & Mary Howard
Nov. 27 Sarah dau. of Thomas & Ann Parsley
Dec. 21 George son of Joshua & Sarah Hazell
Jan. 7 John son of George & Elenor Hudnoll
Jan. 10 W^m son of Edward & Edith Lawrance
Jan. 13 Alice dau. of Thomas & Mary Bell
Jan. 27 Robert son of Emanuell & Mary Drake
Jan. 27 Elizabeth dau. of W^m & Elizabeth Saulsbury
Feb. 12 W^m son of W^m & Ann Rogers
Mar. 22 John Cloakelane, a foundling
Mar. 24 Elizabeth dau. of Thomas & Grace Kingsley

1689.

April 14 Ann dau. of John & Ann Orsburn
April 21 Henry son of W^m & Sarah Reeve
June 2 Elizabeth dau. of Thomas & Elizabeth Hopkins
July 7 Edward son of Edward & Hannah Wilmore
July 11 Elizabeth dau. of John & Sarah Haynes
Aug. 18 Elizabeth dau. of Gilbert & Jane Brandon
Oct. 27 Susanna dau. of W^m & Elizabeth Kemp
Nov. 1 Elizabeth dau. of Samuell & Mary Hayward
Nov. 19 W^m son of Ralph & Ann Meadowes
Feb. 20 Jone Dowgate, a foundling
Mar. 9 Thomas son of Thomas & Grace Kingsly

1690.

Mar. 25 Elizabeth dau. of James & Elizabeth Coale
April 6 Edward son of Edward & Edith Lawrance
May 1 Imanuell son of Imanuell & Mary Drake
May 13 Hannah dau. of W^m & Elizabeth Hannock
June 8 Martha dau. of John & Ann Orsburn
June 15 Hannah dau. of W^m & Ann Rogers
June 15 Edward son of Richard & Elizabeth Elliott
June 15 Peter son of Peter & Elizabeth Tonby
June 26 John son of John & Elizabeth Withinbrook
Sep. 27 Elizabeth dau. of W^m & Ann Crane
Dec. 24 Sarah dau. of W^m & Elizabeth Dickinson
Dec. 26 Mary dau. of Gilbert & Jane Brandon
Feb. 8 Rose dau. of Thomas & Elizabeth Warren
Mar. 15 Thomas & Hannah son & dau. of Thomas & Abigall Pilkinton
Mar. 15 John son of Thomas & Ann Parsley
Mar. 24 John son of Edward & Edith Lawrance

1691.

April 3 Sarah dau. of Samuell & Mary Howard
April 5 Samuell son of W^m & Alce Saulsbury
April 20 Teverca dau. of Thomas & Elizabeth Hopkins
May 1 Samuell son of John & [*blank*] Alder
May 27 W^m son of W^m & Elizabeth Kemp
May 29 Ann dau. of Edmund & Ann Kidby
Oct. 27 Samuell son of Georg & Elenor Hudnoll
Dec. 22 Thomas son of John & Elizabeth Withinbrook
Feb. 3 Wm Dodson Court

Feb. 7 Martha dau. of Thomas & Elizabeth Warren
Feb. 12 Shusella dau. of Thomas & Grace Kingsly
Mar. 24 Orpwood son of Richard & Gartroot Dawsonn

1692.

Mar. 27 James son of W^m^ & Elizabeth Saulsbury
April 6 John son of W^m^ & Sarah Reeve
April 10 Phebe dau. of W^m^ & Phebe Peart
April 10 Elizabeth dau. of Nicholas & Sarah Goble
April 12 Daniell son of W^m^ & Elizabeth Dickeson
April 15 Elizabeth dau. of John & Mary Hawkins
May 9 Ann dau. of Samuell & Mary Howard
July 10 John son of Thomas & Mary Parriot
Aug. 13 Isabella dau. of W^m^ & Elizabeth Kemp
Sep. 28 Lyddia dau. of Silvester & Lyddia Ives
Oct. 6 John son of Samuell & Mary Quested
Oct. 9 Mary dau. of John & Mary Turner
Nov. 6 Mary dau. of James & Elizabeth Clegg
Nov. 8 John son of John & Hester Spark
Nov. 15 Katharine dau. of Benjamyn & Ann Knight
Nov. 27 W^m^ son of Cornelius & Elizabeth Needham
Dec. 16 Prisiila dau. of John & Katharine Wilson
Dec. 27 Frances dau. of John & Ann Orsburn
Jan. 15 W^m^ son of Robt & Martha Player
Jan. 29 W^m^ son of John & Mary Williams
Feb. 19 Roger son of Thomas & Elizabeth Hopkins
Mar. 5 Thomas son of Richard & Elizabeth Elliott
Mar. 12 Cornelius son of Cornelius & Ann Davis
Mar. 15 Lewis son of Nicholas & Sarah Goble

1693.

April 2 Joseph son of W^m^ & Sarah Reeve
April 4 W^m^ son of W^m^ & Phebe Pairt
May 10 Joseph son of Joseph & Katharine Gravenor
June 22 Margrett dau. of Samuell & Mary Howard
Aug. 11 John son of John & Mary Hawkins
Nov. 7 Henry son of Robert & Hannah Price
Jan. 4 Grace dau. of Robert & Grace Conningsby
Jan. 7 Charles son of George & Ellenor Hudnall
Jan. 21 Thomas son of Windsor & Elizabeth Pasmore
Feb. 1 Elizabeth dau. of William & Alice Saulsbury
Feb. 9 Ann dau. of Benjamin & Ann Knight
Feb. 16 Elizabeth dau. of John & Elizabeth Lankisheir
Feb. 27 Mary dau. of Edward & Mary Rich
Mar. 18 Martha dau. of Nicholas & Sarah Goble
Mar. 21 Mary dau. of John & Ann Osbourn

1694.

June 30 James son of Samuell & Elizabeth Newton
Aug. 13 Elizabeth dau. of Hanibal & Elizabeth Hall
Sep. 16 Elizabeth dau. of Thomas & Elizabeth Warren
Sep. 23 Damerus dau. of Robert & Hannah Price
Sep. 26 Henry son of John & Margrett Rogers
Sep. 30 Thomas son of Thomas & Mary Parrott
Oct. 7 Elizabeth dau. of William & Phebe Piart

Oct. 7 William son of Peter & Elizabeth Tonby
Oct. 24 Sarah dau. of Peter & Clarance Russheare
Nov. 9 Martha dau. of John & Mary Hawkins
Nov. 26 William son of Samuell & Mary Howard
Feb. 6 Mary Dowgate, a foundling
Feb. 12 Seth son of Seth & Mary Jermy
Feb. 24 Henry son of Nicholas & Sarah Goble
Feb. 27 Bernice dau. of Gilbert & Jane Brandon
Mar. 6 Bridgett dau. of Robert & Grace Conningsby
Mar. 8 Mary dau. of Joseph & Elizabeth Cook
Mar. 10 Ann dau. of Edward & Mary Rich

1695.

April 14 Henerritta dau. of Benjaman & Ann Knight
June 13 Richard son of Joseph & Kathrine Gravinnour
June 21 Henry son of John & Elizabeth Lankisbeire
Aug. 18 John son of Robert & Hannah Price
Aug. 22 John son of John & Margrett Smith
Sep. 15 Thomas son of William & Sarah Reeve
Dec. 23 Suanna dau. of Daniell & Suanna Wallis
Feb. 1 John son of John & Elizabeth Heald
Feb. 28 Sarah dau. of John & Sarah Price
Mar. 1 Nicholas son of Nicholas & Sarah Goble
Mar. 8 Windsor son of Windsor & Elizabeth Pasmore

1696.

Mar. 29 Thomas son of William & Ann Skelton
May 14 Mary dau. of James & Kathrine Clark
May 24 Richard, a foundling
June 1 Ann dau. of John & Elizabeth Moore
June 14 William son of Seth & Mary Jermy
July 5 Elizabeth dau. of Thomas & Elizabeth Rawlins
July 31 Bathsheba dau. of Gilbert & Jane Brandon
Aug. 16 Sandys son of Benjamin & Ann Knight
Nov. 1 Henry son of Richard & Sarah Clark
Jan. 3 Stephen son of Stephen & Elizabeth Alltree
Mar. 2 James son of Daniell & Suanna Wallis
Mar. 7 Robertu dau. of Thomas & Philipa Parrott

1697.

Mar. 25 Henry son of Henry & Rebeckah Cooper
April 25 Amy dau. of Bennett & Amy Morris
April 28 Jane dau. of William & Phebee Peirt
May 16 William son of John & Elizabeth Heald
May 16 William son of Thomas & Ann Poole
Aug. 8 Hanna dau. of Edward & Edith Lawrance
Sep. 3 Justinian son of John & Elizabeth Bracegirdle
Sep. 26 John son of Winsor & Elizabeth Pastmore
Oct. 8 Edwin son of John & Kathrine Thornicraft
Nov. 3 Margrett dau. of Henry & Sarah Parnell
Nov. 19 Sarah dau. of James & Ruth Whitchurch
Nov. 21 Elizabeth dau. of Benjamin & Anne Knight
Nov. 22 Elizabeth dau. of Henry & Elizabeth Nobbs
Feb. 12 William son of John & Elizabeth Read

1698.

April 13 Johanna dau. of John & Elizabeth Tille
May 10 Hannah dau. of Nicholas & Sarah Goble
July 20 Ann dau. of Fredrick & Rebecca Bode
Aug. 22 Ann dau. of Thomas & Dorothy Denning
Sep. 18 Samuel son of John & Elizabeth Heald
Sep. 25 Sarah dau. of Thomas & Ann Poole
Oct. 31 Thomas son of Henry & Sarah Parnell
Nov. 25 Thomas son of Thomas & Elizabeth Warren
Jan. 15 Elizabeth dau. of Benjamin & Ann Knight
Feb. 19 Mary dau. of Robert & Ann Wilkison

1699.

April 1 Phebe dau. of William & Phebe Pirt
April 4 Charles son of Gilbard & Jane Brandon
April 9 Henry son of Henry & Elizabeth Knobbs
April 9 William son of Thomas & Elizabeth Rawlins
April 16 William son of Thomas & Suannah Marshall
April 23 William son of John & Judith Fleece
May 22 William son of John & Ruth Gibson
July 9 Sarah dau. of Robert & Mary Parnell
July 17 Elizabeth & Sarah daus. of William Man; two parish children
Aug. 31 Penelope dau. of Nicholas & Sarah Goble
Sep. 2 Suannah dau. of Charles & Elizabeth Yeoman
Sep. 3 William son of William & Sarah Reeve
Sep. 17 Henry son of Henry & Mary Figgs
Sep. 24 Ann dau. of Thomas & Dorothy Danning
Sep. 29 Edward son of Abraham & Elizabeth Cardall
Oct. 20 Elizabeth dau. of William & Elizabeth Waters
Nov. 19 Richard son of Richard & Sarah Clarke
Dec. 14 Thomas son of Thomas & Susannah Pead
Mar. 3 Thomas son of Thomas & Anne Poole

1700.

April 8 Benjamin son of Benjamin & Anne Knight
May 12 Hester dau. of Henry & Hannah Beesley
Aug. 7 Windsor son of Windsor & Elizabeth Pasmer
Sep. 2 John son of Willaby & Elizabeth Merchant
Oct. 9 Rebeccah dau. of William & Jane Robinson
Nov. 17 Martha dau. of Cannon & Mary Mountlow
Dec. 20 John Walbrook, left in the parish
Dec. 27 Sarah dau. of Henry & Sarah Parnel
Dec. 29 Mary dau. of Joseph & Anne Hollymore
Feb. 18 Elizabeth dau. of William & Elizabeth Rolshouk
Mar. 19 Margaret Dodson, a foundling

1701.

April 20 Elizabeth dau. of Thomas & Dorothy Denning
April 23 Christopher son of Henry and Mary Figgs
May 12 Mary dau. of Thomas & Ann Pool
June 24 William son of John & Sarah Pack
Aug. 21 Susanna dau. of Thomas & Susannah Pead
Oct. 24 Mary dau. of Nicholas & Elizabeth Moseley
Nov. 2 Anne dau. of Young & Katherine Herring

Dec. 16 Anne dau. of Henry & Martha Sivedall
Jan. 22 William son of William & Jane Booth
Feb. 12 John son of Cannon & Martha Mountlow
Mar. 12 George son of George & Mary Janson

1702.

April 19 George son of Henry & Hannah Beasly
April 19 John son of Robert & Anne Jones
June 21 Richard son of Joseph & Anne Hallymore
June 30 Joseph & Benjamin, twins, sons of Thomas & Anne Pool
July 13 James son of John & Sarah Pack
Aug. 4 William son of William & Margaret Peart
Sep. 24 Elizabeth dau. of Thomas & Katherine Ayloffe
Oct. 8 John son of John & Martha Gilbert
Nov. 19 Anne dau. of Nicholas & Elizabeth Mosely
Dec. 1 Mary Lane, a foundling
Dec. 13 Mary dau. of John & Sarah Paine
Jan. 14 William son of William & Elizabeth Rolshouk
Jan. 21 John son of Reginald & Lucy De Boyville

1703.

Mar. 30 Elizabeth dau. of John & Anne Hewson
May 11 Samuel son of Samuel & Mary Smith
June 28 Martha dau. of Thomas & Susanna Pead
July 18 John son of Elizabeth & William Waters
Aug. 23 John son of Elizabeth & George Upton
Sep. 7 William son of John & Ruth Gibson
Sep. 12 Mary dau. of William & Margaret Tims
Sep. 14 Nicholas son of Nicholas & Mary Jackman
Oct. 9 Mary dau. of Dr George Colebrook & Martha his wife
Dec. 3 Thomas son of Thomas & Anne Hooper
Dec. 12 Robert son of Young & Catherine Herring
Jan. 11 Richard son of Joseph & Anne Hallimore
Feb. 8 Grace dau. of Daniel & [*blank*] Davis
Mar. 5 Elizabeth dau. of George & Mary Johnson
Mar. 8 Henriette Violle dau. of John & Margaret De Raffau

1704.

April 2 William son of John & Mary Held
April 28 Anne Slutter dau. of John & Sarah Pack
May 18 Peter son of Reginald & Lucy De Boyville
May 31 Martha dau. of John & Martha Gilbert
June 27 Elizabeth Barnes dau. of Joseph & Elizabeth Bradbury
July 17 Mary dau. of Thomas & Mary Nicholls
Aug. 18 Agnis dau. of Benjamin & Anne Knight
Aug. 21 Martha dau. of George & Martha Colebrook
Aug. 24 Elizabeth dau. of Daniel & Elizabeth Dickenson
Sep. 8 Katherine dau. of William & Elizabeth Rolshouk
Sep. 29 Hannah dau. of William & Elizabeth Waters
Oct. 1 Abraham son of John & Sarah Pain
Oct. 28 Francis son of [*blank*] & Mary Wood
Oct. 31 Letitia dau. of William & Mary Timms
Nov. 15 Thomas son of Thomas & Elizabeth Facer
Jan. 19 Thomas son of Thomas & Anne Hooper
Mar. 11 Francis son of Francis & Isabella Tresset

1705.

Mar. 25 Roger son of James & John [*sic*] Egan
May 8 Henry son of Samuel & Mary Smith
May 13 Mary dau. of Nicolas & Mary Jackman
May 20 John son of John & Ruth Gibson
May 31 Honour dau. of John & Sarah Pack
June 24 Ester dau. of George & Mary Johnson
July 8 Anne dau. of Thomas & Elizabeth Finchley
July 23 Humphry son of Joseph & Mary Atkins
Aug. 2 Charles son of John & Martha Gilbert
Aug. 13 Jane dau. of John & Jane Hall
Sep. 9 George son of George & Elizabeth Upton
Oct. 19 Anne dau. of William & Elizabeth Waters
Oct. 21 Anne dau. of William & Anna Bethia Steel
Oct. 31 Elizabeth dau. of Richard & Elizabeth Stobbins
Dec. 13 Susannah dau. of Henry & Mary Figges
Dec. 16 Thomas son of John & Hannah Pickard
Dec. 30 Samuel son of Thomas & Elizabeth Facer
Dec. 30 John son of John & Mary Heald
Jan. 29 Margaret dau. of Margaret and William Timms
Feb. 4 Hannah dau. of Callow & Hannah Cary
Feb. 6 Samuel son of John & Anne Hewson
Feb. 12 René son of Reginald & Lucy De Boyville
Feb. 26 Samuel son of Samuel & Anne Baker
Feb. 27 Anne dau. of Nathan & Anne Pool
Mar. 6 Mary dau. of Young & Catherine Herring

1706.

April 14 Isabella dau. of Francis & Isabella Trest
April 25 Anne dau. of Richard & Susannah Nurse
May 20 Robert son of Robert & Anne Davy
June 2 James son of Edmond & [*blank*] Hiller
June 2 Nicholas son of Nicholas & Mary Jackman
July 12 Sarah Alley, a foundling
Sep. 12 George son of George & Martha Colebrook
Sep. 24 George son of George & Elizabeth Upton
Nov. 5 John son of John & Jane Hall
Dec. 17 William son of John & Mary Johnson
Dec. 26 Anna Maria dau. of Richard & Anna Mounteny
Jan. 16 Robert son of John & Martha Gilbert
Feb. 2 Mary dau. of Daniel & Elizabeth Dickson
Mar. 13 Thomas son of Thomas & Elizabeth Facer

1707.

April 1 Susannah dau. of William & Anna Bethia Steel
April 30 John Graves son of William & Ruth Alexander
May 9 Mary dau. of Samuel & Mary Smith
May 25 Abraham son of Abraham & Eleanor Williams
May 25 John son of Samuel & Anne Baker
July 16 Eleanor dau. of Richard & Susannah Nurse
Aug. 6 Edward son of Samuel & Margaret Owen
Aug. 22 Mary dau. of Nicholas & Mary Jackman
Aug. 30 Sarah dau. of John & Sarah Parry
Sep. 8 John son of Benjamin & Anne Knight
Oct. 9 John son of John & Sarah Pack

Oct. 13 Nathaniel son of Nathaniel & Anne Pool
Oct. 14 Mary dau. of John & Mary Hopkins
Oct. 18 William son of George & Elizabeth Upton
Jan. 6 Mary dau. of John and Hannah Pickard

1708.

April 11 Anne dau. of Thomas & Elizabeth Facer
April 23 Hannah dau. of John & Jane Hall
May 7 Ruth dau. of William & Ruth Alexander
May 16 Martha dau. of Joseph & Jane Lowe
June 13 Ellistone son of William & Anna Bethia Steel
July 9 Radman son of Henry & Mary Figges
Aug. 17 Josiah son of George & Martha Colebrook
Oct. 21 Mary dau. of Richard & Assenter Beavis
Nov. 28 Young son of Young & Catherine Herring
Dec. 28 Catherine dau. of Samuel & Mary Dexter
Jan. 6 Robert son of John & Martha Gilbert
Jan. 16 Joseph son of Edward & Jane Farmer
Jan. 25 Elizabeth dau. of John & Susannah Townsend
Mar. 13 Elizabeth dau. of John & Susannah Pack
Mar. 14 Samuel son of Samuel & Anne Baker

1709.

Mar. 27 Sarah dau. of Francis & Isabella Trest
April 5 Anne dau. of Randolph & Margaret Fernley
April 26 John son of Nicholas & Mary Jackman
May 8 William son of Thomas & Mary Smith
May 8 Sarah dau. of John & Mary Law
May 19 Robert son of Robert & Elizabeth Mayour
June 8 Mary dau. of John & Sarah Parry
June 26 Hannah dau. of Daniel & Mary Browne
June 30 John son of John & Hannah Pickard
July 17 Elizabeth dau. of John & Eleanor Williams
July 17 James son of Joseph & Elizabeth Ridgeway
Sep. 15 James son of George & Margaret Edwards
Sep. 25 Elizabeth dau. of William & Anna Bethia Steel
Sep. 28 Mary dau. of Joseph & Mary Adkins
Oct. 2 Michael son of George & Jane Hall
Nov. 21 Elizabeth dau. of Gabriel & Elizabeth Tabourdin
Jan. 12 William son of Thomas & Elizabeth Facer
Jan. 17 John son of John & Jane Hall
Feb. 26 Elizabeth dau. of Elizabeth & Hezekiah Walker
Mar. 11 Elizabeth dau. of Henry & Elizabeth Kingdom

1710.

April 4 Elizabeth dau. of John & Martha Gilbert
May 5 Francis son of Francis & Anne Huddleston
May 22 Henry son of Henry & [*blank*] Searse
May 26 Susannah dau. of John & Susannah Townsend
May 26 William son of John & Margaret Gittons
June 10 Sarah dau. of Nicholas & Sarah Jackman
June 13 Dorothy dau. of John & Elanor Williams
July 17 Anna dau. of George & Martha Colebrook
Aug. 6 Mary dau. of Henry & Mary Figges
Sep. 3 Saint George son of John & Sarah Pack

Sep. 17 Mary dau. of Webb & Elizabeth Fleming
Oct. 18 Thomas son of Richard & Susannah Nurse
Nov. 16 Elizabeth dau. of Edward & Jane Farmer
Nov. 19 William son of Samuel & Anne Baker
Nov. 23 Hannah dau. of John & Hannah Pickard
Dec. 27 Mary dau. of John & Jane Hall
Mar. 22 Mary dau. of John & Susannah Townsend

1711.

April 3 Thomas son of Hezekiah & Elizabeth Walker
April 15 Mary dau. of Daniel & Mary Browne
April 17 Gabriel son of Gabriel & Elizabeth Tahourdin
April 17 Edmond son of Alexander & Sarah Young
May 3 William son of Robert & Anne Davey
May 8 Anne dau. of John & Anne Jones
May 11 Thomas son of Thomas & Margaret Obinson
May 17 Samuel son of Samuel & Sarah Marriold
May 25 Catherine dau. of Young & Catherine Herring
May 27 Thomas son of Thomas & Elizabeth Facer
June 2 Francis Hill, a foundling
Oct. 28 Anne dau. of Nicholas & Sarah Jackman
Dec. 16 Frances dau. of John & Eleanor Williams
Jan. 6 George son of George & Sarah Biggs
Feb. 19 Anne dau. of John & Hannah Pickard
Feb. 24 John son of John & Frances Wright
Mar. 9 Joseph son of Thomas & Elizabeth Finchley
Mar. 11 Anne dau. of John & Anne Seaborn
Mar. 16 George son of Web & Elizabeth Fleming

1712.

April 2 John & Bridget son & dau. of George & Bridget Bennet
May 9 Isaac son of Samuel & Martha Le Fever
May 18 Sarah dau. of Alexander & Sarah Young
July 7 Henry son of Henry & Mary Figges
Aug. 10 Margaret dau. of George & Margaret Edwards
Sep. 4 Christian dau. of Francis & Ann Huddleston
Oct. 5 Anne dau. of Samuel & Ann Baker
Dec. 8 Ann dau. of Francis & Ann Cooper
Feb. 22 Margaret dau. of Samuel & Sarah Mariot
Feb. 22 Sarah dau. of John & Eleanor Williams

1713.

Mar. 26 John Hall
April 1 Thomas Stanley Brown son of Daniel & Mary
April 9 Elizabeth dau. of John & Elizabeth Townsend
April 10 Elizabeth dau. of John & Hannah Pickard
June 21 Francis son of Francis & Ann Huddleston
July 12 Sarah dau. of George & Sarah Biggs
July 13 William son of William & Ann Steel
July 21 George son of Samuel & Tomasin Thorn
Sep. 13 Elizabeth dau. of Hezekiah & Mary Walker
Oct. 25 Elizabeth dau. of Niccolas & Mary Jackman
Nov. 22 Elizabeth dau. of George & Bridget Bennet
Feb. 24 Samuel son of Samuel & Ann Baker
Feb. 28 Thomas son of Edward & Jane Farmer

1714.

May 9 Ann dau. of Henry & Mary Figges
May 30 Elizabeth dau. of Thomas & Elizabeth Facer
June 16 Yate dau. of Lancelot & Priscilla Bromwich
Aug. 15 Martha dau. of John & Elizabeth Townsend
Aug. 15 Stephen son of Samuel & Hannah Charman
Aug. 15 Mary dau. of John & Ann Seaborn
Nov. 29 Thomas son of Joseph & Margaret Tompson
Jan. 2 Obadiah son of William & Martha Roberts
Feb. 28 William son of George & Bridget Bennett
Mar. 1 Margaret dau. of Nicholas & Sarah Jakeman

1715.

April 3 Thomas son of John & Sarah Buckland
May 12 Elizabeth dau. of Michael & Mary Howard
May 24 Stephen son of Martin & Anne Lyon
June 16 Samuel son of John & Jane Hall
July 24 Phillis dau. of John & Eleanor Williams
Aug. 19 Charles son of James & Mary Susannah Portalis
Oct. 6 John son of John & Elizabeth Townsend
Oct. 21 Frances dau. of Benjamin & Frances Greive
Nov. 9 Lydia dau. of Henry & Lydia Smith
Dec. 21 Martha dau. of Jonathan & Martha Johnson
Mar. 22 Anna Maria Facer

1716.

April 27 George son of Henry & Mary Figges
April 28 James son of James & Lydia Jackson
May 6 Elizabeth & Anne daus. of Daniel & Mary Brown
June 3 Hannah dau. of John & Mary Phillips
June 10 Charles son of John & Elizabeth Breed
June 17 Martha dau. of William & Martha Roberts
July 4 Thomas Earl son of Samuel & Mary Anger
July 19 John son of John & Sarah Buckland
Aug. 28 Samuel son of Samuel & Jane Hall
Oct. 15 Samuel son of John & Mary Wattlington
Nov. 13 Winefrid dau. of Martin & Anne Lyon
Nov. 24 Mary dau. of George & Mary Biggs
Nov. 30 Catherine dau. of Catherine & Robert Knap
Dec. 28 Thomas son of Samuel & Anne Baker
Jan. 11 Henrietta dau. of James & Mary Susannah Portalis
Feb. 12 Joseph son of Joseph and Margaret Thompson
Mar. 17 Ann dau. of Benjamin & Rebeccah Narling

1717.

May 9 John son of John & Elizabeth Solley
June 2 Mary dau. of Edward & Mary Lloyd
June 2 Richard son of Richard & Willaby Clerk
June 18 Mary dau. of Thomas & Margaret Obinson
July 6 John son of John & Bethiah Unwin
Sep. 4 Anne dau. of Samuel & Mary Watlington
Oct. 25 Carlton son of Samuel & Johanna Stevens
Dec. 12 John son of Jacob & Mary Bell
Dec. 15 William son of Robert & Mary Harris

Dec. 27 William son of Edward & Elizabeth Newton
Jan. 5 Sarah dau. of William & Martha Roberts
Jan. 14 Mary dau. of John & Jane Hall
Jan. 17 Henry son of Henry & Lydia Smith
Feb. 16 John son of John & Grace Tiflin
Mar. 24 Hannah dau. of [*blank*] & Hanah Charman, widow

1718.

Mar. 24 Henry son of Henry & Mary Figges
Mar. 30 Elizabeth dau. of [*blank*] & Ann Latham
June 8 Joseph son of John & Sarah Buckland
June 26 Mary dau. of John & Mary Watlington
July 9 Nicholas son of Nicholas & Mary Jackman
July 29 Thomas son of Thomas & Mary Philips
Oct. 6 Richard Thomas son of a poor woman brought to bed in the street
Nov. 23 Barsheba dau. of Edward & Mary Lloyd
Dec. 21 Mary dau. of William & Sarah Pig
Dec. 25 William son of John & Bethiah Unwin
Mar. 17 John son of John & Mary Nottingham

1719.

April 19 George son of George & Sarah Biggs
May 14 Hannah dau. of John & Mary Watlington
Nov. 8 John son of John & Sarah Buckland
Jan. 31 Catherine dau. of Roger & Catherine Lloyd
Feb. 26 William son of Thomas & Elizabeth Nichols

1720.

Mar. 27 Charles son of John & Bethiah Unwin
April 20 Mary dau. of William & Ann Natt
April 25 John son of John & Mary Watlington
June 19 Emme dau. of William & Sarah Pigg
July 3 Mary dau. of Edward & Elizabeth Ansell
July 10 Henry son of Thomas & Elizabeth Dixson
July 24 Mary dau. of William & Mary Reeves
July 27 Joseph son of Joseph & Sarah Underwood
July 31 John son of John & Ann Maylard
Aug. 12 Samuel son of Samuel & Jane Hall
Oct. 25 Elizabeth dau. of William & Johanna Crips
Nov. 22 Peter Warren
Dec. 11 Sarah dau. of James & Mary Goodson
Dec. 22 John son of John & Elizabeth Dod
Jan. 27 Sarah Sparling; born in 1697
Mar. 1 Mary dau. of Thomas & Mary Philips
Mar. 1 John son of John & Mary Watts
Mar. 5 John son of John & Mary Marshal
Mar. 13 Edward son of John & Mary Watlington

1721.

Mar. 26 Sarah dau. of William & Elizabeth Friend
Mar. 29 William son of James & Hannah Witworth
April 21 John son of John & Elizabeth Bowlton
May 26 Elizabeth dau. of Richard & Martha Round
June 2 Martha dau. of William & Martha Banks

June 18 John son of William & Bethiah Unwin
July 3 Henry son of William & Rebecca Andrews
Oct. 4 Henry son of George & Sarah Roffey
Nov. 19 Jane dau. of Edward & Mary Lloyd
Dec. 24 John son of Thomas & Elizabeth Dixon
Jan. 14 Samuel son of John & Elizabeth Dodd
Jan. 19 Anne dau. of John & Anne Tapsfeild
Mar. 8 Samuel son of John & Sarah Buckland
Mar. 23 Margaret dau. of William & Sarah Pig

1722.

Mar. 31 Eleanor dau. of Thomas & Mary Philips.
June 20 Anne dau. of William & Hannah Prowdman
June 24 Elizabeth dau. of Roger & Mary Lloyd
July 14 John son of John & Anne Mallow
Aug. 31 Prudence dau. of Theophilus & Elizabeth Beynon
Sep. 16 John son of Richard & Martha Round
Sep. 23 Anne dau. of Joshua & Mary Beleanea
Oct. 4 Mary dau. of John & Mary Watts
Oct. 9 Hannah dau. of Moses & Carolina Lee
Dec. 4 Joseph son of Samuel & Jane Hall
Jan. 1 Elizabeth dau. of Thomas & Elizabeth Dixon
Feb. 3 George son of John & Bethiah Unwin
Mar. 10 Brandon son of Roger & Mary Lloyd
Mar. 17 Mary dau. of Thomas & Catherine Horabin
Mar. 17 Richard son of George & Sarah Roffey

1723.

April 7 John son of John & Elizabeth Dodd
May 30 James son of William & Mary Bayly
June 6 Jane dau. of Richard & Jane Peirce
July 10 John son of Thomas & Mary Philips
July 17 Deborah dau. of John & Anne Tapsfeild
July 21 Elizabeth [*blank*], a foundling
July 27 John son of John Allen, dec[d], by Jane his wife
Aug. 20 Anne dau. of Anne & Anthony Rivers
Sep. 19 Robert son of Robert & Margaret Bromfeild
Dec. 15 John son of John & Elizabeth Mills
Dec. 22 Elizabeth dau. of Thomas & Elizabeth Gibson
Jan. 31 James son of William & Bethiah Unwin

1724.

May 3 James son of James & Elizabeth Ennis
May 21 William son of William & Mary Bayly
May 29 Barsheba dau. of Edward & Mary Lloyd
June 4 George son of John & Jane Price
June 28 Mary dau. of Henry & Anne Peacock
July 8 James son of George & Mary Rawlinson
July 26 Robert son of Nicholas & Sarah Cuttle
Aug. 2 Richard son of Richard & Jane Peirce
Sep. 13 Mary dau. of George & Elizabeth Mitcham
Sep. 14 John son of Joseph & Mary Dickinson
Oct. 11 Mary dau. of [*blank*] Chebsey
Oct. 11 George son of [*blank*] Peat
Nov. 1 Elizabeth dau. of Elizabeth & Henry Bell

Nov. 3 Anne dau. of Samuel & Elizabeth Sandeforth
Nov. 15 Edward son of John & Sarah Buckland
Nov. 19 Julian dau. of William & Hannah Prowdman
Dec. 6 Barbary dau. of Marke & Mary Tallbatt
Dec. 10 Allexsander son of Samuel & Ann Follett
Dec. 27 Margaret dau. of George & Elizabeth Ham
Feb. 14 Paul son of John & Bethiah Unwin
Mar. 7 David son of David & Sarah Matthews
Mar. 12 John son of Richard & Susanah Browne

1725.

April 11 Mary dau. of William & Elizabeth Hopper
May 23 Solloman son of John & Frances Schooler
June 13 Margarett dau. of John & Margarett Smallman
June 13 Ann dau. of Solomon & Elizabeth Butcher
June 15 Mary dau. of John & Ann Tapsfield
Aug. 19 Richard son of Thomas & Mary Phillips
Sep. 5 Samuel & Ann son & dau. of John & Martha Shaw
Sep. 26 Sarah dau. of Thomas & Ann Whitchurch
Oct. 17 Ann dau. of Hans Felix & Ann Schonholte
Dec. 28 Mary dau. of John & Elizabeth Dodd
Dec. 28 Lucey dau. of Thomas & Elizabeth Simson
Dec. 28 Brandon dau. of Edward & Mary Lloyd
Feb. 9 Mary dau. of Samuel & Elizabeth Sandeforth
Feb. 13 Henry son of Henry & Ann Pecock
Feb. 16 Mary dau. of Henry & Rebeckah Andrews

1726.

April 12 Bethiah dau. of John & Bethiah Unwin
April 21 Jane dau. of James & Lidia Stevenson
June 8 Mary dau. of Thomas & Ann Brown
July 18 John son of John & Hannah Randal
July 22 John son of John & Mary Pitts
July 28 Lockton son of Henry & Elizabeth Bell
Aug. 21 Elizabeth dau. of James & Elizabeth Ennis
Sep. 6 Hannah dau. of William & Hannah Prowdman
Sep. 18 James son of James & Elizabeth Lee
Oct. 2 Henry son of William & Giner Miller
Oct. 7 John son of Joseph & Elizabeth Cooke
Oct. 15 Elizabeth dau. of John & Mary Bankes
Oct. 23 Sarah dau. of Thomas & Elizabeth Bafton
Dec. 18 Ann dau. of John & Ann Lewis
Jan. 22 Catherine dau. of John & Sarah Hanson
Jan. 27 Hannah dau. of Thomas & Ann Whitchurch

1727.

Mar. 27 George son of George & Mary Oliver
April 16 William son of Edward & Lidia Reves
May 19 Henry son of John & Faith Cocks
Aug. 4 Sarah dau. of John & Ann Tapsfield
Sep. 7 Samuel son of Samuel & Elizabeth Torin
Sep. 24 Nathaniel son of Jn° & Bethiah Unwin
Oct. 4 Thomas son of John & Hannah Randal
Oct. 20 Mary Ann dau. of James & Alice Harden
Nov. 15 Mary dau. of Robt & Elizabeth Tompson

Nov. 22 Sarah dau. of William & Ann Sparkes
Nov. 26 Elizabeth dau. of Jn° & Elizabeth Dodd
Dec. 1 William son of William & Hannah Prowdman
Jan. 14 Mary dau. of Stanford & Mary Navil
Feb. 6 Mary dau. of Thomas & Mary Phillips
Mar. 3 Elizabeth dau. of Geor. & Eliz. Mitchiel
Mar. 15 Edw[d] Spencer son of Henry & Sarah Field

1728.

May 2 Edmond son of Henry & Ann Peacock
May 19 Ann dau. of Thomas & Ann Whitchurch
June 14 Deb. Moriah dau. of Jn° & Mary Smith
June 25 Gilbert son of Roger & Mary Lloyd
July 4 Richard son of James & Martha Prince
Aug. 8 John son of Jn° & Faith Cock
Sep. 8 Grace dau. of William & Giner Miller
Dec. 22 Sarah dau. of Will[m] & Mary Faircloath
Feb. 7 John son of Joseph & Ann Bradford
Mar. 16 Mary dau. of James & Eliz. Junis

1729.

April 13 Mary dau. of Felix & Ann Schonholtz
May 11 Eliz. dau. of George & Eliz. Bradshaw
June 20 Samuel son of William & Hannah Prowdman
July 18 Sarah dau. of John Kick & Sarah Knott, a bastard
Aug. 24 David son of David Barton & Elizabeth Dixon, a bastard
Nov. 25 Kironhappuch dau. of Thomas & Jemima Prockter
Dec. 12 Thomas son of John & Faith Cock
Dec. 25 Eliz. dau. of Tho[s] & Ann Whitchurch
Dec. 25 Ann dau. of Cliffard & Jane Leatherland

1730.

April 3 Sarah dau. of Tho[s] & Sarah Smith
May 10 Sarah dau. of Tho[s] & Sarah Kent
May 24 Joseph son of James & Elizabeth Ridgeway
May 24 Henry son of Henry & Sarah Feild
June 6 Elizabeth dau. of John & Bethiah Unwin
June 30 Frances dau. of George & Sarah Roffee
Nov. 11 Thomas son of Thomas & Neaomi Hinxman
Dec. 2 Elizabeth dau. of Edward & Mary Pettil
Dec. 22 Rich[d] son of Thomas & Mary Phillips
Dec. 28 Thomas son of Thomas & Francies Martin
Feb. 14 John Vollintine son of John & Martha Stead
Feb. 14 Edward son of Mathew & Francies Smith
Mar. 11 Eliz. dau. of John & Faith Cock
Mar. 18 Rebeckah dau. of Thomas & Sarah Wragg
Mar. 21 John son of Mathew & Mary Hatch

1731.

April 12 Mary dau. of John & Mary Barratt
April 25 Margaret dau. of James & Elizabeth Junis
May 30 Jane dau. of Thomas & Ann Whitchurch
June 20 Joseph son of Tho[s] & Sarah Kent
July 4 William son of Will[m] & Hannah Prowdman

Aug. 9 James son of John & Bethiah Unwin
Aug. 22 Ann dau. of Nathaniael & Mary Kinch
Oct. 18 Christian Merriman, an adult person
Dec. 1 Ann dau. of James & Eliz[th] Costin
Dec. 19 Mary dau. of Charles & Jane Atkins
Feb. 8 Edward son of Joseph & Mary Farmer

1732.

Mar. 30 Eliner dau. of Thomas & Mary Phillips
April 30 Deborah dau. of Joseph & Eliz. Ridgway
May 24 Elizabeth dau. of William & Elizabeth Peacock
June 6 Mary dau. of John & Faith Cock
June 30 Robert son of David & Mary Tayler
Aug. 16 Sarah dau. of Thomas [*blank*]
Dec. 13 Job son of William & Ann Archer
Dec. 28 Martha dau. of John & Martha Stead
Feb. 11 William son of William & Elizabeth Thorowgood
Mar. 20 Charles son of Charles & Jane Atkins

1733.

April 22 George son of George & Elizabeth Mitchael
April 29 Richard son of Edward & Margaret Bagster
May 6 Edward son of George & Giner Lloyd
May 18 John son of John & Faith Cock
Aug. 26 Frances dau. of Mathew & Frances Smith
Oct. 7 Lidia dau. of Paul & Mary Archer
Nov. 15 Edward son of Thomas & Francies Martin
Nov. 25 Ann dau. of William & Mary Whipham
Mar. 15 Ann dau. of Rich[d] & Ann Somes

1734.

April 20 Lambert son of Lambert & Mary Kraner
May 26 Thomas son of Joshua & Francies Manwood
June 26 Richard son of Thomas & Mary Phillips
July 8 Hannah dau. of William & Sarah Corsey
July 14 Mary dau. of Thomas & Mary Dumbreak
Sep. 6 Margarett dau. of Girolomo & Mary Franciseoni
Sep. 29 John son of Charles & Jane Atkins
Oct. 9 Agnis dau. of Thomas & Agnis Curtis
Oct. 13 Hannah dau. of William & Hannah Prowdman
Nov. 10 Margaret dau. of John & Ann Trigg
Nov. 15 Isaac son of William & Elizabeth Thorogood
Jan. 31 Isabellah, a foundling
Feb. 19 John son of John & Ann Brandon

1735.

May 4 Elizabeth dau. of Edw[d] & Margaret Bagster
May 11 Carthrine dau. of George & Elizabeth Groves
July 6 Job son of Paul & Mary Archer
Oct. 12 Elizabeth dau. of George & Elizabeth Mitchel
Oct. 12 Elizabeth dau. of Edward & Elizabeth Jones
Oct. 22 John son of John & Francies Scooler
Nov. 14 Liddia dau. of William & Elizabeth Thorogood

Nov. 28 James son of John & Ann Brandon
Dec. 14 Francies dau. of Thomas & Francies Martin
Feb. 27 Mary dau. of William & Mary Whipham

1736.

April 25 Joseph son of Thomas & Mary Marshall
May 15 Ann dau. of Michael & Ann Barraud
July 14 William son of William & Hannah Prowdman
July 23 Thos son of Thos & Sarah Henry
Aug. 16 Anthony son of Anthony & Elizabeth Frost
Oct. 28 Ann dau. of Joseph & Ester Garrad
Nov. 28 John son of William & Elizabeth Thoroughgood
Dec. 5 John son of Edward & Arabellah Hamlin
Jan. 15 Mary dau. of John & Ann Trigg
Feb. 10 Elizabeth Mary dau. of John & Mary Ester Turner
Mar. 20 Hannah Carolina dau. of John & Mary Crudee

1737.

Mar. 27 Robert son of Absolom & Elizabeth Robinson
July 7 Elizabeth dau. of John & Elizabeth Farrell
July 31 Richard son of Richard & Carthrine Swanell
Aug. 7 Jane dau. of John & Mary Scott
Oct. 23 George son of George & Elizabeth Groves
Oct. 30 Anna Mariah dau. of Thomas & Mary Coleman
Nov. 25 William son of William & Hannah Prowdman
Nov. 27 John son of John & Sarah Hurry
Dec. 27 William son of William & Mary Whipham
Mar. 8 Mary dau. of Lambert & Mary Craner

1738.

May 10 William son of John & Martha Cock
Sep. 3 James son of William & Elizabeth Thorowgood
Sep. 6 John son of Edward & Margaret Bagster
Oct. 22 Benjaman son of John & Ann Trigg
Oct. 29 William Prowdman
Nov. 2 Martha dau. of Paul & Mary Archer
Nov. 27 Pheaby dau. of Richard & Carthrine Swannell
Jan. 17 Ann dau. of Edwd & Elizabeth Newman
Mar. 9 Margarett dau. of Richard & Elliner Ashley

1739.

April 22 Camm Jemmima dau. of John & Mary Grudee
May 25 Francies dau. of Thos & Francies Martin
June 11 John son of John & Martha Cock
July 12 Thomas son of William & Margrett Pond
Sep. 9 Sarah dau. of George & Elizabeth Mitchael
Nov. 6 Francis & Henry sons of Blunt & Ann Rogers
Jan. 21 John son of Edward & Elizabeth Newman

1740.

April 20 Elizabeth dau. of Francies & Dorothy Edward
May 14 John son of William & Mary Whipham
June 12 Henry son of Henry & Susannah Lee

Aug. 25 James son of John & Martha Cock
Aug. 29 Rachiel dau. of John & Rachiel Lane
Dec. 10 Mary dau. of Blunt & Ann Rogers
Dec. 12 Elizabeth dau. of John & Elizabeth Dod
Jan. 14 William son of William & Margarett Pond
Feb. 13 Henry son of Henry & Jane Bodher
Feb. 24 John son of John & Sarah Baker
Feb. 27 William Strengfellow son of Thomas & Frances Quincy
Mar. 11 Susannah dau. of Thomas & Susannah Boothby
Mar. 15 Cathrine dau. of John & Cathrine Hewlett

1741.

April 13 Samuel Mony son of Samuel & Emm Baker
May 13 Frances John son of John & Mary Ennes
May 29 Ely Evisson son of Thos & Ann
June 28 Hannah dau. of Mathew & Hannah Morley
Aug. 16 Ester dau. of Ester & Joseph Garrad
Sep. 16 Sarah dau. of William & Mary Whipham
Nov. 13 John Spearman son of John & Elizh Dod
Feb. 14 James son of Edward & Deborah Samuel
Mar. 2 Sarah dau. of William & Abbigal Jones
Mar. 7 Martha dau. of Richard & Carthrine Swannell
Mar. 21 Elizabeth dau. of John & Rachael Lane

1742.

Sep. 1 George son of Paul & Mary Archer
Oct. 13 Susannah dau. of George & Elizabeth Mitchael
Nov. 17 Jams Bride son of Richd & Jane
Nov. 19 Thos Norris
Jan. 19 William son of William & Hannah Prowdman
Feb. 9 Ann Cruchly dau. of Cruchly & Mary Cole
Feb. 25 William son of William & Ann Cowdrey

1743.

April 14 Ann Maria dau. of John & Mary Head
July 19 Edward Baptist, a foundling
July 28 Thos Henshman son of Thos & Jane
Aug. 12 Rachiel dau. of Henry & Elizabeth Edwards
Nov. 20 Charles son of Charles & Elizabeth Walker
Mar. 9 Samuel son of (late John) & Elizabeth Dod
Mar. 19 Carthrine dau. of John & Rachiel Lane; born 23 Feb.

1744.

Mar. 25 John son of Thomas & Susannah Boothby
June 3 John son of Christopher & Mary Crouch
July 20 Ann dau. of John & Mary Ann Norris
Aug. 31 Christiana dau. of Henry & Christiana George
Dec. 25 Carthrine dau. of Charles & Eliz. Walker
Dec. 26 Richard son of Richd & Jane Neale
Mar. 20 Sophia dau. of Arthur & Ellinor Hannum

1745.

June 2 William son of Paul & Mary Archer
Nov. 3 Sarah dau. of Jacob & Mary Cuff

Nov. 11 Frances son of Frances & Ann Gigner
Jan. 19 James son of James & Mary Steward
Feb. 3 John son of Charles & Elizabeth Walker
Mar. 12 William Jennings
Mar. 14 Margaret Bradley

1746.

June 11 Phillip son of Thomas & Mary Ann Noris
June 13 Ann dau. of John & Rachael Lane
June 15 John son of late Thomas & Ann Jennings
July 29 William son of Nathanael & Jane Cambden
Aug. 3 Richard son of Richard & Elizabeth Bradshaw
Aug. 20 Mary dau. of Arthur & Illinor Hannum
Oct. 15 John son of Jacob & Mary Cuff
Nov. 9 John son of Richard & Rebecca Sunderland
Jan. 18 Edward son of Edw[d] & Jane Coster
Feb. 1 Richard son of William & Sarah Upton
Feb. 1 Ann dau. of Thomas & Elizabeth Hutchins
Feb. 19 William son of Frances & Ann Gigner

1747.

June 3 Hezekiah son of Hezekiah & Elizabeth Walker
June 12 Joseph son of Joseph & Elizabeth Hoskins
June 18 Mary dau. of Walter & Mary Staniford
June 29 George son of George & Elizabeth Tregea
July 2 Phillip son of Richard & Jane Neale
Aug. 27 Robert son of Rob[t] & Elizabeth Browne
Sep. 3 Paul son of Paul & Mary Archer
Sep. 3 Robert Browne
Dec. 3 Mary Ann dau. of Patience & Thomas Camden
Mar. 6 Ester dau. of Thomas & Ester Martin
Mar. 9 Martin son of Frances & Ann Gigner

1748.

April 3 George son of William & Elizabeth Cobby
May 29 Susan dau. of John & Rachiel Lane; born 1 May
July 27 Sarah dau. of Hezekiah & Elizabeth Walker
Aug. 17 Jane dau. of Nathaniel & Jane Cambden
Aug. 28 Edward son of Arthur & Elliner Hannum
Oct. 11 Thomas son of Thomas & Margaret Parkes
Nov. 16 Joseph son of William & Sarah Upton
Nov. 20 John son of James & Elizabeth Holmes
Nov. 28 Susanah dau. of James & Mary Rogers
Jan. 1 Elizabeth dau. of Thomas & Mary Ann Noris
Feb. 22 Thomas son of Thomas & Elizabeth Hutchins
Mar. 15 Elizabeth dau. of Robert & Ann Streatfeild

1749.

June 14 James son of Frances & Ann Gigner
July 5 Elizabeth dau. of Joseph & Elliner Crouch
Sep. 3 Robert son of Thomas & Patiens Cambden
Oct. 1 James son of John & Ann Mills
Oct. 12 George Leapidge, Buried
Mar. 23 Mary Ann dau. of Henry & [*blank*] Dixon

1750.

April 8 Sarah dau. of John & Ann Turner
April 11 Frances dau. of William & Rebecca Tate
June 24 James son of Hizekiah & Elizabeth Walker
Aug. 3 Arthur son of Arthur & Ellinor Hannum
Aug. 8 Mary dau. of William & Ellizabeth Gobby
Aug. 8 Richard son of Richard & Frances May
Aug. 26 Thomas son of Thos & Sarah Brockley
Aug. 29 John son of Frances & Ann Gigner
Sep. 7 Sarah dau. of the Revd James & Jane Townley
Sep. 23 Sandeforth son of Robert & Ann Streatfeild
Oct. 3 Nathaniel son of Nathaniel & Jane Camden
Nov. 2 Mary Carroliner dau. of James & Hannah Miller

1751.

July 20 Mary dau. of John & Elizabeth Anderson
Aug. 25 Mary dau. of Jeremiah & Margaret Hopkins
Oct. 20 Elizabeth dau. of William & Margaret Crouch
Oct. 22 Richard son of Richard & Frances May
Nov. 3 Rebecka dau. of William & Rebecka Tate
Nov. 24 Robert son of Thomas & Mary Ann Noris
Dec. 22 Edward son of Edward & Ann Pistor

1752.

Jan. .. Robert son of Frances & Ann Gigner
Jan. 26 Mary Ewell dau. of John & Cartherine Woollett
Feb. 9 Thomas son of Thos & Mary Martha Browne
Feb. 23 James son of Arthur & Ellinor Hannum
April 14 William son of William & Mary Wilde
June 12 Margarett dau. of Thomas & Margarett Parkes
June 24 Thomas son of Thomas & Elizabeth Hutchins
June 24 Thomas son of Thomas & Ester Martin
June 28 Martha dau. of John & Mary Scott
Oct. 15 James son of James & Elizabeth Norton
Oct. 29 Edward son of Joseph & Elliner Crouch
Dec. 17 John son of Richard & Frances May
Dec. 17 Martin son of Martin & Elizabeth Carr
Dec. 26 Elizabeth dau. of Thomas & Elizabeth Elliott

1753.

April 26 John son of John & Elizabeth Mallett
Aug. 19 Margarett dau. of William & Margt Crouch
Aug. 29 Mary dau. of Nathaniel & Mary Thomas
Sep. 16 Joseph son of Samuel & Elizabeth Bishop
Oct. 3 George son of William & Mary Frost
Oct. 28 Mary dau. of David Pugh, a bastard
Nov. 11 John son of John & Elizabeth Anderson
Dec. 23 Anna dau. of Richard & Frances May

1754.

Jan. 4 Eliz. dau. of Henry & [*blank*] Dixon
Mar. 19 William son of George & Mary Browne
May 26 John son of John & Ann Mills

REGISTER OF BURIALS FROM JUNE 11, 1686.

1686.

June 11 Hester dau. of William & Hester South
June 17 John Smallpeice
June 17 Susanna Deale
June 18 Thomas son of Thom. Blow
June 20 Marey Katherine wife of John Adam, clarke
June 30 Ann dau. of W^m & Elizabeth Baker
July 11 Nickolas Cross
July 27 Susanna dau. of W^m & Elizabeth Dickason
Aug. 12 Susanna Kindall
Aug. 23 Sammuell son of Samuell & Marey Howarde
Aug. 31 Rose wife of John Duggdall, in new churchyard
Sep. 2 Elizabeth Baker
Sep. 11 Sarah wife of Joseph Kendall
Sep. 12 Margerett Wrighte
Oct. 3 Ruth dau. of Roberte & Elizabeth Radforde
Oct. 17 Joseph son of Jeams & Amy Mecum
Oct. 29 Thomas son of Thomas & Ann Beadell
Oct. 31 Marey dau. of William & Elizabeth Kempe
Nov. 3 Jane Dudley
Nov. 15 Richarde son of Richarde & Marey Maninge
Dec. 26 Isack Rutton from Oxforde
Jan. 9 John son of John & Ann Osburne
Jan. 16 Marey dau. of Thomas & Hester Hooper
Jan. 24 Henerey son of Matheiwe & Barberey Berisfeild
Jan. 28 Mr William Drinkwater
Feb. 16 Marey Cross
Mar. 2 George Berman
Mar. 13 Marey Memler

1687.

May 12 Elizabeth dau. of W^m & [*blank*] Winter
June 8 Thomas Foukes
Aug. 5 Hannah dau. of W^m & Hannah Smith
Aug. 18 Joseph Vaughan
Aug. 28 John & Mary Dennington
Sep. 10 Elizabeth Brown
Sep. 22 Ann Lloyd
Sep. 22 Ann Cross
Oct. 6 Mary dau. of James & Ame Markham
Oct. 21 Mr John Sadler
Oct. 31 Thomas Drant
Nov. 1 Mrs Rebecca Rutton
Nov. 3 Rebecca dau. of George & Elenor Hudnoll
Nov. 16 Elizabeth Appelby
Dec. 4 Ann dau. of Gilbert & Jane Brandon
Dec. 24 John Rumbell
Jan. 6 Susanna wife of John Beard

Jan. 10 Alice dau. of Samuell & Elizabeth Smith
Jan. 29 Frisewith dau. of George & Mary Knocker
Feb. 24 Thomas Fisher
Feb. 27 Samuel Tuckworth
Mar. 11 Sarah Hamon
Mar. 13 Thomas son of [*blank*] Parsley & [*blank*] his wife
Mar. 21 Joseph Vaughan son of Joseph Vaughan & Ann

1688.

Mar. 25 William son of William & Sarah Reeve
Mar. 26 Edward Reynolds
Mar. 27 Alice dau. of William & Hannah Smith
April 4 Jeremiah son of Jeremiah & Victory Wright
April 6 Isaac son of Daniel & Mary Withers
April 10 Hannah dau. of William & Elizabeth Dickeson
June 7 Henry Shengelton
July 24 Elizabeth dau. of Jeremiah & Victoria Wright
Aug. 2 Mr Wm Woodroffe
Sep. 4 Wm son of Thomas & Dorothy Jarrad
Sep. 30 Penelope dau. of Christopher Moore
Oct. 5 George son of George & Mary Knocker
Oct. 26 Mary dau. of Michaell & [*blank*] King
Oct. 27 Mr Isaac Rutton
Dec. 27 Thomas son of Samuell & Mary Howard
Dec. 29 Isachar Redding
Jan. 9 Wm son of Edward & Edith Lawrance
Feb. 17 John son of John & [*blank*] Farcclough
Feb. 27 Susanna Stoe
Feb. 28 Wm son of Wm & Elizabeth Kemp

1689.

April 1 Wm son of Wm & Ann Rogers
April 7 John Pitson
April 12 Benjamyn son of Theophilus & Elenor Redding
April 21 Jane Hilman wife of Thomas Hilman, senior
May 12 John son of George & Elenor Hudnoll
May 15 John son of Thomas & [*blank*] Cooper
June 13 Wm son of Edward & Edith Lawrance
June 23 Elizabeth dau. of Thomas & Grace Kingsly
Aug. 19 John Collett
Sep. 20 Elizabeth dau. of Gilbert & Jane Brandon
Oct. 18 Wm Crane
Nov. 7 Elizabeth wife of Andrew Prime
Dec. 8 Hannah dau. of Christopher & Penelope Moor
Dec. 28 Mary wife of John Only
Mar. 10 Rebecca Stanyforth, bur. at Bethlem
Mar. 11 Thomas son of Thomas & Grace Kingsly
Mar. 18 Elizabeth Luddington

1690.

Mar. 26 Elenor Meaverell
April 2 Margary Rennalls
May 29 Capt Ralph Benton
June 22 Elizabeth dau. of John & Judith Pairt
July 29 Samuell Clark, Mr Clark's kindsman

Aug. 23 Thomas Banfeild
Aug. 27 Henry Ford, M[r] Siar's man
Sep. 25 Elizabeth dau. of Samuell & Mary Howard
Sep. 29 Sarah Ludington
Oct. 18 Daniell Gurney
Oct. 30 John Onely
Nov. 9 Imanuell Drake
Nov. 11 Roger Denington
Nov. 20 Samuell son of Samuell & Mary Pippitt
Dec. 9 Sarah dau. of Samuell & Sarah Gauder
Dec. 15 John son of W[m] & Judith Floid
Feb. 25 Joseph & Thomas sons of John & Margarett Wormlayton
Mar. 13 W[m] Eyeon
Mar. 18 John son of John Adam, clark

1691.

April 6 Mary Hart
April 19 Thomas son of W[m] & Elizabeth Kemp
May 3 Samuell son of John & [*blank*] Alder
May 14 Hannah dau. of W[m] & Ann Rogers
May 24 Elizabeth Knocker
June 10 W[m] son of W[m] & Elizabeth Kemp
June 10 Ann Cuming
June 29 Ann wife of John Eldredg
Aug. 16 Thomas son of Theophilus & Elenor Redding
Sep. 25 Sarah dau. of W[m] & Elizabeth Dickeson
Dec. 8 Penelope wife of Christopher Moore
Dec. 17 W[m] Gurney
Jan. 12 M[r] James Coale
Feb. 7 Rose dau. of Thomas & Elizabeth Warren
Feb. 7 W[m] Dodsons Court
Feb. 8 John son of John & Mary Williams
Feb. 12 M[rs] Elizabeth Fowler
Feb. 21 Mary Wharton, widow
Mar. 15 Thomas Hooper
Mar. 19 Sarah Beard
Mar. 24 Ann dau. of John Beard

1692.

April 5 Edward son of Richard Elliott
April 10 John son of W[m] & Sarah Reeve
May 3 Elenor Gurney
May 20 Ann dau. of Margarett Benton
July 8 Lyddia dau. of Samuell Stevens
July 19 Ann wife of W[m] Allin
Sep. 14 Elizabeth Wood
Oct. 11 Phebe dau. of W[m] & Phebe Pairt
Oct. 20 John Holwell
Oct. 21 Elenor Fleming
Nov. 16 Thomas Mabley
Dec. 5 W[m] son of Cornelius & Elizabeth Needham
Dec. 22 M[r] James Whitchurch
Jan. 7 Prissilla dau. of John & Katharine Wilson
Jan. 29 Martha dau. of John & Ann Orsburn
Feb. 4 John son of Thomas & Ann Parsley
Feb. 22 Elizabeth dau. of John & Elizabeth Ludington
Mar. 20 Dauiell son of W[m] & Elizabeth Dickeson

1693.

April 2 Martha dau. of Thomas & Elizabeth Warren
April 15 John Cosh
April 27 Sarah dau. of Joshua & Sarah Hazell
June 8 Roger Murthwaite
July 4 John Appleby
July 13 William Terry
July 14 Margrett dau. of John Adam, clark
July 23 James son of Theophelus & Ellenor Redding
July 28 Sarah dau. of Samuell & Mary Hayward
Aug. 1 Joanna Hackett
Aug. 7 George Richbell
Aug. 14 Richard son of George & Phebe Knocker
Oct. 29 Thomas Worbaton
Nov. 23 Mr Edward Whitchurch
Dec. 28 Sarah Tillitt
Jan. 10 Elizabeth King
Jan. 13 Joseph son of Christopher More
Feb. 9 Thomas Cooper
Mar. 6 Anthony Hudnall
Mar. 11 Robert Annis

1694.

Mar. 28 Sarah dau. of John & [*blank*] Haines
April 6 Rebecca wife of John Beard
April 21 Thomas Withinbrook
June 28 Elizabeth Richball
July 2 James son of Samuell & Elizabeth Newton
July 17 Martha dau. of Margrett Benton
July 26 Mary Spawl
Sep. 13 Margrett dau. of Samuell & Mary Howard
Sep. 16 Thomas Langham
Sep. 28 Thomas son of Henry & Mary Cole
Oct. 8 Damerus dau. of Robert & Hannah Price
Oct. 14 Jone Withers
Oct. 17 Joseph son of William Reeves
Oct. 31 Margrett dau. of John & Margrett Wormlayton
Nov. 18 John Taylor
Nov. 29 William son of Samuell & Mary Howard
Dec. 11 Thomas Palmer
Jan. 5 Elizabeth Barner
Jan. 11 Suanna Edgley
Jan. 27 Elizabeth Mead
Feb. 10 Thomas Alley
Feb. 12 Thomas son of Thomas & Mary Parrott
Mar. 5 Henry son of Nicholas & Sarah Goble
Mar. 9 Mary dau. of John & Elizabeth Luddington
Mar. 10 Ann Hudnoll

1695.

April 3 Mary Man
April 17 Edward Wire
April 22 James Rudd
April 26 Peter Toobe
July 23 Mathew Burisfeild

Sep. 5 Bernice dau. of Gilbert & Jane Brandon
Sep. 9 Margrett Smith
Nov. 4 John son of Michell King
Nov. 24 Anthony Stockbridg
Dec. 11 Sarah Jackson
Dec. 25 Suanna dau. of Daniell Wallis
Jan. 3 Henry Dickson
Mar. 15 Windsor Pasmore

1696.

April 12 John son of Robert & Hannah Price
April 23 Mrs Sarah Blackmore
May 20 George Smith
May 21 Richard, a foundling
May 27 Ann dau. of James Clark
July 1 William son of Seth & Mary Jermy
July 2 Ann dau. of John Moore
July 9 Elizabeth dau. of Nicholas & Sarah Goble
July 16 John son of Edward Lawrance
July 23 Mr Ralph Whitchurch
July 29 Richard Glanford
Aug. 5 Jane Duckworth
Aug. 15 Margrett dau. of John & Mary Horton
Aug. 16 Daniell Smith
Aug. 21 James Strong
Aug. 24 Sandys son of Benjamin & Ann Knight
Oct. 26 Mary dau. of John Osbourn
Nov. 10 John Freeman
Dec. 3 John Rutton
Dec. 4 John son of Daniell Petty
Jan. 11 Joseph son of Joseph Knowls
Jan. 12 A dau. of Otheniell Westmacott
Jan. 22 Nathaniell Larking
Feb. 12 Thomas son of William & Sarah Reeve
Feb. 26 Mary Cooledge
Mar. 2 Ann Maxfeild
Mar. 5 Joseph Reeve
Mar. 14 Bennett Wallett
Mar. 14 John Heald
Mar. 17 Rebeckah Furness

1697.

April 6 John son of Thomas Parrott
April 22 Margrett Wormlayton
May 13 Jarvis Byfeild
June 3 William son of John & Elizabeth Heald
June 10 Mosses son of Richard Glandford
June 25 A female child of William Dickerson's
July 23 Nicholas son of Nicholas Goble
Aug. 6 Elizabeth Kemp
Sep. 20 Jane dau. of John Faircloath
Nov. 18 Bathsheba dau. of Gilbert & Jane Brandon
Nov. 24 Margrett dau. of Henry & Sarah Parnell
Nov. 30 William Baker
Nov. 30 Margrett Emmerton
Dec. 10 Mrs Mary Heyward

Jan. 7 Benjamin Bridges
Jan. 14 A female child of Daniell Pettie's
Jan. 26 Elizabeth Stevens
Jan. 28 Anthony Young
Feb. 6 Elizabeth dau. of Benjamin & Ann Knight
Mar. 20 Thomas Whiteing

1698.

Mar. 26 Sarah dau. of James & Ruth Whitchurch
April 17 Ann Gess
May 14 Mary Thatcher
June 3 William Munday
July 10 Elizabeth Cole
Sep. 2 Jone Taylor
Sep. 15 Elizabeth Buffett
Oct. 1 Elinor Hudnall
Oct. 12 Francis Read
Oct. 20 Richard Banks
Dec. 30 Mr William Wilkison } father & son
Dec. 30 Mr Robert Wilkison }
Feb. 14 Martha Burrum
Feb. 22 Mathew Coles
Feb. 24 Robert Stevens
Mar. 19 Thomas Parrot
Mar. 20 Martha Appleby
Mar. 23 Robert Radford

1699.

April 11 William Dickerson
April 24 Thomas Sparkmon
May 31 Mrs Mary Haybourn
June 18 Mary Lucas
June 21 Otheniell Westmacott
July 22 Elizabeth Dent
Aug. 14 Sarah Tidcomb
Aug. 31 Ebenezer Glandford
Sep. 14 John Read
Sep. 21 Mary Sparks
Oct. 17 Thomas Parnell
Oct. 18 Francis Scorfeild
Oct. 21 Amy Aris
Oct. 26 William Marshall
Oct. 27 Barbary Goodinch
Nov. 10 Sarah Browne
Nov. 17 Thomas Warren
Nov. 21 Margret [*blank*]
Jan. 10 Benjamin Lipecomb
Feb. 12 Jane Munday
Feb. 15 Phebe Pert
Feb. 24 Mary Warren
Feb. 29 Mr Samuell Howard

1700.

April 25 William Reeve
May 12 Richard Nicholls
July 16 Thomas Knight

Sep. 16 William Rawlins
Sep. 20 Elizabeth Merchant
Sep. 27 Elizabeth Rawlinson
Oct. 2 Arthur Tirel
Oct. 6 Barbary Buryfield Goodinch
Nov. 9 M[rs] Katherine Faircloth
Nov. 15 John Merchant
Jan. 12 Joseph Aris
Jan. 16 Elizabeth Todd
Jan. 26 M[rs] Elizabeth Foulks
Feb. 9 Penelope Goble
Feb. 27 Mary Cross
Mar. 14 Henry Allen
Mar. 18 William Gibson

1701.

April 3 Martha Mountlow
April 10 Mary Hallimore
April 12 Hannah Goble
April 15 Mary Abraham
April 22 Elizabeth Rosshouk
June 1 Elizabeth Fisher
June 6 Mary Lawrence
June 10 Margaret Unitt
June 12 Edward Farmer
Aug. 1 Anne Poulton
Sep. 21 Mary Pippitt
Sep. 21 Thomas Facer
Oct. 2 Jane Legrand
Oct. 26 Nicholas Goble
Nov. 26 John Gibson
Dec. 10 Thomas Cannon
Dec. 21 Rebeccah White
Feb. 12 John son of Cannon Mountlow

1702.

April 1 Paul Thomas
April 23 Thomas Finchley
June 25 Mary Picer
July 27 Joseph Pool
Aug. 26 John son of Benja. Pulinson
Sep. 24 Richard Turner, a pensioner
Oct. 16 Mary Uthwait, bur. at Deptford
Dec. 3 Mary Lane, a foundling
Dec. 5 John son of John & Sarah Pack, bur. at Enfield
Mar. 17 Jane Harris, bur. at Sutton in Surry
Mar. 19 Anne dau. of Thomas & Dorothy Denning

1703.

Mar. 30 Elizabeth dau. of John & Anne Hewson
April 13 John Haines
May 23 Samuel son of Samuel & Mary Smith
May 30 George son of George & Mary Janson
June 24 David Adams
Aug. 9 Joseph son of Walter & Phillis Hide

Aug. 29 Mary dau. of Edward & Sarah Leake
Aug. 31 Ann Parsley
Sep. 29 Thomas Dowell
Dec. 13 Thomas son of Thomas & Anne Hooper
Dec. 30 Sarah Snell
Jan. 23 Richard son of Joseph & Anne Hallimore
Mar. 3 Elizabeth Hacket

1704.

April 4 John son of George & Elizabeth Upton
May 6 Mary Cooper
May 13 Mary dau. of John & Sarah Paine
June 25 William Cheesman
June 25 Samuel Stevens
June 28 Rachel dau. of Edward & Sarah Leak
July 11 Benjamin son of Benja. & Mary Howell
July 14 Susannah dau. of Jonathan & Susannah Bower
July 16 Mary Key, a foundling
July 19 Mary dau. of Thomas & Mary Nicholls
Aug. 4 Hannah dau. of James & Mary Davis
Aug. 14 Charles son of Gilbert & Jane Brandon, bur. at Padington
Aug. 14 Elihu son of Thomas & Elizabeth Grandford
Aug. 15 Anne Parsand
Oct. 22 A stillborn child of Edm. & Rebeccah Hilliard
Nov. 19 Isabella Fowke, from St Swithin's
Jan. 1 Christian Finch
Jan. 6 Adonijah son of Thomas & Eliza. Grandford
Mar. 13 Deborah dau. of John & Deborah Scofield

1705.

April 3 Francis Wright
April 20 Michael son of Michael & Elizabeth Cross
April 27 Frances dau. of Michael & Eliza. Cross
May 2 Mary French
May 2 Robert son of Young & Katherine Herring
May 11 Thomas son of Thomas & Elizabeth Facer
June 24 John Gabriel son of John & Margaret De Raffou
June 28 Sarah Harris
July 5 William Crisp
July 26 Joseph Hollimore
Aug. 11 Bethiah dau. of Thomas & Eliz. Glandford
Aug. 18 Jane dau. of John & Jane Hall
Aug. 20 Humphry son of Joseph & Mary Atkins
Sep. 5 Mary Smith
Dec. 6 John son of John & Ruth Gibson
Mar. 11 Anne dau. of Nathaniel & Anne Pool

1706.

Mar. 25 Samuel son of Samuel & Anne Baker
May 3 Susannah Fletcher
May 24 Thomas son of John & Hannah Pickard
June 4 William Salisbury
June 20 Sarah Goble
June 23 Benjamin son of Benjamin & Mary Howell
June 23 Richard son of Benjamin & Mary Howell

July 26 Blaze Clerk
Aug. 18 John Harison
Sep. 20 Hugh Dean
Oct. 13 Mary Smith
Jan. 15 William son of George & Mary Johnson
Feb. 7 Sarah dau. of John & Esther Dashwood
Feb. 13 Pereeda dau. of Samuel & Elizabeth Underwood
Feb. 18 John Snell
Mar. 2 Margaret Sharp

1707.

Mar. 26 Thomas son of Thomas & Elizabeth Facer
Mar. 26 Thomas Smith
June 11 Abraham son of John & Sarah Paine
June 15 William son of Edward & Sarah Leak
July 24 Joseph son of James & Margaret Morton
Aug. 29 John Pain
Oct. 4 Sarah dau. of John & Sarah Perry
Oct. 24 William son of George & Eliza. Upton
Nov. 4 Lott Rawlins
Nov. 10 Nathaniel son of Natha. & Aune Pool
Dec. 9 William Honor
Dec. 12 Nicholas Anett
Dec. 19 Simon son of James & Rachell Mallorke
Jan. 6 Richard son of Rich[d] & Catherine Bradshaw
Jan. 15 Esther Crosby
Jan. 27 Ruth Whitechurch
Jan. 28 Mary dau. of Sam. & Mary Smith
Mar. 23 Francis Appleby

1708.

Mar. 29 Elizabeth dau. of Edward & Jane Farmer
April 2 Benjamin son of Joseph & Elizabeth Ridge
May 19 Phillip son of John & Anne Gardner
June 2 John son of John & Susannah Townsend
June 2 Sarah dau. of James & [*blank*] Whitchurch
June 9 Gabriel son of Benjamin & Mary Howel
June 22 George Norman
Sep. 13 Jacob Asselin
Sep. 16 Dorothy Byfield
Oct. 13 Robert son of Robert & Anne Davy
Oct. 21 Anne Jackman
Oct. 22 Thomas Feild
Oct. 24 Elizabeth Obbinson
Oct. 24 Thomas Fox
Nov. 11 Mary dau. of Thomas & Elizabeth Grandford
Nov. 12 Anne dau. of Robert & Anne Davy
Nov. 18 Anne Hilditch
Nov. 18 Anna dau. of John & Margaret De Raffou
Jan. 3 William Smith, a pensioner
Jan. 3 Randolph Took
Jan. 4 Joan Lewis
Jan. 25 Anne dau. of Thomas & Elizabeth Facer
Feb. .. Joshua Hazel
Mar. 8 Elizabeth Gifford

Mar. 13 Edward son of Edward & Margaret Francis
Mar. 17 Samuel son of Samuel & Anne Baker
Mar. 21 Elizabeth dau. of Joshua & Elizabeth Hazel

1709.

April 21 Joseph son of John & Mary Varndell
April 21 George Hudnall
May 9 William son of Thomas & Mary Smith
May 16 John son of Nicholas & Mary Jackman
Aug. 4 Ruth dau. of Thomas & Elizabeth Grandford
Sep. 4 Edward Francis
Sep. 26 Elizabeth Elliot
Sep. 29 James son of George & Margaret Edwards
Sep. 30 Elizabeth dau. of William & Anna Bethia Steel
Oct. 10 Elizabeth White
Nov. 21 Mary dau. of John & Hannah Pickard
Nov. 25 Daniel son of Edward & Sarah Leak
Nov. 25 Anne dau. of Thomas & Mary Moreton
Nov. 26 Michael son of Michael & Mary Christmas
Dec. 2 Liddia Hill
Dec. 21 Francis Hannel
Jan. 15 William son of Thomas & Elizabeth Facer
Jan. 15 Hannah Smith
Jan. 18 Praxis Shorter
Jan. 20 John son of John & Jane Hall
Jan. 30 Thomas Lightfoot
Feb. 12 Anne Norman
Feb. 13 John son of Thomas & Rebeccah Manning
Feb. 23 Rebeccah dau. of John & Mary Leapidge
Feb. 26 Anne dau. of John & Margaret Gittins
Mar. 1 John son of John & Mary Leapidge
Mar. 1 Mary dau. of John & Mary Leapidge
Mar. 6 Elizabeth dau. of John & Susannah Townsend
Mar. 11 Elizabeth dau. of Henry & Elizabeth Kingdom
Mar. 12 Isabella Trist
Mar. 19 William Damsell

1710.

Mar. 28 Joseph Atkins
Mar. 30 Anne Wheeler
April 4 Elizabeth dau. of John & Martha Gilbert
April 7 Elizabeth dau. of Hezekiah & Eliza. Walker
April 27 Nicholas son of Nicholas & Mary Jackman
May 19 Francis son of Francis & Anne Huddleston
May 23 Margaret Francis
May 27 Susannah dau. of John & Susannah Townsend
May 30 Robert son of Anthony & Mary Sackfeild
June 13 Sarah dau. of Nicholas & Mary Jackman
June 13 William son of John & Margaret Gittons
July 9 Robert son of Robert & Anne Davy
July 17 Mary Smith
Sep. 19 Peregrine son of Vicinion & Elizabeth Bradshaw
Oct. 15 Judith Young
Oct. 23 Mary Vaughan
Oct. 29 Elizabeth Campbell
Dec. 28 George son of George & Elizabeth Lane

Jan. 2 Mary Reeves
Jan. 18 Elizabeth Lane
Jan. 18 Philippa Parrot
Jan. 25 Isaac son of Cuthbert & Susannah Bland
Jan. 26 Mary Rawlins
Feb. 2 George Upton
Mar. 8 Thomas Smith
Mar. 20 Mehetabel King

1711.

April 3 Henry son of Henry & Mary Cooper
May 18 Joseph son of Edward & Sarah Leak
May 20 Edward son of Alexander & Sarah Young
May 21 John Oliver
May 24 Robert Taylour
June 2 Charles Facer
July 24 William Wilkinson
Sep. 27 William Vanfleet
Oct. 18 Jane Brandon
Oct. 19 [*blank*] Townsend
Dec. 19 Elizabeth Smith
Jan. 2 Ruth Barnet
Jan. 16 Elizabeth Cook
Feb. 10 Thomas Russel
Feb. 13 John Plumer
Feb. 17 Nathanael Edwards
Feb. 24 Robert Player
Mar. 6 John Aris
Mar. 9 Hannah Andrews
Mar. 22 Elizabeth Stinton
Mar. 23 Edward Dashwood

1712.

Mar. 26 Mary Stinton
April 9 Bethiah Varnoll
April 21 John Bennet
April 21 Mary Hall
May 18 Hannah Potts
May 22 Sarah Goodinch
June 9 Daniel Andrews
June 21 Elizabeth Tudor
July 16 John Scorfield
July 19 John Simms
Aug. 21 John Leapidge
Sep. 22 Elizabeth Hickson
Oct. 3 Jane Hall
Oct. 5 Robert Carter
Oct. 7 Catherine Herring
Oct. 7 Onesiphorus Collaber
Oct. 17 Anne Baker
Oct. 25 Elizabeth Dashwood
Nov. 20 M[rs] Dickinson
Nov. 26 Elizabeth Baynham
Dec. 27 Isaac Bland
Jan. 3 Rebecca Pickering
Jan. 23 John Baker
Feb. 12 Ann Pickard

1713.

Mar. 27 Thomas Rogers
Mar. 29 Jenkin Lewis
July 28 William son of W[m] & Ann Steel
Aug. 24 Ann Roberts
Sep. 6 William Steel
Sep. 10 Christian Huddleston
Oct. 30 Elizabeth Jackman
Nov. 5 Thomas Sparks
Nov. 6 Henry Morgan
Nov. 12 Elizabeth Pickard
Jan. 4 Sarah Biggs
Jan. 8 John Marsh
Jan. 9 Hannah Hazel
Jan. 31 Mary Reeves
Feb. 11 Joseph Finch
Feb. 14 Elizabeth Townsend
Feb. 29 Jane Lane
Jan. 4 William Reynolds
Jan. 27 George Charagehead
Mar. 7 M[rs] Woollet -

1714.

April 6 Hannah Vetory
April 28 Frances Hudlestone
June 5 Elizabeth Facer
June 20 Thomas Waldron
June 26 Edward Leak
June 30 Robert Player
Aug. 7 William Lepidge
Aug. 11 Matthew Berisford
Aug. 15 Sarah Haines
Aug. 19 Elizabeth Farmer
Sep. 12 Stephen Charman
Oct. 1 Florence Phips
Oct. 28 John Lodington
Nov. 1 John Adam, clerk
Nov. 12 Samuel Baker
Nov. 19 John Fairclough
Nov. 23 Mary Bunden
Nov. 26 Henry Dixson
Nov. 30 John Taylor
Dec. 7 Mary Price
Dec. 18 James Bado
Feb. 11 Mary Cane
Feb. 27 Elizabeth Coupeland
Mar. 6 Samuel Cosins Wood
Mar. 16 Hannah Cunnick
Mar. 17 Margaret Jakeman
Mar. 20 Thomas Wickersham

1715.

Mar. 29 Mary Bates
April 27 Benjamin Knight
May 6 James Reynolds
May 12 Mary Woodley

May 17 William Wood
May 30 James Harford
June 1 Robert Wooding
June 10 Frances Caroline De Raffoe
June 18 Elizabeth Hassell
June 23 Samuel Hall
July 14 Martha Berrisford
July 20 Sarah Leak
July 26 John Horn
Aug. 9 Joan Latham
Aug. 25 Charles Portalis
Nov. 14 Lydia Smith
Dec. 4 Mary Edwards
Dec. 7 Jane Dashwood
Jan. 24 Judeth Waters
Jan. 29 Judeth Gibson
Feb. 12 Samuel Tibbs
Feb. 22 Catherine Brewer
Mar. 3 Alice Hargrave
Mar. 18 George Hargrave

1716.

Mar. 26 Anne Sibbaus
April 7 George Biggs
May 3 Martha Harrison
May 11 Sarah Sparks
May 26 James Stevenson
June 2 Widow Thomas
June 20 John Raffoe
July 5 William Church
July 29 Nathanael Hughes
Aug. 6 Thomas Earle Anger
Sep. 2 Samuel Hall
Sep. 15 Richard Sibley
Oct. 17 Thomas Taylor
Dec. 29 Anthony Jennings
Jan. 19 William Paine
Jan. 26 Lukenar Jones
Feb. 5 James Marsh
Feb. 17 John Mountague
Feb. 19 John Baptist
Feb. 26 Hannah Dixon
Mar. 11 Sarah Sparks
Mar. 16 Anne Fullies

1717.

Mar. 27 Richard Reading
April 29 Samuel Rogers
May 5 Mary Dicker
July 2 Mary Lloyd
July 2 Richard Annet
July 18 Edward Underhill
July 30 John Unwin
July 30 William Underhill
Aug. 15 Timothy Roberts
Aug. 20 Mary Cane

Nov. 14 Mrs Berrisford
Dec. 7 A man found dead in St Antholin's churchyard
Jan. 6 Anne Brown
Jan. 11 Sarah Roberts
Jan. 12 William Williams
Feb. 7 John Buckland
Mar. 1 Elizabeth Brown

1718.

April 26 John Haler
May 1 Jane Lloyd
May 8 Ann Stevenson
May 22 Thomas Whittingham
May 30 Henry Smith
June 3 Carolina Goble
June 24 Mary Gregory
June 28 Mary Watlington
July 21 Thomas Pig
Aug. 11 Frances Huddlestone
Sep. 2 A poor man that came to be passed
Sep. 11 Elizabeth Trainter
Oct. 27 Grace Edwards
Nov. 19 Susanna Wright
Dec. 6 James Smith
Dec. 27 Richard Helsom
Dec. 31 John Knight
Jan. 11 Susanna Fosset
Jan. 11 Mary Posleton
Jan. 16 A foundling
Mar. 22 Henry Geary

1719.

Mar. 26 John Nottingham
Mar. 26 Margaret Obbinson
May 15 Deborah Scofeild
June 3 Catherine Buneau
June 6 Mary Buckly
June 29 Joseph Warren
July 1 Sarah Helsom
Aug. 14 Elizabeth Proctor
Sep. 6 Elizabeth Smith
Sep. 25 Mary Kenton
Oct. 16 Sarah Hunt
Nov. 1 Robert Bryden
Nov. 2 Mary Oliver
Nov. 3 John Castle, a foundling
Nov. 17 Ann Knight
Dec. 1 Elizabeth Maycock
Dec. 6 Alice Wheeler
Dec. 22 Thomas Obbinson
Feb. 1 Elizabeth Foden
Feb. 3 Mary Grover
Mar. 2 Mary Hitchin

1720.

April 2 Benjamin Kinton
April 10 Thomas Dixson
May 4 Mary Natt
May 8 Mary Allen
June 3 Henry Proctor
June 7 Waldive Willington
June 11 Samuel Smith
Aug. 5 Ann Poston
Aug. 11 John Joy
Aug. 21 Francis Stinton
Sep. 9 Cornelius Cloribus
Sep. 11 Thomas Glew
Nov. 26 Peter Warren
Jan. 5 Hester Witworth
Feb. 8 Martha Willington
Feb. 8 John Corker
Feb. 14 John Berdmore

1721.

Mar. 26 Elizabeth Potts
Mar. 29 Rebecca Cooper
April 2 John Marshal
May 11 Dorothy Bayfeild
June 3 Thomas Prowdman
Aug. 1 Henry Andrews
Aug. 15 John Varndal
Sep. 23 Edward Reeves
Oct. 7 Catherine Vanfleet
Oct. 11 James Bradshaw
Nov. 6 Sarah Gerrard
Dec. 6 Dorothy Reed
Dec. 10 Hannah Whitworth
Dec. 12 Mary Col
Jan. 2 John Rogers
Jan. 9 John Dixson
Jan. 20 Henry Roffey
Jan. 21 Henry Figges
Jan. 25 William Tanner
Jan. 30 Samuel Dodd
Feb. 16 Hannah Byfeild
Feb. 26 Mary Phillips
Feb. 26 Elizabeth Morthweild
Feb. 27 Jane Lloyd
Mar. 1 Sarah Hassel
Mar. 7 Mary Hitchcock

1722.

Mar. 25 Anne Roberts
April 13 Elizabeth Round
May 3 [*blank*] Herring
June 12 Jane Edwards
July 7 Anne Prowdman
July 8 Richard Beasly
Aug. 12 John Mallon

Aug. 21 Elizabeth Stevenson
Sep. 24 William Pig
Oct. 6 James Masters
Oct. 9 Elizabeth Bradshaw
Oct. 9 John Naylor
Oct. 28 Michael Christmas
Oct. 29 George Leapidge
Nov. 8 William Vanfleet
Nov. 20 John Dodd
Dec. 2 John Edwards
Dec. 25 Richard Hawkes
Jan. 3 Mary Goodey
Jan. 9 [*blank*] Glew
Jan. 28 Margaret Pig
Feb. 5 Samuel Buckland
Feb. 22 Mary Welsh
Feb. 28 Samuel Hall
Mar. 5 Hannah Wheat
Mar. 6 Rebecca Wilson
Mar. 8 Mary Hall
Mar. 21 Brandon Lloyd
Mar. 24 Jane Lee

1723.

April 8 Joseph Warren
May 4 Anne Belcanca
May 27 Catherine Vickars
May 31 Roger Lloyd
June 9 Jane Peirce
June 19 Anne Bowden
July 10 Elizabeth Bell
July 23 Deborah Tapsfeild
Aug. 14 Mathew Beresford
Sep. 10 William Prowdman
Oct. 13 Bersheba Lloyd
Oct. 25 Catherine Housman
Nov. 6 Martha Willington
Nov. 24 Alice Crofts
Nov. 30 John Varndal
Nov. 30 Elizabeth Lloyd
Dec. 29 Elizabeth Sparkes
Jan. 15 John Mills
Jan. 19 Mary Horabin
Jan. 31 Elizabeth Hoard
Feb. 1 Deborah Wooding
Feb. 8 Hannah Woodley
Feb. 12 Mary Allen
Mar. 3 Robert Cassmore

1724.

April 15 Thomas Facer
May 17 Elizabeth Dixson
July 2 Mary Peacock
July 3 John Till
July 12 Michael Varndal
July 18 Mary Warren

Aug. 8 James Rawlinson
Aug. 12 Elizabeth Orton
Aug. 13 George Price
Aug. 20 Thomas Dixson
Sep. 19 Mary Powel
Oct. 14 Grace Boulton
Oct. 23 Sarah Carter
Dec. 22 Ruth Reeves
Dec. 23 Allexander Follett
Dec. 29 Ann Robertson
Feb. 12 Archobell Jackman
Feb. 25 Sarah Reeve
Feb. 25 Ann Mallard

1725.

April 2 William Vanfleet
April 15 Edward Schoenholte
May 30 Henry Woodley
May 30 Elizabeth Hassell
June 3 Richard Lambert
June 6 James Hunt
June 13 Anthony Cross
Aug. 11 Edward Buckland
Sep. 27 William Henderson
Sep. 30 William Bumstead
Oct. 18 Elizabeth Cloribuss
Oct. 18 William Horabin
Nov. 7 John Pettett
Nov. 11 Sarah Whitchurch
Dec. 3 Jacob Cooke
Dec. 5 Martha Dodd
Dec. 9 Lucey Simson
Jan. 10 Henry Cooper, sexton
Jan. 12 Solomon Scooler
Feb. 15 Cosier Varndal
Feb. 20 Richard Phillips
Mar. 7 John Barker
Mar. 9 William Miller

1726.

Mar. 28 Mary, a foundling
Mar. 28 Anthony, a foundling
Mar. 31 Mary Grover
April 17 Bethiar Unwin
April 26 Mary Sandeforth
June 6 Samuel Wheat
June 7 A foundling
June 11 Rachael Willis
June 16 Abigal Sallsberry
July 31 Peter Hawkins
Aug. 9 Mary Hickman
Aug. 25 Lockton Bell
Sep. 9 Elliner Phillips
Sep. 14 Hannah Prowdman
Sep. 16 Robert Wooding
Sep. 23 James Lee

Oct. 4 Ann Stinton
Oct. 12 John Joseph Harden
Oct. 30 Ann Varndal
Dec. 16 William Gould
Dec. 28 Theodorit Vanfleet
Dec. 31 Sarah Goble
Jan. 8 John Penn
Feb. 13 Hannah Whitchurch
Feb. 18 Mary Miller
Mar. 4 William Miller
Mar. 5 John Newbury
Mar. 22 Elizabeth Stone

1727.

April 9 Ann Lewis
April 30 Henry Peacock
May 6 George Oliver
May 16 Sarah Paine
Aug. 7 Sarah Tapsfield
Aug. 18 Elizabeth Milles
Aug. 22 Thomas Horabin
Sep. 9 Thomas Baker
Sep. 21 John Sanders
Oct. 13 Richard Squaril
Oct. 15 Ann Latham
Nov. 9 Mary Miller
Nov. 12 Nicholis Bigsby
Nov. 19 Benjaman Harling
Nov. 19 Frances Reynolds
Nov. 19 Mary Hawkins
Nov. 29 Caleb Ashborn
Dec. 10 Bentishah Wood
Dec. 12 James Randal
Dec. 13 William Prowdman
Dec. 29 [*blank*] Andrews
Jan. 5 Samuel Woolf
Jan. 27 Thomas Elliott
Feb. 1 Elizabeth Wittingham
Feb. 8 James Gould
Feb. 10 Mary Phillips
Feb. 11 Ralph Walton
Feb. 16 Peter Mitchiel
Feb. 23 John Crofts
Mar. 9 William Barksdale
Mar. 14 Samuel Wittingham
Mar. 17 Elizabeth Mitchiel
Mar. 19 [*blank*] Weatherly

1728.

April 18 Robert Wheate
May 12 Ann Russell
May 13 Robert Wooding
June 2 William Hawkins
June 9 Elizabeth Jordon
June 22 Hannah Lambert
June 22 Ann, a foundling

July 17 Peter Hawkins
July 20 Rich[d] James
Aug. 28 Elizabeth Baker
Sep. 5 Thomas Marston
Sep. 8 Henry Cock
Sep. 29 John Bell
Nov. 3 M[rs] Latham, a pen[r]
Nov. 8 Joseph Bradford
Dec. 24 Sarah Rosswell
Jan. 13 John Hanson
Mar. 6 Deborah Howell

1729.

May 8 Joyce Webster
May 11 William Gravile
May 16 Edward Farmer
July 19 Mary Varndal
Aug. 4 Charles Saunders
Sep. 1 David Barton
Sep. 22 John Moore
Sep. 28 Ann Bigsby
Oct. 18 Thomas Mitchiael
Oct. 30 Meriam Robins
Nov. 18 Elizabeth Dodd
Dec. 5 Samuel Salter
Dec. 21 Elizabeth Dorrington
Jan. 2 Ann Leatherland
Jan. 6 [*blank*] Seabon, a pen[r]
Jan. 8 John Ridges
Jan. 8 Johanah Heah
Jan. 18 Mary Humble
Jan. 25 Mary Gray
Feb. 1 John Cock
Feb. 2 Ann Bradshaw
Feb. 8 Katherine Faircloath
Feb. 9 Elizabeth Whitchurch
Feb. 20 John Bradford
Feb. 23 Mary Bradshaw
Feb. 23 Mary Clarke
Mar. 3 Elizabeth Peppett
Mar. 4 John Hickson
Mar. 8 Mary Atkins
Mar. 8 Thomas Cock
Mar. 15 John Dodd

1730.

Mar. 31 Thomas Organ
April 17 Hanah Usher
April 24 Ann Scooler
July 22 Mary Preston
July 22 Jane Farmer
July 31 Henry Medcalf
Dec. 22 Nathaniel Redin
Dec. 24 Richard Phillips
[*blank*] William Scooler
[*blank*] James Pigg

Dec. 28 Elliner Sacketts
Feb. 2 George Woosly Lloyd
Feb. 7 John Osbond
Feb. 22 Mary Jackman
Feb. 25 John Mercer
Mar. 16 Mary Hodgkins
Mar. 19 James Bradshaw
Mar. 22 Rob[t] Wooding

1731.

May 25 Patience Browne
June 20 Judith Prowdman
June 22 Ruth Mortimoore
June 22 Elizabeth Pettit
July 6 Rich[d] Costin
July 23 Joseph Kent
July 26 Samuel Prowdman
July 26 William Prowdman
July 28 Rebecca Rag
Aug. 19 James Unwin
Aug. 19 Frances Wilde
Sep. 10 Thomas Townsend
Sep. 17 John Harwood
Sep. 21 Elizabeth Sharpe
Sep. 21 Elizabeth Dickenson
Oct. 9 John Wooding
Oct. 24 Mary Pettet
Oct. 28 William Basire
Oct. 28 James Bradford
Nov. 7 John Notcutt
Dec. 5 John Morse
Jan. 13 Edward Farmer
Jan. 13 Mary Moorse
Jan. 28 Frances Saunders
Mar. 14 Edward Hodgkins
Mar. 15 Sarah Haris & Ann Haris

1732.

Mar. 29 Martha Gunston
April 1 Jane Haris
April 23 Elizabeth Sammon
May 2 Valentine Horsey
May 19 Lucey Graves
May 26 Elizabeth Peacock
June 26 [*blank*] Barratt
July 20 Rebecca Lloyd
July 20 Ann, a foundling
Aug. 16 Sarah Martin
Oct. 19 Ann Varndel
Nov. 9 Thomas Horabin
Nov. 26 Elizabeth Walker
Nov. 30 Mary Hassleden
Dec. 7 [*blank*] Cock
Dec. 20 Charles Parry
Dec. 20 Elizabeth Bradshaw
Dec. 21 Elizabeth Pigg

Jan. 28 Samuel Dormon
Jan. 28 Mary Nims
Jan. 30 Elizabeth Barnett

1733.

April 20 Sarah Saunders
May 2 Amelia Carr
May 6 Andrew Bayley
May 8 John Barratt
June 5 John Hodgkins
June 20 Mary Ryves
July 6 John Cock
Aug. 12 William Ryves
Sep. 28 John Barratt
Oct. 18 Charles Drake
Oct. 31 Kerthrine Noble
Nov. 29 Mary Atkins
Dec. 10 Mary, a foundling
Jan. 6 [*blank*] Herring
Jan. 20 Elizabeth Boulton
Feb. 14 Elizabeth Hickson
Mar. 23 Elizabeth Lambert
Mar. 23 Prudence Wotton

1734.

April 1 Mary Yews
April 11 James Wallis
May 19 Johannah Dorington
May 23 Elizabeth Hurrey
June 6 Ann Arnold
July 14 Mary Downs
July 14 Edward Lloyd
Aug. 21 Jane Warmsley
Sep. 1 Robert Tower
Oct. 11 Edward Mason
Nov. 1 John Robins
Nov. 18 Isaac Thorogood
Dec. 1 Deborah Ridgway
Dec. 29 Ann Haddock
Feb. 14 Ann Costin
Mar. 2 Thomas Hodgkins
Mar. 4 Sarah Hull

1735.

Mar. 30 John Buckland
[*blank*] John Pigg
April 22 Mary Marshall
May 30 Frances Smith
Aug. 22 Carthrine Groves
Aug. 23 Elizabeth Stanton
Aug. 28 Cadwallider Hinde
Sep. 18 John Brandon
Oct. 5 Elinor Phillips
Oct. 18 Carthrine Hackett
Nov. 14 Lidda Thorogood

Nov. 16 Carolina Chelteaham
Dec. 4 John Haris
Dec. 9 Thomas Warmsley
Dec. 12 Hannah Rock
Dec. 29 Frances Hurrey
Jan. 19 Lidda Adams
Jan. 26 James Giles
Feb. 5 Mary Clarke
Mar. 4 John Varndel
Mar. 9 Martha Giles

1736.

April 2 Elizabeth Ridgway
April 14 Thomas Fox
May 15 Thomas Buckland
May 20 Ann Dorington
June 4 Henry Fairway
June 15 Sarah Orton
June 17 William Edwards
June 27 Ann Giles
July 19 William Prowman
July 20 Mary Christmas
July 21 Rachiel Toms
Aug. 3 Mary James
Aug. 5 Ann Barrand
Aug. 5 Sarah Scoller
Aug. 7 John Haris
Sep. 1 Elizabeth Bagster
Sep. 5 Samuel Johnson
Oct. 7 Anthony Frost
Nov. 2 Ann Garrad
Nov. 4 Theodotia Saunders
Nov. 7 Ann Hinkes
Nov. 14 Charles Marriott
Nov. 24 Faith Cock
Jan. 9 John Gibson
Mar. 10 Ann Bankes
Mar. 24 Avis Milet

1737.

Mar. 25 [*blank*] Marshal
Mar. 30 James Mortimer
Mar. 31 Deborah Haris
April 13 Samuel Hallaburton
April 15 Dorothy Pinner
April 19 Walter Yerbury
April 21 John Hamlin
April 26 Robt Roberson
June 28 Jane Mortemore
June 28 John Tobin
July 1 Samuel Baker
July 17 Elizabeth Bradley
July 19 Edward Hannum
Aug. 10 Francies Martin
Oct. 25 Thos Phillips

Dec. 25 Elizabeth Cock
Dec. 29 Frances Scooler
Jan. 10 Hannah Phillips
Mar. 17 Elizabeth Lodington
Mar. 20 John Scooler, a pen[r]

1738.

April 7 Ralph Jones
April 11 Mary Pigg
April 12 [*blank*], pentioner
April 26 Tho[s] Walker
May 14 Edward Wallis
June 15 Gilbert Brandon
July 30 William Hunt
Aug. 16 James Ridgway
Aug. 16 Christian Walker
Sep. 27 James Burdied
Oct. 22 Eliz. Facer
Oct. 25 Mary Crannen
Nov. 22 Jesper Payne
Dec. 5 Mary Whipham
Dec. 18 William King
Dec. 24 John Cock
Jan. 4 John Allcorne
Feb. 4 Ann Newman
Mar. 12 Master Hezekiah Newton & Master Walker Newton

1739.

April 16 Ann Bodington
April 18 Francics Driver
April 19 Mary Robins
April 23 Ann Wooding
May 9 Richard Hobbs
May 28 William Green
June 13 John Cock
July 12 John Mallard
Aug. 5 John Smith
Aug. 13 Elizabeth Wilkinson
Nov. 18 Elizabeth White
Nov. 24 Francics & Henry Rogers
Nov. 29 Francics Dunn
Dec. 4 James Ashley
Jan. 8 William Mason
Feb. 2 [*blank*] Herring
Feb. 6 John Bradshaw
Feb. 21 Sarah Almott
Feb. 26 Nathaniel Phillips
Mar. 6 William Jarvis
Mar. 7 Philip Hackett
Mar. 16 Elizabeth Moore

1740.

April 14 James Mitchal
April 15 Jane Jeyne

April 17 Elizabeth Allen
April 23 James Moore
May 18 Elizabeth Webb
May 21 John Whipham
May 27 Nicholis Jackman
June 26 Mathew Yates
June 27 Eliz. Dickson
July 10 John Hall
July 26 Ann Smith
Aug. 10 Rachal Mills
Aug. 28 James Cock
Sep. 5 Martha Colebrook
Sep. 24 Mary Deacon
Oct. 6 John Buckland
Jan. 25 Lambert Kranen
Jan. 27 Dorothy Appleby
Feb. 9 Thomas Newman
Feb. 13 Mary Varndell
Mar. 9 James Hackett
Mar. 20 Edward Walford
Mar. 24 Christopher Poitrues

1741.

April 5 Francis Walford
May 11 Elizabeth Lucas
June 1 Frances John Ennis
June 21 John Newman
June 25 Francies Preist
June 26 Eliz. West Walker
Sep. 5 Ester Garrad
Sep. 12 Ann Searl
Sep. 23 Susanah Saward
Oct. 30 Mary Newman
Nov. 14 Ann Myers
Dec. 5 Thomas Pond
Dec. 11 Jane Faulconer
Jan. 4 Mary Phillips
[*blank*] Mary Cobley
Jan. 13 Mary Peirson
Jan. 25 George Lane
Feb. 7 Mary Rawlins
Feb. 28 Ann Varndell
Mar. 10 Joseph Hunt
Mar. 21 Elizabeth Mitchell

1742.

April 1 Martha Swannell
April 6 Mary Clarke
April 7 Caleb Lambert
May 4 Cathrine Faulconer
May 7 Elizabeth West Walker
May 23 Robert Goadby
June 12 Ellinor Fox
June 27 Elizabeth Alewood

July 28 Elizabeth Whiting
Aug. 11 Elizabeth Sergeant
Sep. 13 Elleanor Crossman
Oct. 28 William Willson
Nov. 28 Susan[h] Boothby
Feb. 6 Frances Saunders
Feb. 15 Jane Porter
Mar. 20 Francis Pond
Mar. 23 Ann Cruchlecot

1743.

Mar. 29 Frances Faulconer
April 1 Ann Ratcliff
April 4 John White
April 19 Elizabeth Ridgway
April 21 [*blank*] Reader
April 24 John Ennes
May 23 William Trussley
May 26 Benj[n] Pullingson
July 8 Mary Higgs
July 10 William Wallis
Aug. 17 Edward Baptist, a found.
Aug. 25 Rachael Edwards
Sep. 6 Ann Smallpiece
Dec. 18 Ann Miller
Jan. 5 Samuel Steadwell
Jan. 8 William King
Jan. 14 Rebec. Leapidge
Jan. 23 George Grome
Jan. 24 Mary Ennes
Jan. 30 Thomas Crossman

1744.

April 6 Mary Newman
April 17 William Bagster
April 30 William Thoroughgood
May 13 John Smallpiece
June 10 Jane Stanton
June 29 Mary Hunt
July 2 Edward Wise
July 19 Thomas Saunders
July 20 Daniel Hodgkin
July 25 Isaac Hooper
Aug. 16 Richard Gray
Dec. 9 Debor. Maria Grandon
Dec. 30 Mary Blower
Dec. 31 [*blank*] Fox
Feb. 2 Young Herring
Feb. 5 John Gobby, a pen[r]
Feb. 16 James Whitchurch, Esq[r]
Mar. 11 Sarah Wignall
Mar. 12 Mary Applebie
Mar. 14 Joseph Haynes

Mar. 31 Sarah Mitchell
Mar. 31 Sarah Elmer
April 6 Bridgett Barker
Oct. 24 Susannah Mitchael
Nov. 10 William Dolman
Dec. 4 John Yews
Dec. 11 Mary Ann Hall
Dec. 18 Henry Willson
[*blank*] John Sale
Dec. 22 Mary Pennard
Jan. 1 Richard Winn
Jan. 9 Mary Smith
Feb. 7 Isaac Cooke
Feb. 9 Elizabeth Green
Feb. 14 Charles Garrard
Feb. 16 John Hall
Feb. 18 John Walker

1746.

May 9 Edward Jennion
May 25 Grace Williams
July 4 John Moore
Aug. 9 Joseph Roswell
Aug. 27 Edward Mitchael
Sep. 7 William Archer
Sep. 8 Susannah Thompson
Sep. 28 Mathew Smith
Oct. 8 Martha Barr
[*blank*] John Horey
Oct. 19 William Thoroughgood
Nov. 4 Rebecker Flackett
Nov. 28 John Wood
Dec. 17 Margaret Farnly
Jan. 26 Ann Young
Feb. 1 Ann Whipham
Feb. 9 Ann Hodgkins
Feb. 22 Vicesamas Bradshaw
Feb. 22 Rich[d] Bradshaw
Mar. 16 Elizabeth Parinson

1747.

Mar. 25 Sarah Gobbing
April 3 Joseph Farmer
April 15 Elliner Jobins
April 23 Charles Bull
May 3 Joseph Hoskins
May 23 Deborah Haynes
June 26 Mary Stamford
Oct. 16 William Allin
Oct. 21 James Millit
[*blank*] John Ingram
Oct. 30 Patient Newman
Nov. 1 Jane Tayler

Nov. 8 Ann Jennings
Nov. 12 Elizabeth Ledgett
Nov. 22 Edward Coston
Jan. 6 Elizabeth Wallis
Jan. 17 George Tregea
Jan. 31 Mary Millett
Feb. 1 James Hooper
[*blank*] Elizabeth Tayler
Feb. 25 William Hasleton
Mar. 17 Rachiel Oldfield

1748.

June 24 William Haynes
July 24 Isabell Cooke
July 29 Paul Archer
Aug. 30 John Mills
Sep. 3 Thomas Younge
Sep. 17 William Bruff
Oct. 9 Richd Swanell
Oct. 23 Ann Raggett
Oct. 31 Samuel Squier
Nov. 4 John Noble
Nov. 9 Thomas Parkes
[*blank*] Joseph Ridgway
Dec. 6 Elizabeth Dixon
Dec. 15 Ann Knight
Dec. 31 Hannah Fearnly
Jan. 26 Henry Mott
Jan. 31 Isabelah Williams
[*blank*] Elizabeth Grover
Feb. 9 Sarah Haynes
Feb. 22 James Ashworth
Feb. 28 Henry Moon
Feb. 28 Martha Collier

1749.

Mar. 26 Hezekiah Walker
April 23 John Lane
April 23 William Prowdman
May 14 Sarah Walker
May 14 [*blank*] Swanell
June 28 Elizabeth Crossman
Aug. 27 Elliner Steward
Sep. 13 Maynard Smith
Oct. 12 George Leapidge
Nov. 17 Elizabech Ennis
Jan. 8 John Tayler
Jan. 10 Thomas Hutchins
[*blank*] [*blank*] Lane
Jan. 28 Rebeckah White

1750.

May 3 Thomas Horabin
May 20 Susanna Cowley

July 29 John Wotton
Aug. 20 Richard May
Aug. 29 William Durson
Oct. 26 Edward Wilde
Dec. 31 Hannah Browne
Jan. 13 Ann Poole
Feb. 13 Thos King
Feb. 19 Edward James

1751.

April 28 John Cornelious
May 7 John Fenly
May 12 Mary Saunders
July 9 William Jones
July 14 Mary Brookes
July 19 Sarah Hall
Sep. 13 Mary Hopkins
Sep. 18 Anna Maria Jennion
Sep. 29 Mecklin Powles
Oct. 1 Susannah Cary
Nov. 19 Frances Falconer

1752.

Feb. 8 James Lamen
Mar. 22 Ambruss Raggett
Mar. 24 Mary Attfield
Mar. 27 John Dixon
May 3 Sarah Dobson
May 6 Rebecca Tate
June 17 Ann Chambers
June 27 Richard Hester
June 30 Hester Martin
July 11 Johnothan Furnley
July 12 Mary Whipham
July 28 Thomas Huntson
Aug. 2 Samuel Goldsmith
Aug. 21 Hannah Wood
Oct. 13 William Martin
Oct. 19 Sarah Coker
Oct. 24 Ester Jervis
Nov. 17 Thomas Martin
Dec. 2 Theresa Falconer
Dec. 14 Thomas Martin

1753.

Jan. 19 Sarah Beachcroft
Jan. 28 Thomas Young
Mar. 11 Jane Goulding
Mar. 22 Mary Blake
April 12 Thomas Manger
April 26 Lucey Hunt
May 6 Mary Gobby
Aug. 24 Margaret Huges
Sep. 14 Ann Pott

Sep. 23 Mary Hannum
Sep. 28 Ann Hannum
Oct. 21 John Rider
Oct. 27 Peter Sergeant
Oct. 28 John Meliett
Nov. 2 Margaret Hannum
Nov. 29 Jane Winn
Dec. 23 Jonas Bull

1754.

Jan. 11 Eliz. Dixon
Jan. 20 John Brann
Jan. 21 Dorothy Hardwick
Jan. 24 Elizabeth Browne
Feb. 17 Thomas Hallaway
Mar. 25 William Robins

INDEX OF PERSONS.

A

B

C

D

E

F

G

M

N

O

P

Q

R

S

T

U

V

W

Y

ERRATA.

(*Blank*); *add* Richard, 132; Robert, 160.
Goddard, John; *for* 60 *read* 59, 66.
Goodall, Robert; *for* 49 *read* 50, 65.

INDEX OF PLACES.

J

K

L

M

N

O

P

Q

R

London: Mitchell and Hughes, Printers, 140 Wardour Street, W.

The Harleian Society.

INSTITUTED FOR THE PUBLICATION OF INEDITED MANUSCRIPTS RELATING TO GENEALOGY, FAMILY HISTORY, AND HERALDRY.

PRESIDENT—HIS GRACE THE DUKE OF MANCHESTER.

PUBLICATIONS.

VOL.

I.—The Visitation of London, in 1568, by Cooke. Edited by J. J. HOWARD, Esq., LL.D., F.S.A., and G. J. ARMYTAGE, Esq., F.S.A.

II.—The Visitation of Leicestershire, in 1619, by Lennard and Vincent. Edited by JOHN FETHERSTON, Jun., Esq., F.S.A.

III.—The Visitation of Rutland, in 1618, by Camden. Edited by GEORGE J. ARMYTAGE, Esq., F.S.A.

IV.—The Visitations of Nottingham in 1563 and 1614. Edited by GEO. W. MARSHALL, Esq., LL.D., F.S.A.

V.—The Visitations of Oxford, 1574 and 1634. Edited by W. H. TURNER, Esq.

VI.—The Visitation of Devon in 1620. Edited by the Rev. F. T. COLBY, D.D., F.S.A.

VII.—The Visitation of Cumberland in 1615. Edited by JOHN FETHERSTON, Esq., F.S.A.

[The preceding Seven Works are out of Print.

VIII.—Le Neve's Catalogue of Knights. Edited by GEORGE W. MARSHALL, Esq., LL.D., F.S.A. £1 : 1 : 0

IX.—The Visitation of Cornwall, 1620. Edited by Col. VIVIAN and Dr. H. H. DRAKE. £1 : 1 : 0

X.—The Registers of Westminster Abbey. Edited by Colonel CHESTER, D.C.L., LL.D. £1 : 1 : 0

XI.—The Visitation of Somersetshire in 1623. Edited by the Rev. F. T. COLBY, D.D., F.S.A. £1 : 1 : 0

XII.—The Visitation of Warwickshire. Edited by JOHN FETHERSTON, Esq., F.S.A. £1 : 1 : 0

XIII.—The Visitations of Essex in 1552, 1558, 1612, and 1634. Part I. Edited by WALTER C. METCALFE, Esq., F.S.A. £1 : 1 : 0

XIV.—The Visitation of Essex, consisting of Miscellaneous Pedigrees, and Berry's Pedigrees. Part II. With general Index. £1 : 1 : 0

XV.—The Visitation of London, 1633-4. Vol. I. Edited by J. J. HOWARD, Esq., LL.D., F.S.A., and Colonel CHESTER, D.C.L., LL.D. £1 : 1 : 0

XVI.—The Visitation of Yorkshire in 1564. Edited by the Rev. C. B. NORCLIFFE, M.A. £1 : 1 : 0

XVII.—The Visitation of London, 1633-4. Vol. II. Edited by J. J. HOWARD, Esq., LL.D., F.S.A. *[In the Press.*

XVIII.—The Visitation of Cheshire in 1580. Edited by J. PAUL RYLANDS, Esq., F.S.A. £1 : 1 : 0

XIX.—The Visitation of Gloucestershire, in 1623, by Chitting and Phillipot as deputies to Camden. Edited by Sir JOHN MACLEAN, F.S.A., and W. C. HEANE, Esq. *[In the Press.*

The Publications of the Society which are in print can be obtained, by Members *only*, at the prices above mentioned, on application to Messrs. MITCHELL and HUGHES, 140 Wardour Street, W

Entrance Fee: Half-a-Guinea. Annual Subscription: **One Guinea.**

PROSPECTIVE PUBLICATIONS.

The Visitations of Bedfordshire in 1566, 1586, and 1634. To be Edited by F. A. BLAYDES, Esq.

The Registers of Durham Cathedral. To be Edited by Captain WHITE, F.S.A.

The Visitation of Dorsetshire, in 1623, by St. George and Lennard as deputies to Camden. To be Edited by J. PAUL RYLANDS, Esq., F.S.A.

The Visitation of Shropshire, in 1584, by Lee as deputy to Cooke. To be Edited by J. PAUL RYLANDS, Esq., F.S.A.

List of Knights with their Arms, from Hen. VII. to James I. To be Edited by Sir JOHN MACLEAN, F.S.A.

The Visitation of Hertfordshire, in 1572, by Cooke. To be Edited by WALTER C. METCALFE, Esq., F.S.A.

The Visitations of Worcestershire in 1569 and 1634.

The Visitations of Hampshire, in 1530, 1552, 1575, and 1622, by Benolte, Hawley, Cooke, and Philipot as deputy to Camden.

The Visitations of Sussex, in 1530, by Benolte; 1574, by Cooke; and 1633, by Philipot and Owen as deputies to St. George and Burrough.

The Book of Heirs from 1 Edward I. to 17 Henry VI. To be Edited by Sir JOHN MACLEAN, F.S.A.

Persons wishing to join the Society should apply to GEORGE J. ARMYTAGE, Esq., F.S.A., Hon. Sec., Clifton Woodhead, near Brighouse.

REGISTER SECTION.

PUBLICATIONS.

Vol. I.—THE REGISTERS OF ST. PETER'S, CORNHILL, LONDON. Part I., A.D. 1538 to 1666. Edited by Granville Leveson Gower, Esq., F.S.A. £0 : 10 : 6

Vol. II.—THE REGISTERS OF CANTERBURY CATHEDRAL. Edited by Robert Hovenden, Esq. £0 : 10 : 6

Vol. III.—THE REGISTERS OF ST. DIONIS BACKCHURCH, LONDON. Edited by the late Colonel J. L. Chester, D.C.L., LL.D. £0 : 10 : 6

Vol. IV.—THE REGISTERS OF ST. PETER'S, CORNHILL, LONDON. Part II., A.D. 1666 to 1754. Edited by Granville Leveson Gower, Esq., F.S.A. £0 : 10 : 6

Vol. V.—THE REGISTERS OF ST. MARY ALDERMARY, LONDON. Edited by the late Colonel J. L. Chester, D.C.L., LL.D. £1 : 1 : 0

Vol. VI.—THE REGISTERS OF ST. THOMAS APOSTLE, LONDON. Edited by the late Colonel J. L. Chester, D.C.L., LL.D. £1 : 1 : 0

Vol. VII.—THE REGISTERS OF ST. MICHAEL, CORNHILL, LONDON. Partly Edited by the late Colonel J. L. Chester, D.C.L., LL.D. £1 : 1 : 0

Vol. VIII.—THE REGISTERS OF ST. ANTHOLIN, BUDGE ROW; AND ST. JOHN BAPTIST ON WALLBROOK, LONDON. £1 : 1 : 0

PROSPECTIVE PUBLICATIONS.

THE REGISTERS OF ST. JAMES, CLERKENWELL, LONDON.

THE REGISTERS OF CHRIST CHURCH, NEWGATE STREET, LONDON.

THE REGISTERS OF ST. SEPULCHRE'S, LONDON.

AND MANY OTHERS.

The Publications of the Register Section will be supplied to Members on payment of an extra Subscription of One Guinea, and can be obtained, by Members *only*, from Messrs. Mitchell and Hughes, 140 Wardour Street, W., at the above Prices.

Forms of Application, and all other particulars, may be obtained by applying to George J. Armytage, Esq., F.S.A., Hon. Sec., Clifton Woodhead, near Brighouse.

www.ingramcontent.com/pod-product-compliance
Lightning Source LLC
Chambersburg PA
CBHW030350270326
41926CB00009B/1038

* 9 7 8 3 3 3 7 0 4 7 8 2 5 *